Philosophy and Anthropology

Key Issues in Modern Sociology

Anthem's **Key Issues in Modern Sociology** series publishes scholarly texts by leading social theorists that give an accessible exposition of the major structural changes in modern societies. These volumes address an academic audience through their relevance and scholarly quality, and connect sociological thought to public issues. The series covers both substantive and theoretical topics, as well as addressing the works of major modern sociologists. The series emphasis is on modern developments in sociology with relevance to contemporary issues such as globalization, warfare, citizenship, human rights, environmental crises, demographic change, religion, postsecularism and civil conflict.

Philosophy and Anthropology

Border Crossing and Transformations

Edited by
Ananta Kumar Giri
and John Clammer

ANTHEM PRESS
LONDON · NEW YORK · DELHI

Anthem Press
An imprint of Wimbledon Publishing Company
www.anthempress.com

This edition first published in UK and USA 2014
by ANTHEM PRESS
75–76 Blackfriars Road, London SE1 8HA, UK
or PO Box 9779, London SW19 7ZG, UK
and
244 Madison Ave #116, New York, NY 10016, USA

First published in hardback by Anthem Press in 2013

British Library Cataloguing-in-Publication Data
A catalogue record for this book is available from the British Library.

Library of Congress Cataloging-in-Publication Data
The Library of Congress has catalogued the hardcover edition as follows:
Philosophy and anthropology : border crossing and transformations / edited by
Ananta Kumar Giri and John Clammer.
pages cm. – (Key issues in modern sociology)
Includes bibliographical references.
ISBN 978-0-85728-512-6 (hardcover : alk. paper)
1. Philosophical anthropology. 2. Anthropology–Philosophy.
I. Giri, Ananta Kumar. II. Clammer, J. R.
BD450.P47238 2013
128–dc23
2013043347

ISBN-13: 978 1 78308 355 8 (Pbk)
ISBN-10: 1 78308 355 7 (Pbk)

Cover image © Jagdish Mohanty 2013

This title is also available as an ebook

For E. E. Evans-Pritchard, Chitta Ranjan Das and Mrinal Miri

CONTENTS

NOTES ON CONTRIBUTORS

Prasenjit Biswas is an associate professor in the Department of Philosophy, North Eastern Hill University, Shillong, India.

Marcin Brocki teaches in the Institute of Ethnology and Cultural Anthropology, Jagiellonian University in Krakow, Poland. His main research interests are in theory and methodology of anthropology and anthropology of the body. His recent books include (in Polish): *Antropologia społeczna i kulturowa w przestrzeni publicznej* (Social and cultural anthropology in public space, 2013), *Antropologia. Literatura, dialog, przeklad* (Anthropology: Literature, dialogue, translation, 2008), *Język ciała w ujęciu antropologicznym* (Body language in anthropological perspective, 2002).

Vaclav Brezina is a senior research associate at the ESRC Centre for Corpus Approaches to Social Science (CASS), Lancaster University. His research interests are in the areas of philosophy of social sciences, corpus linguistics and sociolinguistics.

John Clammer is currently a special advisor to the rector, United Nations University, Tokyo. He has taught in many universities around the world and is the single author of sixteen books, including such seminal works such as *Difference and Modernity: Social Theory and Contemporary Japanese Society* (1995) and *Diaspora and Belief: Globalisation, Religion and Identity in Postcolonial Asia* (2009).

Fred Dallmayr is Packey J. Dee Professor in the Departments of Philosophy and Political Science at the University of Notre Dame. He holds a Doctor of Law degree from the University of Munich and a PhD in political science from Duke University. He has been a visiting professor at Hamburg University and at the New School for Social Research in New York, and a fellow at Nuffield College in Oxford. During 1991–92 he was in India on a Fulbright research grant. His main fields are modern and contemporary political philosophy and comparative and cross-cultural studies. Some of his recent publications are: *Between Frankfurt and Freiburg* (1991), *Beyond Orientalism* (1996), *Dialogue Among Civilizations* (2002), *Small Wonder* (2005) and *In Search of the Good Life* (2007).

Robert Feleppa is a professor of philosophy at Wichita State University, Kansas. His areas of specialization are philosophy of social science and Buddhist philosophy. In addition to his work on the anthropology of development, he is interested in the psychology and philosophy of emotion, particularly as these bear on our understanding of emotion and intuition in Zen Buddhism.

Heidrun Friese is teaching at the Johann Wolfgang Goethe University, Frankfurt am Main and is currently working on a research project on 'The Limits of Hospitality' at the European University Viadrina, Frankfurt (Oder). Her research interests include social and political theory, Europe and European integration, (cultural) identities, time, history and memory, concepts of space, borders and transnationalism, friendship and hospitality. Recent publications include 'Europe's Otherness: Cosmopolitism and the Construction of Cultural Unities', in Gerard Delanty (ed.), *Europe and Asia Beyond East and West: Towards a New Cosmopolitanism* (2006); 'Cultural Identities', in Gerard Delanty (ed.), *Handbook of Contemporary European Social Theory* (2006); *Europa: costituzione e movimenti sociali* (co-edited with Giuseppe Bronzini, Antonio Negri and Peter Wagner) (2003); *Identities: Time, Boundaries and Difference* (edited) (2002); *Europa politica: Ragioni di una necessità* (co-edited with Antonio Negri and Peter Wagner) (2002); and *The Moment: Time and Rupture in Modern Thought* (edited) (2001).

Ananta Kumar Giri is currently on the faculty of Madras Institute of Development Studies, Chennai, India and has taught and done research in many universities in India and abroad including the University of Kentucky, USA; Aalborg University, Denmark; the University of Freiburg, Germany and MSH, Paris. He has an abiding interest in social movements and cultural change, criticism, creativity and contemporary dialectics of transformations, theories of self, culture and society, and creative streams in education, philosophy and literature. Giri has written and edited around two dozen books in Odia and English, including *Global Transformations: Postmodernity and Beyond* (1998); *Sameekhya o Purodrusti* (Criticism and the vision of the future, 1999); *Patha Prantara Nrutattwa* (Anthropology of the street corner, 2000); *Conversations and Transformations: Toward a New Ethics of Self and Society* (2002); *Self-Development and Social Transformations? The Vision and Practice of Self-Study Mobilization of Swadhyaya* (2008); *Mochi o Darshanika* (The cobbler and the philosopher, 2009); *Sociology and Beyond: Windows and Horizons* (2012); and *Knowledge and*

Human Liberation: Towards Planetary Realizations (2013). For his contribution to knowledge and society, Giri was awarded the *Barata Jyoti* (India Glory) award in 2012.

Susantha Goonatilake has taught or researched at, among others, the Universities of Exeter, Sussex, Malaya, Trondheim, Linkoping, Philippines, Columbia, the New School for Social Research, the Institute of Developing Economies, Japan, and the Institute of Social Studies, The Hague. Goonatilake is a fellow of the World Academy of Arts and Sciences. He is a former general president of the Sri Lanka Association for the Advancement of Science and is president of the 164-year-old Royal Asiatic Society, Sri Lanka. He has published widely and his books include *Cultural Consequences of the Shift to Asia* (forthcoming); *A 16th Century Clash of Civilizations: The Portuguese Presence in Sri Lanka* (forthcoming); *Recolonisation: Foreign Funded NGOs in Sri Lanka* (Sage); *Anthropologizing Sri Lanka: A Civilizational Misadventure* (Indiana); *Toward a Global Science: Mining Civilizational Knowledge* (Indiana); *Merged Evolution: The Long Term Implications of Information Technology and Biotechnology* (Gordon and Breach); *Technological Independence: The Asian Experience* (UNU); *Evolution of Information: Lineages in Genes, Culture and Artefact* (Pinter Publishers); *Aborted Discovery: Science and Creativity in the Third World* (Zed); *Crippled Minds: An Exploration into Colonial Culture* (Vikas); *Food as a Human Right* (UNU); *Jiritsu Suru Ajia No Kagaku-Dai San Sekai Ishiki Karano Kaiho* (Ochanomizu Shobo, Tokyo); and *Al-Iktishaf al-mujahad; al-'ilm wa-l-ibda' fi al-'alam al-thalith* Suzantha Ghunatilik Tarjamahu 'afif al-Razaz (Center for Arabic Studies).

Heike Kämpf is a professor of philosophy at the Technical University of Darmstadt, Germany. He studied philosophy, ethnology and history in Münster, Germany. Publications include *Tauschbeziehungen: Zur anthropologischen Fundierung des Symbolbegriffs* (1995); *Helmuth Plessner: Eine Einführung* (2001); and *Die Exzentrizität des Verstehens: Zur Debatte um die Verstehbarkeit des Fremden zwischen Hermeneutik und Ethnologie* (2003).

Lars Kjaerholm taught anthropology at Aarhus University, Denmark.

Kai Kresse is an anthropologist working on the Swahili coast. He studied philosophy, African studies and literature in Hamburg (gaining an MA in philosophy), and social anthropology in London (MSc and PhD). Currently, he is vice-director for research at Zentrum Moderner Orient in Berlin, and was lecturer in social anthropology at the University of St Andrews (2002–2009). He has published widely on knowledge, philosophy and intellectual practice in Africa, on Islam in East Africa, and also on

African literature, cultural philosophy and the work of Ernst Cassirer. His monograph *Philosophising in Mombasa: Knowledge, Islam and Intellectual Practice on the Swahili Coast* (2007) was published by Edinburgh University Press and the International African Institute and won an Honourable Mention for the Herskovits Prize in 2008. He has co-edited the volumes *Knowledge in Practice: Expertise and the Transmission of Knowledge* (2009); *Struggling with History: Islam and Cosmopolitanism in the Western Indian Ocean* (2007); *Reading Mudimbe* (2005); *Symbolisches Flanieren: Kulturphilosophische Streifzüge* (2001); and *Sagacious Reasoning: In Memory of H. O. Oruka* (1997). He is also a co-editor of the online journal *Polylog: forum für interkulturelle Philosophie* (www.polylog.org). In 2005, he was Evans-Pritchard lecturer at All Souls College, Oxford.

Kasper Lysemose currently holds a position as postdoc at Aarhus University, Denmark. His main interests lie in phenomenology, philosophical anthropology, philosophical hermeneutics and the history of philosophy. He wrote his PhD on the philosophy of Hans Blumenberg and is currently working in a research group on a project entitled *Existential Anthropology: Inquiring Human Responsiveness*. He has published articles on Kant, Husserl, Cassirer, Heidegger, Gehlen, Blumenberg and others.

Ivan Marquez was born in Puerto Rico. He has a PhD in philosophy from Indiana University–Bloomington. He has taught at Indiana University, California State University, University of Puerto Rico, and Bentley University. Currently he is assistant professor in the Department of Philosophy at Texas State University–San Marcos and Senior Research Fellow at Bentley University. He has published on social and political philosophy, ethics, metaphysics, epistemology, philosophy of education and Latin American thought. He is editor of *Contemporary Latin American Social and Political Thought: An Anthology* (Rowman and Littlefield, 2008). Recent research interests include Latin American thought, culture and history, metaphysics of development and its connection to ethics, Marxism and climate change, performativity of discourse, and sociocultural history of analytic philosophy.

João de Pina-Cabral is professor of social anthropology at the University of Kent, Canterbury, UK. From 1986–2012, he was also research professor at the Institute of Social Sciences at the University of Lisbon, where he was scientific director from 1997–2003. He was founding president of the Portuguese Association of Anthropology (1989–1991) and president of the European Association of Social Anthropologists (2003–2005). He was Malinowski memorial lecturer in 1992 and Stirling memorial lecturer in 2003.

He is an honorary member of the Royal Anthropological Institute, of the Royal Academy of Moral and Political Sciences, Madrid and of the Academy of Sciences, Lisbon. He has carried out fieldwork and published extensively on the Alto Minho (Portugal), Macau (China) and Bahia (Brazil). He has been visiting professor in Brazil (USP, Unicamp), France (EHESS), Macau, Mozambique (U. E. Mondlane), Spain (Barcelona), United Kingdom (St Antony's College, Oxford) and the United States (University of Chicago).

Gernot Saalmann is currently lecturer at the Department for Sociology, University of Freiburg, Germany. His research interests are sociological theory (practice), sociology of knowledge and religion, cultural anthropology (music and film) and globalization (with a focus on India). Recent publications in English include *Classical Sociological Theories* (2011); 'Arguments Opposing the Radicalism of Radical Constructivism', *Constructivist Foundations* 1, 3 (2007); 'The Encounter, Exchange and Hybridisation of Cultures', in D. Schirmer, G. Saalmann, C. Kessler (eds), *Hybridising East and West* (2006).

Peter Skalník was born in 1945 in Prague. He specializes in political anthropology and African studies and has keen interest in the history of anthropology. He has done fieldwork in four continents. He has edited 20 books (among them *Early Writings of Bronislaw Malinowski, The Early State, The Study of the State, Outwitting the State*) and dozens of chapters and articles. At present he is a Research Associate in the University of Hradec Králové and an Extraordinary Professor in the University of Wrocław. He is a Chevalier of the Ordre des Palmes Académiques and served as the Czechoslovak and Czech ambassador in Lebanon.

Piet Strydom is a retired member of the School of Sociology and Philosophy, University College Cork, Ireland, and associate editor of the *European Journal of Social Theory*. Major publications include *Contemporary Critical Theory and Methodology* (2011); *New Horizons of Critical Theory: Collective Learning and Triple Contingency* (2009); *Risk, Environment and Society* (2002); and *Discourse and Knowledge* (2000). He edited *Philosophies of Social Science* (2003, with Gerard Delanty) as well as special issues of the *European Journal of Social Theory* and the *Irish Journal of Sociology*.

Daniel Šuber is lecturer of sociology at the University of Lucerne, Switzerland. His research interests are epistemology, sociology of culture, religion and knowledge. He received his PhD from the University of Konstanz, Germany. His PhD work, published in 2007, examines the ideological traces of the tradition of German *Lebensphilosophie* in classical social theorists.

He specializes in the field of social and cultural theory, visual sociology and sociology of religion. He is co-editor of *Religion and Politics: Cultural Perspectives* (2005), of *Erleben, Erleiden, Erfahren: Zur Konstitution sozialen Sinns jenseits instrumenteller Vernunft* (2008), and of *Retracing Images: Visual Culture after Yugoslavia* (2012). He has contributed chapters on the sociology of knowledge, phenomenological theory, visual sociology in the Balkans, and the history of sociology. He has just published a German introduction to the sociology of Émile Durkheim (2012). Currently he is finishing a research project of the visual culture in Serbia.

Betsy Taylor is a cultural anthropologist whose recent research is on emerging forms of civil society and social movements, community-based natural resource management, place-based planning, globalization and sustainability. Her scholarly writings engage questions of environmental imaginaries and identities, the construction of identity (gender, class, place, ethnicity, religion), the constitution of public space, regimes of knowledge and the articulation of local/professionalized knowledges, participatory action research and public involvement strategies. She is currently senior research scholar with the Alliance for Social, Political, Ethical and Cultural Theory, at the Virginia State and Polytechnic Institute. She has also served as research director for the Appalachian Center and on the faculty of the Social Theory program at the University of Kentucky. She has worked on projects for community-driven, integrated development and participatory action research in Appalachia and India – including health, agriculture, forestry, culture and environmental stewardship. In addition to numerous scholarly articles, she is co-author (with Herbert Reid) of *Recovering the Commons: Democracy, Place, and Global Justice* (2009).

Introduction

PHILOSOPHY AND ANTHROPOLOGY IN DIALOGUES AND CONVERSATIONS

John Clammer and Ananta Kumar Giri

Philosophy and anthropology have long been intellectual companions. In European continental philosophy in particular, the boundaries between the two disciplines have always been very porous. One thinks at once of the largely German project to construct a philosophy of man and of human's place in nature (a project broadly known as philosophical anthropology), the constant border crossings between anthropology and philosophy of notable individuals such as Paul Cassirer and Martin Heidegger, and the importation into British analytical philosophy by way of Ludwig Wittgenstein of concerns that can only be called anthropological. Although from the other side of the disciplinary boundary anthropology has rarely been reflective about its own philosophical presuppositions, in practice anthropologists constantly bring particular and often unexamined philosophical and ontological positions to their supposedly empirical analyses. For example, anthropologies inspired by Durkheim are deeply rooted in Kantian philosophy, Evans-Pritchard's ideas are stamped with R. G. Collingwood's Hegelian philosophy, Max Gluckman was stimulated by Whitehead's process philosophy, and Pierre Bourdieu drew inspiration from Wittgenstein and Pascal, among others. An earlier generation of anthropologists had no hesitation about exploring the philosophical notions of 'primitive' man (Radin [1927] 1957).

Yet the fuller implications of shifting philosophical influences in anthropology are rarely addressed. In this volume we propose that the implications of these influences call on the one hand for a deeper investigation of the philosophical presuppositions of anthropology, and on the other for a deep questioning of the philosophical presuppositions themselves from the comparative-cultural view of anthropology and in particular of ethnography. Indeed, as a comparative inquiry into the human condition, anthropology can bring to this questioning a singular creativity and a viewpoint rarely, if ever, explored by philosophers themselves – their own hidden or taken-for-granted cultural and ontological presuppositions and their own social location as cultural producers of a particular kind of (in some Western societies in particular) legitimate, if often marginalized, form of discourse. Our resulting project is not mutual critique, but a form of dialogue, a conversation in which a dialectical illumination can take place and ideally the whole basis of that conversation be moved onto new ground.

To take an instance of this: consider for a moment the current hegemonic tendency in anthropology and sociology, traceable mainly to Nietzsche through Foucault, to conceptualize all things social as solely or ultimately matters of power. This framework tends to result in an ethnocentric picture of ethics as simply a form of (witting or unwitting) subterfuge, and leaves little room to consider the ethical dimension of human existence, in its many cultural expressions, as a dimension of being-in-the-world in its own right. Yet at the same time there are some current philosophical trends that call these anthro-philosophical assumptions into serious question (cf. Clammer 2005). Take, for example, those deriving from Levinas and some aspects of Derrida, not to mention seriously neglected non-Western philosophical traditions such as those deriving from the thought of Gandhi or the Buddha and his many later commentators, including the seriously philosophical analyses of figures such as the Japanese Zen monk Dogen (LaFleur 1985) or the members of the Kyoto School of Japanese philosophy (Blocker and Starling 2001).

Consequently, addressing anthropologies through philosophies and reciprocally philosophies through anthropologies (and note that we deliberately use both these terms in the plural) renders open to question current trajectories in which both disciplines often move un-self-critically in the realm of the taken-for-granted. With this in mind, this collection of original essays is designed to stimulate creative crossings and intersections between the two disciplines that question most closely the nature of the human being-in-the-world, and to explore historically, analytically and inventively the borderlands of anthropology and philosophy and the transformations that potentially await them both when they enter into a more sustained conversation with each other.

This project began as a panel at the European Association for Social Anthropology conference in Vienna. What the organizers had expected to be a rather small and possibly marginal workshop in relation to the mainstream themes of the larger conference, evolved into an all-day panel with a standing room–only audience. Stimulated by this overwhelming response that clearly signalled a hunger within the profession to discuss the philosophical underpinnings of our discipline, we have subsequently invited a number of additional authors to contribute original essays to this collection. Our hope and expectation is that it will not so much represent a summing up of an already established subfield, but rather will provide the stimulus for fresh and creative thinking within anthropology, a deeper questioning of the largely unexplored fundamental philosophical underpinnings of the field, and the basis for a fresh dialogue with philosophers around areas and topics of common interest.

At the workshop and in subsequent discussions with authors and potential authors, it became very clear that the project could not proceed on the basis of attempting some kind of systematic 'comparison' of anthropology and philosophy. In fact both sides of the equation represent very diverse traditions with major internal differences and debates within each subject. Just as anthropologists are separated from one another by their individual theoretical stances or even the 'schools' to which they adhere, so philosophers are deeply divided not only on the basis of their principal areas of interest (ethics, aesthetics, epistemology, the philosophy of history and so on), but also and more importantly by their general orientation to their subject – analytical and linguistically oriented philosophers in particular having very little professional traffic with their colleagues working in more phenomenological directions or busy exploring entirely new fields of emerging interest such as environmental philosophy. The study of non-Western philosophies in the European and North American academy is, if taken seriously at all, relegated to programmes in Oriental, Asian or African studies and is rarely undertaken in the context of philosophy departments.

This volume both questions this rigidity of intellectual and disciplinary boundaries and attempts to bypass it by means of encouraging many voices and many perspectives to offer fresh and, we hope, thought-provoking approaches to the dialogue between anthropology and philosophy. Our initial assumption was indeed that there are many largely unexplored points of contact, worth exploring not only out of a purely intellectual interest, but because the issues raised touch directly and relevantly on many significant issues of fundamental existential import. These are questions largely suppressed in professional technical philosophy and its anthropological counterpart – issues of the human place in the world, of how meaning systems are constructed and validated, of the nature of rights, rationality, ethics and aesthetic criteria. The exploration of these issues also suggests ways in which the two disciplines might be revised and enriched, and how indeed they might look back to their original roots in the pursuit of a holistic understanding of the human species in its social, cultural and environmental settings, and in the pursuit of the wisdom that makes meaningful, fulfilling and responsible that human existence.

The chapters that follow provide many and diverse perspectives on these issues, all hinging on the basic assumption that both disciplines are in fact pursuing complementary, if not identical, projects – that of illuminating the meaning of being human, the 'species being' of which Karl Marx talked a century and a half ago, and which has been revived in recent discourse by David Harvey in the context of social justice and possible human futures, and of the critique of globalization (Harvey 2002). These debates stand in a long tradition of philosophical anthropology with its roots in the Enlightenment and earlier, and which has born a variety of fruit, ranging from philosophies of being in their Heideggerian, existentialist, phenomenological and theological forms to discussions of rationality, human rights, the philosophy of law and contemporary debates about the meaningfulness of broad synthetic concepts such as 'human nature', the 'self' and 'culture', and even of nature in the context of postmodernist deconstructionism and the challenge of sociobiology. These issues, which clearly transcend the conventional boundaries between anthropology and philosophy, are not of simply academic interest. They spill over very directly into sociology (in particular the sociology of knowledge and areas of sociology which are inherently comparative, such as sociologies of art or of ethics), into psychology and psychiatric practice, into religious studies and very much into debates about the universality or otherwise of human rights, and from there into the very interesting questions raised by proponents of animal rights, deep ecology and the status of notions of the individual, the self and rights in Asian religious and philosophical traditions, and in particular Buddhism (for a good example see Keown, Prebish and Husted 1998). They raise indeed very fundamental questions, such as the status of anthropocentrism. While in Western philosophy this issue has surfaced almost exclusively in the context of environmental philosophy (Fox 1990), it is a foundational issue in Buddhist and Taoist thinking, from which position it deeply interrogates the epistemological and ontological assumptions of mainstream Western philosophy while also raising important interpretative issues for anthropologists working in societies where those belief systems are extant and where the practical consequences of belief are worked out in daily practice and ritual (from the philosophical side, see Hall and Ames 1998; from the anthropological, Schipper 1993). The studies that follow are of necessity themselves explicitly or implicitly comparative, not only as regards the relationship between anthropology and philosophy, but equally in terms of bracketing the assumptions of the mainstream Western world view when other systems of thought, explanation and rationality are foregrounded. We hope that one of the results of this book will be to draw far more scholarly attention on the part of both philosophers and anthropologists to the extraordinary richness and relevance of Asian and African philosophies to both their disciplines, since these are systems which cross the boundaries between belief and analytical investigation, between religion and philosophy, and between cognitive systems and systems of practical morality, and speak in so many respects to our current global crises, including our relationship with the environment.

Themes and Variations

As the readers will see, the volume is divided into three parts. The first lays out some of the main groundwork by situating anthropology and philosophy in relation to one another via an exploration of the concept and practice of philosophical anthropology.

Part I begins with 'The Project of Philosophical Anthropology', by John Clammer, who like many other authors in this section presents to us the key works of the pioneers of philosophical anthropology as an intellectual movement in nineteenth- and early twentieth-century Germany: Scheler, Plesner and Gehlen. But Clammer also presents Foucault's critique of the apparent ahistorical essentialism of Scheler's philosophical anthropology. Clammer pleads for a rapprochement between naturalistic anthropology and philosophical anthropology, which is already historicized. This also reverberates with the spirit of Piet Strydom's contribution in Chapter 6, which pleads for bringing together 'naturalistic and historicist motifs in anthropological thought'. In the second chapter, 'The Self-Preservation of Man: Remarks on the Relation Between Modernity and Philosophical Anthropology', Kasper Lysemose discusses self-preservation at the heart of the enterprise of modernity and philosophical anthropology. But self-preservation involves care. Lysemose refers to Heidegger and writes, 'Instead of calling this structure *Exentricität*, Heidegger calls it *Sorge*. With this well-chosen word the relation of the eccentric anthropological structure to the principle of self-preservation becomes clearer: 'At the centre of man's Sorge – or 'care' – lies man's own being.'

Lysemose's discussion of the relationship between modernity and philosophical anthropology is broadened by Ivan Marquez's essay, 'Whither Modernity? Hybridization, Postoccidentalism, Postdevelopment and Transmodernity', which presents to us the cross-currents between philosophy and anthropology in Latin America. Marquez proposes 'concrete syncretism' as a way of moving creatively beyond the current predicament of modernity, which could revitalize both philosophy and anthropology.

Clammer, Lysemose and Strydom discuss Scheler, Plesner and Gehlen as pioneers of philosophical anthropology. But for Vaclav Brezina, confining the project of philosophical anthropology to these writers would be too narrow. He writes in his contribution, 'Philosophical Anthropology and Philosophy in Anthropology': 'It seems more useful […] to conceive of the role of philosophy in the inquiry about the human condition in terms of a dynamic model of *philosophy in anthropology* rather than in terms of a single discipline such as *philosophical anthropology*. The philosophy-in-anthropology model [...] leaves the involvement of philosophy in the anthropological debate open to philosophical speculation, hence accommodating all major approaches to the issue (essentialism, existentialism, culturalism and naturalism).' Such a spirit of engagement is creatively carried forward in Heike Kämpf's subsequent contribution, 'The Engagement of Philosophy and Anthropology in the Interpretive Turn and Beyond'. Writes Kämpf:

> One of the most interesting and fruitful anthropological discussions of philosophy occurred within the so-called 'interpretive turn' in anthropology. This turn was inspired by philosophy and initiated a reconsideration of philosophical concepts. In particular, the reconsideration of the hermeneutic notion of 'understanding' led to new anthropological readings of the works of Martin Heidegger, Hans-Georg Gadamer and Paul Ricoeur. At the same time this anthropological discussion had its impact on philosophy. On the one hand, hermeneutic and analytic philosophy came closer together while questioning the possibilities of understanding alien cultures: Peter Winch and Richard Rorty dealt with the problem of understanding cultural differences in referring to the philosophy of language. On the other hand, hermeneutic philosophy, being traditionally occupied with the interpretation of texts and historical events, found itself involved in questions concerning social behaviour and cultural differences. Thus a dialogue between anthropology and philosophy occurred, which caused a reformulation of the concept of 'understanding' and simultaneously initiated new attempts to conceptualize the cultural and social reality.

Kämpf nurtures the ground for an anthropology of the contemporary enriched by the confluence of both philosophy and anthropology. Such a creative engagement with the contemporary is at work in the final contribution of Piet Strydom in this section, 'Mediation through Cognitive Dynamics: Philosophical Anthropology and the Conflict of Our Time'. Writes Strydom, 'The old question of philosophical anthropology has made a strong reappearance. This event is accompanied by the urgent demand to come to a better understanding of its core problematic and how the latter could possibly relate to the contemporary situation, particularly to the polarization and conflict of our time.' For Strydom, the conflict that we face is the opposition between naturalism and idealism. Strydom discusses Quine's work as an example of strong naturalism, and Heidegger's as strong idealism. Naturalism today is being vigorously pursued by the biosciences, where there is a tendency towards reductionism. Similarly, idealism tends to be one-sided.

In this context, the central philosophical–anthropological problem is to 'arrive at creative yet responsible ways of crossing the borders and mediating between the naturalistic and historicist – both humanistic and antihumanistic – sides of the image of the human being so as to find a balanced constellation of modes of thinking, of developing and applying knowledge, and of culturally, socially and politically arranging collective forms of life.'

Strydom's foundational interrogation of the dualism between naturalism and idealism in philosophical anthropology is followed by a foundational interrogation of anthropocentrism of philosophy and much of philosophical anthropology. In his essay, 'Philosophy as Anthropocentrism: Language, Life and *Aporia*', Prasenjit Biswas insightfully discusses the work of Wittgenstein and Heidegger. Rarely do we see these two philosophers discussed together. Biswas discusses them with creative insights and helps us learn from both of them in creative border crossing between philosophy and anthropology. Biswas finds anthropocentrism in both Wittgenstein and Heidegger and discusses the work of Giorgio Agamben as a way of transforming such anthropocentric limitations.

The above reflections and meditations in Part I create a hunger and thirst in us to seek out the important sources of philosophical anthropology. Contributions in Part II help us in this. It begins with Ananta Kumar Giri's contribution on Kant. Giri discusses pathways of pragmatic anthropology in Kant's work, animated as it was by a model of popular philosophy. Giri also discusses the dualistic foundation of Kantian anthropology and the need to cultivate nondual modes of thinking and practice in anthropology, not just confined to the academic discipline. This spirit of overcoming dualism and realizing creative holism is embodied in the pioneering work of Wilhelm Dilthey, and in the subsequent contribution, 'Dilthey's Theory of Knowledge and its Potential for Anthropology', Daniel Šuber presents Dilthey's holistic theory of knowledge as different from the '(neo-) Kantian, i.e. *dualistic*' version. For Šuber, Dilthey worked from

> certain, namely *holistic*, ideas about the givenness of 'life' in human consciousness. They are maybe best expressed in his unusual term 'life nexus', which presumes that life is never given to us as a compendium of a multitude of separate aspects, but only as a 'structural coherency' where functions as 'willing', 'feeling' and 'thinking' are immediately and inextricably present. This notion of 'life' is holistic in that it '*encompasses* our representations, evaluations, and purposes, and it exists *in the connection* of these constituents'.

Šuber's presentation of sources of philosophical anthropology in Dilthey is followed by Peter Skalník's discussion of creative relationship between philosophy and anthropology in Malinowski, one of the pioneers of modern anthropology. This is then followed by Lars Kjaerholm's insightful discussion of the semiotic theories of Charles Sanders Peirce. Kjaerholm draws our attention to 'some problems in bringing it to bear in cultures where there are other ontologies which are incompatible with Peirce's classes of possible signs'. As he writes, 'To point to just one example, the problem becomes acute in Victor Turner's studies of symbols, since (as we see in the Indian material) what to our minds are symbols may in the Indian understanding be indices – direct representations of deities and not symbolic representations of them. If the interpretation, the ground, which any given culture refers to in its interpretation of signs, is not brought to bear in an analysis of its signs, then we run the risk of importing our own ontology in the analysis of other cultures. An example is the *yantra*, the geometric design which is thought in a very real sense to represent a particular deity. The *yantra* and its accompanying sound formula, its *mantra*, together are a deity, not a symbol for one.'

Kjaerholm's elaboration of Peircian semiotics and its application for anthropology is followed by Betsy Taylor's presentation of the work of Paul Ricoeur and his crucial significance for a mutually enriching dialogue between philosophy and anthropology. In her creative engagement with Ricoeur, Taylor brings the 'notion of humanness as ecological' to the fore and explores how Ricoeur's notions of text, world, body and action might help us understand the complex and heterogeneous temporalities of humans as ecological beings. Building upon Ricoeur's notion of narrative, Taylor shows us how there is not a circling but a spiralling of 'narrative prefiguration, configuration and refiguration – a mutual incitement between text and the world through which subjectivity passes with a certain capacity for becoming more itself, precisely through its dislocation, expansion and refiguration by texts'. There is a dynamic relationship between text, world and action that gives rise to a new temporality, which Taylor calls 'sedimentary temporality'. In her words:

> What I am calling sedimentary temporality appears as the capacity of subjectivity *to accrue being over time* through co-participation in meaning and action in the world. However, this accrual does not, in any simple way, *enstructure an architecture for the self*. It is not a developmental sense of self, like the Freudian, in which strata are laid down in the psyche – like geological strata predictably or catastrophically building from geological processes of deposition. To shift the hermeneutic circling of text and action, of text and world from a vicious circle to a virtuous circle, Ricoeur speaks of the 'wagers' that are anything but certain, and are frail because they are always subject to 'fault'.

Given the key significance of temporality in anthropology, Taylor's elaboration of sedimentary temporality presents us with an alternative conceptualization of the human, temporal and social. Taylor also discusses the work of commons, which are 'enmeshed interdependencies between communities of beings', where 'we feel connected to commons not just as an "I" having an "it". Rather, we experience them in ways that transgresses first and third person, singular and plural. Our sense of ownness with them requires an (inter)subjectivity that has pronominal hybridity and fluency across "I", "we", "thou", "you", "it", "them".'

If Taylor presents us gifts of insights from Ricoeur, Gernot Saalmann helps us understand the philosophical transformation of anthropology in the works of Clifford Geertz, who creates transformative possibilities in both anthropology and philosophy through a creative combination of 'analytic philosophy and the hermeneutic tradition'. In the subsequent contribution, Marcin Brocki presents us with insights from Mikhail Bakhtin, whose notions of alterity, dialogue, heteroglossia and carnival have been used extensively by anthropologists. For Brocki, 'The discovery of Bakhtin's idea of dialogism coincided with a crisis of representation and a so-called "literary turn" in ethnography.' Anthropologists, Brocki tells us, have used Bakhtin's notion of 'polyphony' but have broadened it. For Brocki, polyphony, in the research practice of ethnography, relates 'both to the reality being examined [...], the dialectics of field research, and "multiple" authorship of ethnographic texts'.

This discussion on Bakhtin is followed by discussion of the work of Slovenian philosopher Slavoj Žižek and his significance for anthropology. Belief is a key concern in anthropology, and in our volume João de Pina-Cabral discusses this with regard to works of philosophers such as Quine as well as some people's beliefs in Mozambique about albinos – light-skinned people. Kjaerholm develops Žižek's insightful notion of belief by proxy thus:

> The first pilgrim was a man who had sinned against Aiyappan, and in order to be cleansed of his sin, which resulted in a serious skin affliction, he entered the *sanctum sanctorum* of Aiyappan's temple and literally merged with the statue representing Aiyappan, thus illustrating what the 'ideological' goal of this pilgrimage is supposed to be: the merging of the subject/individual, or dividual if you will, with the divine universal soul, as in so many other types of Hindu worship. [...] This might seem hard to believe by Westerners, and many times I have been questioned at conferences about this – 'Do they really believe in this? Are they really possessed?' and so on – and with Žižek's idea about belief-by-proxy, we can now answer that maybe nobody in India 'really' believes it, but the belief is still there, since they believe there are some who believe it.

The contributions discussed so far present us with sources of philosophical anthropology from the Western philosophical tradition. In our volume we were eager to have more global philosophical sources for creating a global philosophy and anthropology. Susantha Goonatilake discusses the border crossing between anthropology and Buddhist philosophy. For Goonatilake, 'There is always intertwined in Buddhism an observational element which combines with the philosophical elements.' Though the thrust on observation exists alongside belief in gods and goddesses, 'outside such cultural furniture, the observational could stand on their own – as in descriptions of meditation. […] A good observational metaphor used in Buddhism is that one should be like the lotus leaf floating on water, being both within water as well as outside it. This observational injunction would be ideal for participant observation, the person, the observer being both within the water of other human beings as well as being above it.'

In his essay, Goonatilake pleads for a reverse ethnocentrism, but here he wants to build on traditions of contempt: 'Even at the nadir of Sri Lanka, European civilization – at least certain aspects of it – was looked at with contempt by the Sinhalese.' But reverse ethnocentrism is as much a danger to anthropology as planetary conversation as the colonial ethnocentrism. For border crossing and mutual critique, our positions of pride and contempt need a flow of *Karuna* (compassion) from Buddhist paths.

From these contributions in Part II we come to Part III, where contributors discuss several instances of mutual border crossing and dialogue between philosophy and anthropology at work. It begins with Kai Kresse's contribution on the dialogue between philosophy and anthropology in Africa and his ethnography of anthropology and philosophy. This is followed by João de Pina-Cabral's fascinating essay on belief at the border crossing of philosophy and anthropology. He examines the belief of some people in Mozambique that albinos (light-skinned black people) do not die, but taking cues from Davidson and Quine (especially his notion of a garden of belief), urges us not to dismiss such beliefs as irrational. Pina-Cabral's essay is followed by Robert Feleppa's contribution, where he also brings insights from philosophy and anthropology to think about the predicament of development, culture and indigenous knowledge. The last essay in this section discusses important practical and normative issues; Heidrum Friese discusses friendship from a philosophical and anthropological perspective.

The volume concludes with an insightful afterword from Fred Dallmayr, who revisits the notion of philosophical anthropology, especially the meaning of being human. Dallmayr tells us, 'What we are experiencing today is not, to be sure, a high tide of old-style humanism, but the tentative resurgence of a subdued, self-critical and non-Eurocentric (that is, non-hegemonic) view

of the "human" on the far side of absolute affirmation and absolute negation.'
Dallmayr seeks to clear a path 'beyond anthropocentrism and anti-humanism,
a path which also avoids derailment into (biological or idealistic) modes of
reductionism.' Going beyond biological and idealistic reductionism is a motif
in our volume, especially in the contribution of Piet Strydom, and building
upon this we should aim at a philosophical anthropology which seeks to realize
humanity as a seeking whole building upon weak naturalism, weak ontology,
weak structuralism and weak anthropology.

New Directions

In this volume we explore many themes at the borderlands of dialogue and
conversation between philosophy and anthropology. While there has been
some overture to philosophy in anthropology, as we discuss in the beginning,
this volume makes a contribution to this anthropological engagement with
philosophy by bringing both old and new interlocutors together, including
Kant, Plesner, Wittgenstein, Heidegger, Peirce, Dilthey, Bakhtin, Ricoeur,
Žižek, Geertz and Buddha. It presents a much broader picture of the
anthropological engagement with philosophy than is currently available in the
field, which is still rather Eurocentric.

   A single volume, even one as large as this, cannot exhaust all the possibilities,
but we hope that this collection opens up new territory, suggests directions
for rethinking older but unexplored linkages and refreshes thinking about the
historical importance of philosophical influences on and in anthropology.
While sociological theory has remained closer to its philosophical roots and
much more explicit in its connections to, and even overlap with, philosophy
proper, anthropology for the most part has been shy to explore its own
relationship to its sister discipline, with which it shares so much in common.
Recent systematic discussions of anthropological theory are interesting in
this respect. While one fairly representative systemic coverage (Moore 2000)
does not in any way directly discuss the relationships between anthropology
and philosophy, a number of the individual chapter authors do find that
in practice it is necessary to draw on a language of ethics and virtue; and
indeed it is significant to note the extent to which discussions of ethics have
re-entered anthropology in the last decade (for example, Howell 1997), as
more recently have analyses of ontology (Clammer, Poirier and Schwimmer
2004). This indirect form of acknowledgement of the philosophical debt of
anthropology appears in a number of significant recent monographs. Michael
Jackson, for example, refer to 'Existential Anthropology', drawing on the
earlier philosophical work of Jean-Paul Sartre and Maurice Merleau-Ponty –
the work of the latter in particular having many significant implications for

anthropology (Jackson 2005). James Weiner explicitly draws on the work of Heidegger, as well as his own anthropological critique of Merleau-Ponty, in his studies of the Papua New Guinea life worlds (Weiner 2001). Likewise, engaged scholars such as Veena Das and Betsy Taylor also embody a deeply philosophically situated engagement with anthropology in their creative use of Wittgenstein and Merleau-Ponty respectively (see Das 1999, 2007; Taylor this volume; and Reid and Taylor 2010).

It is, in short, difficult to keep philosophy out of anthropology, and extremely fruitful when it is explicitly let in. Resistance in fact seems to come more from the philosophical side despite boundaries becoming more porous with the belated admission of continental philosophy into the mainstream curriculum. This is a situation more or less forced on philosophy by the rise to general cultural prominence of the leading French intellectuals Foucault, Derrida, Lacan and Althusser, and by the broader discovery or rediscovery by sociology and cultural studies of a wide range of thinkers who in practice straddle disciplinary boundaries: Merleau-Ponty again, Levinas, Martin Buber, Bourdieu, Habermas, Benjamin, Barthes and Adorno, to name some of the most prominent. At the same time the English-speaking philosophical world has become more aware of work in contemporary French language philosophy. This itself straddles the boundaries between philosophy understood in the narrow, technical sense that has prevailed for so long in many, if not most, British and North American philosophy departments (for example, Badiou 2004; Rancière 2007) and the work of French anthropologists that raises not only the equally narrow technical questions of conventional anthropology, but also addresses wider global and existential questions (Augé 1999). This move is also fuelled by the recognition that some of the universally acknowledged leading philosophers, when read from a wider perspective, are as much engaged with issues that bear upon the social sciences as they are with philosophy alone in a narrow technical sense – Wittgenstein being an excellent example of this broad-ranging intelligence at work, an intelligence with an awareness of the much broader implications of philosophical ideas for a huge range of human interests and communication (for example, see Clammer 1976 and Finch 1995).

Huge resources for the exploration of the human condition exist in this border region between philosophy and anthropology, and hopefully this volume has pointed to some of the most significant ones. We are also aware that the volume points beyond itself to relatively unexplored areas of the connections between anthropology and philosophy. There are at least five that we would immediately identify. The first of these is aesthetics. Philosophical aesthetics, we would suggest, suffers from severe myopia in its understanding of what constitutes art, and is perhaps the most ethnocentric of all the branches of

Western philosophy. Art is of course a social product and as such is rooted in the cultural context of any given society. The universalist assumptions of philosophical aesthetics are called deeply into question by a comparative and anthropological approach to art (Coote and Shelton 1992). This should not be read as a rejection of Western aesthetics. It is rather a suggestion that, as Marshall Sahlins (1996) has so cogently argued, Western thought systems are simply forms of local knowledge that, because of contingent historical events, have become hegemonic. They are no doubt valid within their own cultural context, but are not necessarily universalizable. The area of aesthetics is a particularly rich one, as handled with sensitivity it opens up questions of representation, power, ontology, belief, the cultural and social structuring of expression and of emotion, of fantasy and imagination. These deeply interesting and fundamental issues in the human sciences suggest a highly fruitful cross-border dialogue between anthropology and philosophy in which neither a purely empirical nor a wholly abstract approach can shed sufficient light, but in which the ethnographic data of anthropology and the conceptual rigour of philosophy, when brought together, do indeed create a new form of philosophical anthropology.

Much the same can be said about other areas of potential dialogue. Perhaps first among these is ethics, an area which, while traditionally the preserve of philosophy, has attracted increasing anthropological and sociological attention in recent years (for example, Smart 1999; Bauman 1994, 1995). The subject of ethics raises some questions parallel to those raised by aesthetics and indeed a number of scholars have attempted to establish an intimate relationship between the two (for example, Maffesoli 1990; Quarles van Ufford and Giri 2003). But beyond that particular project lie major questions of the universality of values, of relativism, of human nature, of the possible material basis of ethical beliefs, of religion as a source of values and behavioural standards, and of the criteria by which ethical or non-ethical behaviour can be judged or evaluated. These questions in turn merge with questions of the anthropology and philosophy of law and human rights (from an anthropological perspective, see Cowan, Dembour and Wilson 2001), and back again to aesthetics in the context of debates about obscenity or pornography (Young 2005). Here again we find a border area in which a profoundly fruitful dialogue can take place when an interdisciplinary perspective is actively embraced.

Recent anthropological discoveries of the idea of 'indigenous knowledge' likewise suggest areas of comparative philosophy and especially of the comparative philosophy of science (or rather sciences), including those of medicine, agriculture and meteorology (Sillitoe 1998). This topic has special significance for the area of environmental philosophy, a newly emerging area that has its own close links with ethics, ontology, the philosophy of science and even aesthetics. Many environmentalists are now looking to the traditional knowledge of preindustrial societies for clues to environmental restoration and forms of ecological consciousness that are in harmony with nature and are nonexploitative of natural resources. The centrality of environmental issues is one that is dawning more rapidly on anthropology with its vast database of information on traditional ecological practices, but only very slowly on philosophy. But as it does so, the links to empirical knowledge of the ecosystem will become vital as will knowledge of the links between ecological and social systems. Any reading of contemporary work in environmental philosophy quickly demonstrates the inherently interdisciplinary nature of the project, such as the journal *Environmental Ethics* or the controversial but important work of Henryk Skolimowski (1981, 1992).

The question of the environment takes us in turn into the territory of Asian, African and Latin American philosophy. The Eurocentrism of mainstream philosophy is seen clearly in its denigration of non-Western forms of philosophy as not being 'real' philosophies at all, but some form of religion or subphilosophical systems of thought. The result has been the marginalization of the rich philosophical traditions of China, India, Japan, of Islam, and of almost the entire philosophical output and heritage of Africa and much of Latin America. Interestingly, it is the environmental question that has brought a great deal of Asian philosophy back into mainstream Western philosophical discourse (Callicott and Ames 1989). A number of the contributions to this book attempt to bring Asian and African philosophy back into a central place. And this is a valid project not only on intellectual and postcolonial grounds, but also precisely because when one explores those philosophies, the links between what is understood as 'philosophy' in those traditions and what we today understand as anthropology are very much closer than in the Western philosophical tradition (for African philosophy, see Eze 1997). Significantly, a contemporary volume of Latin American essays on the philosophies of science and social science is entitled *Antropología del presente* (Althabe and Schuster 1999). The issue here is not only, as a matter of intellectual justice and fair play in what is supposedly an era of globalization, to re-establish the legitimacy and interest of non-Western philosophies, but to indicate that they also raise fundamental questions for that Western philosophical (and by extension, anthropological) tradition. One of the most important of these is the question of anthropocentrism. Central to Buddhist philosophy and to most contemporary ecological philosophy is the idea that an anthropocentric world view is a distortion of humans' true ontological status, and lies at the root of our present environmental crisis. While some would consider this primarily a philosophical issue, it has profound implications for anthropology. For can there indeed be an anthropology beyond anthropocentrism, one rooted in a much more ecological and decentred ontology in which humans are simply one species among the myriad others that co-inhabit our planet?

While Asian philosophies have been for the most part rooted in religious traditions of great antiquity, something true equally of many African thought systems, it is also necessary to remember that they and Latin American philosophy were shaped in the context of colonialism and the imposition of both alien thought systems (religious, philosophical, sociological) and alien institutions that embodied and reproduced these systems (universities, churches, systems of mapping, administration and management of resources). The latest manifestations of the philosophies of those continents continues to be shaped by postcolonial interactions – of Latin America with Spanish and French philosophy, of francophone Africa also with French philosophy, of anglophone Africa and Asia with British and North American philosophy, and francophone Asia (Vietnam and the other states of Indo-China) with French thought. At the same time all these areas have been exposed to the theological philosophies and anthropologies expounded by introduced religious systems, Catholic and Protestant Christian, Buddhist, and of course for much of Africa and Asia, Islam. In much the same way that anthropology has been implicated in complex ways with colonialism (Asad 1975), so has philosophy, although this latter subject has received little attention from this perspective.

While not purporting to answer all of these questions, we offer this volume in a spirit of invitation –invitation to a dialogue between the two disciplines most centrally addressing the human condition. This dialogue and the disciplinary, ethical and aesthetic boundary crossing that it entails suggests many creative openings for fresh work in both philosophy and anthropology and in the rich zone of interaction between them which this volume hopes to inspire, and in doing so begin the mapping process of new territories of both intellectual and practical inquiry. It also, we hope, addresses questions of even wider import. In the current global context the roles of both the humanities (represented here by philosophy) and the social sciences (here anthropology) have been questioned and their relevance to the challenges now facing humankind debated. We intend that this volume will both serve as a bridge between the humanities and social sciences on the one hand, and demonstrate their combined relevance in a world of increasing risk and complexity on the other. In a real sense, anthropology is the most 'humanistic' of the social sciences, and its traditional concern not only with social organization, but also with myth, ritual, art and belief systems places its interests clearly within the compass of the humanities as normally understood. There has been much talk in the academy of interdisciplinary studies, but few actual moves to embody that intention in actual cooperative and transdisciplinary programmes of research and teaching.

While not deliberately foregrounded in this volume, we hope that its contributions will indeed illustrate how transdisciplinary dialogue can take place, the intellectually fruitful outcome of such dialogue, and its manifold ways of speaking to current issues – of identity, the nature of selfhood, the individualistic basis of liberalism, of emerging issues in ethics and technology, of the cultural location of human rights, of climate and environmental justice, and even the nature of globalization itself. What the world may need at this moment is a new philosophical anthropology: one that transcends narrow anthropocentrism, that is alert to the continuities of humans and nature, that places issues of social, gender and environmental justice at its heart, and which seeks not only to describe, but also to create new forms of being human that provide the basis for a sustainable future. Implicit in many of the essays that constitute this book are the seeds of such thinking, and so we offer it not only in the guise of an academic text, but also as a basis for new conversations about human futures.

References

Althabe, Gerard and Félix Gustavo Schuster, eds. 1999. *Antropología del presente*. Buenos Aires: Edicial.

Asad, Talal, ed. 1975. *Anthropology and the Colonial Encounter*. London: Ithaca Press and New York: Humanities Press.

Augé, Marc. 1999. *An Anthropology for Contemporaneous Worlds*. Translated by Amy Jacobs. Stanford: Stanford University Press.

Badiou, Alain. 2004. *Infinite Thought: Truth and the Return of Philosophy*. Translated by Oliver Feltham and Justin Clemens. London and New York: Continuum.

Bauman, Zygmunt. 1994. *Postmodern Ethics*. Oxford and Cambridge, MA: Blackwell.

_____. 1995. *Life in Fragments: Essays in Postmodern Morality*. Oxford and Cambridge, MA: Blackwell.

Blocker, H. Gene and Christopher I. Starling. 2001. *Japanese Philosophy*. Albany: State University of New York Press.

Callicott, J. Baird and Roger T. Ames, eds. 1989. *Nature in Asian Traditions of Thought*. Albany: State University of New York Press.

Clammer, John. 1976. 'Wittgensteinianism and the Social Sciences'. *Sociological Review* 24 (4): 775–91.

_____. 2005. 'Beyond Power: Alternative Conceptions of Being and the (Asian) Reconstitution of Social Theory'. *Asian Journal of Social Science* 33 (1): 62–76.

Clammer, John, Sylvie Poirier and Eric Schwimmer, eds. 2004. *Figured Worlds: Ontological Obstacles in Intercultural Relations*. Toronto and London: Toronto University Press.

Coote, J. and A. Shelton, eds. 1992. *Anthropology, Art and Aesthetics*. Oxford: Oxford University Press.

Cowen, Jane K., Marie-Benedict Dembour and Richard A. Wilson, eds. 2001. *Culture and Rights: Anthropological Perspectives*. Cambridge: Cambridge University Press.

Das, Veena. 1999. 'Wittgenstein and Anthropology'. *Annual Review of Anthropology* 27: 171–95.

_____. 2006. *Life and Words: Violence and the Descent into the Ordinary*. Berkeley: University of California Press.

Eze, Emmanuel Chukwudi, ed. 1997. *Postcolonial African Philosophy: A Critical Reader*. Oxford and Cambridge, MA: Blackwell.

Finch, H. L. 1995. *Wittgenstein*. Rockport, MA: Element.

Fox, Warwick. 1990. *Towards a Transpersonal Ecology: Developing New Foundations for Environmentalism*. Boston and London: Shambhala.

Hall, David L. and Roger T. Ames. 1998. *Thinking from the Han: Self, Truth and Transcendence in Chinese and Western Culture*. Albany: State University of New York Press.

Harvey, David. 2002. *Spaces of Hope*. Edinburgh: Edinburgh University Press.

Howell, Signe, ed. 1997. *The Ethnography of Moralities*. London and New York: Routledge.

Jackson, Michael. 2005. *Existential Anthropology: Events, Exigencies and Effects*. Oxford: Berghahn.

Keown, Damien V., Charles S. Prebish and Wayne R. Husted, eds. 1998. *Buddhism and Human Rights*. Richmond: Curzon.

LaFleur, William, ed. 1985. *Dogen Studies*. Honolulu: University of Hawaii Press.

Maffesoli, Michel. 1990. *Au creux des apparences: Pour une éthique de l'esthétique*. Paris: Plon.

Moore, Henrietta L., ed. 2000. *Anthropological Theory Today*. Cambridge: Polity Press.

Quarles van Ufford, Philip and Ananta Kumar Giri, eds. 2003. *A Moral Critique of Development: In Search of Global Responsibilities*. London and New York: Routledge.

Radin, Paul. (1927) 1957. *Primitive Man as Philosopher*. New York: Dover.

Rancière, Jacques. 2007. *The Future of the Image*. Translated by Gregory Elliot. London: Verso.

Reid, Herbert and Betsy Taylor. 2010. *Recovering the Commons: Democracy, Place, and Global Justice*. Urbana: University of Illinois Press.

Sahlins, Marshall. 1996. 'The Sadness of Sweetness: The Native Anthropology of Western Cosmology'. *Current Anthropology* 37 (3): 395–415.

Schipper, Kristofer. 1993. *The Taoist Body*. Translated by Karen C. Duval. Berkeley: University of California Press.

Sillitoe, Paul. 1998. 'The Development of Indigenous Knowledge: A New Applied Anthropology'. *Current Anthropology* 39 (2): 223–52.

Smart, Barry. 1999. *Facing Modernity: Ambivalence, Reflexivity and Morality*. London and Thousand Oaks: Sage.

Skolimowski, Henryk. 1981. *Eco-Philosophy: Designing New Tactics for Living*. London: Marion Boyars.

_____. 1992. *Living Philosophy: Eco-Philosophy as a Tree of Life*. London: Arkana.

Weiner, James. 2005. *Tree Leaf Talk: A Heideggerian Anthropology*. Oxford: Berg.

Young, Alison. 2005. *Judging the Image: Art, Value, Law*. London and New York: Routledge.

Part I

NURTURING THE FIELD: TOWARDS MUTUAL FECUNDATION AND TRANSFORMATION OF PHILOSOPHY AND ANTHROPOLOGY

Chapter 1

THE PROJECT OF PHILOSOPHICAL ANTHROPOLOGY

John Clammer

The notion of a philosophical anthropology has almost entirely dropped out of contemporary intellectual discourse, both in philosophy and in anthropology. Among the few places where it is alive as an active concept or form of intellectual inquiry is in Christian (mainly Roman Catholic) theology. There are reasons for this absence, which we will shortly elaborate on, but the virtual disappearance of the idea of a philosophical anthropology is an unfortunate one, as it is potentially a notion that can not only provide a bridge between anthropology and philosophy – linked as we shall see by many common concerns – but also an intellectual space in which many fundamental questions of human existence have been and can still be posed. This essay proposes to look at the history of the idea of a philosophical anthropology, its contemporary ramifications and usages, and both its shortcomings and potential as an organizational centre for the key existential questions marginalized in much mainstream Western philosophy and almost entirely absent from the discourse of contemporary anthropology.

In a rare survey article on the concept published in the *Encyclopaedia Britannica*, its authors, the Swiss philosopher Georges Paul Gusdorf and the American anthropologist Mary Elizabeth Tiles, suggest that the word 'anthropology' was first used in German universities in the sixteenth century to refer to the systematic study of man as both a physical and moral being:

> Philosophical anthropology is thus, literally, the systematic study of man conducted within philosophy or by the reflective methods characteristic of philosophy; it might in particular be thought of as being concerned with questions of the status of man in the universe, or the purpose or meaning of

human life, and indeed, with the issues of whether there is any such meaning and of whether man can be made the object of systematic study. (*Encyclopaedia Britannica* 1993, 550)

Such a broad definition inevitably suggests that what actually is seen as falling within the scope of philosophical anthropology varies in time and space and with current conceptions of the nature, concerns and methods of philosophy. It is no surprise to discover that recent philosophical anthropology has flourished mainly in continental Europe, with its strong traditions of existential and phenomenological approaches to philosophy leading to a preoccupation with philosophies of being (that of Heidegger for example) and its active Catholicism (and here we are referring principally to Germany, France and to a lesser extent Spain), and hence to an emphasis on ontology, rather than in the English-speaking world, with its emphasis on analytical philosophy and a corresponding preoccupation with epistemology.

Essentially, then, philosophical anthropology was and to some extent still is considered to be the 'philosophy of man', and as embodying Humanist concepts or indeed as being the philosophical expression of Humanism, especially during and after the European Renaissance. Correspondingly, the central concern has been the concept of human nature. This common thread has itself undergone numerous mutations as the intellectual and cultural environments surrounding this perennial debate have themselves evolved. The medieval concept of the 'great chain of being' and its implication of the potential perfectibility of human beings was by the Renaissance being challenged by growing knowledge in the natural sciences (especially in biology, which began to demonstrate the continuities between humans and the rest of nature), by philosophical debates about rationality or rationalities (fuelled by the discovery of other flourishing civilizations), and by the discovery of other religions in which the anthropocentrism of the monotheistic paradigms of the Near East and Europe was very directly challenged. With these contextual shifts came quite naturally corresponding shifts in notions of human nature, from medieval ones of a fixed and universal nature, to Renaissance and post-Renaissance ones of plasticity and autonomy, and indeed to the idea of humans as having no fixed nature at all, a trend that culminated in the West in existentialism and later in postmodernism. The idea of philosophical anthropology as humanism and of humans as the centre of things has consequently been challenged on many fronts – from comparative religion and the ethnographic data of anthropology, from the natural and especially the biological sciences, from relativistic thinking and the antifoundationalism and radical constructivism of much recent social and cultural theory. This has led a whole cohort of critics, from postmodernists to structuralists and from Althusser to Foucault, to an antihumanist position in which any talk of human nature can only describe either a pre- or nonscientific conception of anthropology, a form of religious mystification or an illegitimate form of essentialism.

From this reading Western philosophy can be seen as a reflective process throughout which, from late antiquity onwards, differing views of humankind were worked out, from the early investigations of Plato and Aristotle, through the essentially theological ruminations of the medieval philosophers, to the beginnings of a more critical investigation of humans as the focal point of philosophy (rather than, for example, of logic or proofs for the existence of God). This began with Michel de Montaigne and Giambattista Vico in the eighteenth century (Vico's *Scienza Nuova* was published in 1725) and proceeded via Descartes to the philosophers of the eighteenth-century Enlightenment including David Hume in England, with his empiricist investigations of human knowledge and perception, and of course Kant, whose grappling with similar problems (but with very different solutions to the British empiricists and idealists) led him to devote a whole volume of his work to philosophical anthropology. By the nineteenth and early twentieth centuries, pivotal figures became not so much philosophers – with the exception of Edmund Husserl, whose work has had a profound impact on the later philosophies of Heidegger, Sartre and Merleau-Ponty – as linguists (Gottlob Frege and Ferdinand de Saussure), investigators of the psychic realm (Freud in particular and subsequently Foucault), political economists (of which Marx, with his notions in his early work of 'species being', is clearly the key figure) and even anthropologists themselves, with the 'antihumanism' of Lévi-Strauss playing a major role in the 'death of man' debates that occurred in Western discourse in the 1960s, paralleled by the 'death of God' debates going on in radical theology at around the same time.

Seen from this point of view, philosophical anthropology is actually the thread that ties together very disparate forms of Western philosophy, widely separated by time. The 'anthropological question', sometimes suppressed, sometimes denied, is actually what unifies philosophy. And anthropology, which has had an ambiguous relationship with philosophy, preferring on the whole to ally itself with the natural sciences, sociology or linguistics, actually by its very nature raises philosophical questions: these are in fact at its heart. The movement by anthropology into the social merely masks this inevitable conclusion. Studies of the early origins of anthropology (Slotkin 1965) show very clearly that until the nineteenth century it was actually very difficult to separate anthropology and philosophy, even physical anthropology, since both addressed essentially the same questions. A parallel discussion of the philosophies of Asia – of Japan (Piovesana 1997; Paul 1993), China

(Hall and Ames 1998) or India (Hiriyanna 1964), for example – would throw up a structurally similar history, but with a very different content, the metaphysics of Buddhism, Taoism and Hinduism being radically different from those prevailing in the mainstream West. While discussions of logic and other technical matters most certainly do occur, and where contact with the West and with Western philosophies and religions has greatly modified what might have been the natural course of indigenous philosophical development, the 'problem of man' prevails too, but in an interesting way. The nonanthropocentrism of much Asian philosophy (the main exception being the schools emerging from Confucianism) posits a very different relationship and set of causal processes between humans and their total environment (which inevitably contains the spiritual as well as the social and the natural or material environments) than that found in Western philosophy. The more recent challenges of deep ecology, with its profound links to Buddhistic forms of thought, in a sense unifies the current concerns of both forms of philosophy while provoking both to a fresh engagement with nature and with the human place within it.

The Trajectory of Philosophical Anthropology

The mostly Continental provenance of philosophical anthropology can best be understood by its origins in the German speaking world and its continued usage there by German philosophers, especially those influenced by phenomenology, and by its translation into various varieties of the 'philosophy of the person' among French Catholic and to a lesser extent Spanish philosophical theologians. Michael Landmann suggests that the term itself was first used in 1596 by the theologian Otto Cassmann with reference to the supposed double nature of mankind – as both bodily and spiritual beings – common to the theology of the time, and that another form of dualism has since crept into the human sciences. He argues that while physical anthropology and ethnology explore the 'external' characteristics – biological and cultural – of human beings, philosophy critiques this supposed knowledge and suggests that 'man' him or herself is a 'problem' that raises fundamental questions about being and what if anything distinguishes the human race from other forms of existence inhabiting the universe (Landmann 1955, 6). The supposition must therefore be that 'scientific' anthropology contains (usually unexplored) assumptions about what human beings really *are*. This debate gives rise on the one hand to forms of entirely non-naturalistic positions (suggesting that there is an inner core or essence of human beings, the depiction of which requires no recourse to cultural or biological factors) and on the other to naturalistic anthropologies (suggesting that humans are both the makers of and are shaped by culture, and that biological, genetic and environmental factors influence, even if they do not determine, human behaviour and social organization). The picture is complicated, as Landmann goes on to point out, by the self-interpretation of peoples: the classical Greek conception of human beings as essentially rational beings was both indeed a *conception* (and almost certainly a highly gendered one, as it is not clear if women were always included in this 'conception of man') and also, in Weberian terms, an ideal type, which as such acted to express in concrete terms that self-image in philosophy, sculpture, architecture, ritual, and social organization. This is true, but the question is: to what extent? While idealist philosophers would argue that self-conception is fundamental – a culture will 'express' itself in its art, poetry and religion – this can easily become a highly romanticized and abstract notion, one that would be vigorously contested by materialist philosophers who would see real cultural and social development as deriving from economic and technological factors, of which the 'expressions' would be epiphenomenal. In practice very few modern social scientists would draw the lines so clearly. Even Weber, so often charged with proposing an idealist model of the origins of capitalism (the famous 'Protestant ethic' theory), was in fact perfectly aware of the material factors and discussed them at length.

Marx and Engels, in their critique of Feuerbach's influential *The Essence of Christianity* (1841) contained in their *The German Ideology* (1846), attack him not for his position on religion, but for the fact that he essentially does not go far enough: by grounding his theology in anthropology rather than in a spiritualized notion of the self, he has made a big step in the right direction, but not enough to contain 'real, historical men' or to overcome the idealist tendency to see the 'sensuous' world around him, and nature in particular, as eternally given rather than as socially constructed. The main point of contention between many proponents of a philosophical anthropology and those who are satisfied with a purely naturalistic one is exactly this fault line: between the ability to satisfactorily confine the scientific study of humans to the empirically determinable on the one hand, and the desire to seek out the special and defining qualities of human beings on the other – a 'philosophy of life', exemplified perhaps in the work of Martin Heidegger, whose whole philosophy is primarily an ontology, an attempt to place being at the centre of the entire philosophical enterprise (Heidegger 1961). The result is that a great deal that appears under the sign of philosophical anthropology is closer to what might be called 'wisdom literature' than it is to either conventional naturalistic anthropology or to most forms of technical philosophy, with the exception of existentialism, with which it shares many links and common questions. This can be clearly seen in the philosophical anthropology of Max Scheler, seen by many as one of the principle promoters of the idea, whose conception of the subject as a basic science of the essence and essential constitution of man places him in a quasi-theological camp that sees humans in the context of the eternal, and leads to his rejection of naturalistic anthropology and evolution as unnecessary to a true understanding of human nature (Scheler 1927, 1960). The outright rejection of philosophical anthropology for its apparently irredeemable essentialism by thinkers such as Foucault stems from this ahistorical idealism, rarely rooted in the actual experience of peoples.

But need this dichotomy between naturalistic anthropology on the one hand, feeling little need to raise philosophical questions about its epistemological and ontological assumptions, and an idealist and largely essentialist philosophical anthropology on the other, be the only option? I think not, and in going on to review some of the possibilities still inherent in philosophical anthropology, I will suggest that it is more than possible to suggest a rapprochement between the two, and to actually make the stronger case that they require each other. Naturalistic anthropology, innocent of its philosophical underpinnings, is shallow and falls far short of its avowed intention to be a synthesizing science of humanity; philosophical anthropology, bereft of substantive empirical and ethnographic foundations, floats in an intellectual no man's land of pop theology, new ageism and marginality in relation to mainstream philosophy. To bring the two together, however, is to open up areas of creativity in anthropology and philosophy where the truly human in all its variety is not alien to philosophy and the fundamental existential issues to which philosophy points enrich and deepen anthropology, helping it beyond the purely sociological and the self-limitations this imposes on its path to becoming a genuinely human and humane science.

There are in fact several significant points of contact. One of the principal reasons why philosophical anthropology has continued to flourish in continental Europe is the influence of phenomenology. In the sense that this word was used by Edmund Husserl (as opposed to the earlier Hegelian usage), it referred to a method of pure description, one intended to move beyond assumptions by bracketing all presuppositions and hence allowing phenomena to appear in all their innocence, as it were. This descriptive method, difficult as it is to actually apply in practice, has nevertheless given rise to numerous offshoots that have proved to be more significant than the parent: existentialism; the subtle and still underestimated philosophy of Merleau-Ponty; the sociological phenomenology of Alfred Schutz especially, as embodied in his seminal work *The Phenomenology of the Social World* ([1932] 1967); a large number of works in philosophical theology; and, perhaps most significantly, a whole flourishing school of psychiatry largely originating in the work of the Swiss psychiatrist Ludwig Binswanger. Binswanger was originally a student of Freud who broke away to form his own tendency after encountering the philosophical work of Husserl and Heidegger, concluding that psychiatric disorders could only be approached by grasping the life worlds of the disturbed to provide a descriptive picture of the whole patient, and that this broad context was necessary to transcend the individualist and largely context-free methods of classical psychoanalysis. As he put it, his thoughts led him 'beyond psychology, psychoanalysis and biology [...] to arrive at an Anthropology' (Binswanger 1957, 89). This approach led Binswanger to reject the mind/body distinction in favour of a holistic approach that saw the human person as a totality: 'Through philosophical anthropology Binswanger hoped to provide an analysis of human existence that would make analyses of specific human existences possible; he hoped that *philosophical anthropology would make existential analysis possible*' (Kohl 1965, 167, italics in the original). An entire school of existential and phenomenological psychiatry now exists following this lead; Husserl's influence has thus been wide and deep despite his lack of direct disciples. He has been the inspiration for the antinaturalistic philosophical anthropology of Max Scheler, much of the work of Heidegger and Merleau-Ponty (and to a lesser extent Jean-Paul Sartre), and a continuing tradition of work in philosophical anthropology by German philosophers such as Erich Rothacker. In *Kulturanthropologie* (1948), Rothacker attempts to supplement Wilhelm Dilthey's philosophy of history with an analysis of humans not only as carriers of culture, but to locate culture in basic structural 'essences' of human beings, arising from the fact that, whereas other animals are dominated by their natural environments, humans can achieve mastery through creativity. Likewise, a great deal of philosophical theology and its derivatives were inspired by Husserl, including the philosophies of life of the two prominent Spanish existentialists Miguel de Unamuno and José Ortega y Gasset (for a bibliography and survey of the literature from 1939 until the mid-1960s, see Farber 1966, 163–228, which includes discussion of Italian, Dutch, Latin American, Danish and other less known literatures of work deriving from phenomenology).

While phenomenology has had very little direct impact on anthropology, especially in its Anglo-Saxon forms, an interesting but unexplored point of contact is through Husserl's notion of phenomenological 'reduction', or the identification of pure conscious experiences leading to radical or 'pure' description, which constitutes the methodological basis of phenomenology in the strict sense. While this 'suspension', including that of belief and other forms of ideological colouration, is not exactly a description of the ethnographic method, it is in some ways close to it, as it is to Weber's notion of the separation of fact and value and of meaningful action, which provided the starting point for Alfred Schutz's phenomenological approach to social life. Husserl's concept of meaning-endowing experiences is there brought into a dialogue with Weber to construct a model for the analysis of intersubjective understanding, ideal-typical social categories and a developed interpretative sociology. Here there is substantial common ground with ethnography, the division between anthropology and philosophy being less substantive than clouded by the artificial separation of disciplines and their canonical literatures.

Elaborations and Ramifications

At this point we could simply agree that philosophical anthropology is an interesting but minor theme in the history of (mainly European) thought, with little substantive connection to what anthropologists actually do. This I think is a rather narrow-minded view, as a deeper exploration of the interfaces between anthropology and philosophy soon throws up the fact that many of the fundamental theoretical issues in anthropology are in fact among those that have traditionally fallen within the province of philosophical anthropology. Here I will pick out what I would consider to be some of the most significant of these: the 'rationality' debate; debates about the nature or existence of human nature and the associated issues of concepts of the person and of individualism; symbolism and humans as symbolizing creatures; the challenge of structuralism; the meaning of culture; the significance of the emergence of anthropological interest in the self, the body and emotions; the probable impact of ideas arising in environmental anthropology and sociology about the nature of human beings in relationship to nature; and the challenge of non-Western anthropologies that under the regime of globalization have arisen to contest the hegemony of the Western versions. Quite a list in fact.

In his now classic 1937 ethnography *Witchcraft, Oracles and Magic Among the Azande*, Edward Evans-Pritchard raised a fundamental philosophical problem for anthropology. Given that the Azande belief in witchcraft-as-causality is to most (and certainly to almost all Western anthropologists) irrational and certainly 'nonscientific', a major problem of interpretation arises. If one adopts the Zande position, then an accurate descriptive account of their culture is possible, but at the rather high price for the anthropologist to pay of going cognitively native. If, however, one prefers to regard their beliefs as just exotically fascinating but with no basis in any known system of scientific causality, then the absolutely central belief system of the entire culture has to be regarded as absurd, and so a highly biased or even comical account of the Zande will necessarily emerge. How does one transcend the horns of this dilemma? Within anthropology a number of possible answers, none wholly satisfactory, have been suggested. One could of course simply become a relativist or pluralist, but this of course makes the possibility of any real communication between cultures remote or impossible, and in any cases raises serious philosophical problems about the status of knowledge: is it, as some extreme sociologists of knowledge might suggest, always contextual? If so, then of course there is no 'truth', only socially constructed 'truths', a conclusion that some postmodernists might happily embrace at the level of theory, though few actually seem to at the level of practice (Hollis 1970). This same problem has been unwittingly raised by the recent promotion of 'indigenous knowledge' (e.g., Sillitoe 1998) as the way for anthropologists to meaningfully engage with the pressing development problems of the contemporary age. But, then, is indigenous knowledge simply a local means of more effectively delivering universalist and top-down development solutions? Or, much more radically, are all indigenous knowledges philosophically equal, meaning, as Marshall Sahlins (1996) has suggested, Western anthropology and Western knowledges are simply specific local knowledges that as a result of certain contingent historical factors (colonialism for example) have become effectively hegemonic, at least as concerns the sciences? If Sahlins is correct, then potentially there are many knowledge systems and many anthropologies made increasingly available to all of us as the result of globalization, and capable of interrogating the West in much the same ways that Western anthropology has been interrogating the rest. Other possibilities reside in an older anthropological universalism or in the claim that native anthropologists are exempt from this problem as they already presumably accept the local value system and system of knowledge. But it is doubtful if this is true, not only because unthinking acceptance of the local cultural values renders the native anthropologist as nonobjective as the foreigner and possibly more so, but equally because the epistemological status of that local knowledge is still left in doubt. Are the natives 'rational'?

While a Lévy-Bruhl would have no problem in answering this in terms of 'participation' and the like, this does not really let us off the hook. The dilemma still remains: a contextual position that argues that there are in effect many rationalities (the status of which is defined not by its contrast with other rationalities, but by its internal consistency) or a universalist one that suggests that we are all equally rational because we share the same brain structures, can communicate and translate each other's languages and are all members of one species – the relatively minor cultural variations found within being much less significant than the commonalities. Each position has its own philosophical problems and practical consequences. The first, in assuming essentially that rationality equals culture, presumes a unified and consistent cultural 'system', which experience and ethnography equally show to be highly problematic – cultures being in fact messy, unfinished, contested and stratified entities, even if they exist at all in any coherent sense, which some anthropologists now seem to seriously doubt (Fox and King 2002).

The second, while it makes such useful concepts as that of human rights possible, has to assume that cultural differences are fairly insignificant, a position that some might argue is only possible precisely because the hegemony of certain globalized systems of economy, language, law and so forth has effectively marginalized the alternatives so that, if they can survive at all, can only do so on the far edges or in the interstices of the modern world system. The rationality debate in fact raises questions that fall directly within the purview of philosophical anthropology: are we one species? Is there a common system of rationality shared by the whole human species (excepting the insane)? Is communication really possible between communities and can translation ever really succeed? The fact that these questions and others like them have been answered variously by the likes of Chomsky, Lévi-Strauss and Foucault by shifting the ground to suggest either a biological hardwiring (for Chomsky that makes language and translation possible) or a form of structuralism in which cultural differences are simply the reshuffled elements in a common and finite pack of cards, does not make the problem go away, but simply suggests another philosophical permutation to a perennial problem of human identity.

It is really in this context, although not necessarily posed in the form of questions about rationality, that the intense debates about human nature that have raged in or around the social sciences are to be sited (although, interestingly enough, studiously ignored by most anthropologists for whom these questions are actually fundamental). These issues have in fact been the perennial subject matter of philosophical anthropology, given new life by three fresh factors: the challenge of sociobiology, political developments including debates over the universality of human rights and the problems of multiculturalism, and, probably as a result of globalization, a rising concern with identity. The first of these factors (arising principally from the work of the biologist Edward O. Wilson in his book *Sociobiology* (1975) and popularized in his more free-ranging *On Human Nature* (Wilson 1982), in which he applied insights from the social insects and higher apes to a range of broadly anthropological questions including aggression, hierarchy, the incest taboo, homosexuality, territorial conflict, altruism, sex differences, religion and the evolution of civilizations) suggests not that there is no 'human nature', but that there indeed is, albeit one formed and conditioned not so much by culture as by biology. The storm of protest that broke around this thesis illustrates not only profound ideological differences and indeed irrationalities (a deep fear of behaviour being explained in fundamentally biological and ethological terms), but the centrality of the issue itself and its implications, including that of whether we as a species (I assume anthropocentrically that a dog or higher ape are not reading this) are, despite many forms of cultural conditioning, fundamentally aggressive. The shrill rejection of sociobiology in some quarters may have rather less to do with its truth or otherwise than with the bleak and, in a sense, determined character of human nature that it posits.

But while biology has provided one line of approach to the issue of the existence and qualities of human nature, politics suggests another. In his survey of arguments pertaining to human nature from a political science perspective, Christopher Berry suggests, in a discussion that in fact goes well beyond politics and actually embraces all of the human sciences, that the topic is essential because it informs debate in relation to human rights, to the old question of the perfectibility of humans, freedom versus constraint, the possibility of a universalist political theory and the whole nature of politics as a project to justly order human society (Berry 1986). To be able to review the various contending positions, Berry finds it necessary to call on anthropology to inform political theory in this respect. This is because the problem of relativism is equally acute in political science as it is in cultural studies, perhaps more so as the issue of human rights hangs on being able to establish a reasonable concept of the unity of the human species, as do concepts of development enshrined in such documents as the UN's programmatic Millennium Development Goals, and where actual political systems generate aggression that takes highly destructive collective forms. As Berry and others point out, whether this purported unity (and one required ideologically by the very concept of the United Nations or of human rights) is posited on the grounds of biosocial facts, by the fact that languages despite their surface differences presuppose a common underlying structure, or by the requirements of rationality, matters less than the requirement to indeed find or assert such a structure (Berry 1986, 77; Hollis 1979). There are really three questions here: that of the unity or existence of a universal human nature, that of the basis for the belief in or against such a conception, and that of the issue of whether it actually matters. If for political, aesthetic, ecological or other reasons we wish to believe in the brother/sisterhood of humankind because that belief works a lot better than its alternatives in promoting a peaceful, just and pleasant world, does it really matter whether human nature objectively exists? By desiring it to exist we have perhaps brought it into existence – it might indeed exist as an evolutionary goal rather than as a current empirical given.

This latter position seems in fact to be that of the philosopher Richard Rorty, whose defence of liberalism is based on the idea that human solidarity or community is all that is necessary. Liberalism, while requiring a sense of community, does not need the notion of a common human nature (Rorty 1982, 207) and pragmatism is the appropriately corresponding philosophical position, as 'loyalty to our fellow humans does not require something permanent and ahistorical […] which guarantees convergence to agreement' (Rorty 1982, 171). But a problem with this, as Berry argues (1986), is that it is ethnocentric: the values of Western bourgeois liberalism are taken to be the norm, a claim both not rooted in anthropology and strangely ahistorical itself. One fallback position adopted by both philosophers (for example, John Finnis in his 1980 *Natural Law and Natural Rights*) and by a mostly earlier generation of anthropologists (for example G. P. Murdoch 1945) has been simply to list the supposedly common characteristics of all human cultures – either as general categories (for Finnis these are life, knowledge, play, aesthetic experience, friendship, practical reasonableness and religion) or (for Murdoch) as a list including such diverse elements as athletic sports, dancing, joking, law, marriage, mealtimes, toolmaking and visiting.

The work of Lévi-Strauss can be seen as an attempt to bypass these approaches altogether by rooting his approach in the idea of structure – to concentrate on not the contents of categories, but on the relations between them. These it is argued will prove to be a large but limited range of universal forms, the role of the anthropologist being to 'grasp beyond the conscious and always shifting images which men hold, the complete range of unconscious possibilities' (Lévi-Strauss 1968, 23). Universalism, then, lies not (as with Murdoch) in a list of features, but in the underlying structures derived from a concept of linguistics, and which provide finite permutations of the elements involved, whether these be (as in Lévi-Strauss's own principle examples) kinship, myth or cooking, or any other category of cultural activity. This has led, of course, to charges of 'antihumanism' – structuralism implies that people essentially are manipulated by the forms rather than manipulate them and are thus 'unfree'. Lévi-Strauss's work consequently has certain formal correspondences with sociobiology in that both locate 'human nature' not in some unalienable essence of man, but in the forms and evolutionary processes that frame humanity. Freedom is thus not freedom from but freedom within the 'limitations' (they are in fact just as much opportunities) of biology and structure. Here, then, we find a form of philosophical anthropology very different from that of the German tendency, a concern not with essences, but with forms and process (but for a phenomenological critique of Lévi-Strauss see Géras 1970).

The work of Michel Foucault provides an interesting counterpoint to the Lévi-Straussian approach. In his unpublished introduction to a French edition of Kant's *Anthropology*, most of which later appeared in the introduction to *Les mots et les choses* (1966), Foucault launches an attack on attempts to establish an anthropology – not in the sense of Lévi-Strauss, but in the form of the philosophical anthropology of Sartre and Merleau-Ponty, and behind them of Husserl himself. Since Nietzsche, Foucault argues, the death of God signals the death of man, so the Kantian question 'what is man?' is redundant and the whole Husserl/Sartre/Merleau-Ponty lineage negated. The primary question of philosophical anthropology consequently cannot be asked. In its place Foucault proposed, of course, 'an archaeology of the human sciences': 'In essence *Les mots et les choses* maintains that every period is characterized by an underground configuration that delineates its culture, a grid of knowledge making possible every scientific discourse, every production of statements. Foucault designates this "historical a priori" as an episteme, deeply basic to defining and limiting what any period can – or cannot think' (Eribon 1992, 158). Foucault, then, is not attacking naturalistic anthropology – indeed he argues that ethnology and psychoanalysis stand in a place apart: they are 'counter-sciences' that 'ceaselessly "unmake" that very man who is creating and recreating his positivity. [...] One may say of both of them what Lévi-Strauss said of ethnology: that they dissolve man' (Foucault 1966, 379–81). Foucault's critique, then, is not of anthropology as such, but of the forms of idealist philosophical anthropology stemming from Kant. The central questions however remain the same. Berry wisely suggests at the conclusion of his book,

> What final conclusion can be drawn? The most sensible would be that we should not expect too much from a concept of human nature. [...] Indeed a self-denying ordinance is in order. Knowing that recourse to human nature is not going to end dispute then it should not pretend to that role. One can certainly ask theorists what view of Man is held and ask that they be clear what that view is and what they think follows from it. But no theorist should think that articulating a view of man is going to disarm criticism [...], for the critic is also a theorist to whom the same principle applies. (Berry 1986, 140)

If the debates around the notion of human nature identify what is undoubtedly the central problem of philosophical anthropology, there are clearly many other points of contact between anthropology and philosophy that also throw up fundamental questions. Since the mid-1980s there has been an upsurge in anthropology of a whole new group of issues that can broadly be defined as philosophical in nature: a preoccupation with the self, with concepts of the person and personal identity, with individualism and collectivism, with the emotions, with therapy and medical anthropology, and with the body – concerns mirrored equally in sociology, suggesting a broader social shift away from functionalism, structuralism and Marxism to a more subjectivist approach to sociocultural life and phenomena. Interesting as this is in itself, each of these categories of enquiry raises philosophical issues as significant as, and indeed related to, the classical concerns of philosophical anthropology.

Some related examples might suffice. The first is the emergence of a preoccupation with the self. While some might argue that this is symptomatic of a retreat from political engagement and transformative action in/on the world, it nevertheless raises significant issues. An entire volume, for instance, is devoted to this issue by Anthony Cohen (1994), in which he argues that the individual exists (and not just as a relational self) and that individual self-consciousness and a notion of agency are necessary to explain a whole range of traditional anthropological themes such as naming, ethnicity and socialization. The most contentious part of his thesis is undoubtedly the claim that the notions of culture and society should be treated from the self upwards, an interesting kind of reductionist argument. That there are selves beneath roles is hardly an original position to take, and in fact Cohen's whole model fits within a whole trend of anthropologizing that stems from the seminal work of Marcel Mauss by way of Louis Dumont (especially Dumont 1986) and which is well expressed in the debates about the person, selfhood and individuality that arose in the 1980s (Carrithers, Collins and Lukes 1985). It is in the work of Brian Morris, however, that the issue of personal identity in anthropology is systematically linked to philosophy (Morris 1991). What distinguishes Cohen and Morris in terms of their approaches is that while Morris, despite being an anthropologist, confines himself to the Western philosophical, psychological and sociological traditions, Cohen, in arguing in effect for the universality of the concept of the individual, provides a much wider ethnographic and comparative perspective. But at the heart of the matter is the key philosophical question about the nature of personal identity: are individuals (who clearly exist in a biological sense) monads, simply points in a network of social relationships, known only to themselves through some form of subjective introspection, available to knowledge and sociological investigation only as they perform and behave as agents; or do they not even exist at all, as strict Theravada Buddhists would have to argue?

These are not just theoretical questions, as in practice they shape psychological and in particular psychiatric practice, underpin many forms of political theory and practice (Western liberalism as opposed to forms of collectivist communism, Hobbes as opposed to Rousseau), and fundamentally shape both a society's self-image and the practice of anthropology as it applies to those societies. Nowhere is this latter point seen more clearly than in Japan where a self-image deriving from Buddhism, Shinto and other nativist folk traditions has given rise to an indigenous model of a feeling-based culture with a special relationship to nature, a hierarchical but nonclass society and a real but diffused spirituality entirely different from that of monotheistic Western religions, and a unique claim to being the original postmodern society (Clammer 1995).

This self-conception has given rise to a distinctive form of native anthropology, and also to intense debate among the wider Japanological community as to the legitimacy of this form of indigenous ideology: is it just a self-serving and nationalist myth or does it actually reflect real distinctiveness in the culture being so characterized? These questions raise yet another fundamental one: can there be anthropology beyond anthropocentrism? In the major religious traditions of Asia, especially in Buddhism and Hinduism, we find a weak or nonexistent sense of the self – a self that is actually impermanent, is constantly recycled but not as an unchanging or individual essence, and is really just the reflection of innumerable other entities and relationships, rather than something that exists in itself as a self-subsistent entity. Such an understanding shifts the entire ground of anthropological discourse, and for this reason Cohen's argument does not go far enough. To adduce ethnographic examples of individualism from around the globe does not prove the existence of the individual. In the Eastern traditions the self 'exists' as a sort of fiction, as a theoretical and pragmatic construct enabling the temporary carrier of an identity to function as a social being, rather as a character in a novel or film is the subject or carrier of a narrative and as such exists imaginatively, but possesses no concrete identity outside of the *maya* (illusion) of the novel or movie, real as the character may seem to the reader or viewer.

Any attempt to construct a philosophical anthropology that is truly universal must confront this comparative challenge or face the charge (and a legitimate one for many of the existing varieties) of ethnocentrism and quite possibly also gender bias. The recent concern in anthropology with questions of the self, the body and the emotions clearly indicate that a more comprehensive model of the human person (however that notion itself is constructed) was urgently needed and waiting to be born. The interesting thing, however, is the increasing convergence between these contemporary approaches and philosophy, compared with the older traditional ethnographic concerns. The questions of kinship or socialization raise few immediately pressing philosophical questions; those of ritual and symbolism or of totemism raise far more; issues of self, body and feeling, of aesthetic experience and of psychiatric models raise many and unavoidable ones. They also suggest a new content for philosophical anthropology itself. No longer satisfied with an ahistorical search for the 'essence' of humanity, a much richer picture of the constitution of the human begins to emerge: embodied, feeling, sensing, hoping, dying, symbolizing, as much irrational as rational, embedded in nature and with a constantly fluctuating balance between what seem to be the constants of human cultures and inner/outer exploration, leading in many cases to the challenging or transgressing of those constants or at least their endless modification. These questions, which anthropology is becoming less embarrassed about asking, are in fact the most interesting and basic ones. These questions touch most directly on the contingencies and uncertainties of the human condition and, far from fleeing from a concern with social justice and social transformation, provide a basis for those fundamentals, but one that avoids and transcends the economism of older approaches both Marxist and capitalist, each of which in their technologism reveal an impoverished conception of humanity and its potentials.

It is exciting that anthropology has, at the turn of the century, rediscovered much of its own potential, too, as it has moved away from its earlier sociologism to embrace issues of ethics, aesthetics, human futures, the great moral issues encapsulated in that inadequate term 'development', embodiment, the emotions, sexuality rather than kinship, psychiatry, and consumption rather than the exchange relationships of traditional economic anthropology. While it has long had an interest in issues of human–environment relationships, the current ecological crisis and the challenges to notions of human identity posed by deep ecology is rightly moving those concerns back to centre place, not only in anthropology but in philosophy too, where questions of the 'nature of nature' are taking hold (for example Sopher 1995), and in doing so raising significantly the issues of biologism, of social constructivism and of humanity as part of/over against nature. The appearance on the international stage not only of Asian philosophy but of African (Eze 1997) and Latin American (Althabe and Schuster 1999) forms, with their critiques of Western concepts of culture, science, race and identity, has also broadened the basis of comparative philosophy and brought it closer to the traditional concerns and area interests of anthropology. In an important foundational text for discussions of the relationships between philosophy and the social sciences, Peter Winch (1965) – in discussing problems of meaningful behaviour, the relationship between concepts and actions, the possible status of social studies as science and in significantly introducing Wittgenstein into debates about the philosophy of the social sciences – still privileges epistemology as not only pivotal to philosophy, but to the understanding of society, too. In this respect Winch remains within the dominant postwar Anglo-Saxon tradition of philosophy.

Continental philosophical anthropology on the other hand has always been more concerned with ontology, both in its German and in many of its French expressions (for example, Jolif 1967). With the revival in anthropology of the idea of ontology (Clammer, Poirier and Schwimmer 2004) the convergence is made even more complete. Is there, then, a future for philosophical anthropology? I think so, if it is seen as both the interface between the concerns of philosophy and of anthropology on the one hand, and on the other as the site of discussion of the fundamental existential issues that confront all humans as individuals and all cultures as collectivities: their finiteness and fragility as well as their resilience, their creativity, but also of the ecological, biological and psychological boundaries within which that creativity in all its forms – aesthetic, political, social and economic – is expressed. Seen in these terms the dialogue is far from over. Indeed, given the challenges of globalization, conflict and ecology that now confront us, its necessity is all the more pressing.

References

Althabe, Gerard and Félix Gustavo Schuster, eds. 1999. *Antropología del presente*. Buenos Aires: Edicial.

Berry, Christopher J. 1986. *Human Nature*. London: Macmillan.

Binswanger, Ludwig. 1957. *Sigmund Freud: Reminiscences of a Friendship*. New York: Grune and Stratton.

Carrithers, Michael, Steven Collins and Steven Lukes, eds. 1985. *The Category of the Person: Anthropology, Philosophy, History*. Cambridge and New York: Cambridge University Press.

Clammer, John. 1995. *Difference and Modernity*. London and New York: Kegan Paul International.

Clammer, John, Sylvie Poirier and Eric Schwimmer, eds. 2004. *Figured Worlds: Ontological Obstacles in Intercultural Relations*. Toronto and London: Toronto University Press.

Cohen, Anthony P. 1994. *Self-Consciousness: An Alternative Anthropology of Identity*. London and New York: Routledge.

Dumont, Louis. 1986. *Essays in Individualism: Modern Ideology in Anthropological Perspective*. Chicago: Chicago University Press.

Encyclopaedia Britannica. 1993. 'Philosophical Anthropology'. Vol. 25: 550–61.

Eze, Emmanuel Chukwudi, ed. 1997. *Postcolonial African Philosophy*. Oxford and Cambridge, MA: Blackwell.

Farber, Marvin. 1966. *The Aims of Phenomenology: The Motives, Methods and Impact of Husserl's Thought*. New York: Harper and Row.

Finnis, John. 1980. *Natural Law and Natural Rights*. Oxford: Clarendon Press.

Foucault, Michel. 1966. *Les mots et les choses*. Paris: Gallimard. English translation by Alan Sheridan, 1973. *The Order of Things: An Archaeology of the Human Sciences*. New York: Vintage.

Fox, R. G. and B. J. King, eds. 2002. *Anthropology Beyond Culture*. Oxford and New York: Berg.

Géras, N. M. 1970. 'Lévi-Strauss and Philosophy'. *Journal of the British Society for Phenomenology* 1 (3): 50–60.

Hall, David L. and Roger T. Ames. 1998. *Thinking from the Han: Self, Truth and Transcendence in Chinese and Western Culture*. Albany: State University of New York Press.

Heidegger, Martin. 1961. *An Introduction to Metaphysics*. Translated by Ralph Manheim. New York: Doubleday.

Hiriyanna, M. 1964. *Outlines of Indian Philosophy*. London: George Allen and Unwin.

Hollis, M. 1970. 'The Limits of Irrationality'. In *Rationality*, edited by Bryan Wilson, 214–20. New York: Harper and Row.

Hollis, M. 1979. 'The Epistemological Unity of Mankind'. In *Philosophical Disputes in the Social Sciences*, edited by S. C. Brown, 225–32. Brighton: Harvester Press.

Jolif, J.-Y. 1967. *Comprendre l'homme: Introduction à une anthropologie philosophique*. Paris: Les Editions du Cerf.

Kohl, Herbert. 1965. *The Age of Complexity*. New York: New American Library.

Landmann, Michel. 1955. *Philosophische Anthropologie*. Berlin: Walter de Gruyter.

Lévi-Strauss, Claude. 1968. *Structural Anthropology*. Translated by C. Jacobson and B. Scheopf. London: Allen Lane.

Morris, Brian. 1991. *Western Conceptions of the Individual*. Oxford and New York: Berg.

Murdoch, G. P. 1945. 'The Common Denominators of Culture'. In *The Science of Man in the World Crisis*, edited by R. Linton, 123–42. New York: Columbia University Press.

Paul, Gregor. 1993. *Philosophie in Japan: Von den Anfängen bis zur Heian-Zeit*. Munich: Iudicium

Piovesana, Gino. 1997. *Recent Japanese Philosophical Thought 1862–1996*. Richmond: Japan Library.

Rorty, Richard. 1982. *Consequences of Pragmatism*. Brighton: Harvester Press.

Rothacker, Erich. 1948. *Kulturanthropologie*. Berlin: Bouvier Verlag.

Sahlins, Marshall. 1996. 'The Sadness of Sweetness: The Native Anthropology of Western Cosmology'. *Current Anthropology* 37 (3): 395–415.

Scheler, Max. 1927. *Die Stellung des Menschen im Kosmos*. Darmstadt: Reichel.

———. 1960. *On the Eternal in Man*. Translated by B. Noble. New York: Harper and Row.

Schutz, Albert. (1932) 1967. *Der sinnhafte Aufbau der sozialen welt*. Vienna: Julius Springer. Translated by George Walsch and Frederick Lehnert, 1967. *The Phenomenology of the Social World*. Chicago: Northwestern University Press.

Sillitoe, Paul. 1998. 'The Development of Indigenous Knowledge: A New Applied Anthropology'. *Current Anthropology* 32 (2): 223–52.

Slotkin, James Sydney, ed. 1965. *Readings in Early Anthropology*. London: Methuen.

Sopher, Kate. 1995. *What is Nature? Culture, Politics and the Non-human*. Oxford and Cambridge, MA: Blackwell.

Wilson, Edward O. 1975. *Sociobiology: The New Synthesis*. Cambridge, MA: The Belknap Press.

———. 1982. *On Human Nature*. New York and London: Bantam Books.

Winch, Peter. 1965. *The Idea of a Social Science and its Relation to Philosophy*. London: Routledge and Kegan Paul, New York: Humanities Press.

Chapter 2

THE SELF-PRESERVATION OF MAN: REMARKS ON THE RELATION BETWEEN MODERNITY AND PHILOSOPHICAL ANTHROPOLOGY

Kasper Lysemose

> *Naked existence* could in itself be the fulfilment of a task of infinite importance. The imperative concerning this task is essentially incomprehensible and can only be alluded to in a symbolic way, because we *are* this imperative.
>
> —Gehlen ([1940] 1993, 72)[1]

It would probably be too bold a statement to say that philosophical anthropology is the philosophy of modernity. There is, however, an important and close relation between the two. It is the aim of this article to draw attention to this relation.[2] This will be done by examining the following hypothesis: the *tertium comparationis* between philosophical anthropology and modernity is to be found in the principle of self-preservation.

The idea that philosophical anthropology is a movement with a particular close connection to modernity is not new. It has been stressed by the German philosopher Odo Marquard in his *Schwierigkeiten mit der Geschichtsphilosophie* (Difficulties with the philosophy of history, 1965). Here Marquard focuses on philosophy of history as a specific modern type of philosophy. The background for this focus is the observation that the human life-world has been overlooked in scholastic and metaphysical philosophy. Premodern philosophy had thus abandoned man in his attempt to find orientation. Marquard often reminds us of the Hegelian insight that if philosophy has nothing to do with reality, this is reality's own problem. This does not mean – as one might immediately think – that philosophy should stay in its ivory tower with a good conscience. On the contrary! If philosophy does so, it will have grave consequences for reality, since philosophy is – or, rather, was thought to be – the primary discourse whereby man could find meaning and reason in his life-world.

The philosophy of history arising during the Enlightenment is precisely an attempt to correct an alleged ivory-tower syndrome in previous philosophy. It is an intellectual endeavour seeking to give human life orientation through a sense of historical direction. Marquard, however, has – as the title of his book indicates – difficulties with the way this is done. These difficulties have two main sources: firstly, the philosophy of history is a mono-narrative. This means that it tells one universal history – mankind's history of progress and freedom. Secondly, it is revolutionary. This means that it wants to make a radical break with a repressive past and jump into a promising future. According to Marquard, it hereby fails at providing orientation in the life-world of human beings. Firstly, this life-world has a plurality of narratives which are excluded in the perspective of the philosophy of history. Secondly, man needs his past as a reservoir of experience to form his expectations of the future. Traditions and institutions are, no doubt, not the ultimate good (*summum bonum*) that the philosophy of history places at the end of its mono-narrative. Nevertheless, they are an anthropological necessity.

Due to his difficulties with the philosophy of history, Marquard's attention is drawn towards a competing modern philosophical formation: philosophical anthropology. Like the philosophy of history, it is characterized by a turn toward the life-world. Its perspective on it is not, however, from the standpoint of history, but from that of nature. Instead of asking what man can make of himself, philosophical anthropology asks what nature has made of man. It is, in other words, more concerned with what man cannot change than with what is at his disposal. In Marquard's own sceptical anthropology this is conveyed as a focus on the finitude of man.

As will be apparent, Marquard takes the turn towards the human life-world to be a characteristic feature of philosophical formations in modernity. This is not without plausibility. But it is obviously a very general characterization. And it does not clarify the intimate relation between precisely philosophical anthropology and modernity. This article can be seen as a supplement to Marquard's account on this particular point. By stressing the importance of the principle of self-preservation, it is possible to give a more philosophically potent – although, needless to say, not indisputable – description of the relation.

That such a description would still be in accordance with Marquard can be seen from the fact that he often characterizes modernity as the conservative age. The reason for this is Marquard's anti-utopianism. For a finite being like man it is not only impossible to start with a clean slate, but also not desirable. It would leave man without any orientation. Luckily, traditions and institutions exempt man from this unbearable situation. Between the lines of his historical account, Marquard thus unfolds a polemic directed against the Frankfurt School. It might very well be, he argues, that repression and injustice are incorporated in our traditions and institutions. But to demand that man should 'wake up' from an immersion in an alleged *Verblendungszusammenhang* or should legitimize all normativity through *Herrschaftsfreie Dialog* expresses a hyper-rationality, which is not in accordance with the *conditio humana*. Behind the promising word 'emancipation' lurks the danger of losing what little chance of orientation an indeterminate being like man has – *fiat utopia, pereat mundus*.

This line of thought points toward a philosophical-anthropological concept of conservatism. Conservatism is usually associated with its political sense. In the present context, however, this is a secondary level. The debate between neoconservatism and critical theory belongs to this level. At the primary level conservatism is about the fundamental rationality of preserving what is. Precisely this rationality is expressed in the concept of self-preservation. To understand the constitutive role this principle has for both modernity and for philosophical anthropology is to understand the fundamental relation between the two.

I. The Principle of Self-Preservation

The idea that the principle of self-preservation is constitutive for modernity was put forth in the 1970s by notable philosophers such as Hans Blumenberg, Dieter Henrich and others (see the eminent collection of articles in Ebeling 1976). This idea might at first sound unfamiliar. For it is common philosophical school teaching that the principle of modern philosophy is that of subjectivity. With his turn towards the *cogito* Descartes is the father of modern philosophy – so we are informed. And of course subjectivity plays a significant role in modern philosophy. This is in many ways also true of premodern philosophy, though. What is really new is not the principle of subjectivity, but a new interpretation of this principle – namely through the principle of self-preservation. This principle is in turn of a more universal scope than that of subjectivity. It is a general ontological principle with applications in all ontological fields, subjectivity being only one of them.[3] In this light it would be more appropriate to proclaim Spinoza as 'the father of modern philosophy', were it not that this category is of dubious historiographical value and the source of many futile discussions. But what makes Spinoza interesting in this context anyway is his elevation of self-preservation to a universal metaphysical principle. This can be observed in his doctrine of *conatus* which states that every particular thing strives at preserving its own being to the extent that it has the power to do so (see Spinoza [1677] 1999, pars tertia, propositio VI).

For an elaboration on the meaning of the principle of self-preservation one can distinguish between negative and positive determinations. The principle receives its negative determinations in the historical process where it is advanced to be the principle of modernity. When modernity proclaims self-preservation as the principle of its own rationality, this is at first a purely negative self-understanding. It is established through rejection of significant aspects of the philosophical and theological tradition. Hence the negative determinations are important for the understanding of the *genesis* of the principle. This does not, however, suffice for a *systematic* elaboration. The history of modernity is, in one of its most fundamental aspects, the history of the attempts to elucidate what its own founding principle positively means and what implications it has for various regional ontologies.

a) Negative determinations of the principle of self-preservation

Regarding the negative determinations of the principle of self-preservation, two aspects have been emphasized: the negation of theological absolutism (Blumenberg) and the negation of teleology (Robert Spaemann).

i) The negation of theological absolutism

The notion of theological absolutism plays a significant role in Blumenberg's description of the genesis of the modern age. It denotes a complex of ideas in late medieval theology revolving around an extreme emphasis on the omnipotence of God. Among these ideas is voluntarism, contingency, nominalism and the separation of faith and knowledge. The most extreme expression of God's omnipotence is possibly the doctrine of *creatio continua*. This doctrine amounts to an ontological depravation of the world. The world has no immanent power to sustain itself. The only reason for its existence is God's will to continuous creation. Without these merciful acts of will, the world would immediately turn into nothing. The doctrine of *creatio continua* is, in other words, a case of entirely transitive preservation. And it is also a doctrine which, in its pragmatic and existential implications, is unbearable. It is consequently an act of self-assertion when modernity negates this doctrine – and theological absolutism as a whole – and claims an immanent-worldly force of intransitive and reflexive preservation (i.e., self-preservation).

It is obvious that creation and preservation are the same under the conditions of *creatio continua*. Descartes, who adheres to this doctrine and thereby displays his belonging to late medieval thought, states this very clearly in the third meditation of his *Meditationes de prima philosophia* (1641). This identity is dissolved when self-preservation becomes the principle of modernity. As part of this process the growing ontological depravation of the world is reversed. Instead of lingering on the verge of nothingness in every moment, an immanent force of self-preservation is ascribed to the world and to the particular beings in the world. This is clearly not the same as to say that the world has the capability to bring itself into existence. It has merely the ability to preserve this existence – which in itself is an absolute contingency. To phrase it somewhat emphatically (and with an allusion to the anthropological consequences): it is not necessary that the world exists, but the world has in it the ability to 'care' about this unexplainable fact.

Even though the concept of self-preservation is meant as a universal principle, it has particularly intriguing implications in the specific ontological field of subjectivity. Here it entails that subjectivity is occupied with the preservation of its own existence, though it is not itself responsible for this existence and cannot account for it. Subjectivity cannot be a spectator to its own coming into existence. From the inner-subjective – or phenomenological – point of view, existence is, so to speak, always already there. The coming-into-existence of subjectivity is of a fully prereflexive nature. It is, as Dieter Henrich puts it in his theory of subjectivity, 'the ground in consciousness' (*Der Grund im Bewußtsein*). In his analysis of subjectivity and self-preservation as constitutional and interrelated principles of modernity, Henrich writes, 'Self-consciousness only comes into being in a context which is not intelligible as a result of the power and activity of self-consciousness itself. And it comes into being in this context in such a way, that it knows about this dependency in a primordial way. Therefore self-consciousness must comprehend itself in light of the necessity of self-preservation' (Henrich 1976, 100). As will appear below, this train of thought is very adaptable into a philosophical-anthropological context.

ii) *The negation of teleology*

It has been asserted by Spaemann that a distinctive trait of modernity is an 'inversion of teleology' (see his contribution in Ebeling 1976). This inversion is to be understood as a consequence of the principle of self-preservation. Already Spinoza states this very clearly when he claims that the strive to preserve itself is the real essence of everything ([1677] 1999, pars tertia, propositio VII). Obviously this is a denunciation of the Aristotelian teleology in medieval scholasticism. All change has its driving force from the effort to preserve and *not* from an actualization of any inherent and essential *telos*. The strive towards bringing that into being which does not yet exist is reversed towards preserving the being of that which already exists. Not the realization of essence, but the securing of existence is – to put it paradoxically – the 'essence' of all things.

This inversion of teleology is in a way prepared by the syndrome of theological absolutism. The speculative highlighting of God's omnipotence corresponds to the diminishing possibility for reason to gain any insight into the order of creation. For what now became the *human* reason, God increasingly became a *deus absconditus*. Given that there is no limit to what God can do, every theo-logical attempt at reducing his *potentia absoluta* to a reliable *potentia ordinata* is an illegitimate and intrusive act. In scholasticism the notion of the substantial forms in particular things had been upheld. Theological absolutism suspends the veto right of these forms against God's interference in their inner nature (see Marquard 1984, 33). The Aristotelian metaphysic of essence was thus replaced by a metaphysic of radical contingency. For human reason this meant ignorance regarding the essence of things – first and foremost their teleological structure. God's creative will is overwhelmingly abundant and human understanding must be economical. The latter must proceed according to principles of selection and reduction of complexity. It must construct a *nominal* order that does not necessarily reflect any *ontological* order, but solely serves pragmatic interests. There is, however, a significant difference between the late medieval period and modernity in this respect. Whereas the nominalistic limitation of human knowledge is a disappointment to the medieval mind, modernity no longer has any expectation of insight into the essence of things. This historical process of resignation paves the way for grasping the creative possibilities of man. And this in turn is an important background for anthropological thought within modernity.

b) Positive determinations of the principle of self-preservation

Regarding the positive determinations of the principle of self-preservation, it must be noted that it is an open question what a full theory of self-preservation should look like. This is no wonder since such a theory would be the foundational theory of modernity. Accordingly, no complete systematic elaboration can be the ambition in the present context. Nevertheless the following points can be made.

i) Self-preservation is not a particular, but a universal principle

This point has already been stressed above. It means that all ontological fields are understood through the principle of self-preservation. In this way it is possible to see interesting connections between Spinoza's concept of *conatus*, Hobbes's concept of the state, Newton's concept of *inertia*, Kant's concept of reason, etc. The consequences for each ontological field differ, as do the interpretations of the principle itself. But despite all differences, it is fairly easy to comprehend the common ground: a notion of self-preservation and the attempt to give it a positive determination and an adequate elaboration.

ii) Self-preservation is not a naturalistic but a rational principle

Within ordinary language the word 'self-preservation' is often used in a naturalistic sense. It has connotations such as 'egotism' or 'survival of the fittest'. As a principle of modernity it must be understood as a rational principle (see Manfred Sommer's contribution in Ebeling 1976; and Sommer 1977). Or rather, as Blumenberg puts it, it is not a new rational principle among others, but the principle of a new conception of rationality itself (Blumenberg [1969] 1976, 146). That self-preservation does not imply a naturalistic view becomes especially evident when the role of the principle within transcendental philosophy is considered. For Kant reason *is* self-preservation. Accordingly, Kant identifies the moral law with the self-preservation of reason ([1786] 1999, 60ff.). Evidently, this suggests that self-preservation is not meant as an empirical but as a transcendental principle of reason.

iii) Self-preservation is not a substantialistic but a functionalistic principle

In a typological approach it is possible to distinguish between two main interpretations of self-preservation: the substantial and the functional interpretation. The substantial interpretation claims: self-preservation is a concept covering all forms of strategies whereby the self ensures its own preservation. In this view there is the self on the one side and self-preservation on the other. The self has in itself nothing to do with self-preservation. But it is forced to preserve itself because of outer circumstances. Self-preservation is, in other words, secondary to the self. The functional interpretation claims on the contrary: the self is a concept covering forms of strategies which all are a function of self-preservation. Self-preservation is accordingly not something secondary to the self. The self *is* self-preservation. Or as Husserl writes, 'I am not first and then afterwards do I preserve myself; being is self-preservation' (Husserl [1929–35] 1973, 367). The difference between these two interpretations might sound subtle. But it does lead to vastly different implications in the systematic elaboration to say either *the self preserves itself* or *the self is self-preservation*.

iv) Self-preservation is not a static but a dynamic principle

It may seem that the principle of self-preservation is against change and growth: it can evidently only give rise to a general condition of *status quo*.

This is indeed the accusation put forth by Friedrich Nietzsche. During his study of Spinoza's philosophy Nietzsche came to acknowledge the fundamental importance of the principle of self-preservation for modernity. But Nietzsche did not approve of this. He sensed nihilism at the root of it – a will to nothing. Of course Nietzsche did not want to return to any form of Aristotelian teleology. Instead he developed his own principle of will to power – a principle of growth and expansion – in direct opposition to self-preservation (for an informative interpretation of Nietzsche on this point, see Abel 1998). It is, however, questionable whether self-preservation actually is a static or even nihilistic principle, as implied by Nietzsche. On the contrary, it might very well be that self-preservation implicates the *necessity* of change, growth and expansion. Without the ability to change, grow and expand, a system – to phrase it in Luhmann's terms – cannot sustain itself. It must perform *funktionale Ausdifferenzierung*. Self-expansion (*Selbststeigerung*), then, is not an alternative to self-preservation but an integral part of it. This has immense importance for the interpretation of modernity. As is well known, a widespread view is that the founding principle of modernity is the will to power (Heidegger, Foucault, etc.). On the basis of this it is possible to give a devastating critique of modernity as being ruled by a blind and pure will aiming at nothing but its own total supremacy. This will to power has, however, been interpreted without its relation to self-preservation. When this is done, it is possible to defend the legitimacy of the modern age – or *Die Legitimität der Neuzeit* (the title of one of Blumenberg's most influential books). In this perspective modernity is not ruled by a will to power running wild. It has its genesis in the self-assertion of man against theological absolutism, leading to the principle of self-preservation.

II. Philosophical Anthropology

When did philosophical anthropology arise? If we follow Marquard's exposition there are at least three answers (1995, 143): Philosophical anthropology is as old as philosophy itself, it belongs specifically to modernity or it is a movement that took its beginning in Germany between the two world wars. In the present context I shall follow Marquard's view that it belongs specifically to modernity. I shall, nevertheless, focus on the German tradition of philosophical anthropology. For it seems that the principle of modernity – self-preservation – becomes explicit in this particular form of philosophical anthropology. Before delving into this matter, I shall sketch a brief historical outline of philosophical anthropology in Germany.

It makes good sense to distinguish between two generations of philosophical anthropologists in Germany: the generation before World War II and the generation after World War II. This is not an exact line of demarcation, since many philosophical anthropologists were active both before and after the war. But World War II signifies a shift in the intellectual environment in Germany which also had impact on philosophical anthropology.

The classical philosophical anthropologists are often said to be Max Scheler, Helmuth Plessner and Arnold Gehlen. The founding year is 1928, when Scheler published *Die Stellung des Menschen im Kosmos* and Plessner *Die Stufen des Organischen und der Mensch*. At that time both were working at the university in Cologne. The founding of philosophical anthropology was not a common effort, though. From the beginning it was affected by a strong rivalry. Consequently, philosophical anthropology became much less a school than critical theory or phenomenology. It was (and is) a highly heterogeneous movement – but nonetheless recognizable as *one* movement. If Scheler and Plessner had written the initial works of this movement, Gehlen wrote the most frequently read: *Der Mensch* (1940). At the time Gehlen's book stood as the culmination of the first generation of philosophical anthropologists.

Philosophical anthropology is not only in itself a diverse movement. It also 'infiltrates' other philosophical movements. It would, for example, be reasonable to mention the work of Ernst Cassirer from the neo-Kantian movement as a part of philosophical anthropology. In addition there is an interesting and tense connection between phenomenology and philosophical anthropology – and not only because Scheler and Plessner both had their role to play within phenomenology. In contrast to these phenomenological outsiders, both the father of phenomenology, Husserl, and its most important heretic, Heidegger, rejected – in different ways – the idea of philosophical anthropology. The intricacy of this matter increases when it is noted that Husserl nonetheless rejected Heidegger's *Sein und Zeit* as a form of philosophical anthropology *and* that Heidegger's own 'children' – Löwith, Jonas and Arendt – each developed forms of philosophical anthropology in opposition to Heidegger. Karl Löwith's *Das Individuum in der Rolle des Mitmenschen* (1928), Hannah Arendt's *The Human Condition* (1958) and Hans Jonas's *The Phenomenon of Life* (1963) are all important contributions to philosophical anthropology.

Philosophical anthropology is – as the name indicates – a philosophical movement. But it was infused with the biology of the time. Among the important background biologists were Jakob von Uexküll, Hans Driesch, Adolf Portmann and Louis Bolk. All had an influence on the classical authors of philosophical anthropology and may in fact themselves, in various degrees, be counted as part of the movement.

Two obvious misunderstandings of the relation between philosophical anthropology and biology must be avoided. Firstly, it is often said that philosophy has a foundational relation to particular sciences. It is dubious if this is true at all, but it is certainly not true in this case. It is rather so that philosophical anthropology has an adoptive relation to biology. This means that philosophical anthropology selects and incorporates insights from contemporary biology. Secondly, this does not imply that philosophical anthropology is a scientific form of philosophy. The framework of philosophical anthropology is not scientific but philosophical. Otherwise, philosophical anthropology would be a dilettantish mode of thinking – trying to do what professional biologists clearly do better. Instead philosophical anthropology uses biology as a medium to reflect upon when considering the general question of man's position in the world. This question in turn is not a scientific question and will never be answered in scientific discourse.

Admittedly, philosophical anthropologists of the first generation were closer to the sciences in their self-understanding than this suggests. And it could be argued that they did actually at times appear somewhat dilettantish from a scientific point of view. In any case, the mode of reception in which they have an importance today is not scientific but philosophical. In this respect the classical philosophical anthropologists are still utterly relevant. In line with this the philosophical nature of philosophical anthropology is emphatically stressed in the second generation of philosophical anthropologists. Here the *Geltungsanspruch* is a far cry from the sciences, as is quickly perceived when reading, for example, Hans Blumenberg, Peter Sloterdijk or Odo Marquard. These three authors are responsible for some of the most important philosophical-anthropological literature in Germany after World War II. Blumenberg's *Arbeit am Mythos* (1979) and *Höhlenausgange* (1989) are major anthropological works, as are his posthumously published *Beschreibung des Menschen* – an almost one thousand-page investigation of the possibility of a phenomenological anthropology. Sloterdijk's three-volume work *Sphären* (1998–2004) appears on the same grand scale. Marquard, in contrast, has no inclination to write major works. His sceptical disposition finds expression in minor and often amusing writings – hereby prolonging a connection to essayism pertaining to philosophical anthropology since Montaigne.

III. Man without Essence

The formative years of philosophical anthropology lie between the two world wars. In Germany this was a time of crisis. It was a time with a widespread loss of orientation, and the disbelief in the Weimar Republic was considerable – especially among intellectuals. Book titles such as the following indicate the general uneasiness of the period: *Untergang des Abendlandes* (The decline of the West, Oswald Spengler 1918–22), *Was bleibt unser Halt?* (What remains to hold on to? Rudolf Eucken 1919), *Die Weltkatastrophe und die deutsche Philosophie*

(The world catastrophe and the German philosophy, Wilhelm Wundt 1920), *Die geistige Krise der Gegenwart* (The contemporary spiritual crisis, Arthur Liebert 1924), *Das Unbehagen in der Kultur* (Civilization and its discontents, Sigmund Freud 1930). This list could easily be expanded, but it suffices to give an impression of the cultural environment. It is no wonder that such an environment gave rise to fundamental questions about the relation between the individual and the whole – on the grandest scale about *Die Stellung des Menschen im Kosmos* (The human place in the cosmos). World War I had shattered the optimistic belief in historical progression – and, if we follow Marquard's view, this naturally gave rise to a more sceptical and anthropologically oriented mode of thinking. And in fact it seems that it became utterly questionable (*Fragwürdig*) what man is. All the traditional answers (a rational being, a moral being, a free being, etc.) had lost their plausibility. It is consequently a dominant aspect of the philosophical anthropology arising during this time that it does not primarily present itself as a new and better theory of man. On the contrary, it understands itself as a philosophical reflection on the historical experience of the loss of all such theories. Man had – so it seemed – lost any normative self-understanding. As Scheler states, 'It can be said that man at no point in history has become so problematic for himself than is presently the case' (1928, 14).

This does not mean that there was no knowledge of man. On the contrary! Both the historical and the natural sciences had gained an overwhelming factual knowledge. But the historicizing and the naturalization of man had only contributed to the general bewilderment. Consequently, in 1929 Heidegger notices that we know more and more about man, but less and less about what man is. 'No age has known so much and so many different things about man as ours (…). But also no age has known less than ours of what man is. Never before has man become as problematic (*fragwürdig*) as is the case in our time' (Heidegger [1929] 1991, 209; the quote ends with a reference to Scheler's book from the year before).

Heidegger writes this in *Kant und das Problem der Metaphysik* (1929). In this book Heidegger interprets Kant's philosophy as a mode of thinking on the verge of breaking through to the fundamental question in philosophy, according to Heidegger: *what is being?* But Kant turns away and fails at establishing a 'fundamental ontology'. In Kant's own understanding, however, the fundamental question in philosophy is *not* that of being but that of man. All philosophical questions are contained in the one big question: *what is man?* Philosophical anthropology is in accordance with Kant on this point – and in opposition to and competition with Heidegger. But Kant's big question is subject to an important transformation within philosophical anthropology. Due to the cultural situation sketched above this question is transformed into the minor question: *how is the existence of man possible?* The loss of essence – a characteristic of modernity as such – is the acute historical experience at the root of philosophical anthropology. And it is therefore no wonder that the shift from essence to existence is very dominant in this context. An answer to the question about the essence of man should consequently not be expected from philosophical anthropology. Rather a reflection on that which is at the centre of man's 'eccentric care': the utter contingency of his own existence.

It may be appropriate to remark that philosophical anthropology was not the only movement where the shift from essence to existence took place. This was even more explicit in existentialism. The famous dictum ascribed to Sartre – existence comes before essence – comes to mind. At the basis of this common view there is a deep rivalry between existentialism and philosophical anthropology. The opposition may be seen as the re-enactment of the old opposition between philosophy of history and anthropology. On the background of the experience of loss of essence, existentialism focuses on freedom and choice – and in this sense, radical historicity. Man is an indeterminate being. He cannot cling to any pregiven nature or order of things. Consequently, he must determine himself. On the same background philosophical anthropology has a different focus – not on the historicity of man but the nature of man. This sounds, of course, very essentialist. And indeed the main accusation against philosophical anthropology is that it clings to an idea of anthropological invariables. This criticism has been put forth especially by existentialist thinkers and by critical theorists: what lies behind the heading *The Nature of Man* is the conservative ideology of the bourgeoisie. The focus on the nature of man is, however, more intricate than this criticism implies. The project of philosophical anthropology is to understand how a being without a nature is possible within nature. The aim is to establish a philosophy of nature or of life, and in this framework to develop categories that make the description of an indeterminate and unfathomable being possible.

To some degree the fascination of existentialism and philosophical anthropology is the same. They both deal with questions revolving around man and his situation in the world. In Kantian terms: they are not modes of philosophy *nach dem Schulbegriff* (the scholastic concept of philosophy), but *nach dem Weltbegriff* (the worldly concept of philosophy). But the radical, juvenile and even revolutionary pathos in existentialism is absent in philosophical anthropology. Philosophical anthropology is sceptical, pragmatic and even conservative. In short – and to formulate the matter a bit rakish – philosophical anthropology is existentialism for grown-ups!

All the central categories in classical philosophical anthropology (Scheler's *Weltoffenheit*, Plessner's *Exzentrizität*, Gehlen's *Mängelwesen*, etc.) express the absence of any essential human nature. They do this with a different emphasis and consequently with very different systematic implications. Nevertheless, they are all in accordance with the modern principle of self-preservation. There is no natural teleology for man. There is no essence to realize. Instead there is the contingent existence of man, the improbable continuation of this existence – and a fundamental care to preserve this existence.

In this perspective it is also easily seen that Heidegger's concept of *Sorge* could be interpreted as a genuine anthropological category, even though Heidegger would not agree to this. In his view what may appear as anthropology in *Sein und Zeit* is only a path to articulating the question of the meaning of being (see Plessner [1928] 1975, x). Nonetheless, it is not illegitimate to benefit from his insights in an anthropological context. And if this is done, a striking resemblance between Heidegger's *Dasein* and Plessner's *Exzentrizität* presents itself. *Dasein* is defined by Heidegger as a being which, in its being, cares about this very being – or as it is phrased in the German original: 'Das Dasein ist Seiendes, dem es in seinem Sein um dieses selbst geht' (Heidegger [1927] 1993, 191). Obviously this *in* and *um* corresponds to Plessner's concept of man being both centred and eccentric. Instead of calling this structure *Exzentrizität*, Heidegger calls it *Sorge*. With this well-chosen word the relation of the eccentric anthropological structure to the principle of self-preservation becomes clearer. At the centre of man's *Sorge* – or 'care' – lies man's own being. Man *is* not merely his own being, but is revolving around it as well. In this way, revolving around and distanced from his own being, this very being loses its self-evident character. In other words, it loses its anonymous premodality and enters the modality of contingency. As stated above: at the centre of man's eccentric care lies the utter contingency of man's existence.

All that man 'cares' about is his own existence. He simply *is* this care – he *is* self-preservation. From this follows that if man stopped *revolving around* his own being, but simply *became* this being, he would no longer be human. Hypothetically it could be imagined that man became so successful at ensuring his own existence that this existence would no longer be given in the modality of contingency, but either re-enter the pre-modality of self-evidence or gain the godly modality of necessity. Either way, the implosion of man into his own centre would be the end of man. As Blumenberg instructively puts it:

> If the self-preservation of *Dasein* is successful, then *Dasein* will find that the centre of its own care is empty. This does not only imply that *Dasein* wouldn't know what to do with itself. It would find nothing where it had presupposed that which it was all about in its ecstatic caretaking. The paradox is that *Dasein* is *Sorge* and only can free itself from this at the cost of ceasing to be anything at all which it could care about. (Blumenberg 1987, 217–16)

Only as eccentric does man *have* a centre. This centre is man's own being. If man is absorbed into his own centre, he loses that which he *is* 'all about'.

If we leave Plessner's concept of eccentricity and Heidegger's concept of care, and turn towards Gehlen's mode of philosophical anthropology, the importance of the principle of self-preservation becomes explicit. At the entrance to his philosophical anthropology Gehlen poses his so-called anthropo-biological question: 'What is the content of the anthropo-biological question? It is nothing else but the question about the conditions of existence of man' (Gehlen [1940] 1993, 11). This question becomes acute when man is thought of as a deficient being – or in Gehlen's terms, a *Mängelwesen*. Man is born premature, naked, unprotected, exposed and utterly helpless. In contrast to animals, man is unspecialized and has no complete instincts, only residues thereof. For beings with strong instincts it is pregiven how they should attempt to preserve their existence. Man's residual instincts abandon him without this self-evidence. The primary concern for man is therefore how to preserve himself. He is forced to invent strategies that relieve him from his situation and establish the continuation of his unlikely existence. Gehlen interprets all forms of human action in this perspective (i.e., as functions of self-preservation). This goes both for basic physiological and morphological characteristics and for advanced 'spiritual' forms such as language, art and society.

Especially, Gehlen's analysis of society has given rise to considerable debate. This is worth mentioning since the sociological discourse, perhaps clearer than any other, highlights the significance of the principle of self-preservation for the interpretation of modernity. The central concept is that of institution. Again, a simplified opposition between philosophical anthropology on the one hand and existentialism and critical theory on the other is illustrative. The latter two philosophical formations agree – despite all differences – on a critical attitude towards institutions. They are both anti-institutional and antibourgeois modes of thinking. This stems from a strong insistence on individual freedom and autonomy. Institutions are seen as limits for the individual and even as repressive and totalitarian. As opposed to this, philosophical anthropology looks at institutions as a compensation for the deficiencies of man. They provide orientation and stability, thereby relieving man of his helplessness. In short: what philosophical anthropology interprets as anthropological necessities from the point of view of self-preservation, existentialism and critical theory hold as nothing but the ideological affirmation of *das Man*.

In 1965 Adorno and Gehlen met on German national radio to discuss the question, 'Is sociology a science about man?' (Grenz 1974). This highly illuminating debate can to some degree be seen as a competition about who has the most pessimistic view on man in society. Adorno's pessimism is well known. Society and its institutions are governed by the principle of self-preservation. This absorbs man in a dialectic of power over nature and objectification of the self, and leads eventually to the organization of society as a repressive context of delusion (*Verblendungszusammenhang*). Gehlen's way of outbidding Adorno's pessimism lies in his will to accept the institutions of society, even if they deprive man of all autonomy. Institutions may very well turn man into a blind appendix to the machinery of society, but the alternative – the basic anthropological situation – is always worse in Gehlen's opinion. The destruction of institutions is a utopian dream – and not a pretty one, should it come true.

Neither Adorno nor Gehlen seem to present an acceptable sociological interpretation of modernity. Adorno's harsh criticism of society is surely too extreme. But it challenges Gehlen's view on society in a way that makes his no less extreme position explicit. This gives rise to the suspicion that Gehlen's almost cynical affirmation of institutions is not anthropologically well founded. The preservation of man no longer lies in the hands of man. Instead it is in the hands of his institutions. Of course, these institutions are in a way the prolonged hand of man. But in Gehlen's theory they take on a strong independence. In consequence they bear resemblance to the theological absolutism which gave rise to self-preservation as the principle of modernity. The outcome of this 'institutional absolutism' appears to be a form of second nature – although man never had a first one. Institutions, as Gehlen perceives, seem to establish a functional equivalent to the role instincts play for animals. They determine man's being thoroughly, and subsequently annihilate his indeterminate being. They close his world-openness (*Weltoffenheit*) and force him to adapt completely to a cultural environment (*Umwelt*). Eventually they obliterate any consciousness of the contingency of his own existence.

These difficulties with Gehlen's 'hard' theory of institutions make it attractive to opt for a 'soft' one. Such a theory can be found in Plessner's view on society. Plessner is concerned with a sociological theory which preserves the constitutive anthropological contingency. What must be preserved in this sense is, however, not only the consciousness of the possibility *not to be*. It is the consciousness of the possibility *to be otherwise* as well. Both meanings of contingency are at the centre of man's self-preservation – and Plessner seems, in contrast to Heidegger, to stress in particular the latter meaning of the concept.

According to Plessner's general philosophy of life, all life has a position. Man, however, is not firmly fixed in his position. In Nietzsche's words, man is 'das noch nicht festgestellte Thier' (the not-yet-determined animal) ([1886] 1999). No determination of his position can give answer to the question *what is man?* As an eccentric being he is outside his own position and therefore too elusive to receive any exhaustive description. He is, as Plessner also puts it, an unfathomable being (*Unergründlichkeit*) or a *homo absconditus*.

Plessner's central sociological idea is to use the concept of *role* (or *mask*) to account for the adequate institutional relations between unfathomable and eccentric beings. This suggests itself because the semantics of role imply at least one aspect of huge anthropological importance: a role – perceived *as* a role – shows that it hides something. This allows an unfathomable being to do two things: to present itself *and* at the same time present itself in a way that shows its own possibility of being otherwise. In this way a role is a way for the individual to preserve others' as well as his own consciousness of the contingency of his existence. It is a way in which he can become visible and actual – for others and for himself – without being absorbed into this visibility and actuality. The *noch nicht festgestellte Thier* can experiment with his position – he can *sich verstellen* (deceive/pretend). The surplus of consciousness, which he has as a result of the eccentric distance to his own position, thus opens a way of self-preservation different from that of the animals. As Nietzsche observes: 'As a means for the preserving of the individual, the intellect unfolds its principal powers in deception (*Verstellung*), which is the means by which weaker, less robust individuals preserve themselves – since they have been denied the chance to wage the battle for existence with horns or with the sharp teeth of beasts of prey' (Nietzsche [1873] 1999, 876).

Notes

1 I have translated all German quotations for the occasion, in a few cases relying on authoritative translations.
2 The article is meant as an introduction to philosophical anthropology. It is written with an interdisciplinary context in mind, rather than the philosophers already well versed in this tradition. The perspective is a very broad historical one seeking to position philosophical anthropology within the general framework of modernity.
3 It should be noted that Henrich sees the *reciprocal* relationship between self-preservation and subjectivity as the constitutive feature of modernity. To give the *primacy* to self-preservation – as it is done here – is more in accordance with Blumenberg's outlook.

References

Abel, Günter. 1998. *Nietzsche*. Berlin: Walter de Gruyter.
Blumenberg, Hans. (1969) 1976. 'Selbsterhaltung und Beharrung. Zur Konstitution der neuzeitlichen Rationalität'. In *Subjektivität und Selbsterhaltung*, edited by Hans Ebeling, 144–207. Frankfurt: Suhrkamp Verlag.
_____. 1987. *Die Sorge geht über den Fluß*. Frankfurt: Suhrkamp Verlag.
Ebeling, Hans, ed. 1976. *Subjektivität und Selbsterhaltung*. Frankfurt: Suhrkamp Verlag.
Gehlen, Arnold. (1940) 1993. *Der Mensch*. Frankfurt: Vittorio Klostermann.

Grenz, F. 1974. *Adorno's Philosophie in Grundbegriffen: Auflösung einer Deutungsprobleme*. Frankfurt: Suhrkamp Verlag.

Heidegger, Martin. (1927) 1993. *Sein und Zeit*. Tübingen: Max Niemeyer Verlag.

_____. (1929) 1991. *Kant und das Problem der Metaphysik*. In *Gesamtausgabe*, vol. 3. Frankfurt: Vittorio Klostermann.

Henrich, Dieter. 1976. *Selbstverhältnisse*. Stuttgart: Reclam Verlag.

Husserl, Edmund. (1929–35) 1973. *Zur Phänomenologie der Intersubjektivität*, part 3, edited by Iso Kern (*Husserliana* vol. XV). Den Haag: Martinus Nijhoff.

Kant, Immanuel. (1786) 1999. 'Was heißt: sich im Denken orientieren'. In: *Ausgewählte und kleine Schriften*. Hamburg: Felix Meiner Verlag.

Marquard, Odo. (1965) 1973. *Schwierigkeiten mit der Geschichtsphilosophie*. Frankfurt: Suhrkamp Verlag.

_____. 1984. 'Das gnostische Rezidiv als Gegenneuzeit'. In *Religionstheorie und politische Theorie*, vol. 2, edited by Jacob Taubes, 31–6. Munich: Wilhelm Fink Verlag.

_____. (1991) 1995. 'Der Mensch "Diesseits der Utopie"'. In *Glück im Unglück*, 142–55. Munich: Wilhelm Fink Verlag.

Nietzsche, Friedrich. (1873) 1999. 'Ueber Wahrheit und Lüge im aussermoralischen Sinne'. In *Kritische Studienausgabe*, edited by Giorgio Colli and Mazzino Montinari, 873–90. Munich: De Gruyter.

_____. (1886) 1999. *Jenseits von Gut und Böse*. In: *Kritische Studienausgabe*, vol. 5, edited by Giorgio Colli and Mazzino Montinari, 9–243. Munich: De Gruyter.

Plessner, Helmuth. (1928) 1975. *Die Stufen des Organischen und der Mensch*. Berlin: Walter de Gruyter.

Scheler, Max. 1928. *Die Stellung des Menschen im Kosmos*. Darmstadt: Otto Reichl Verlag.

Sommer, Manfred. 1977. *Die Selbsthaltung der Vernunft*. Stuttgart-Bad Cannstatt: Friedrich Frommann Verlag.

Spinoza, Baruch de. (1677) 1999. *Ethik in geometrischer Ordnung dargestellt*. Lateinisch-Deutsch. Hamburg: Felix Meiner Verlag.

Chapter 3

WHITHER MODERNITY? HYBRIDIZATION, POSTOCCIDENTALISM, POSTDEVELOPMENT AND TRANSMODERNITY

Ivan Marquez

1. Introduction: Philosophical Anthropology and Modernity

Western philosophy has had a long engagement with the philosophical-anthropological issue of the nature of and prospects for humanity. Aristotle, for instance, placed humans within a functional, organic, cosmic totality, where the part–whole relation between humans and the rest of nature ascribed the *telos* and proper flourishing of humans. Many seventeenth-century philosophers – rationalists like Descartes, materialists like Hobbes and empiricists like Locke – defined humans as rational, self-interested and atomistic. With eighteenth-century French Enlightenment thought – especially the idea of progress in the work of de Saint-Pierre, Turgot, Voltaire, d'Holbach, Helvetius and Condorcet – and nineteenth-century German idealism, especially Hegel, human nature itself is placed within the dimension of time (i.e., in history) signalling the birth of modernity as the master narrative of philosophical anthropology. According to this modern narrative, humanity was developing through its own linear historicity towards the ultimate fulfilment of its own nature. However, also beginning in the nineteenth century with German romanticism and continuing into the twentieth century with phenomenology and existentialism, the character of this human historicity itself became one of the central concerns of much of philosophical anthropology. To some extent, these Romantic, phenomenological and existentialist reflections on philosophical anthropology began to undermine the very notion of a single, substantive, human nature unfolding in a single ineluctable path of historical progress. Also, some work in anthropology did likewise (see Boas 1911). The combined effect of these reflections was a critique that put in doubt the philosophical-anthropological core of modernity. Modernity was now (and still is) in crisis.

This essay will look at Latin American contributions to the efforts to move forward out of this crisis of modernity, a crisis that is as much philosophical as it is epochal. Postmodern discourses have laid out the general critiques of modernity's essentialist, universalist and teleological claims about humanity in general and reason in particular (see Habermas [1985] 1987). However, for the most part, these postmodern discourses have remained Eurocentric in their analyses and otherwise have not been able to transcend the problematic in a way that goes beyond a weak celebration of difference and fragmentation. Furthermore, the very fragmentation of our current times has not been in turn problematized in ways that highlight the systemic and differential effects of such fragmentation and the problems that it poses to specific individuals, communities, societies and cultures, with regard to their sources of meaning and identity, and to the production and reproduction of networks of asymmetric power relations in which they participate.

Modernity's progressive Hegelian notion of world history and its Enlightenment emancipatory goal of the actualization of universal reason, individual freedom and equality have been widely discussed. However, with some exceptions in anthropology (Asad 1973; Wolf 1982), what has been lacking is a discussion about modernity's underside of European and later US world domination, making clear how modernity is simultaneously a universal and abstract philosophical discourse, a world-historical project of European provenance, and a particular and concrete imperial world-system (see Dussel 1995, 1996; Mignolo 2000, 2011). An emphasis on the geopolitics of the philosophical discourse of modernity would put at our disposal a counterdiscourse to Francis Fukuyama's triumphalist and univocal 'end of history' discourse (1992) and to Samuel P. Huntington's elitist and combative 'clash of civilizations' discourse (1996). This counterdiscourse would offer an alternative framework to understand the past, present and possible futures of modernity – one that explains modernity in relation to other discourses and processes, such as occidentalism, colonialism, developmentalism and capitalism.

The rest of this essay will endeavour to do two things simultaneously: 1) to examine Latin American contributions to this counterdiscourse of modernity, specifically as developed by Néstor García Canclini, Walter Mignolo, Arturo Escobar and Enrique Dussel; and 2) to show how the present and future of modernity might lie in hybridization, postoccidentalism, postdevelopment and transmodernity as defined respectively by these four authors.

2. Néstor García Canclini on Hybridization

In his seminal book *Hybrid Cultures: Strategies for Entering and Leaving Modernity* (1995 [1989]), the Argentine anthropologist Néstor García Canclini shows how aspects of modernity and tradition have interacted in Latin American societies. Canclini's main claim is that in many places in Latin America modernity does not replace tradition *tout court*, but rather it is woven into the fabric of life in myriad ways. Sometimes aspects of modernity do replace traditional ways. At other times, aspects of modernity are rejected and tradition is upheld. And, finally, at still other times, aspects of modernity and tradition are woven together to create new hybrid forms of human expression and life.

One important thing that follows from this state of affairs, according to Canclini, is that social life, at least in Latin America, is currently constituted by multitemporal spaces. These multitemporal spaces, in turn, are constituted by material and symbolic practices, sometimes coexisting in more or less functional and harmonious ways and sometimes in struggles for hegemony, being sites of agency and contestation for subjects with their own diverse identity claims, needs and wants.

Instead of rejecting modernity or the idea of the temporality of human life, Canclini helps us make the case for multiple modernities and temporalities. It is one of Canclini's hopes that the understanding, acceptance and creative use of these conditions of modern sociability will create individual and collective lives that are rich in subjectivity and robust in agency. In order to maximize the chances that this will be the case, he deploys poststructural and post-Marxist analyses, especially of the cultural field, using insights from Gramsci, Bourdieu, Foucault, Baudrillard and Lyotard among others. What emerge from these analyses are accounts of the workings of 'material cultures' that among other things allow us to understand modernism, modernization and modernity as distinct but mutually interrelated phenomena, simultaneously operating in diverse spaces and temporalities.

Canclini's general perspective allows us to deconstruct the seemingly monolithic Eurocentric model of the discourse of modernity, opening it up to multiple possibilities and permutations. By transcending a traditionally rigid discourse of modernity, we can be guided by a more fine-grained analysis of modern life that puts a premium on creativity, richness and functional adequacy above all else. And thus, in a way, it becomes possible to continue being modern without being held captive by an *idée fixe* of what modern culture and society should or should not be.

Finally, I believe that the time is right to turn Canclini's framework of analysis to the task of understanding US and European societies themselves in these terms, thus, in a certain sense, transcending the postcolonial moment by taking the next bold step of provincializing the US (see Nussbaum 2008; West 1989; Zinn 1980) and Europe (see Anderson 1983; Chakrabarty 2000; Judt 2005; Taylor 2004). Provincializing the US and Europe would allow us to see them from the outside as local, heterogeneous, heterodox and partly heteronomous phenomena instead of as the unique embodiment of the world spirit unfolding in universal history.

3. Walter Mignolo on Postoccidentalism

In his broad-spanning book, *Local Histories/Global Designs: Coloniality, Subaltern Knowledges, and Border Thinking* (2000) the Argentine semiotician Walter Mignolo explores the modernity/coloniality link in many different guises.

One of Mignolo's main claims is that modernity cannot be properly understood independently of the colonization of the Americas, especially Latin America. According to him, modernity and coloniality are mutually implicated. Modernity emerges as the hegemonic discourse of the coloniality of power, operating both as organizing principle and legitimator.

However, Mignolo is keen to highlight that modernity itself was shaped and enabled by the European encounter with the other of the Americas and by the possibilities brought on by the colonial world-system. Furthermore, he points out that the metanarrative of modernity, resulting in part from the colonization of the Americas, created an 'occidentalism' as well as its colonized Other. Simply put, the idea of the West/the Old World/Europe was co-created with the idea of the West Indies/the New World/(Latin) America as a central feature of this metanarrative of modernity, setting the terms of what he refers to as the 'colonial difference'.

An important component of Mignolo's account of modernity is his description of the changes to the function of time and space within modernity. On the one hand, modernity as a project inserts itself in a temporality that ceases to be cyclical or simply linear, becoming instead progressively linear and univocally historic, thus, colonizing time. On the other hand, modernity as a project unhinges itself from a spatiality tied to a specific physical place or to a given, naïvely conceived, geographic territory, opting instead for a new notion of constructed space that is part of a geopolitics of knowledge connected to a coloniality of power, exerting itself within a particular historical framework. Space is thus constructed as a site for the operation of knowledge-power in general and differential knowledge-power relations within a world-system in particular. This colonized space of modernity goes by the name of 'occidentalism'.

However, modernity not only imposes itself on the colonial other that it creates in order to better dominate it, but it is also influenced and shaped by it and thus emerges in part from its interaction with the other. Notwithstanding the bidirectionality of this relationship between the modern and the colonial, given the coloniality of power (i.e., the structures of domination and subjugation that are in place and the power differential that they embody), the colonial is influenced and shaped a lot more strongly by the modern than vice versa.

According to Mignolo, the modern/colonial world that has existed since the fifteenth century has created local histories that respond to global designs that have changed across time, each new design displacing but never fully eliminating the preceding ones. The first global design was of Spanish provenance based on the project of Christian evangelization or Christianization. The second was of French and British origin based on the project of a secular civilizing mission or the spread of 'civilization', based on universal reason. The third came out of the United States based on the project of development and modernization. The fourth and present one comes out of global capital and it is based on globalized marketization.

One way to contend with the present crisis of modernity is through postoccidentalism. Mignolo defines postoccidentalism as a way of transcending occidentalism. Postoccidentalism is not one single thing but represents several things. It is a critical engagement with the modern/colonial world from the point of view of local histories in Latin America. These efforts try among other things to reinstate traditional, local and subaltern knowledges into the general legacy of modernity, creating a more complete totality that includes elements that had been supressed by colonial global designs. It is also a reflection about the nature of Latin America in its own terms. Furthermore, it is a creative overcoming of repressive or totalizing categories defining relations among geopolitical players, thus eliminating colonial difference and opening up the field of possibilities for the future. It involves attempts to deconstruct modernity in general and occidentalism in particular, thus provincializing Europe. Finally, it involves creating the conditions from a peaceful pluriversal world by a process of delinking from the hegemonic geopolitical discourse of knowledge-power, leading to decolonial epistemic shifts that make it possible to bring forth other epistemologies, other principles of knowledge and understanding, and consequently other economies, politics and ethics.

For Mignolo, the main epistemological tool of this postoccidental reason is 'border thinking'. Border thinking comes from people who are in a position to inhabit liminal spaces, which allows them to see things simultaneously from the inside and the outside, and through that process, enabling them to transcend the inner logics governing particular systems, a transcendence that can entail rejecting them, substituting them for other logics or creating new syntheses that incorporate diverse elements which were previously seen as mutually exclusive or contested.

Ultimately, Mignolo hopes that border thinking will help us undergo an epistemic shift and break away from the rule of Western epistemology, opening up the field to the possibility of thinking otherwise, intercultural dialogue and pluriversality (as opposed to universality) as the new universal project. This, for him, is what lies beyond modernity.

4. Arturo Escobar on Postdevelopment

In his groundbreaking book *Encountering Development: The Making and Unmaking of the Third World* (1995), the Colombian anthropologist Arturo Escobar examines the changing functioning of development discourses and practices in Latin America. Using a poststructuralist framework, Escobar traces the development of development as a discourse of knowledge-power.

Development discourse represents the post–World War II reconfiguring of modern world capitalism with its centre in the US. In the 1950s and 1960s development was conceptualized by means of a modernization theory of liberal slant, tying ideas of growth and development to the beneficial effects of capital, science and technology. In the 1960s and 1970s dependency theory critiqued from a Marxist perspective the structural flaws of development and modernization initiatives, claiming in effect that these initiatives were part of a global world-system divided according to centre and periphery, where the periphery was kept in a state of structural underdevelopment by the very workings of a global capitalism geared toward developing and enriching the centre(s). Since the late 1980s a poststructuralist critique of the very notion of development has taken centre stage, analysing the history of development as part of modernity's efforts since the eighteenth century to create a system of knowledge-power that makes a 'Third World' in the process of dominating it. Development becomes the key idea shaping social reality and action during this period of modernity, guiding initiatives of social transformation in ways that match the needs and wishes of global capitalism.

In a way, the poststructuralist analysis of development continues the Marxist dependency theorists' interest in how the context of political economy shapes the phenomena of development, but they deepen this analysis by engaging in an examination of how discourse itself produces and reproduces these phenomena. Escobar points out that the poststructuralist emphasis on discourse is not at the expense of a Marxist consideration of the material conditions of production and reproduction of society, because for the poststructuralist social reality is already always constituted by discourse and there is no reality to speak of that is not already discursive reality. The task of critique, then, is to examine development as a discursive formation to see which objects are constituted by it, to which actions it gives primacy, which kinds of subjectivities and agencies are enabled by it, who can speak for reality within it, and in whose benefit. An analysis of this kind contests the terms of development themselves and opens the discursive field to new possibilities of being and becoming.

This radical critique of development discourse leads certain practitioners, like Escobar, to formulate the need and the desirability of a 'postdevelopment' era. Postdevelopment entails the unmaking of the 'development' and 'underdevelopment' dyadic world and the creation of alternate spaces where development is not the central organizing principle of social life. It also involves giving primacy to endogenous local knowledge over exogenous expert knowledge. Postdevelopment tries to go beyond development by thinking independently from the modern capitalist discourse about alternative visions of the economy, democracy and society. The most promising starting point to think and live otherwise is, according to Escobar, the new popular/grassroots social movements, given that these movements are involved in an ongoing articulation of local needs, aspirations and identities from within communities against hegemonic powers, and in the creation of new local knowledges and the reassertion of old local knowledges in contestation with expert knowledges deployed by hegemonic powers. Postdevelopment, then, represents a search for new ways to reimagine and construct life-worlds, sometimes as representative of an 'alternative development' and other times as a more radical 'alternative to development'; life-worlds which break the hegemonic hold of the development discourse, asserting and embodying diverse, divergent and autochthonous conceptions of the good life.

As a response to the crisis of modernity, this postdevelopment approach heralds an new era guided by the principle that 'another world is possible' – a world that is rich in human and nonhuman biodiversity, a hybrid world, a world that is participatory and democratic, a world that is decolonial, a world that accepts and promotes difference in subjectivity and agency, a world that is primarily local and sustainable but also networked, a world of multiple economies of scale instead of a single economy of growth, a world that respects vernacular cultures as sources of noncapitalist values and nonmarketable human goods, a world that sees those cultures as alternative discourses of knowledge-power, a world of multiple but intertwined histories, multiple space-times, multiple worldviews and multiple anthropologies, and a world of multiple modernities and alternatives to modernity.

5. Enrique Dussel on Transmodernity

In his foundational triad of books, *Philosophy of Liberation* ([1977] 1985), *The Invention of the Americas: Eclipse of 'the Other' and the Myth of Modernity* ([1992] 1995) and *The Underside of Modernity: Apel, Ricoeur, Rorty, Taylor, and Philosophy of Liberation* (1996), the Argentine philosopher Enrique Dussel develops a sustained critique of modernity and Western reason. The positive outcome of this critique is a new conception of 'philosophy of liberation' with a new historical project of 'transmodernity'.

For Dussel, modernity has two significations. The primary and positive signification of modernity is as rational emancipation, whereby the force of reason as critical process opens up new possibilities of human development. A secondary and negative signification of modernity is as a myth that justifies an irrational praxis of violence. According to Dussel, the myth follows these steps:

(a) Modern civilization understands itself as most developed and superior, since it lacks awareness of its own ideological Eurocentrism. (b) This superiority obliges it to develop the most primitive, uneducated, barbarous extremes. (c) This developmental process ought to follow Europe's, since development is unilineal according to the uncritically accepted developmental fallacy. (d) Since the barbarian opposes this civilizing process, modern praxis ought to exercise violence (a just colonial war) as a last resort in order to destroy any obstacles to modernization. (e) This domination produces its diverse victims and justifies its actions as a sacrifice, an inevitable and quasi-ritual act. Civilizing heroes transform their victims into holocausts of a salvific sacrifice, whether these victims are colonized peoples, African slaves, women, or the ecologically devastated earth. (f) For modernity, the barbarian is at fault for opposing the civilizing process, and modernity, ostensibly innocent, seems to be emancipating the fault of its own victims. (g) Finally, modernity, thinking itself as the civilizing power, regards the sufferings and sacrifices of backward and immature peoples, enslaveable races, and the weaker sex as the inevitable costs of modernization. (Dussel [1992] 1995, 136–7)

Modernity needs to be overcome by denying its civilizing myth. However, Dussel does not seek to overcome modernity through a postmodern attack on reason itself based on the irrational incommensurability of language games, but rather by a transmodern opposition to the irrational violence of modern reason based on 'the reason of the other' (137).

Dussel claims that the totalizing efforts of modern reason are in contradiction to its own rational ideal and that the limitations of modern emancipatory reason need to be overcome by a liberating reason that affirms the positivity of the alterity and exteriority of the other of modern reason against modernity's effort to define that alterity and exteriority as pure negativity. As he puts it,

> In transmodernity, the alterity, coessential to modernity, now receives recognition as an equal. Modernity will come into its fullness not by passing from its potency to its act, but by surpassing itself through a corealization with its once negated alterity and through a process of mutual, creative fecundation. The transmodern project achieves with modernity what it could not achieve by itself – a corealization of solidarity, which is analectic, analogic, syncretic, hybrid, and mestizo, and which bonds centre to periphery, woman to man, race to race, ethnic group to ethnic group, class to class, humanity to earth, and occidental to Third World cultures. This bonding occurs not via negation, but via a subsumption from the viewpoint of alterity and in accord with Marx's reversal of Hegelian *Aufhebung* through the concept of subsumption.
>
> This subsumption intends neither a premodern project, nor a folkloric affirmation of the past, nor the antimodern project of conservatives, rightists, Nazis, fascists, or populists. Nor does it envision a postmodern project negating modernity and all rationality only to topple into nihilist irrationalism. This transmodern project really subsumes modernity's rational emancipative character and its negated alterity even as it rejects modernity's mythic character and its irrational exculpation of self and inculpation of its victims. (Dussel [1992] 1995, 138)

Dussel sees positive developments in the crisis of modernity. For instance, non-European cultures are rediscovering the value of their own worldviews, reconstructing the history of their own traditions, reflecting on the modern/ colonial crisis in their own terms, and producing new growth in their own cultures, having as their project not the construction of another modernity or even another universal, univocal culture, but the construction of a new pluriverse that will aim to overcome modernity in several ways (Dussel 2010). First, ecologically, it will uphold the postulate of 'perpetual life' and embody the principle of respect for nature as fundamental to the preservation of life. Second, economically, it will go beyond capitalism, abandoning the principle of quantitative growth as definitive of progress and moving instead toward zero quantitative growth and the development of qualitative aspects of human life. Third, politically, it will practice critical republicanism and participative democracy, by means of which the majority of people will become autonomous actors, instead of being ruled by corrupt political elites and financial bureaucracies. Fourth, militarily, it will uphold the postulate of 'perpetual peace' and hence will develop the necessary structures and practices to maintain an internationally egalitarian cosmopolitan order.

6. Coda: Whither Modernity? What Is Next?
An Ethics of Development

It appears to me that the future of modernity is something that will only be settled after the fact. Presently, depending on where one looks, one sees reaffirmations, radical transformations and dismissals of modernity, each with its own vision of human nature and humanity's future. I will end this essay with a brief sketch of my own stance on these matters (for a longer version, see Marquez 2005).

At the highest level of generality, the problem we are now facing in the crisis of modernity is the problem of figuring out the formal and material conditions and possibilities for putting in place and maintaining a dynamics for an ever-developing nontotalizing totality, which would effectively address humanity's three most important concerns for the twenty-first century: globalization (being-one-in-many), democracy (being-many-in-one) and sustainability (being-for-ever). I believe that the nature of this task requires a reconception of ethics, development and the ethics of development. In what follows I will put forward my own proposal for such reconception.

Ethics is ontology, or more precisely, self-directed ontogeny. Ethics is an understanding of human development, its conditions of possibility and the scope of the possibilities of development, given a particular configuration of a given system at time t. Ethics is a 'general economy' of existence that tries to understand and enable human development.

However, following a possibilist-relationalist-functionalist metaphysics and a naturalized poststructuralist perspective, if the being of a being is found in its being-in-relation, if there are many ways of being-relating, and if these relations change constantly, then the potentiality of the human being will be changing constantly and so will be its being. So how then can we proceed if we want to elaborate a stable and general framework to understand, effect and affect human development? How can we get a handle on this protean moving target called humanity?

I suggest that we use a two-pronged approach. On the one hand, there are some meta-stable elements to this object called humanity. We are biological beings, we are conscious bodies, we need food to eat and water to drink, we reproduce, we are born, we grow and we die, and we want to leave behind a population that can do likewise until the heat death of the universe. To this extent, we are stable beings. On the other hand, beyond this basis, human potentiality and the pathways of actualization are many and varied. So how can we do justice to the apparent stability of our potentiality and actualization drive, while at the same time do justice to the variability in potentiality and pathways of actualization? Can we find a way to avoid relativism on the one hand and absolutism on the other? Can we find an evaluatively useful way to be pluralists? I think that a functional analysis of human practices allows us to accept the reality of pluralism without having to accept relativism *tout court*.

There might be different ways to try to achieve a goal, which points in the direction of pluralism, but some ways might be better at achieving it than others. Thus, we do not always have to accept a relativist conclusion. Sometimes there might be equally good ways to achieve a goal – thus, again, in those cases pluralism follows, but not relativism. However, there will be cases where there does not seem to be an easy way to find out if the goals or the pathways to their achievement are commensurable. In these cases, relativism is the right conclusion to embrace. Sometimes this relativism will put us in tragic situations, where no common way of evaluating a system is available and no universally acceptable pathway of actualization is at hand. In those cases, we will simply have to act and live with the consequences. Other times, we can compromise and go forward that way.

At any rate, relativism, just like pluralism, presents us on many occasions with the opportunity not only to make tragic choices, but also to embrace other ways of being and doing and other pathways of becoming. Thus, it allows us to expand our own universe of possibilities of being-in-the-world.

The reality of pluralism and relativism can be seen as an epistemological problem or as an ontological-existential opportunity. It can be seen as humanity's particular way of showing its biodiversity, a biodiversity that individuals can actually acquire within their own lifetime and encode through culture. If we naturalize culture, we can conceive of different cultural practices as each developing different human potentialities to different levels. Different beliefs configure subjectivity and enable agency in different ways and to different degrees.

We should make good use of all of our world's endowment of actualized human potentiality and we should maintain it, for it represents a library of possible human variety, comprising a vast taxonomy of human potentiality, a huge vocabulary of ways of being-in-the-world, a compendium of technologies of the self, an immense toolbox with a whole array of versatile, multi-function, goal-achieving, problem-solving devices. As long as humans continue, more or less, to be genetically what we are now and to inhabit the world that we do now, there is no danger that humans will completely lose access to that potentiality. However, it usually takes the existence of concrete social and cultural practices to actualize much of the human potentiality of individuals, and it takes a very long time to reinvent many of these modalities of existence once they go out of existence and back into the sea of becoming. Cultural practices are the results of viable and successful mutations in human subjectivity and agency, individual and collective. But just as it takes many generations to develop a new kind of viable species, it takes many human generations to develop these new viable and successful ways of being human. Thus, why throw away all that human endowment if it takes so much time and effort to develop it?

We must strive, therefore, to develop a global, sustainable way of life that preserves human and nonhuman biodiversity. Furthermore, we should develop a syncretic approach to life, which allows us to turn many of the seemingly problematic components of human pluralism and relativism into an opportunity to expand every individual's development endowment. A syncretic approach asks for the existence of an inventory of human potentiality in the form of a natural history of humanity, much like it exists in biology for nonhuman life. Also, this syncretic approach will benefit from the elaboration of an always-tentative general economy of existence for the effective individual and collective use of humanity's patrimony of human potentiality and pathways to actuality.

A specific, though general, ethics of development derives from this theoretical understanding of human development. It is one based on three components: 1) sustainability, promoting the long-term existence of the maximum human and nonhuman biodiversity; 2) democracy, promoting human–human relationships that are bidirectional and, to the extent that it is possible, nonimposing; and 3) nonethnocentrism, promoting true modernity, a modernity not predicated upon a nonexistent abstract universality but on concrete syncretism.

This ethics of development would serve as a general framework for individual and collective decision making. The eventual effects of this ethics of development would be the emergence of a global human life that is, in principle, open and fallibilistic, democratic and experimental, pluralistic, and syncretic. The end result would hopefully be the optimization of individual and collective subjectivity and agency across time.

Whither modernity? There.

References

Asad, Talal, ed. 1973. *Anthropology and the Colonial Encounter*. New York: Humanities Press.

Anderson, Benedict. 1983. *Imagined Communities: Reflections on the Origin and Spread of Nationalism*. London: Verso.

Boas, Franz. 1911. *The Mind of Primitive Man*. New York: Macmillan.

Chakrabarty, Dipesh. 2000. *Provincializing Europe: Postcolonial Thought and Historical Difference*. Princeton, NJ: Princeton University Press.

Dussel, Enrique D. (1977) 1985. *Philosophy of Liberation*. Translated by Aquilina Martinez and Mary Christine Morkovsky. Maryknoll, NY: Orbis Books.

_____. (1992) 1995. *The Invention of the Americas: Eclipse of 'the Other' and the Myth of Modernity*. Translated by Michael D. Barber. New York: Continuum.

_____. 1996. *The Underside of Modernity: Apel, Ricoeur, Rorty, Taylor, and the Philosophy of Liberation*. Translated by Eduardo Mendieta. Atlantic Highlands, NJ: Humanities Press.

_____. 2010. 'From Modernity to Transmodernity'. Paper presented at the International Symposium 'Research across Boundaries'. University of Luxembourg, 16–19 June.

Escobar, Arturo. 1995. *Encountering Development: The Making and Unmaking of the Third World*. Princeton, NJ: Princeton University Press.

Fukuyama, Francis. 1992. *The End of History and the Last Man*. New York: Avon.

García Canclini, Néstor. (1989) 1995. *Hybrid Cultures: Strategies for Entering and Leaving Modernity*. Translated by Christopher L. Chiappari and Silvia L. López. Minneapolis: University of Minnesota Press.

Habermas, Jürgen. (1985) 1987. *The Philosophical Discourse of Modernity: Twelve Lectures*. Translated by Frederick Lawrence. Cambridge, MA: MIT Press.

Huntington, Samuel P. 1996. *The Clash of Civilizations and the Remaking of World Order*. New York: Simon and Schuster.

Judt, Tony. 2005. *Postwar: A History of Europe since 1945*. New York: Penguin.

Marquez, Ivan. 2005. Ethics, Development, and the Ethics of Development. *World Futures: Journal of General Evolution* 61, 4: 307–316.

Mignolo, Walter D. 2000. *Local Histories/Global Designs: Coloniality, Subaltern Knowledges, and Border Thinking*. Princeton, NJ: Princeton University Press.

_____. 2011. *The Darker Side of Western Modernity: Global Futures, Decolonial Options*. Durham, NC: Duke University Press.

Nussbaum, Martha C. 2008. *Liberty of Conscience: In Defense of America's Tradition of Religious Equality*. New York: Basic Books.

Taylor, Charles. 2004. *Modern Social Imaginaries*. Durham, NC: Duke University Press.

West, Cornel. 1989. *The American Evasion of Philosophy: A Genealogy of Pragmatism*. Madison: University of Wisconsin Press.

Wolf, Eric R. 1982. *Europe and the People without History*. Berkeley: University of California Press.

Zinn, Howard. 1980. *A People's History of the United States*. New York: Harper and Row.

Chapter 4

PHILOSOPHICAL ANTHROPOLOGY AND PHILOSOPHY IN ANTHROPOLOGY[1]

Vaclav Brezina

Introduction

Who are we as human beings? In what sense are we part of nature (like plants and animals) and in what sense are we different? What is our place in the world? Is there a common meaning to life or is there a series of culturally based meanings? Is there such a thing as meaning of life?

It is probably fair to say that some of the most exciting (as well as challenging) questions are those directly related to the human condition (see the examples above). In today's globalized and warming world, in which an unprecedented opportunity to come together and share perspectives (both online and offline) and the (post-) postmodern isolation of the individual represent two sides of the same coin, these questions seem to be ever more pressing. It is therefore rather surprising to observe that many present-day philosophers show a strange reluctance to address these topics. As Terry Eagleton, himself not a professional philosopher, put it in his recent book on the meaning of life, 'Philosophers have an infuriating habit of analysing questions rather than answering them' (2007, 1).

Are these questions, then, for at least some philosophers, too ambitious to ask? Who else should address them? Were they formulated in an immature state of philosophy when it was not clear that 'what we cannot speak about we must pass over in silence' (Wittgenstein [1922] 2001, 89)? These and similar questions come to mind when we reflect on the possibility of philosophical inquiry about the human condition. The complexity of the issue makes it difficult to find an adequate starting point for the discussion. I therefore suggest transforming these questions into a more general question, namely: what (if anything) can philosophy tell us about us as human beings and about the various aspects of human existence? This chapter attempts to evaluate the question in the context of the current debate within the field sometimes referred to as 'philosophical anthropology'. First, an overview of the literature dealing with the issues explicitly labelled as 'philosophical anthropology' is presented based on data from *The Philosopher's Index*. Next, the term 'philosophical anthropology' is analysed and subjected to critique. In the subsequent section, four major paradigms of the philosophical-anthropological debate are considered and arguments for an autonomous supradisciplinary character of philosophy in the anthropological debate are put forward, introducing the philosophy-in-anthropology model as a basis for philosophical-anthropological enquiries. Finally, this chapter offers a case study (illustrating the philosophy-in-anthropology model) which compares the approach of natural sciences, social sciences and philosophy to the anthropological issue of human sexuality.

'Philosophical Anthropology': An Overview of the Philosophical Debate

Before looking at the individual arguments concerning the major aspects of the philosophical-anthropological debate, we first need to map the ground. The data presented in this section are based on *The Philosopher's Index* (Philosopher's Information Center 2007), an extensive online database collecting information about books, articles and essays published in the field of philosophy.

The Philosopher's Index was searched for the term 'philosophical anthropology' as a descriptor (i.e., a word that captures the main topic of a book or article) for individual decades between 1941 and 2006. The results can be seen in Figure 1. For comparison, the term 'epistemology', which is general enough to guarantee a relatively constant and wide philosophical interest, was also examined (see Figure 2). The results show that whereas there is a steady increase in the number of works which bear the descriptor 'epistemology' throughout the individual periods, the interest in the issues explicitly labelled as 'philosophical anthropology' peaks for the first time in the 1970s and marks a dramatic increase only recently (i.e., in the period 2001–2006).

The gradual increase in the number of publications with the descriptor 'epistemology' can be explained by the growth in the production of philosophical literature over time and a more comprehensive excerption policy of *The Philosopher's Index* in recent years. No such explanation, however, can account for the dramatic increase in the number of works with the descriptor 'philosophical anthropology' in the period of 2001–2006. The data thus point to an unprecedented rise in interest in issues labelled as 'philosophical anthropology'.

Figure 1. 'Philosophical anthropology' in *The Philosopher's Index*

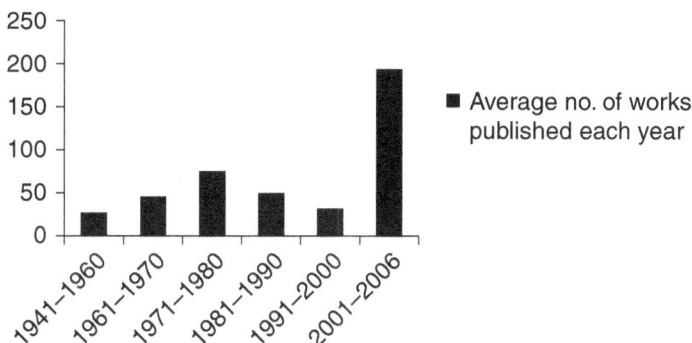

Figure 2. 'Epistemology' in *The Philosopher's Index*

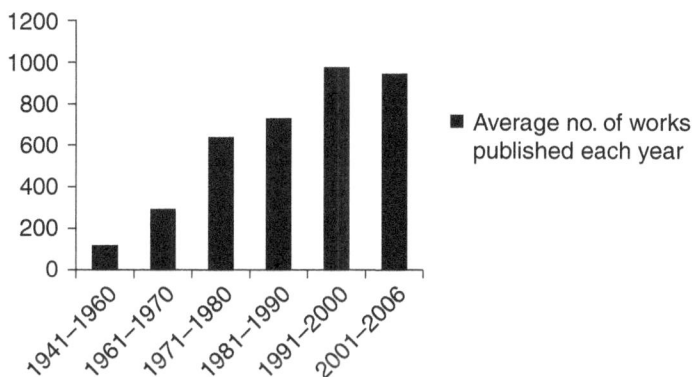

The question which naturally arises next is: what range of issues does the debate involve? For general mapping of the philosophical ground, we can look at the most frequent co-descriptors that occur in *The Philosopher's Index* together with the descriptor 'philosophical anthropology'. Table 1 presents the ten most frequent co-descriptors which characterize the whole period of 1941–2006 (left column) and the top ten co-descriptors which reflect the current debate (right column).

As can be seen from Table 1, there is a fair amount of overlap between the two lists. The commonalities include descriptors such as 'man', 'culture', 'philosophy', 'phenomenology' and 'person'. This suggests that the basic notions connected with 'philosophical anthropology' have remained relatively stable over time. The unique items in the 2001–2006 list, on the other hand, include references to the concept of human 'life', the physical aspect of human existence ('body'), the diachrony of social coexistence ('history') and two key philosophical disciplines ('hermeneutics' and 'ethics').

Table 1: Ten most frequent co-descriptors occurring together with the label 'philosophical anthropology'

	1941–2006			2001–2006		
	Co-descriptor	Total	Per cent of records	Co-descriptor	Total	Per cent of records
1	man	424	14%	culture	90	9%
2	culture	300	10%	life	60	6%
3	philosophy	215	7%	history	44	5%
4	psychology	192	6%	man	44	5%
5	phenomenology	184	6%	phenomenology	41	4%
6	human nature	170	5%	hermeneutics	37	4%
7	freedom	158	5%	ethics	35	4%
8	existentialism	154	5%	person	35	4%
9	metaphysics	148	5%	philosophy	34	4%
10	person	144	5%	body	33	3%

Note: The shaded words are co-descriptors that occur in both lists.

Philosophical Anthropology: What's in a Name?

The word 'anthropology' appears in English for the first time in the late sixteenth century. The *Oxford English Dictionary* records the first use of this term in the general sense of 'the science of man, or of mankind'. The following are a couple of early examples of the word used in English:

> **1593** R. HARVEY *Philad.* 15 Genealogy or issue which they had, Artes which they studied, Actes which they did. This part of History is named Anthropology.
>
> **1656** BLOUNT *Glossogr.*, *Anthropology*, a speaking or discoursing of men. (Simpson 1989, under 'anthropology')

The term 'philosophical anthropology' came into existence much later, when Max Scheler and Helmut Plessner both published their anthropological studies in the late 1920s under the name of 'philosophische Anthropologie' (Krois 2005). In a narrow, historical sense therefore, the term 'philosophical anthropology' is used to denote the movement in German philosophy initiated in 1920s with the aim of integrating knowledge about human beings from all relevant disciplines and providing philosophical synthesis and interpretation of this knowledge. Pappé ([1967] 2006) suggests that the twentieth century was a favourable time for philosophical anthropology of this kind, as this project 'presupposes a developed body of scientific thought, and accordingly, in its program it aspires to a new, scientifically grounded metaphysics' (317). Although philosophical anthropology competed in the first half of the twentieth century with other anthropologically oriented philosophical projects such as existentialism, phenomenology, *Lebensphilosophie* and Heidegger's philosophy of *Dasein*, it also derived inspiration from all these. The most often quoted representatives of the 'philosophische Anthropologie' movement are Max Scheler, Helmuth Plessner and Arnold Gehlen (Rehberg 1988), but as Pappé ([1967] 2006) shows, this movement was broad enough to accommodate many other thinkers with interests directed towards psychology, biology, sociology, theology and the study of culture.

Philosophical anthropology in this sense became an organizing if not syncretic discipline with somewhat reductionist programmes, critical of traditional metaphysics, while at the same time creating a metaphysics of its own. It sought to discover human nature (as a part of 'Nature') rather than the supernatural essence of humanity; or as Gehlen put it, its aim was the 'universal theory of man', which inquires into the 'independent being "man"' ([1940] 1988, 7). The following passage from Gehlen offers an example of an insight typical for 'philosophische Anthropologie':

> Man is an acting being. In a narrower sense, he is also 'undetermined' – he presents a challenge to himself. One might also say that he is a being who must form attitudes. Actions are the expression of man's need to develop an attitude toward the outside world. To the extent that he presents a problem to himself, he must also develop an attitude toward himself and make something of himself. […] We shall see that many of the isolated statements about man are really developments of one basic point of view – that man represents Nature's experiment with an acting being. ([1940] 1988, 24–5)

Apart from this narrow meaning of 'philosophical anthropology' (i.e., a specific movement in continental, originally German, philosophy), the term has also been used in a more general sense. After all, the inquiry about the human condition is an ancient one (cf. Radhakrishnan and Raju 1966) and can embrace a wide range of issues and perspectives. Pihlström thus, for instance, proposes the following general definition:

> By the expression, 'philosophical anthropology', I am not referring to any particular school, since the concept may be used to cover any general philosophical reflection on what it is to be a human being. Hence, it need not be restricted to the German philosophical-anthropological movement, influenced

by *Lebensphilosophie*, phenomenology, and existentialism, which is mainly associated with the work of Max Scheler, Helmuth Plessner, and Arnold Gehlen, and flourished, roughly, from the 1920s to the 1960s [...]. (2003, 260)

Similarly, Rescher defines (his) philosophical anthropology as 'the philosophical study of the conditions of human existence and the issues that confront people in the conduct of their everyday lives' (1990, 1). Pihlström and Rescher are careful not to use terms such as 'essence', 'human nature' or Gehlen's 'independent being' in their definitions in order to avoid the trap of metaphysical presuppositions. The potential disadvantage of these definitions, however, lies in the fact that, at the end of the day, we are left with a very general idea that philosophical anthropology has something to do with human beings and that the approach is philosophical (whatever this may mean).

So far, we have seen that there are (at least) two very different ways in which the term 'philosophical anthropology' can be understood. Neither of them seems to do full justice to the philosophical inquiry about the human condition. The use of the term can be either too narrow (when 'philosophical anthropology' is used to refer to a very specific movement in continental philosophy) or, on the contrary, too vague, in which case 'philosophical anthropology' can mean almost anything and hence possibly nothing.

Further, it can be argued that the term 'philosophical anthropology' itself may be potentially misleading. Its surface similarity to terms such as 'political anthropology', 'economic anthropology', 'medical anthropology', 'linguistic anthropology', etc. may create an impression that 'philosophical anthropology' belongs among their ranks, being comparable in the scope and level of analysis. However, these disciplines are either topical specializations within sociocultural anthropology (Hannerz 2001) or, as is the case with linguistic anthropology, an independent (interdisciplinary) anthropological field, the fourth branch of anthropology within the Boasian paradigm (Duranti 2001). What political anthropology, economic anthropology, medical anthropology and linguistic anthropology have in common is their specialized character, empirical orientation (in the sense of collecting data during fieldwork) and interdisciplinary potential. Philosophical inquiry into the human condition is, in contrast to this, by its very nature a general theoretical enterprise with little interdisciplinary potential as it operates on an autonomous level.[2] We should therefore avoid confusing philosophical inquiry into the human condition with the specialized anthropological subdisciplines, as the label 'philosophical anthropology' would, wrongly, invite us to do.

Philosophical Anthropology and Philosophy in Anthropology

Pihlström (2003), following Kannisto (1984), distinguishes four major philosophical conceptions of humanity, which he calls essentialism, naturalism, existentialism and culturalism. Essentialism, according to Pihlström, presupposes that there exists 'a timeless, unchanging, immutable, metaphysical essence of humanity' (261). Naturalism, on the other hand, is a reductionist, antimetaphysical position, which perceives humankind as part of the contingent natural world discoverable by individual specialized disciplines (biology, chemistry, psychology, sociology, etc.). Existentialism, which stresses the importance of human existence over essence, maintains that 'we are radically free to make our decisions [about our lives] in the concrete material and historical circumstances' (262). Finally, culturalism perceives human beings as rooted not in a pregiven, universal, metaphysical essence (as does essentialism), but in human-constructed cultural environment.

All these conceptions are based on different philosophical traditions and can give us an overall picture about the major frameworks of the philosophical-anthropological inquiry. At this point, we should ask: what is the role of philosophy in this inquiry? The answer will differ with regard to each particular framework.

Essentialism and existentialism

In traditional Aristotelian philosophy, essence (*what* a thing is) and existence (*that* a thing is) were conceived of as two inseparable aspects of every being. The positions of essentialism and existentialism have indeed many features in common, yet at the same time they can be seen as philosophical counterparts. In general, both essentialism and existentialism perceive philosophy as central to the inquiry of what is to be a human being. While for essentialists the role of philosophy is to find the constant, unchanging human essence (i.e., the answer to the question of what all people, regardless of the epoch and culture in which they live, have in common), for existentialists, the primary fact is that we (as human beings) exist – we live in or are 'thrown into' the world. The existentialist framework allows us to say about the human being what in the medieval theological context was said about God: that his (her) essence is his (her) existence.

Existentialism offers profound anthropological insight, often through the analysis of situations in which individual human beings finds themselves. As Jackson succinctly put it in the preface to his *Existential Anthropology*: 'Our task is thus to explore human being-in-the-world through our ever-changing capacity to create the conditions of viable existence and coexistence in relation to the given potentialities of our environment' (2005, xv).

Essentialism, on the other hand, offers generalizations which are intended to capture the fundamental characteristics of humankind. Some criticize essentialism precisely for its philosophical generalizations, which are often seen as inadequate for a description of the dynamic character of humanity (cf. Sayer 2000). The position that once one is a human being one has a certain set of characteristics is unpopular, especially among social scientists who often argue in favour of a culturally, socially and individually constructed human identity.

Culturalism

Culturalism perceives human beings within the framework of cultural variability. It can be understood as a reaction to essentialism and its static and 'totalitarian' (in a broad sense) view of the human condition. Nevertheless, it is far from simple to assess the role of philosophy in the culturalist paradigm, since philosophy has traditionally been connected with the essentialist programme, which looks for the common features of humanity. The problem becomes even clearer when we look at the basic essentialist argument, here clearly expressed by Raju:

> Similarly, if we are to understand man's essential nature for a philosophy of life, it is not enough to understand the cultural achievements of the East and the West. There is something still deeper and more basic than achievements; and that has to be accepted as common to all men, Eastern or Western. Without such faith in the universality of men, comparative philosophy will be of little use. Why should we compare if there is very little in common? Habit and custom, which are the basis of culture and civilization, i.e. of the achievements of man, are only second nature; human nature as such is primary even in respect to them. (1966, 43)

As is apparent from the quote above, essentialists are not content with talking about what Raju calls 'second nature', but seek something beyond this: the primary nature or essence. They are suspicious of what is particular (i.e., mutable, historical and culture based) and presuppose the universal (i.e., immutable, ahistorical and supracultural) order *ante res* or *in rebus*.

However, the distinction between particularity and universality suggested above is probably too crude and needs some rethinking. Let us take as an example human linguistic ability. All people have the ability to learn at least one language, but which particular language they will learn depends on the environment into which they are born. Chomsky suggested that this is due to an inborn, universal grammatical capacity (competence) which is eventually fine-tuned to become the particular language which an individual person speaks (Chomsky 2000; cf. McGilvray 2005). In this case, the universal linguistic competence does not stand against linguistic (and cultural) variability, but remains open to it.

Chomsky's suggestion is far from uncontroversial; nevertheless, the same open dialectics between the universal and the particular is present even in the traditional Aristotelian definition of the human being as *zóon logon echón*. The term *logos* had many meanings in ancient Greek philosophy. In the *zóon logon echón* account, it stands primarily for the rational element in humans. Again, as in the case of the universal linguistic capacity proposed by Chomsky, the particular form, which the universal *logos* takes on in various cultures and various individuals, is left open by the philosophical definition. Cultural as well as individual variability can thus, as these examples show, be compatible with universal philosophical insight.

But what sort of universality is at play here? One might suspect that once the universality has lost its basis in the essence ('primary nature') of the human being, it is only a vague and unclear notion with no real foundation. Hacker, influenced by Wittgenstein, suggests that we should look for the foundation in the 'grammar' (in a broad Wittgensteinian sense) of how we talk (and think) about ourselves:

> [...] especially when operating at a high level of generality, there is an intrinsic interest in detecting the most general structural features of our thought. For the ways in which we think about ourselves and our fellow human beings, the concepts we use in expressing or reporting our inner lives and describing those of others, and the distinctive forms we invoke in explaining our own behaviour and that of others, have very general structural features of which we are not ordinarily aware. (2007, 12–13)

This certainly is not the only philosophical solution to the problem of universality within the culturalist paradigm (cf. Pihlström 2003). At this point, it is sufficient to say that philosophy can retain its irreplaceable position in the inquiry about the human condition (different, though, from how either essentialists or existentialists conceive of it), even when cultural variability is considered.

Naturalism

The paradox of naturalism lies in the fact that philosophy in fact withdraws itself from the debate about the human condition by philosophical metareflection. Naturalism thus invites other disciplines to fill in the place which philosophy traditionally occupied in the anthropological debate. Biologists, chemists and psychologists (possibly also sociologists and social anthropologists, depending on the version of naturalism) are supposed to report on their individual findings which replace a single all-embracing answer to the question about the human condition. The aim here is first and foremost to avoid any 'supernatural' (metaphysical) answer. However, one might suspect that this actually means throwing out the baby with the bathwater.

By this move, philosophy is marginalized, or rather marginalizes itself, in the anthropological debate. The reductionist position of naturalism which itself can be argued philosophically, thus leaves philosophy with little (if anything) to say about human beings. This can be clearly illustrated with Quine's naturalistic position:

> Such is my option. It is part and parcel of empirical science itself, with rational reconstruction intruding only at the conjectural interstices or where complexities of historical accident becloud the schematic understanding we are seeking. The motivation is still philosophical, as motivation in natural science tends indeed to be, and the inquiry proceeds in disregard of disciplinary boundaries but with respect for the disciplines themselves and appetite for their input. Unlike the old epistemologists, we seek no firmer basis for science than science itself. (1995, 16)

Quine opts for an interdisciplinary empirical science as a suitable replacement for traditional philosophy. This leaves philosophy ('rational reconstruction' in Quine's words) with the Cinderella role of occasional clarification of our knowledge. Nevertheless, Quine emphasizes that the motivation for this enterprise is still in some sense philosophical, which suggests that philosophy is seen as a general framework-providing discipline.

Philosophy in anthropology: A model

As shown above, the four approaches differ considerably in what role they ascribe to philosophy in the philosophical-anthropological inquiry. For essentialism it is philosophy (not biology, sociology or sociocultural anthropology) that assumes the key position in the ultimate quest for the essence of humanity. Existentialism is more concerned with the simple fact that we exist and the consequences that follow from this. Culturalism is a position which tries to reconcile individual and cultural variation with the universality of philosophical insight. Naturalism, which stands at the other end of the spectrum, puts the traditional tasks of philosophy on the agenda of other disciplines.

Having seen that there is not one single way in which philosophy is perceived to be involved in the inquiry about what is to be a human being, it seems rather misleading to assume that all issues concerning humanity should come under one single philosophical discipline such as philosophical anthropology. For in each individual approach to the philosophical-anthropological inquiry discussed above, philosophy's role and the nature of its involvement in the anthropological debate differ significantly.

Moreover, as I argued above, philosophical debate about the human condition does not fit easily into the interdisciplinary picture of the present-day specialized sciences (social, behavioural, cognitive, biological, etc.) since this debate operates on a different level of generality (see 'Sex, Sexuality and Lovemaking: A Case Study' below). There is arguably a considerable difference between philosophical inquiry about humanity and traditional (Boasian) anthropology as an empirical, research-based discipline. Although it might not always be clear at first sight (especially in today's interdisciplinary environment), anthropology as an empirical discipline (be it biological, social or linguistic anthropology, or archaeology) has not only certain limits imposed on it by the topic of the inquiry (human beings), but also certain standard procedures, methods and research policies (see Bernard 2006). There are, however, no standard procedures in philosophy, as the four major conceptions of humanity demonstrate. Philosophy can be closely involved in the anthropological debate, as essentialists would have it, or can stand outside it, as naturalists would prefer.

This is not to imply that there is (or ought to be) no communication between philosophy and the specialized anthropological disciplines. The culturalist paradigm is especially favourable to this kind of interaction, as it tries to reconcile the universality of philosophical insight with the particularity of empirical experience. Philosophy can (and in my opinion should) be kept up to date by empirical anthropology so that philosophical thought does not float in an abstract vacuum. Philosophy, on the other hand, can bring important insights which are of great value to understanding individual observable phenomena from a broader perspective.

In conclusion, it seems more useful (for the reasons stated above) to conceive of the role of philosophy in the inquiry about the human condition in terms of a dynamic model of philosophy-in-anthropology rather than in terms of a single discipline such as philosophical anthropology. The philosophy-in-anthropology model maintains that philosophical thought may undoubtedly make a considerable contribution to the anthropological debate. On the other hand, this model does not require from philosophy any particular kind of involvement. There are three main aspects of the proposed model:

1   it leaves the involvement of philosophy in the anthropological debate open to philosophical speculation, hence accommodating all major approaches to the issue (essentialism, existentialism, culturalism and naturalism);

2   it respects the autonomy of philosophy and its supra-disciplinary character; and
3   it is open to the fruitful interaction between empirical anthropology and
    philosophy (once their respective roles are clarified).

Sex, Sexuality and Lovemaking: A Case Study

This section offers a short case study which illustrates the basic principles of
the philosophy-in-anthropology model. It comments on and compares three
types of anthropological discourse related to sex, sexuality and lovemaking.
The first of the analysed texts represents the treatment of the topic from
the perspective of human biology (natural science), the second text is a
contribution to the topic from the perspective of social anthropology (social
science) and finally the third text explores the topic from the philosophical
perspective (philosophy in anthropology). The case study tries to show that:

1   there are different levels of the anthropological debate, each with a
    particular focus and specific vocabulary;
2   philosophy's contribution to the anthropological debate (if we decide that
    such contribution is possible and desirable, see the discussion above) must
    be sought on an autonomous level; and
3   the interaction between philosophy (representing the universal viewpoint)
    and other specialized disciplines (representing a particular viewpoint) is
    possible within the framework of the philosophy-in-anthropology model.

A brief terminological remark ought to be made first: when Cameron and
Kulick (2003) review the terms which are employed both in common usage
and (social) sciences to refer to various aspects of human sexuality, they admit
that there is much polysemy and overlap. Apart from the relatively well-
established pair of terms *sex* ('biological phenomenon of dimorphism' [4])
and *gender* ('sociocultural "being a woman" [or a man]' [4]), Cameron and
Kulick recognize another pair of terms: *sex* ('erotic desire/practice' [1]) and
sexuality ('ways of being sexual' [8], 'socially constructed expression of erotic
desire' [4]). Although the latter pair of terms is not (yet) firmly established in
the scientific discourse, the distinction between 'sex' and 'sexuality' is of great
usefulness since it helps us to distinguish between the treatment of the topic in
natural and social sciences (which, as we shall see, influences the viewpoint and
hence the quality of understanding). For the purpose of the discussion below,
the distinction between the terms 'sex' and 'sexuality' will be understood as
suggested in Cameron and Kulick (2003). Further, a third term referring to
a more general (philosophical) treatment of the topic will be used, namely
'erotic love'. This term denotes the sentiment traditionally labelled by the

Greek term *eros*. Finally, the term 'lovemaking' will be employed to refer to a practice of acting upon *eros*.

We can now proceed to the analysis of the individual texts. First, let us have a look at the text representing the treatment of the topic from the perspective of human biology:

[1] The female orgasmic phase, if stimulated by coitus, usually occurs 10 to 20 min. after *intromission* (penetration of the penis into the vagina). [...] An orgasm in either sex can be one of the most intense and pleasurable of human experiences. We talk more about the experience of orgasm later, but now let us look at some physiological changes that occur [...].

1   Strong muscular contractions occur in the outer one-third of the vaginal wall. The first contraction lasts about 2 to 4 s and is followed by rhythmic contractions at intervals of 0.8 s, the same frequency as the muscular contractions during male ejaculation. There can be 3 to 15 of these contractions, and the intensity of the initial ones is greater than that of later ones. The rectal sphincter can also exhibit rhythmic contractions at 0.8 s intervals.
2   The inner two-thirds of the vagina often expand, which facilitates movement of the penis within it. [...]

The experience of orgasm can vary in one woman and among different women. S. Hite reported that this experience often occurs in three stages. First, women experience a sensation of 'suspension' lasting only an instant, followed by a feeling of intense sensual awareness, oriented at the clitoris and radiating upward into the pelvis. In the second stage, there is a sensation of warmth, beginning in the pelvis and spreading to other parts of the body. Finally, there is pelvic throbbing, focusing in the vagina and lower pelvis. (Jones and Lopez 2006, 198–200)

Natural sciences, in this case human biology, can offer detailed information about the mechanism of bodily response to sexual stimulation. In text [1], we are first presented with a meticulously compiled catalogue of physiological reactions, supplemented with information about the times, frequencies and intervals of these reactions. The complex notion of orgasm is then analysed in terms of the individual stages of pleasurable experience. The pleasure is referred to using expressions such as 'intense sensual awareness, oriented at the clitoris', 'warmth, beginning in the pelvis and spreading to other parts of the body' and 'pelvic throbbing'. It is interesting to note that the experience is described in very general terms, which are specified by reference to a particular bodily location. One would be tempted to ask: what kind of intense sensual awareness is at play here? Is the warmth experienced during orgasm the same kind of warmth experienced while, for example, climbing the stairs or drinking hot tea?

For natural science, however, the crucial part of the inquiry lies in describing the *objective* (i.e., measurable, testable and verifiable) aspects of human sexual behaviour and experience. To do that, the natural scientist must take human lovemaking out of its usual context and transpose it into a laboratory environment, in which he/she (as an 'objective observer') has more control over the process (see Schultz et al. 1999).

Studies of sex in humans carried out by natural sciences are of great importance in medical practice and can help us understand major physiological mechanisms behind the sexual act and experience. At the same time, the account of what is going on when two (or more) people are making love is by no means exhausted by their 'carnal geography'.

Second, let us have a look at a short excerpt dealing with the issue of sexuality in the very specific context of Jamaican society, which represents the treatment of the topic from the perspective of social anthropology:

[2] In Jamaica, for reasons we will explore, sexuality is usually conceptually linked with the desire to create children. For both men and women, perceptions of self-identity and social power are contingent upon the expression of sexual potency which is confirmed by the birth of children. Jamaican art, music, and theatre express the vitality of a society in which women, as well as men, achieve social status through their own activity.

This assertive dynamism is analysed first sociologically, then symbolically. Sex and birth are an affirmation by the self, and by the society, that adulthood has been achieved. Once adulthood is achieved, social influence might be extended through sexual relationships, birth of children, and the building of social networks. On the symbolic level, body imagery and meanings attributed to menstruation give us insights into deeper levels of identity. (MacCormack and Draper 1987, 143)

There is no dispute about the fact that human sexual behaviour and sexual desires have become part of a complex, culturally and socially determined normative framework. It is culture that gives a series of muscular contractions a meaning beyond immediate satisfaction of sexual urge and procreation. In the case of Jamaican society discussed in text [2], culture has created a link between self-identity and social power on the one hand, and sexual potency and childbirth on the other. In this process, language and other forms of representation play an essential role. Art, music, theatre, body imagery and symbolic meanings of menstruation mentioned in text [2] not only depict sexual desires and behaviour, but through these sexuality as 'socially constructed expression of erotic desire' (Cameron and Kulick 2003, 8) takes on its particular form. Social anthropology can thus trace the variation in sexual behaviour and the construction of sexual desires across cultures with vocabulary appropriate to its role of comprehensive sociocultural exploration (with 'identity', 'power' and 'symbols' being among its keywords).

Finally, let us have a look at the treatment of the topic from a philosophical perspective (i.e., one of many possible philosophical perspectives):

> [3] What exactly is sexual pleasure? Is it like the pleasure of eating and drinking? Like that of lying in a hot bath? Like that of watching your child at play? Clearly it is both like and unlike all of these. It is unlike the pleasure of eating, in that its object is not consumed. It is unlike the pleasure of the bath, in that it involves taking pleasure *in* an activity, and in the other person who joins you. It is unlike that of watching your child at play, in involving bodily sensations and a surrender to physical desire. Sexual pleasure resembles the pleasure of watching something, however, in a crucial respect: it has intentionality. It is not just a tingling sensation; it is a response to another person, and to the act in which you are engaged with him or her. The other person may be imaginary: but it is towards a person that your thoughts are directed, and pleasure depends on thought.
>
> This dependency on thought means that sexual pleasure can be mistaken, and ceases when the mistake is known. Although I would be a fool not to jump out of the soothing bath after being told that what I took for water is really acid, this is not because I have ceased to feel pleasurable sensations in my skin. In the case of sexual pleasure, the discovery that it is an unwanted hand that touches me at once extinguishes my pleasure. The pleasure could not be taken as confirming the hitherto unacknowledged sexual virtues of some previously rejected person. A woman who makes love to the man who has disguised himself as her husband is no less the victim of rape, and the discovery of her mistake can lead to suicide. (Scruton 2005, 128)

The following are the key philosophical vocabulary items in text [3]: 'sexual pleasure', 'body',[3] 'intentionality', 'person', 'thought', 'making love', 'rape' and 'suicide'. However, some of these words have already appeared in the previous discussion ('pleasure' and 'person' in text [1], 'body' in both texts [1] and [2]) and there is no reason why other words from the list (possibly with the exception of 'intentionality') should not appear in biological and/or socio-anthropological texts (or in any other text for that matter). Nevertheless, what is special about the words above is that these are (as is much of the philosophical vocabulary) common words used in a philosophical context.

Two of these words ('person' and 'body') also rank high on the list of the most frequent co-descriptors occurring together with 'philosophical anthropology' in *The Philosopher's Index* (see '"Philosophical Anthropology": An Overview of the Philosophical Debate' above). 'Person' is the eighth item and body is the tenth item in the list monitoring the current debate (2001–2006). Moreover, the words 'rape' and 'suicide' represent specific vocabulary of 'ethics', which as a co-descriptor is the seventh item in the list.

Let us go back to the main argument in text [3]. Scruton compares sexual pleasure with other kinds of pleasure to point out the specific character of the former. In his inductive reasoning, he recognizes that the crucial feature of sexual pleasure is intentionality (i.e., orientation of our thought) towards another person. Sexual pleasure is thus, according to Scruton, not a self-enclosed and self-generated sensation, but connects two people in a person-to-person relationship which does not involve only the body, but substantially also the mind.

Scruton then continues with an analysis of the interaction between mind and body during lovemaking (sexual act), seeing bodily pleasure as being dependent on the mind (thought) in that a necessary condition for bodily pleasure is the thought of a particular person.[4] This is shown with the thought experiment of mistaken personal identity during lovemaking. The whole discussion eventually gives rise to serious ethical issues of rape and suicide. In this way, Scruton attempts to uncover the complex sphere of erotic love through the analysis of the dialectics between body and mind (with the mind oriented towards another person).

We can leave aside the actual evaluation and possible criticism of Scruton's argument, noting that there is a large body of philosophical literature which offers different positions on the topic (cf. Van Sevenant, 2005; Soble 1998; Vannoy 1994). At this point, it is, however, important to realize that there is a considerable difference between the philosophical and nonphilosophical (biological, socio-anthropological) treatment of human sexuality, which can be seen from the above analysis of the texts.

From a more general viewpoint, it is also interesting to realize that sexuality is universal among humans in spite of the fact that it may take on various culturally (and/or individually) specific forms (see the discussion about text [2] above). Philosophy's contribution to the debate lies in exploring this universality and its limits. The exploration brings in to the debate various ethical issues. As a result, the fact that human beings are capable of erotic love can be considered as one of the candidates for a defining feature of what is to *be* the human being. At the same time, however, sex and sexuality are not restricted to humans (at least not in the broad sense of the word 'sex', see above) and thus we may wonder whether the apparently obvious difference between animal copulation and human lovemaking can be used to define what is to *act as* a human being. As Van Sevenant puts it, 'Sexual, of course. We are sexual beings' (2005, 27).

Conclusion

In conclusion, returning to the original question (what, if anything, can philosophy tell us about us as human beings and about various aspects of human existence?), we have seen that there is no single answer, as philosophy is an enterprise which sets its own limits of sensible debate. Various positions from essentialism to naturalism recognize a different level of involvement of philosophy in the anthropological debate. This dynamism seems to be better accounted for in the philosophy-in-anthropology model rather than in a single discipline such as 'philosophical anthropology'.

Notes

1 I would like to thank Peter Skalník and Dana Gablasova for their invaluable comments on an earlier version of this chapter.
2 This is not to say that philosophical insights cannot be of value in specialized disciplines or that philosophy should not take into account what specialized disciplines have to offer.
3 'bodily sensations'
4 For some contradictory evidence from medical research, see Levin and van Berlo (2004).

References

Bernard, H. Russell. 2006. *Research Methods in Anthropology: Qualitative and Quantitative*. Lanham: Alta Mira Press.

Chomsky, Noam. 2000. *New Horizons in the Study of Language and Mind*. Cambridge: Cambridge University Press.

Duranti, A. 2001. 'Linguistic Anthropology'. In *International Encyclopedia of Social and Behavioral Sciences*, edited by N. J. Smelser and P. B. Baltes. Amsterdam: Elsevier.

Eagleton, Terry. 2007. *The Meaning of Life*. Oxford: Oxford University Press.

Francoeur, Robert T., ed. 1997. *The International Encyclopedia of Sexuality*. New York: Continuum.

Gehlen, Arnold. (1940) 1988. *Man, His Nature and Place in the World*. New York: Columbia University Press.

Hacker, P. M. S. 2007. *Human Nature: The Categorial Framework*. Oxford: Blackwell.

Hannerz, U. 2001. 'Anthropology'. In *International Encyclopedia of Social and Behavioral Sciences*, edited by N. J. Smelser and P. B. Baltes. Amsterdam: Elsevier.

Jackson, Michael. 2005. *Existential Anthropology*. New York: Berghahn Books.

Jones, Richard Evan and Kristin H. Lopez. 2006. *Human Reproductive Biology*. Amsterdam: Elsevier.

Kannisto, H. 1984. 'Filosofisen antropologian mahdollisuudesta'. *Ajatus* 41: 217–35.

Krois, John Michael. 2005. '"A Passion Can Only Be Overcome by a Stronger Passion": Philosophical Anthropology Before and After Ernst Cassirer'. *European Review* 13 (4): 557–75.

Levin, Roy J. and Willy van Berlo. 2004. 'Sexual Arousal and Orgasm in Subjects Who Experience Forced or Non-consensual Sexual Stimulation: A Review'. *Journal of Clinical Forensic Medicine* 11 (2): 82–8.

MacCormack, Carol P. and Alizon Draper. 1987. 'Social and Cognitive Aspects of Female Sexuality in Jamaica'. In *The Cultural Construction of Sexuality*, edited by Patricia Caplan. London: Routledge.

McGilvray, James Alasdair, ed. 2005. *The Cambridge Companion to Chomsky*. Cambridge: Cambridge University Press.

Medina, José. 2004. 'Wittgenstein's Social Naturalism: The Idea of *Second Nature* After the *Philosophical Investigations*'. In *The Third Wittgenstein: The Post-Investigations Works*, edited by Daniele Moyal-Sharrock, 79–92. Aldershot: Ashgate.

Nye, Robert, ed. 1999. *Sexuality*. Oxford: Oxford University Press.

Pappé, H. O. (1967) 2006. 'Philosophical Anthropology'. In *Encyclopedia of Philosophy*, vol. 7, edited by Donald M. Borchert. New York: Thomson–Gale.

Philosopher's Information Center. 2007. *The Philosopher's Index*. Online: http://www.philinfo. org (accessed 17 July 2008).

Pihlström, Sami. 2003. 'On the Concept of Philosophical Anthropology'. *Journal of Philosophical Research* 28: 259–86.

Quine, Willard Van Orman. 1995. *From Stimulus to Science*. Cambridge, MA: Harvard University Press.

Radhakrishnan, S. and P. T. Raju, eds. 1996. *The Concept of Man: A Study in Comparative Philosophy*. Lincoln, NE: Johnsen.

Raju, P. T. 1966. Introduction to *The Concept of Man: A Study in Comparative Philosophy*, edited by S. Radhakrishnan and P. T. Raju. Lincoln, NE: Johnsen.

Rehberg, Karl-Siegbert. 1988. 'Arnold Gehlen's Elementary Anthropology: An Introduction'. In Gehlen, Arnold. *Man, His Nature and Place in the World*, ix–xxxvi. New York: Columbia University Press.

Rescher, Nicholas. 1990. *Human Interests: Reflections on Philosophical Anthropology*. Stanford: Stanford University Press.

Sayer, Andrew. 2000. *Realism and Social Science*. London: Sage.

Schacht, Richard. 1990. 'Philosophical Anthropology: What, Why and How'. *Philosophy and Phenomenological Research* 50: supplement, 155–76.

Schultz W. G. M., P. Van Andel, I. Sabelis and E. Mooyart. 1999. 'Magnetic Resonance Imaging of Male and Female Genitals During Coitus and Female Sexual Arousal'. *British Medical Journal* 319: 1596–1600.

Scruton, Roger. 2005. *Philosophy: Principles and Problems*. London: Continuum.

Simpson, John, ed. 1989. *Oxford English Dictionary*. Oxford: Oxford University Press.

Soble, Alan. 1998. 'Philosophy of Sexuality'. In *Routledge Encyclopedia of Philosophy*. London: Routledge.

Van Sevenant, Ann. 2005. *Sexual Outercourse: Philosophy of Lovemaking*. Leuven: Peeters.

Vannoy, Russell C. 1994. 'Philosophy and Sex'. In *Human Sexuality: An Encyclopedia*, edited by Vern L. Bullough and Bonnie Bullough, 442–9. New York: Garland Publishing.

Chapter 5

THE ENGAGEMENT OF PHILOSOPHY AND ANTHROPOLOGY IN THE INTERPRETIVE TURN AND BEYOND: TOWARDS AN ANTHROPOLOGY OF THE CONTEMPORARY

Heike Kämpf

One of the most interesting and fruitful anthropological discussions of philosophy occurred within the so-called 'interpretive turn' in anthropology. This turn was inspired by philosophy and initiated a reconsideration of philosophical concepts. In particular, the reconsideration of the hermeneutic notion of 'understanding' led to new anthropological readings of the works of Martin Heidegger, Hans-Georg Gadamer and Paul Ricoeur. At the same time this anthropological discussion had its impact on philosophy. On the one hand, hermeneutic and analytic philosophy came closer together while questioning the possibilities of understanding alien cultures: Peter Winch and Richard Rorty dealt with the problem of understanding cultural differences in referring to the philosophy of language. On the other hand, hermeneutic philosophy, being traditionally occupied with the interpretation of texts and historical events, found itself involved in questions concerning social behaviour and cultural differences. Thus a dialogue between anthropology and philosophy occurred, which caused a reformulation of the concept of 'understanding' and simultaneously initiated new attempts to conceptualize the cultural and social reality. I argue that philosophical and anthropological concerns can finally convene in an 'anthropology of the contemporary', to borrow a term from Paul Rabinow.

In the following I will first outline some of the most important aspects and perspectives of the interpretive turn, which conditions and shapes the contemporary discourse. Then I want to focus on two interrelated aspects of contemporary anthropology in relation to philosophy: first, the attempts to reformulate the concepts of knowledge and understanding, and second, the efforts to conceptualize culture as a practice. These efforts call for a theory of performativity, which can serve as a framework for an anthropology of the contemporary.

1. The Interpretive Turn and the Historicity of Reason

Basically, the interpretive turn responded to the positivist orientation of anthropology towards the natural sciences. This situation was identified as a reason for a crisis of anthropological research, as Paul Rabinow and William M. Sullivan point out:

> The conception of the human sciences as somehow necessarily destined to follow the path of the modern investigation of nature is at the root of this crisis. Preoccupation with that ruling expectation is chronic in social science; that *idée fixe* has often driven investigators away from a serious concern with the human world into the sterility of purely formal argument and debate. (1987, 5)

Rabinow and Sullivan turn to a discussion of meaning, understanding and interpretation as constituent moments of human life. Thus, the interpretive turn is not merely to be considered as an introduction of interpretive methods to anthropology. Rather, it challenges the idea of method and inspires a new concept of culture. According to Rabinow and Sullivan culture is to be considered as 'the shared meaning, practices, and symbols that constitute the human world' (1987, 7). Thus to them the notion of cultural meaning becomes the base-point of the whole interpretive project. Rabinow and Sullivan continue to shape the interpretive turn as follows:

> The interpretive turn refocuses attention on the concrete varieties of cultural meaning, in their particularity and complex texture, but without falling into the traps of historicism or cultural relativism in their classical forms. For the human sciences both the object of investigation – the web of language, symbol, and institutions that constitute signification – and the tools by which investigation is carried out share inescapably the same pervasive context that is the human world. (1987, 5–6)

This quotation displays the fundamental and irreducible character of understanding and rests on the Heideggerian ontological turn of hermeneutics. Understanding (*Verstehen*) is regarded as the primordial mode of being in the world. Thus, understanding becomes inseparable from human life. This also implies that interpretation (*Auslegung*) according to Heidegger is to be considered as an explication and development of the ontological understanding. Therefore, understanding is intimately connected to interpretation and should be considered as constituting the human world. As Gadamer points out, this ontological turn discloses the full implications of understanding as an existential possibility and structure. The relevance of this insight for the human sciences is also highlighted by Gadamer:

> If *Verstehen* is the basic moment of human *in-der-Welt-sein*, then the human sciences are nearer to human self-understanding than are the natural sciences. The objectivity of the latter is no longer an unequivocal and obligatory ideal of knowledge. Because the human sciences contribute to human self-understanding even though they do not approach the natural sciences in exactness and objectivity, they do contribute to human self-understanding because in turn they are based in human self-understanding. (Gadamer 1987, 85–6)

The idea of the irreducible and inescapable status of a culturally mediated understanding serves as a common ground for anthropology and philosophy in this discourse. Culture is primarily conceptualized as a web of meanings in which man is always already interwoven. One can say, then, that although *understanding* is regarded as a basic and universal moment of human existence, it is also the condition for the culturally and historically diverting forms of human worlds. This situation of diversity arises as soon as the mediated character of understanding is acknowledged. Even the seemingly immediate understanding is historically situated and culturally mediated. This concept of understanding has initiated a new orientation of anthropological research, as Clifford Geertz underlines. According to him, the interest in interpretation was an effort to redefine anthropology through 'placing the systematic study of meaning, the vehicles of meaning, and the understanding of meaning at the very center of research and analysis: to make of anthropology, or anyway cultural anthropology, a hermeneutical discipline' (Geertz 1995, 114).

In laying emphasis on the mediated character of understanding, anthropology and philosophy argued against the concept of an 'immediate understanding'. Thereby, the possibility to disengage from a historical or cultural situation in order to grasp a foreign life-world is deeply put into question. The consequence of this reformulation is twofold: on the one hand, it overcomes a mentalist view in stressing that meaning is a public concern and created in communication. Understanding, then, requires a public sphere because private meaning is as impossible as a private language, as Wittgenstein suggested. On the other hand, the success of the effort to understand a foreign culture is called into question. First of all, one can state that a mentalist view of meaning is abandoned. Geertz, especially, recognizes the positive consequences of these considerations: understanding requires 'searching out and analyzing the symbolic forms – words, images, institutions, behaviors – in terms of which people actually represent themselves to themselves and to one another' (Geertz 1983, 228).

And Ricoeur argues that understanding is 'mediated by signs, symbols, and texts; in the last resort understanding coincides with the interpretation given to these mediated terms' (1991a, 15). Both philosophy and anthropology are deeply affected by this interdisciplinary discourse insofar as it affects their self-understandings and procedures. Rabinow and Sullivan point out that knowledge has to be seen as inescapably practical and historically situated. As a result of this perspective on knowledge, anthropology is also able to challenge the practice of knowledge in our culture (1987, 2)

This dialectical structure of understanding the own and the other stems from the reformulation of understanding in philosophic hermeneutics as described above: it is not considered as just a type of knowledge but as the fundamental human way of knowing. Thus it is inseparable from living. Hence the human world, the life-world, is reflected on as being constituted, reproduced and transformed within the process of understanding. As a result of these considerations, the division between observation and theory, the collecting of *data bruta* and their interpretation, is questioned. Rather, observation is to be regarded as theory impregnated, given that understanding is irreducible and thus interpretation is already interwoven into any form of perception.

What also becomes clear is that any conceptualization of the cultural and social life immediately affects the anthropological endeavour. In trying to understand, the researcher cannot exclude himself and his scientific project any longer from his conceptualizations; the research does not claim to establish a 'view from nowhere'. The anthropologist and the anthropological undertaking are rather to be considered as being embedded in and being part of a specific culture and a historical situation. For that reason the investigations in the history of anthropology are increasing. They are trying to clarify the present condition and situation of the anthropological research without claiming to free themselves from history. Similar to the intention of this historical research, fieldwork could be also understood as a chance to gain a deeper and more critical self-understanding. This is not necessarily a merely personal enterprise, but helps us to get an insight into the specific features of our time and culture. In that aim anthropology and philosophy are related, insofar as philosophy is involved in the task to understand our present situation. In this sense, for example, Foucault points out that already Kant was involved in this task when he posed his famous question *Was ist Aufklärung?*

Foucault writes in referring to Kant's text, 'It is in the reflection on 'today' as difference in history and as motive for a particular philosophical task that the novelty of this text appears to me to lie' (1987, 163). In particular, Rabinow's recent work on an 'anthropology of the contemporary' contributes to this project (2008, 13).

The interpretive turn finally effects the contemporary so-called 'postmodern' situation of anthropology. This term is applied to very diverse theories and is often used in a polemic mode. But in the sense that Jane Flax introduces the term, in laying emphasis on the purpose 'to explore how theories might be written in post-modern voices – non-authoritarian, open-ended, and process-oriented', it might be convenient in order to refer to some aspects of contemporary anthropology (1990, 3). Since, together with the historicity of reason, the danger of an epistemological imperialism is acknowledged, a special caution, sensibility and critical reflexivity, as well as self-referentiality, are needed in the efforts to understand.

In summarizing one can say that the contemporary debate, which rests upon this interpretive turn, has moved beyond the neat division between philosophy and anthropology. In reflecting on their own cultural conditions of knowledge, anthropological and philosophical concerns are centred around a common idea and a common undertaking. Particularly, Rabinow's project to 'anthropologize the West' is also present in Michel Foucault. Rabinow writes,

> We need to anthropologize the West: show how exotic its constitution of reality has been; emphasize those domains most taken for granted as universal this includes epistemology and economics make them seem as historically peculiar as possible; show how their claims to truth are linked to social practices and have hence become effective forces in the social world. (1996, 36)

On the other hand, Foucault (1991, 12) considers his work as an anthropology of his own culture. Moreover, in writing a history of Western rationality he contributes to the deconstruction of the idea of a timeless, universal reason. One can also mention here the project of Bruno Latour and Steve Woolgar (1986), who were doing fieldwork in laboratories in order to establish an 'anthropology of science', analysing the scientific production of knowledge.

2. The Incommensurability Thesis and Its Impact on Anthropology: Deconstruction, Dialogue and the Dialectics of Understanding

Hermeneutic philosophy destroyed the Cartesian conviction of the universality of reason and questioned the idea that there are universal standards of rationality.

This dubitative attitude also came up in analytic philosophy being confronted with the problem of understanding alien cultures. In his essay 'Understanding a Primitive Society' Peter Winch rereads the famous ethnography by Evans-Pritchard about witchcraft among the Azande. With the Wittgensteinian notion of language games and forms of life he tried to shed new light on the problem of understanding. From Wittgenstein he borrows the idea that forms of life might differ so much that even their standards of rationality might be incommensurable. Concerning the effort to understand a 'primitive' or foreign society, Winch suggests, that it is necessary not only to bracket our prejudices and biases but also to suspend Western standards of rationality. Winch finally suggests broadening the concept of rationality. In order to understand Azande witchcraft, he argues, it should not be considered in terms of a scientific activity. In regarding witchcraft as a form of science (as an early state of science for example), the investigator might completely misunderstand and distort this institution. Instead Winch argues, 'We must, if you like, be open to new possibilities of what could be invoked and accepted under the rubric of "rationality" – possibilities which are perhaps suggested and limited by what we have hitherto so accepted, but not uniquely determined thereby' (1972, 34).

The point Winch wants to make clear is, as Bernstein summarizes, that the specific standards of rationality 'that may be appropriate for scientific activity are not necessarily relevant for understanding the standards of rationality and irrationality in Zande witchcraft' (1983, 103). But Winch also states that the possibilities of grasping forms of rationality different from ours are limited. At the end of his essay Winch suggests another mode of understanding: he turns away from rationality and considers limiting notions, such as birth and death, as serving a possible common ground. An understanding of foreign societies, then, could start with a search for limiting notions and ask how a specific culture is dealing with them, how they are present in social institutions and beliefs. Through this suggestion Winch not only surpasses the focus on rationality, but he also picks up a hermeneutic notion that was already present in Dilthey and Ricoeur. Ricoeur pleads for a 'depth hermeneutic' that is based on the concept of limiting notions: 'In the same way as language games are forms of life, according to the famous aphorism of Wittgenstein, social structures are also attempts to cope with the existential perplexities, human predicaments, and deep-rooted conflicts' (Ricoeur 1991b, 166). As a result, the personal commitment involved in understanding can be qualified.

Although this idea might frame an anthropological approach and might have a heuristic value, it remains questionable whether this idea of a common human condition can and should be universalized. In reference to anthropological investigations and reflections, one might rather arrive at the conclusion that those seemingly universal limiting notions are themselves limited to a specific culture. In thinking about the many different ways death, for example, is considered in various different contexts, one loses the point of comparison and the category death more or less implodes. For example Crapanzano tells us:

> When we speak of death, we tend to naturalize it that we forget that however real our extinction, our death is always embedded in a cultural tradition that moulds it and governs its figurative and rhetorical possibility. [...] Though we give death a fundamental role in the construction of life, meaning and value, it is by no means clear that all other peoples do so. In many societies death is mutely accepted. (2004a, 202)

The search for abstract cross-cultural universals, which could ground the rightness or truth of our knowledge of alien cultures, might be considered as an expression of a specific European will to ground knowledge permanently, as Rorty suggests. But the need to legitimize a specific understanding remains a crucial point for hermeneutic philosophy. So Gadamer distinguishes true or enabling prejudices from disabling prejudices. After stressing the inescapability of the prejudices, or preconceptions defining the human situation, and pointing out that there is no way to overcome prejudice by reflexivity, he puts forward the positive role of the determination by tradition. He argues, 'Detachment or being liberated from tradition cannot be our first worry in our attitude towards the past in which we – who are ourselves historical beings – incessantly participate' (1987, 114).

In summarizing his argument one can say: as preconceptions are to be regarded as a product of the tradition we belong to, and as we seek to understand the historical past and our historically determined present, those inherited preconceptions do not disturb but enable a true understanding. But Gadamer's strategy of legitimizing preconceptions fails if there are different traditions. And if cultures are regarded as being determined or shaped by tradition, a cross-cultural understanding cannot rely on the preconceptions that enable us to understand our own tradition. In stressing that strong concept of an irreducible 'belongingness' to a tradition which marks the 'effective historical consciousness', Gadamer not only questions the possibility of a true understanding of an alien culture, but rather has to consider it as impossible. Although one might question his idea of belongingness and his idea of coherence through tradition, I want to point out here that Gadamer's reflections result in a recognition that different cultures may be regarded as incommensurable.

The idea that incommensurable discourses do exist, and that they cannot and should not be reconciled by an episteme, becomes finally explicit in Rorty's reading of philosophic hermeneutics. According to Rorty, the philosophical attempts to find a permanent and timeless foundation of knowledge and to render all knowledge claims commensurable are rooted in the Kantian heritage, which he tries to surpass. Therefore Rorty distinguishes 'systematic philosophers' from 'edifying philosophers', whose heritage he is trying to make visible and to bring forward. In contrast to systematic philosophers, edifying philosophers are destroying the traditional philosophical vocabulary. Edifying philosophers are critically aware of the possibility that all claims to truth and universality are merely reflecting the historical and cultural situation, a specific form of life and thinking. Therefore, the edifying discourse does not aim at commensurability or try to establish a permanent framework of inquiries. Rather, this discourse is interested in edification (*Bildung*), not in knowledge. The edifying discourse takes us 'out of our old selves by the power of strangeness to aid us in becoming new beings' (1980, 360). And Rorty proceeds, 'The attempt to edify ourselves and others may consist in the hermeneutic activity of making connections between our own culture and some exotic culture or historical period, or between our own discipline and another discipline which seems to pursue incommensurable aims in an incommensurable vocabulary' (1980, 360).

For Rorty, epistemology-centred philosophy, with its search for foundations of knowledge, is to be considered as an episode in European history which is moreover in danger of following a colonial logic while claiming universality and commensurability. These considerations are present in anthropology when, for example, Rabinow (1996, 36) suggests that epistemology should be seen as a historical event. That strong distrust in universalistic claims is produced by the recognition of the historical and cultural embeddedness of knowledge. But that does not automatically lead to the dichotomy of edification and knowledge. Rather, it implies a new concept of knowledge.

In order to make this point clear, I want to take a closer look at Gadamer's concept of *Bildung* being involved in the process of understanding. Rorty's notion of edification is explicitly borrowed from Gadamer's concept of *Bildung* (self-formation, education). *Bildung* for Gadamer expresses the idea that understanding causes a knowledge that cannot be separated from the knower. Understanding is, as the concept of *Bildung* emphasizes, also affecting and changing the one who understands. It could be translated by Polanyi's notion of 'personal knowledge'. And it is exactly that idea of a personal or practical knowledge that holds to be valuable for anthropology in trying to conceptualize culture as a practice, as I will outline in the following part. Now I want to discuss the Heideggerian notion of destruction (*Destruktion*) as it is found in anthropology. This notion is received in anthropology not merely as a method of literal criticism, as deconstructionism established in reference to Derrida, but rather as a means of critical reflection on a traditional, preconceived set of concepts guiding the process of understanding. Thus deconstructionism in a broader sense also responds to the above-outlined critical reflections on epistemology. For that reason deconstruction is not only to be found in postcolonial studies, but also in many contemporary critical reflections concerning inherited anthropological concepts. Gadamer (1995, 57) points out that Heidegger's destruction cannot be considered as mere devastation, but rather as a removal of covering layers consisting of inherited, dominant and hitherto unquestioned conceptualizations in order to grasp the underlying and hidden experience of thought.

Basically, the deconstructive practice indebted to the Derridean reading of Heidegger is involved in the search for fundamental oppositions which support the intelligibility of a given discourse. The thus revealed oppositions are finally displaced, not merely reversed. In a broader sense one can say that deconstruction in anthropology is involved in scattering established relations of meaning and underlying oppositions, thus questioning the established mode of understanding in order to construct new relations and establish a new more just or adequate understanding. The anthropological distrust in the truth and objectivity of inherited preconceptions and frameworks of inquiry produces diverse deconstructionist operations *within* the effort to understand. From a feminist point of view, for instance, Michelle Rosaldo has turned to deconstructionism in order to reach at a better understanding of the social process. In particular, the male/female opposition is subject to deconstruction understood as a means of denaturalization. Rosaldo deconstructs the tendency to think in dualistic terms and binary oppositions: 'I want to deconstruct conceptual frameworks that we use as though they were concrete reflections of the world "out there" in order both to free our moral thinking from assumptions bound to sex and to free feminism from the moralism of our predominantly individualistic modes of sociological understanding' (1987, 281).

To summarize, one can say that binary oppositions are under suspicion because they both imply a hierarchical order of the opposed terms and tend to prevent an understanding of ongoing action and interaction. On the one hand, this notion of deconstruction already points at the effort to conceptualize the social and cultural world as a practice. On the other hand, it becomes obvious that deconstructionism in anthropology does not primarily lead to establishing a metadiscourse, but is woven into the efforts to understand. Destruction is in a way used as a tool to reach a better understanding. From this point of view the critical anthropological deconstructions of inherited frameworks and concepts do not only operate through a historicization of these concepts, revealing their contingent character, but the question of how to transform or use those concepts, if possible, is also posed.

To illustrate this I want to refer to the anthropological discussion of the concept of 'cargo cult'. As Holger Jebens points out, a deconstruction of the term reveals it to be 'an essentially Western creation'. Hence it 'may unwittingly reveal more about ourselves than about those Melanesian ideas and practices to which they were meant to refer to in the first place' (2004, 3). For this reason a lot of genealogical analyses of this concept arose, which show its historical origin and its tendency to contribute to the practice of othering. Crapanzano (2004b, 227) finally states that the concept of 'cargo' reflects European philosophical presuppositions that are not necessarily shared by the 'cargoists' themselves. At the same time it seems not that easy to abandon the concept because it might be useful to signify practices and experiences that would remain otherwise incomprehensible. Facing this problem, Elfriede Hermann (2004, 38) turns to the Derridean notion of writing 'under erasure' (*sous rapture*). This writing convention indicates, according to Hermann, that a concept is at once inaccurate and necessary. This mode of using the concept might open it up for resignifications, encompassing Western as well as non-Western practices and including the voices of those who have been traditionally only written about.

In summarizing let me introduce Plessner's notion of 'eccentricity', signifying an enabling reflexivity, to consider the outlined anthropological responses to the loss of a permanent and timeless foundation of knowledge. With this term I want to refer to a reflective awareness of the historicity and contingency of preconceptions, which are to be transformed in the process of understanding. The reached understanding may never be complete and may remain open-ended, but that is not necessarily to be regarded as a disappointment. In order to illuminate the process of understanding – as incomplete as it might be – anthropologists have, for example, described their experiences in the field. In doing so, anthropology turns away from a theoretical discussion of the reliability and possibility of knowledge and focuses on concrete situations.

These attempts to describe the process of understanding by referring to concrete encounters and conversations occurred as soon as the limits of an interpretive method, which was oriented by the model of the text, were acknowledged. Crapanzano, among others, revealed the limits and problems of a concept of culture as an 'ensemble of texts' and the related concept of understanding as a 'reading of texts'. In focusing on Geertz's interpretation of the Balinese cockfight, Crapanzano points out that such a preconception of the interpretive method forecloses any dialogue and establishes asymmetrical relationships: Crapanzano finds in Geertz's text merely 'a constructed understanding of the constructed native's constructed point of view' (Crapanzano 1986, 74).

The strong emphasis Crapanzano lays on the constructionist proceeding of this mode of interpretation suggests that the understanding Geertz arrives at is neither an understanding from the native's point of view, nor influenced or corrected by this point of view. Rather, it seems to exclude the other and to suppress the voice of the other. Furthermore, Geertz describes the interpretive method in terms of the anthropologist reading over the shoulder of those to whom the text properly belongs: 'It represents a sort of asymmetrical we-relationship with the anthropologist behind and above the native, hidden but at the top of the hierarchy of understanding' (Crapanzano 1986, 74).

The anthropological descriptions and reflections of the process of understanding finally accentuated the dialogical structure of understanding. Particularly, the notion of dialogue, being opposed to monological constructions, is reconsidered. Furthermore, Ricoeur's notion of 'understanding the self by the detour of understanding the other' and Gadamer's concept of 'the fusion of horizons' both had a vital influence in reshaping an anthropological concept of understanding.

3. Culture as a Practice: Towards a Theory of Performativity

The above notions of 'forms of life', 'life-worlds' and the concept of *Bildung* or 'personal knowledge' already suggested that there is a surplus of sense or meaning in the living experience. In this, these concepts help to question the legitimacy of reducing living experiences to abstract symbolic systems and structures. Although the theorists who are abstracting symbolic systems or systems of meaning from living experience are largely aware of the fact that they are creating models in order to understand social behaviour, still the question should be posed whether this way of perceiving and theorizing culture does not simply miss a surplus of sense, but rather misses the most important aspect of the production of meaning and sense.

This suspicion is particularly present in Pierre Bourdieu. He argues for a theory of practice in order to make a specific practical knowledge visible, which consists in a practical mastery and produces a practical intelligibility. Therefore he criticizes a scholastic fallacy that occurs as soon as the 'mind of the anthropologist who conceptualizes practice' is being put in the place of 'the socially constituted practical sense of the agent' (Bourdieu and Wacquant 1992, 123).

Whereas Bourdieu is particularly interested in correcting the intellectual bias of anthropological research, I want to focus in the following on the development of the efforts to conceptualize culture as a practice. Concerning that question, the key ideas in Bourdieu's notion of the scholastic fallacy are: first, practical knowledge cannot be reduced to theoretical knowledge, and second, social activity cannot be considered as a mere application of theoretical knowledge. One has to consider much more, then, the modes of practical mastery that produce a specific practical intelligibility. Therefore, understanding should not be reduced to an intellectual understanding. All in all, these considerations call for a more agency-based approach. This reorientation does not indicate that the subject–object dichotomy is reintroduced or that the notion of the 'constituent subject' is reconsidered. Rather, it is an effort not to reduce actions to a mere application of systems of thought. In this, the idea of 'know-how' (Ryle) and the concept of 'language games' (Wittgenstein) are discussed insofar as they emphasize the *usage* and the *performance* as the processes in which meaning and knowledge emerge. In that, hermeneutics and a philosophy of language that is concerned with the use of language can be reconsidered in their ability to surpass the restriction of understanding to intellectual understanding and the restriction of knowledge to theoretical knowledge. These philosophic approaches are reconsidered in contemporary anthropology in order to formulate a more process-oriented notion of culture and a more practice-oriented notion of meaning. In that, they react against 'the deep-seated intellectualism characteristic of all European thinkers', as Bourdieu puts it in referring to his own work. Interestingly, he names as 'the rare exceptions' of this tradition Wittgenstein, Heidegger and Merleau-Ponty (122). Despite his critical reading of Heidegger, Bourdieu seems to acknowledge Heidegger's attempt to surpass the notion of an intellectual understanding. He refers to the Heideggerian ontological turn in order to overcome the subject–object dichotomy when he states a sort of ontological complicity in the agent's relationship to the world (128).

Rereading Heidegger in the light of the effort to reach at a new concept of culture in relation to practical knowledge accentuates the 'fore-structure' of understanding. In this, Heidegger (1993, 150) stresses that understanding is always already directed towards the usage of things in the mode of 'fore-having'. In doing so, Heidegger lays emphasis on the anticipatory structure of understanding and stresses that understanding signifies an ability, a know-how. At the same time, practical usage produces a practical knowledge, which cannot be reduced to a teachable technique. According to Heidegger (1993, 149), usage, as *Zutunhaben-mit*, effects a specific practical knowledge that can only be acquired in practice. In summarizing one can say that practical knowledge encompasses know-how, competence and the ability to direct actions toward a project, as the term *Vorhabe* indicates. Since practical knowledge is not based on intellectual knowledge of rules or systems, it rather requires a practical sense, acquired in practice and directing practice.

From this angle social behaviour can be reconsidered in its own logic and should not be considered as a mere application of intellectual knowledge. This perspective is underlined by a context-sensitive theory of language, focusing on language use. The anthropological question of how language operates and functions in the social world, being already posed in the anthropological 'ethnography of speaking', points beyond an understanding of language as merely a means for communication or an instrument of intellection. In this context the theories of later Wittgenstein and Austin's 'speech-act' are received in anthropology.

Wittgenstein does not treat language as an instrument of intellection, instead laying emphasis on the use – the practice – of language, which he compares to playing a game. Meaning, according to Wittgenstein, just *is* use. Meaning is produced in language games and not in reference to a nonlingual reality. Furthermore, language is not to be primarily considered as a system with an internal logic, but in reference to forms of life, which are grounding the language games. In other words: language games emerge from a social practice. As the notion suggests, playing a game, according to Wittgenstein, can be regarded as a rule-following activity. But this activity is not to be understood as an application of rules, but much more as an activity being guided by a 'sense for the game', which is comparable to the practical sense mentioned above. This point is brought out particularly by Bourdieu in his critical remarks on ethnomethodology.

So, if practical knowledge cannot be reduced to intellectual knowledge, and thus social behaviour is not to be considered as a conscious, intellectualized rule-following activity, it might be considered as a form of an *embodied knowledge*. This idea is expressed in Maurice Merleau-Ponty's concept of 'corporeality', which puts forward an intentionality of the body. Bourdieu refers in particular to Merleau-Ponty and Heidegger in order to clarify the relationship of *habitus*, as the 'social made body' (Bourdieu and Wacquant 1992, 127), and the field. Habitus and field are interrelated concepts, indicating that the habitus as a system of dispositions correlates to the field because it emerges from that field and at the same time structures the perception of the field. Bourdieu writes,

> In the relation between habitus and field, history enters into a relation with itself:
> a genuine ontological complicity, as Heidegger and Merleau-Ponty suggested,
> obtains between agent who is neither a subject or a consciousness, nor the mere
> executant of a role, the support of a structure or actualization of a function and
> the social world which is never a mere thing, even if it must be constructed as
> such in the objectivist phase of research. (Bourdieu and Wacquant 1992, 128)

Differing from the traditional philosophical view, Bourdieu underlines the socially conditioned character of practical knowledge being embodied in habitus, and the social genesis of practical sense. In this he also differs from the Gadamerian concept of practical knowledge as practical wisdom or ethical knowledge being indebted to Aristotle's concept of *phronesis* (Gadamer 1987, 118). Although Bourdieu sometimes also refers to phronesis, this concept rather involves an ability of ethical judgment, which is not to be considered as a social product, as Gadamer points out. Rather, it is oriented towards justice, which cannot be reduced to a specific social or cultural situation.

The concern with an embodied, practical knowledge is not only present in Bourdieu's concept of habitus, but is also central in the writings of Foucault and Butler, who unfold the idea of an incorporation of social structures and power relations in order to surpass a mentalist or intellectualized view on social processes. Both the notion of *subjectivation* (Butler) and of *assujettissement* (Foucault) signify the power of a social process forming subjects. In this, the idea of a constituent subject, as well as the idea of the primacy of the subjectivity, is surpassed by the question of how subjects are effected in social processes. These concepts differ from the concepts of self-formation (*Bildung*) present in Gadamer and Rorty outlined above insofar as Foucault and Butler accentuate the subjection involved. In particular, the notion of subjectivation displays a critical view on the social process in which subjects are produced as speaking subjects. The notion of subjectivation sheds light on the explicit and implicit censorship involved in subject formation. As Butler puts it, this process is connected to 'producing what will and will not count as a viable speaking subject' (Butler 2004, xix). Thus, marginalization and foreclosures operating in the subject formation are considered.

These reflections on the complex interplay between the cultural sphere, referring provisionally to symbolic systems and the social world, referring provisionally to social interaction and institutionalized social patterns, are finally pointing at a theory of performativity. Such a theory should be considered as a possible frame for an anthropology of the contemporary.

The notion of performance is indebted particularly to Austin's speech-act theory. Austin outlines the idea that language is used in order to 'do things with words'. So, to utter a sentence can be considered as a way of performing an action. Austin calls these utterances 'performative' and suggests that they cannot be considered as true or false, since they do not state facts. Thus, performative utterances are not truth-evaluable, but are either successful in the social sphere or not. Moreover, Austin pays particular attention to those performative utterances he calls 'illocutionary acts'. An illocutionary act is a performative utterance that performs an act *in* saying something. This concept displays a specific force or power of speech-acts, which has been reconsidered especially in Bourdieu and Butler. Bourdieu's concept of the magic of words, indicating that words constitute a socially accepted reality, is clearly influenced by Austin. In reference to Austin he argues that the social position, the socially recognized authority of the actor, decides whether the speech-act is happy or unhappy. According to Bourdieu, then, the power to do things with words stems from the institutionalized authority of the speaking subject.

Moreover, not only performative utterances but also concepts, which contribute to perceiving the world, can be considered as a means to produce the world. This idea is outlined by Bourdieu in the notion of 'symbolic power'. In borrowing a term from Nelson Goodman, Bourdieu understands the symbolic power as the power of 'worldmaking'. Thus, Bourdieu stresses that categories of thought contribute to producing the world. For that reason Wacquant follows, 'If we grant that symbolic systems are social products that contribute to making the world, that they do not simply mirror social relations but help constitute them, then one can, within limits, transform the world by transforming its representations' (1992, 14).

In summarizing, one can say that the idea of performativity leads to a proceduralist view on culture and sheds light on how social identities, relations and hierarchies are produced and reproduced, established and re-established, through performance. Therefore, symbolic systems should be considered as being effected by the social world. In reverse the symbolic systems are to be thought of as effects of the social sphere. Thus, symbolic systems should be considered in their impact on the everyday understanding of social relations, as this understanding contributes to constitute social relations. Furthermore, the notion of performativity also implies that the established social order requires a repetitious performance. It cannot be considered as being established once and for all. So a proceduralist view on culture underpins a theory of cultural and social change: it shows that the established order is also at risk in its need for repetition, which is open to failure and infelicities.

References

Austin, John L. 1962. *How to Do Things with Words*. Oxford: Oxford University Press.

Bernstein, Richard J. 1983. *Beyond Objectivism and Relativism*. Oxford: Oxford University Press.

Bourdieu, Pierre. 1992. 'The Practice of Reflexive Sociology'. In *An Invitation to Reflexive Sociology*, edited by Bourdieu and Wacquant, 217–60. Chicago: Chicago University Press.

Bourdieu, Pierre and Loïc Wacquant. 1992. 'The Purpose of Reflexive Sociology'. In *An Invitation to Reflexive Sociology*, edited by Bourdieu and Wacquant, 61–216. Chicago: Chicago University Press.

Butler, Judith. 2004. *Precarious Life: The Powers of Mourning and Violence*. London, New York: Verso.

Crapanzano, Vincent. 1986. 'Hermes' Dilemma: The Making of Subversion in Ethnographic Description'. In *Writing Culture: The Poetics and Politics of Ethnography*, edited by Clifford and Marcus, 51–76. Berkeley, Los Angeles, London: University of California Press.

———. 2004a. *Imaginative Horizons: An Essay in Literary-Philosophical Anthropology*. Chicago and London: University of Chicago Press.

———. 2004b. 'Thoughts on Hope and Cargo'. In *Cargo, Cult, and Culture Critique*, edited by Jebens, 227–42. Honolulu: University of Hawaii Press.

Foucault, Michel. 1987. 'What is Enlightenment?' In *Interpretive Social Science: A Second Look*, edited by Rabinow and Sullivan, 157–76. Berkeley, Los Angeles, London: University of California Press.

———. 1991. *Von der Subversion des Wissens*. Munich: Hanser.

Flax, Jane. 1990. *Thinking Fragments*. California: University of California Press.

Gadamer, Hans-Georg. 1987. 'The Problem of Historical Consciousness'. In *Interpretive Social Science: A Second Look*, edited by Rabinow and Sullivan, 82–140. Berkeley, Los Angeles, London: University of California Press.

———. 1995. *Hermeneutik im Rückblick*. Tübingen: Mohr.

Geertz, Clifford. 1983. *Local Knowledge: Further Essays in Interpretive Anthropology*. Princeton: Princeton University Press.

———. 1995. *After the Fact: Two Counties, Four Decades, One Anthropologist*. Cambridge, MA: Harvard University Press.

Heidegger, Martin. 1993. *Sein und Zeit*. Tübingen: Mohr.

Hermann, Elfriede. 2004. 'Dissolving the Self–Other Dichotomy in Western Cargo Cult Constructions'. In *Cargo, Cult, and Culture Critique*, edited by Holger Jebens, 36–58. Honolulu: University of Hawaii Press.

Jebens, Holger, ed. 2004. Introduction to *Cargo, Cult, and Culture Critique*. Honolulu: University of Hawaii Press, 1–13.

Latour, Bruno and Steve Woolgar. 1986. *Laboratory Life: The Social Construction of Scientific Facts*. Princeton: Princeton University Press.

Rabinow, Paul. 1996. *Essays on the Anthropology of Reason*. Princeton: Princeton University Press.

———. 2008. *Marking Time: On the Anthropology of the Contemporary*. Princeton and Oxford: Princeton University Press.

Rabinow, Paul and William M. Sullivan, eds. 1987. *Interpretive Social Science: A Second Look*. Berkeley, Los Angeles, London: University of California Press.

Ricoeur, Paul. 1991a. 'On Interpretation'. In Ricoeur, *From Text to Action: Essays in Hermeneutics II*, 1–20. Evanston, IL: Northwestern University Press.

———. 1991b. 'The Model of the Text: Meaningful Action Considered as a Text'. In Ricoeur, *From Text to Action: Essays in Hermeneutics II*, 144–67. Evanston, IL: Northwestern University Press.

Rorty, Richard. 1980. *Philosophy and the Mirror of Nature*. Princeton: Princeton University Press

Rosaldo, Michelle Z. 1987. 'Moral/Analytic Dilemmas Posed by the Intersection of Feminism and Social Life'. In *Interpretive Social Science: A Second Look*, edited by Rabinow and Sullivan, 280–301. Berkeley, Los Angeles, London: University of California Press.

Winch, Peter. 1972. 'Understanding a Primitive Society'. In Winch, *Ethics and Action*, 8–49. London: Routledge and Kegan Paul.

Wacquant, Loïc. 1992. 'Toward a Social Praxeology'. In *An Invitation to Reflexive Sociology*, edited by Bourdieu and Wacquant, 1–60. Chicago: Chicago University Press.

Chapter 6

MEDIATION THROUGH COGNITIVE DYNAMICS: PHILOSOPHICAL ANTHROPOLOGY AND THE CONFLICTS OF OUR TIME

Piet Strydom

Introduction

In the light of a heightened sense of contingency and vulnerability, a pronounced uncertainty has set in since the late twentieth century about human nature and, hence, the image of the human being. This has been fuelled further by the recognition of the inherent ambiguity of these concepts. Awareness of the precariousness of our assumptions about what human beings are like has not only affected intellectuals, prompting philosophers and social scientists to embark on a searching interrogation, but has also penetrated into the policymaking and the public domain. While philosophers and social scientists may still be able, during the process of reflection, to maintain a sense of the difficulty and even impossibility of finding something to take the place of these problematic assumptions, the reaction of many who feel the need for a more secure foundation is to fix on a particular interpretation. The sources of such interpretations are diverse, and as a result we are witnesses to a proliferation of polarization and conflict at a variety of levels in contemporary society – between science and religion, secularists and believers, North and South, winners and losers of globalization, the West and Islamism, and so forth.

Under these conditions, the old question of philosophical anthropology has made a strong reappearance. This event is accompanied by the urgent demand to come to a better understanding of its core problematic and how the latter could possibly relate to the contemporary situation, particularly to the polarization and conflicts of our time. Answering this call is what

I propose to undertake in the following paragraphs. A brief historical overview will provide the background for understanding the contemporary relevance of philosophical anthropology. I will then explore the subject with reference to a selection of tensions and conflicts in contemporary society and possible ways of fruitfully relating to them.

1. Historical Overview of Philosophical Anthropology

The intellectual development to which Max Scheler (1961) eventually gave the name 'philosophical anthropology' had its starting point in the Romantic critique of the Enlightenment, as represented by Kant. The precursor of this critique was Johann Gottfried Herder and its major proponents included Johann Georg Hamann, the Schlegel brothers and Novalis. During the early modern period up until Kant and even Hegel, the question of human nature had been considered as self-evidently philosophical. It was only after the separation of philosophy and anthropology in the early nineteenth century that the problem of philosophical anthropology as such could arise. In romanticism, it took the form of the philosophy of nature, which was regarded as providing the framework for an understanding of the particularity of the human being. As such, it was pitted against what was construed as the philosophy of history of the Enlightenment thinkers as well as against Hegel's attempt to blunt the Romantic assault by reintegrating its main objections once again into the idealistic philosophy of history. From this ambivalent, if not confused, yet nevertheless fecund starting point emerged two distinct traditions, only one of which, ironically, was unfailingly invoked by philosophical anthropology in the rest of the nineteenth and the first half of the twentieth century (Löwith 1964; Schnädelbach 1984).

The first of these two traditions, the Young-Hegelian tradition, was founded by Ludwig Feuerbach (1922), taken up and transformed by Karl Marx (1967, 1969) and others, and later drawn upon by Jürgen Habermas (1973) and his students, such as Axel Honneth and Hans Joas (1988). The second, frequently cited tradition runs from Friedrich Wilhelm Joseph Schelling – who in his last years also had a connection with the Young-Hegelians – to Arthur Schopenhauer (1883) and Friedrich Nietzsche (1972), the latter of whom prepared the way for Martin Heidegger (1961), who made an important contribution to philosophical anthropology although not being a philosophical anthropologist, and for Arnold Gehlen (1956), who put forward an innovative, action-based, systematic yet politically ultraconservative and authoritarian philosophical anthropology.

Beginning around 1830, history and science were mobilized as issues in the name of which philosophy was prised away from idealism. This meant a turn from metaphysics, as well as from the anthropological assumption of the human being as *animal rationale*, toward the real historical conditions under which human beings live and, hence, toward a pursuit of disciplines which engaged empirically with reality. During the decade following Hegel's death in 1831, while struggles were underway to get the various emerging scientific disciplines established in the course of the university revolution, the natural and historical sciences were engaged in competition over their claims to be the leading disciplines. Below the surface, however, a virulent rivalry between two distinct human self-images, one historicist and the other naturalistic, was playing itself out (Schnädelbach 1984). A decisive turning point in this struggle was marked by the naturalization mid-century of the human self-image, due to a range of factors including the internal theoretical and methodological consolidation of science in the context of industrial and economic development. Although feeding off the philosophy of nature, the natural sciences separated from and triumphed over both their Romantic and idealistic impulses so as to enter a postphilosophical situation. Biology, the apparent relevance of which was confirmed and graphically symbolized by Darwinism, led the naturalization drive which left anthropology in a biologized form and several other disciplines acquiring the hallmarks of organismic, evolutionary and social Darwinist thinking. Marx's position exhibits a complex mixture of the major elements: a re-Hegelianized historicist strand with a relational concept of society maintaining a connection with nature, for which scientific credentials are sought.

The naturalistic turn not only strengthened scientific disciplines, both natural and social, but also provided an impetus for an intensified drive to establish the opposing historical or human sciences as distinct and autonomous disciplines. In his *Historik* – a programme for the establishment of history as a science of understanding rather than of explanation – Johann Gustav Droysen (1953) regarded the human being as being defined by history, proposing the latter as its species concept. And on the basis of his view of history as the medium of the acquisition and development of human self-consciousness, Wilhelm Dilthey (1973, 1974) could insist that human beings are able to learn who they are from history alone. Nevertheless, Dilthey's founding of the *Geisteswissenschaften* was not entirely free from naturalistic residues. Not only did his prioritization of understanding over explanation bear out his secret attachment to his naturalistic adversary, but so too did his incorporation of the philosophy of life.

Despite the availability of possibilities to mediate between naturalism and historicism, the division between the natural and the human sciences proposed by Dilthey stimulated a widespread acceptance of the dichotomy of nature and history, with necessity being correlated with the former and freedom with the latter. This unwarranted dualistic thinking was challenged and, indeed, shattered with a vengeance by authors like Schopenhauer and especially Nietzsche, who represented the philosophy of life and, hence, the metaphysics of the irrational. Whereas Schopenhauer (1883) stressed the will to life as an unchangeable subterranean force which needs to be tamed for the sake of happiness, Nietzsche (1972) combined the Schopenhauerian will with an inverted evolutionary theory so as to introduce the notion of the 'overman', which could be attained by the self-transformation of the human being through breeding. Besides the well-known racist ideological and political resonances this line of development engendered all over the Western world, it prepared the ground for the dominant twentieth-century tradition of philosophical anthropology, as coined by Scheler (1961), and significantly pursued by Helmuth Plessner (1980 [1928]) and particularly Gehlen (1956). This whole trajectory presupposes, in general, the confluence of naturalistic anthropology and the metaphysics of irrationality and, in particular, the combination of the philosophy of life and evolutionary theory.

The concomitant insight that the human species, including *Homo sapiens*, forms an inherent part of the natural historical process was taken up in quite a different way in the Young-Hegelian tradition going back to Feuerbach and Marx – a philosophical-anthropological departure largely ignored by the dominant tradition of philosophical anthropology. Of particular interest is the contribution of George Herbert Mead (1974) who, representing Young-Hegelian-inspired action-oriented pragmatism incorporating a sign-mediated concept of knowledge, developed an anthropologically based theory of practical intersubjectivity. Underpinning it was the self-image of the human being as a reflexive actor within the context of a complex of communicatively mediated social relations. This conception cut across both Cartesian and Diltheyean dualisms and thus suggested appropriate means for mediating between the two contending sides in a manner generating very different ideological and political implications and consequences than those suggested by Nietzsche's fusion. Mead's theory is not only broadly in accord with the position Marx developed, but it also complements it by filling out its largely missing social-psychological dimension. It is clear, therefore, why Mead could so readily be taken up by the other tradition – Habermas (1984/87) in particular, followed by Honneth and Joas (1988). Insofar as Gehlen (who in fact imported Mead into Germany, albeit rather selectively) borrowed his central concept from pragmatism, his strictly action-based anthropology, shorn of its elitist and antidemocratic animus, proved to be by no means irrelevant for a more adequate understanding of our anthropological assumptions.

The moral of this rather telescoped historical overview is that philosophical anthropology remains incomprehensible unless attention is paid to the relation between its naturalistic and historicist or humanistic dimensions, to different solutions to their reconciliation, and the concurrent ideological-political implications. It is precisely this core element that accounts for the fact that, far from being a purely historical phenomenon, philosophical anthropology possesses such a high degree of relevance today.

2. The Motives of Philosophical Anthropology

Generally speaking, it could be submitted that philosophical anthropology fulfils the need for the theoretical interpretation of the wide range of fragmented empirical findings produced by the various sciences investigating human beings and their forms of life. The establishment of philosophical anthropology can therefore be dated quite precisely to the early twentieth century in the wake of the institutionalization of physical and cultural anthropology, sociology and psychology. It is in this sense that Habermas (1973, 92) understands it as a 'reactive discipline', that is, a reaction of philosophy to the efflorescence of scientific knowledge which questions the relevance of philosophy itself. According to Scheler, the founder of philosophical anthropology, however, the need calling this hybrid philosophical and scientific enterprise into being cuts still deeper. It was necessitated by a historical crisis which disturbingly mounted in the second decade of the twentieth century. The historical tendency of a progressive increase in human self-consciousness led to a situation, manifested in a disturbing loss of identity, in which the very nature and humanity of human beings became a problem for them. For Scheler, therefore, the aim of philosophical anthropology was the pursuit of interpretative self-certainty or a worldview through the philosophical synthesis of all relevant available empirical knowledge about human beings.

Like Scheler, Plessner ([1928]1980), who independently developed a hermeneutic philosophical anthropology of bodily expressions, similarly stressed the critical, endangered status of human self-understanding. Despite, or precisely because of, the increasing disciplinary knowledge about the formal biological unity of the human species, human beings have lost themselves in that they no longer see fit to take responsibility for their historical level of existence. Instead of seeking a solution in religiously inspired essentialist thinking, as did Scheler, Plessner insisted that the search for meaning and identity was possible only through scientific criticism. The problem of humanity, both as fact and task, can be properly addressed only by considering the possibilities and prospects of human freedom and concomitant practices within the context of the limitations imposed on human beings by causal laws.

From a comparative perspective, the late twentieth- and twenty-first-century situation in certain respects bears a remarkable similarity to the one in which Scheler and Plessner put forward their diagnoses of the historical crisis and offers of means to begin to understand it, if not resolve it. If Nietzsche's denial of any fixity on the part of the human being foreshadowed the earlier crisis, similarly Michel Foucault's (1970) prediction that man is due to disappear set the scene of the contemporary situation of uncertainty. A comparable increase in complexity, questioning of long-standing assumptions, and polarization of social groups and their respective cultures prepared the ground for a widespread perception of heightened contingency, openness of history, and ambivalence. This perception is accompanied by an equally common feeling of the opacity and uncertainty of macroprocesses and their potential outcomes, and of the vulnerability of modern societies. Under these conditions, a pressing and urgent problem no less serious than earlier has arisen which, in turn, has spawned not only a variety of searches for meaning and identity, and attempts at subject formation in cultural, social and political life, but also an awareness among philosophers and social scientists of the need to face up to the challenging question of what human nature and humanity amount to.

This concern with meaning and identity, which, as earlier, requires a synthetic step beyond the limits of science and epistemology, explains why the interpretative approach in its various forms has been in the ascendancy since the 1960s and 1970s. Since then, it has been accepted that interpretation plays a role not only in social life and, by extension, the human and social sciences, but even in the natural sciences. It is important to note, therefore, that while it serves the search for interpretative self-certainty, this approach in actual fact participates in some way or other in the generation of a range of competing and even conflicting proposals, many of which lay claim to providing the most promising solution. Three prominent proposals stand out today. For a growing number who admit only a particular essentialist answer, the solution is to be found in religion or some spiritual domain. For others, who allow a range of different answers by stressing instead the questions to be asked and their corresponding practices, the solution is provided by science. Here knowledge is often pitted against faith. For still others, both faith and knowledge have their own unique and irreplaceable yet circumscribed contributions to make to a larger joint or intersubjective, politically relevant enterprise. This alone possesses the potential to identify and implement the structures and procedures compatible with what is common to all the different parties.

In addition to its general thrust, philosophical anthropology at the time of its original emergence also had two more specific motives (Honneth and Joas 1988, 43–4), which seem to be repeating themselves under contemporary conditions. The widespread conviction in the early twentieth century that science could make a meaningful contribution to social life only if it were related back to the epoch-making cultural crisis of the time makes these motives transparent. The first motive was to overcome disciplinary boundaries by bringing together philosophy and science as well as the various sciences themselves, in so far as they deal with the nature of human beings. Secondly, the search for this synthesis was driven not by an abstract yearning for universal knowledge, but rather by the urgent need for practical understanding, for knowledge which could give direction and guide the living of life. What remained open here, however, was the nature of the practical synthesis or world view implied by this demand.

A consideration of the different aims of the critique of rationalism, on which the lines of thinking relevant to philosophical anthropology converged in the early twentieth century, sheds some light on the available options. The dominant tradition stemming from romanticism, and transformed by Schopenhauer and Nietzsche, tended to side with a retreat to irrationalism. By contrast, the subordinate Young-Hegelian tradition engaged in a critique of rationalism in the name of a higher form or rationality. For example, Mead brought together evolutionary theory, social psychology, sociology and a range of knowledge deriving from other scientific disciplines in his social pragmatism and, given the latter's action orientation, he afforded all of this a unity through a lifelong commitment to ethical reciprocity, social reform, the emancipation of blacks and women, and efforts to advance human cooperation at the global level beyond communities and nation-states. Max Horkheimer's (1970) 'interdisciplinary materialism', his attempt to overcome disciplinary boundaries, proceeded from a critique of the sciences of the time – natural as well as human – and appealed to living, historical-political experience with a view to contributing to a more rationally and humanely organized society – which, of course, does not imply that his premises were in fact such that they allowed an achievement of this order.

Comparatively speaking, in the late twentieth and twenty-first century we witness a similar concern with the overcoming of disciplinary boundaries as in the early twentieth-century situation. What is different today is that the demand for interdisciplinarity has been radicalized. The emphasis has shifted from interdisciplinarity to 'transdisciplinarity' and even 'postdisciplinarity', although there seems to be confusion over what the former means (e.g., Baecker 1995; Giri 2004) and a lack of clarity about whether the latter could be institutionalized and implemented (Gulbenkian Commission 1996). The critique of rationalism is as noticeable today as earlier, as is the related critique of universalism. Also, the earlier critique of epistemology has been renewed, but now given a sharper edge in the form of a critique of science. At present, a comparable general conviction prevails that scientific knowledge is in need of being incorporated into a broader moral-ethical or moral-ethical-political framework.

Correspondingly, an appropriate practical synthesis and understanding is being sought in different directions, such as a world view or practical philosophy. It comes as no surprise, then, that the same questions as before have become the challenge of our time: what practical understanding? What world view? What practical philosophy? The diversity of answers results in such typically contemporary phenomena as: care of the self, individualism, communitarianism, postsecularism, fundamentalism, identity politics, the clash of civilizations, scientism, naturalism, neo-Aristotelianism, discourse ethics, cosmopolitanism and so forth.

This question cannot be answered, however, without acknowledging that anthropological thought inherently involves a configuration of naturalistic and historicist motifs (Schnädelbach 1984, 227) and, hence, that a determination has to be made about the relation between them. For instance, does one of these motifs have priority over the other? The conditions under which this problem has to be tackled today are not dissimilar from those that prevailed in the late nineteenth and early twentieth century when biology enjoyed pre-eminence. Contemporary conditions are set by the efflorescence of the cognitive sciences, such as information theory, cybernetics, artificial intelligence, cognitive biology and increasingly neuroscience, and the concurrent renewal of naturalism. Simultaneously, however, one cannot afford to overlook or ignore the reaction to this development.

3. Mediation through Cognitive Dynamics

The parameters of the discourse in which the question of philosophical anthropology – or, more specifically, of those assumptions about human nature which underpin science, public policy and everyday life – arises today are staked out by the opposition between science and religion (or quasi religion) or, more abstractly, by naturalism and idealism.

Philosophically, the opposition between naturalism and idealism is at present represented in particular by the exceptionally influential lines of development running from Willard van Orman Quine and Martin Heidegger respectively. On the one hand, Quine's (1957, 1960) strong naturalism, which is based on a scientific interpretation of human cognitive abilities, allowed the contemporary naturalistic continuation of the Humean empiricist tradition. On the other, Heidegger (1959, 1961, 1967) introduced the idealist philosophy of the 'history of being', which, by means of ideas such as the new attitude of 'releasement' and 'apocalyptic attention' to the fate of Western civilization, opened the way for a quasi- or pseudo-religious revaluation of the spiritual powers of contemplation or 'thinking'. Implied in each of these two positions is a particular anthropology or image of the human being.

The Quinean line defends a strictly naturalistic image of the human being, the so-called 'scientific image of man' (Sellars 1963, 1), according to which self-understanding is restricted to an objectivistic orientation toward genomic constitution and cognitive functioning shorn of any connotations of intentionality and normativity. Its Heideggerian counterpart propounds an image of the human being as fatefully delivered out to a series of contingently happening epochal interpretations or disclosures of the world. Needless to say, the former interpretation clearly gives priority to the naturalistic motif in anthropological thought, which contrasts sharply with the latter's prioritization of the – albeit no longer humanistically understood – historicist motif.

The concrete filling out of the naturalistic image of the human being is today most vigorously pursued in the natural sciences, particularly in the biosciences which came into their own in the wake of the cognitive revolution. Here the drive toward the naturalization of the mind is guided by a reductionist research programme aimed at explaining the human being, whether the body or mental phenomena, solely in terms of observable biological, particularly genetic and neurophysiological, conditions. This reductionist animus has its more recent roots in James Watson and Francis Crick's (Watson 1981) description of the double-helix structure of DNA and the subsequent discovery of recombinant DNA on the one hand, and in Benjamin Libet's (2004) brain experiments focused on the time lag between neuronal activity and voluntary movement on the other. Central here is the focus on the causal interrelation of biological processes and states according to natural laws. Such causality is regarded as not merely lying behind both the body and the mind, but also as rendering both human nature and self-consciousness, including the freedom of the will, into something epiphenomenal and even illusory.

Not entirely unexpectedly, the proposal for self-optimization through genetic self-instrumentalization implied by this naturalization of the image of the human being called forth a sharp, negative reaction from religion. Not limited to this proposal, church leaders and believers joined forces to launch a concerted attack against science in general. From the religious point of view, science not merely contradicts the biblical vision of the human being as having been created in the image of God, but even pretends to be able to play God itself. This parting of interpretations brought science and religion as two distinct forces of conviction into an animated conflict. Whereas the former laments the obscurantist imposition on research of irrational limits stemming from archaic feelings, the latter fears the opening of floodgates which would lead to the washing away of the foundations of morality. This conflict between scientism and fundamentalism has been overlaid and complicated by the place religion was seen to occupy in the terrorist attacks in the US and their aftermath. The sobering realization that religion was a motivation for the attack contributed not only to the filling of churches, synagogues and mosques, but also to a shift towards the acknowledgement of the existence, both nationally and globally, of the postsecular society with a multicultural and multifaith physiognomy. In the subterranean battle between two opposing visions of the human being, the image of a creature guided by God here asserts its priority over its naturalistic counterpart.

The contemporary social sciences, which have been deeply affected by the cognitive revolution and the development of the cognitive sciences, are likewise internally divided along comparable lines (Strydom 2006, 2007). In anthropology, for instance, Clifford Geertz (1973) was one of the first to criticize the influence of the cognitive sciences on the discipline in the name of the 'thick description' of symbolically mediated meaning. Dan Sperber (1996, 1997), by contrast, has been trying to counter idealistically inclined interpretative approaches by searching for infraindividual explanatory principles in cognitive structures and processes located in the brain. In sociology, a similar divide exists. Stephen Turner (2002) and Niklas Luhmann (1990, 1992), each in his own way, emphatically take a naturalistic position, the former stressing infraindividual neuronal processes in the brain as the basic reference point and the latter metabiologically conceived supraindividual social systems – Luhmann, interestingly, being inspired by Gehlen's anthropology. In opposition to this, Eviatar Zerubavel (1997) and Raymond Boudon (1995), likewise each according to his own terms, adopt a contrasting idealistic position. While the former celebrates a relativistic culturalism, the latter insists on the rational individual and the explanation of social phenomena strictly in accordance with this principle. Although the difference between the distinct lines in anthropology and sociology are not articulated in such terms, it is nevertheless undeniable that these competing positions are underpinned by contrasting images of the human being – naturalistic in one case and historicist and/or humanistic in the other.

Against the background of this tension between forces of conviction in everyday life, between social scientists and between philosophers, the central philosophical-anthropological problem as it presents itself in our time becomes much clearer. The pressing desideratum today is to arrive at creative yet responsible ways of crossing the borders and mediating between the naturalistic and historicist – both humanistic and antihumanistic – sides of the image of the human being so as to find a balanced constellation of modes of thinking, of developing and applying knowledge, and of culturally, socially and politically arranging collective forms of life. Under current conditions, such border crossing and mediation can, and in my view must, be conceived in accordance with the cutting-edge insights of the day – that is, in cognitive terms.

Philosophically, first, the chasm between naturalism and idealism needs to be bridged. Insights gleaned from developments in the past few decades suggest that a bridging mechanism is to be found in what I have elsewhere proposed to call 'operative cognitive forms', which allow mediation between nature and society (Delanty and Strydom 2003, 383). Ontologically, this requires the adoption of a 'weak' or 'soft naturalism' (Habermas 2003, 22; 2005, 157; Strydom 2002, 151) which proceeds from the assumption that there is continuity between natural historical processes and sociocultural forms of life. This entails that learning processes taking place within human sociocultural frameworks are an extension of evolutionary processes such as mutation, selection and stabilization or reproduction. Natural evolution is conceived as a process analogous to sociocultural learning processes. For example, the human mind, an emergent property of natural evolution, is an intelligent adaptive solution to problems which developed within the constraints of reality. This means that naturally evolved structures or forms themselves possess cognitive import. As cognitively significant, natural historical processes give rise to emergent properties such as cognitive structures, frameworks or forms, which in turn make possible sociocultural learning processes and the development and articulation of sociocultural forms of life.

As regards the social sciences, secondly, it is important to note that although such weak or soft naturalism is based on the monistic assumption of a unitary natural and sociocultural world, a crucial qualification applies. This ontological monism does not preclude the possibility of an epistemological distinction between natural historical processes and sociocultural forms of life and, by extension, a methodological distinction between naturalistic and sociocultural disciplines – a distinction applying not only between the natural and social sciences, but also within the social sciences themselves. From this it follows that a strong naturalistic interpretation, which purports to reduce without any residue sociocultural forms to nature and, hence, the social sciences exclusively to neuroscience or biogenetics, is ruled out. While natural evolution gives rise to sociocultural forms of life and therefore would be central to an explanation of them, this does not detract from the fact that sociocultural forms provide frameworks not only for the development of knowledge about the objective world, but at the same time also for the normatively relevant constructive realization of a social world of well-ordered relations by those involved themselves. There is not a scintilla of doubt, of course, that the naturalistic, explanatory type of social science (Sperber, Turner, Luhmann) and the idealistic, interpretative type of social science (Geertz, Zerubavel, Boudon) both have their own particular, if limited, contribution to make. Considering the challenges of our time, however, neither of their implied images of the human being is the appropriate one today. To satisfy the current philosophical-anthropological need, a type of social science is required which, in cooperation with philosophy, mediates between the two so as to comprehend subject formation as a process possessing the potential of establishing fruitful relations between the naturalistic and historicist moments of being human. Elsewhere, I have begun to work in this direction – once in the rights field (Strydom 2000), on other occasions in the environmental risk field (Strydom 1999a, 2002, 2008), and recently at a more general theoretical level in view of the increasing vulnerability of modern society and the pressing need for intercultural communication (Strydom 2006, 2007).

Finally, the forces of conviction guided by opposed visions of the human being and generating some of the most typical conflicts of our time are equally in need of being brought into more fruitful relations with one another – irrespective of whether they are science and religion, secularists and believers, the North and South, winners and losers of globalization, the West and Islamists, and so forth. The already operating mechanism here is 'collective learning' (Miller 1986, 2002; Eder 1988, 1999; Strydom 1987, 2000, 2002, 2009), which takes place in the medium of communication and discourse. Collective learning, of course, by no means excludes conflict, but rather mobilizes it for learning and in the process transforms it from something infinite to something manageable. Generally speaking, such learning involves the interrelation of cognitive structures and social processes, and it manifests itself as a rule-governed or self-organizing transformation that leads from a previous state of the world to a newly constructed state of the world. This transformation process takes the form of learning in the sense of the reorganization of cognitive classifications of reality and thus the reframing the world. Cognitive structures of different scopes at different levels are simultaneously implicated. Let us take twentieth-century environmental conflict as an example (Eder 1996, 162–212) – a very pertinent example in view of the fact that it indicates the dynamic relation between nature and society and thus bears on the articulation of the naturalistic and historicist motifs in anthropological thought. In response to changes in nature contributed to by human practices, the cognitive structures of social actors (e.g., environmental movement representatives, politicians, business executives and ordinary individuals) underwent transformation at the same time as organizational (e.g., social movement, governmental, corporate and civic) frames and, at a still higher level, cultural cognitive models of very wide scope (e.g., ecology taking the place of industrialism) became transformed.

While there is a variety, two types of learning are of particular relevance in the context of the kind of conflict in which forces of conviction get embroiled in contemporary communication society. Both take place in the public sphere, but depending on the configuration of the relations involved they take different forms. Respectively, these two discursive types can be referred to as 'double contingency' and 'triple contingency' learning (Trenz and Eder 2004; Strydom 1999b, 2008, 2009).

In double contingency learning, two parties (e.g., science and religion, secularists and believers, North and South, the Western environmental movement and Third World Network, or Western imperialism and Islamism) relate to each other through competition, contestation, resistance or conflict. Each is itself the product of a collective learning process, whether institutional learning, as in the case of science, religion and the Western alliance of states and corporations, or associational learning, as in the case of social movements. It is characteristic of such institutional and associational learning processes that both involve the erection of boundaries to the exclusion of the other. This defines the conditions of double contingency. Here, the two opposing parties have a self-referential orientation and are willing and able only to adjust their preferences and accommodate to a certain degree under the conditions arising from a confrontation with the opponent. The parties engage in what can be regarded as two distinct logics of collective action which are rather difficult to reconcile. While they could coevolve, these two logics often do eventuate in conflict. Frequently, therefore, the relation is unproductive, giving rise to a stalemate or even to destruction. In such cases, the parties are often not merely unable, but in fact obstinately unwilling, to learn in the sense of making their own peculiar frames, cognitive formats and cultural models more reflexive, abstract and flexible. Instead, they adopt any of a number of strategies: defensively avoiding disagreement; insisting in an authoritarian manner on a predefined consensus; harping ideologically on an endemic and insurmountable antagonism; or regressively rejecting arguments by disqualifying the people who advance them (Miller 1986, 2002). At times, however, it is fortunately also productive in the sense that conflict could be integrative, as sociologists have held for long. The latter is the positive outcome of double contingency learning. Through contestation and conflict the parties learn to accommodate one another and to allow at least a degree of coordination – through tolerance, for instance.

Over and above such an eventuality, however, there are also various examples from the recent past, such as South Africa and Northern Ireland, of a more demanding, less probable, yet much more promising learning process – namely, triple contingency learning. This is a high-level societal kind of learning which is distinct from double contingency learning in that it results from a confrontation and interrelation of the participants before an attentive public in a fully communicatively mediated or discursive public sphere. It is thus a form of discursive learning in which the active participants, whether institutional actors or civil society actors, take each other into account only via a reference to the observing, evaluating, judging, commenting and thus monitoring public. The public is constitutive of the coordinated system of standard setting and 'scorekeeping' (Brandom 2001, 180) perspectives, through which the participants have to pass to be at all able to arrive at an understanding of what they have in common and, especially, of what they disagree about. It is this configuration of communicative relations that I have elsewhere proposed to called 'triple contingency' (Strydom 1999b), as distinct from the classical sociological concept of double contingency. This threefold set of contingently related communicative relations increases and intensifies public communication and resonance. It draws more participants and observers into the situation and renders cultural models reflexive, autonomous and discursively available, thus activating a plethora of cultural resources for self-reflection, self-problematization, translation, connectivity and the transformation of self-understanding. And it compels both participants and observers to resonate by making unequivocal options and communicating those options effectively, while either accommodating themselves to the public or anticipating its response. It harbours the transcending promise of a transformative moment in which a 'creative combination of different forces' (Delanty 2006, 38) occurs. Such an outcome of a process of discursive construction is a collective achievement since the learning carrying it is a cooperative process in which all those involved are required to reach beyond their particular perspectives, without necessarily abandoning them, so as to link up with something larger than themselves and sharable with others. Such learning is made possible by the emergence of micro-, meso- and macrocognitive structures, cognitive formats, discourses, public spheres and a public possessing the epistemic authority of observing, evaluating, judging, commenting and forming opinion. These are the elements of the cognitive mechanism of mediation, transformation and transcendence that is not merely required, but is indeed already contributing to both problem solving and world creation in the context of the many and varied confrontations and conflicts between forces of conviction and their divergent images of the human being in contemporary society, both national and global.

Conclusion

In the above, I have first offered a brief historical reconstruction of the development of philosophical anthropology in order to show, secondly, that its central problematic is as relevant today as it had been in the late nineteenth and early twentieth century. My key argument was that this problematic rests on the configuration of naturalistic and historicist motifs in anthropological thought and concerns the determination of the relative weight of each as well as the relation between them – i.e., a judicious determination which is and remains aware of its ideological and political implications and consequences.

In the earlier case, the dominant philosophical-anthropological tradition to the detriment of itself and the collective organization of social life marginalized and largely ignored a second significant strand. Today, once again, there seems to be a distinct danger of polarization and conflict at a number of different levels, including philosophy, social science and everyday life. My proposal was that were we to be true to the philosophical-anthropological problematic as it presents itself under current conditions, then we would have to approach the matter and search for a solution in accordance with the most advanced development of our day – i.e., adopting cognitive theoretical terms in order to find an appropriate image of the human being. While not diminishing any particular or culturally specific identities, such a cognitively based vision simultaneously stresses the common human ability to learn and to engage in the joint construction of a shared world.

The required border crossing, mediation, transformation and transcendence are best made comprehensible with reference to the nonlinear cognitive dynamics at work in such processes. A start can be made toward the mitigation of the polarization and conflict in everyday life in contemporary society, both nationally and globally, by attending to the philosophical-anthropological problematic in a cooperative process between philosophy and social science. I have argued that, in philosophy, the polarization and conflict can be undone by the adoption of a weak or soft naturalistic position and that the same can be achieved in social science by means of a communication-discourse theoretical, cognitive approach which focuses on studying and facilitating the conditions of collective learning.

References

Baecker, Dirk. 1995. Review of Dean MacCannell and Juliet MacCannell, 'The Time of the Sign'; Brian Rotman, 'Signifying Nothing'. *Soziale Systeme* 1 (1): 156–60.

Boudon, Raymond. 1995. *Le juste et le vrai*. Paris: Fayard.

Brandom, Robert B. 2001. *Making It Explicit*. Cambridge, MA: Harvard University Press.

Delanty, Gerard. 2006. 'The Cosmopolitan Imagination: Critical Cosmopolitanism and Social Theory'. *British Journal of Sociology* 57 (1): 25–47.

Delanty, Gerard and Piet Strydom. 2003. *Philosophies of Social Science*. Maidenhead: Open University Press/McGraw-Hill.

Dilthey, Wilhelm. (1883) 1973. *Gesammelte Schriften*, vol. 1. Stuttgart: Teubner.

_____. 1974. *Gesammelte Schriften*, vol. 5. Stuttgart: Teubner.

Droysen, Johann Gustav. (1858) 1953. *Historik*. Darmstadt: Buchgesellschaft.

Eder, Klaus. 1988. *Die Vergesellschaftung der Natur*. Frankfurt: Suhrkamp.

_____. 1999. 'Societies Learn and Yet the World is Hard to Change'. *European Journal of Social Theory* 2 (2): 195–215.

Feuerbach, Ludwig. 1922 (1842). *Grundsätze der Philosophie der Zukunft*. Stuttgart: Frommann.

Foucault, Michel. 1970. *The Order of Things*. New York: Random House.

Geertz, Clifford. 1973. 'Thick Description'. In *The Interpretation of Culture*, 3–30. New York: Basic Books.

Gehlen, Arnold. 1956. *Urmensch und Spätkultur*. Bonn: Bouvier.

Giri, Ananta Kumar, ed. 2004. *Creative Social Research*. Lanham: Lexington Books.

Gulbenkian Commission. 1996 *Open the Social Sciences*. Stanford: Stanford University Press.

Habermas, Jürgen. 1973. 'Zur Fragen der philosophischen Anthropologie'. In Habermas, *Kultur und Kritik*, 87–236. Frankfurt: Suhrkamp.

_____. 1984/87. *The Theory of Communicative Action*, vol. 1–2. London and Cambridge: Heinemann/Polity Press.

_____. 2003. *Truth and Justification*. Cambridge: Polity Press.

_____. 2005. *Zwischen Naturalismus und Religion*. Frankfurt: Suhrkamp.

Heidegger, Martin. 1959. *Gelassenheit*. Pfullingen: Neske.

_____. 1961. *Nietzsche*, Vol. 2. Pfullingen: Neske.

_____. 1967. *Vorträge und Aufsätze*, vol. 3. Pfullingen: Neske.

Honneth, Axel and Hans Joas. (1980) 1988. *Social Action and Human Nature*. Cambridge: Cambridge University Press.

Horkheimer, Max. 1970. *Traditionelle and kritische Theorie*. Frankfurt: Fischer.

Libet, Benjamin. 2004. *Mind Time*. Cambridge, MA: Harvard University Press.

Löwith, Karl. 1964. *From Hegel to Nietzsche*. London: Constable.

Luhmann, Niklas. 1990. 'The Cognitive Program of Constructivism and a Reality that Remains Unknown'. In *Selforganization*, edited by W. Krohn et al., 64–85. Dordrecht: Kluwer.

_____. 1992. *Die Wissenschaft der Gesellschaft*. Frankfurt: Suhrkamp.

Marx, Karl. (1843–45) 1967. *Writings of the Young Marx on Philosophy and Society*. New York: Anchor Books.

_____. 1969. *Economic and Philosophic Manuscripts of 1844*. New York: International Publishers.

Mead, George Herbert. (1934) 1974. *Mind, Self and Society*. Chicago: University of Chicago Press.

Miller, Max. 1986. *Kollektive Lernprozesse*. Frankfurt: Suhrkamp.

_____. 2002. 'Some Theoretical Aspects of Systemic Learning'. *Sozialer Sinn* 3: 379–421.

Nietzsche, Friedrich. (1885) 1972. *Thus Spoke Zarathustra*. Harmondsworth: Penguin.

Plessner, Helmuth. (1928) 1980. *Gesammelte Schriften*, vol. 1–3. Frankfurt: Suhrkamp.

Quine, Willard van Orman. 1957. 'The Scope of Language in Science'. *British Journal of Philosophy of Science* 8: 1–17.

_____. 1960. *Word and Object*. New York: Technology Press of MIT.

Scheler, Max. (1927) 1961. *Man's Place in Nature*. New York: Noonday Press.

Schnädelbach, Herbert. 1984. *Philosophy in Germany 1831–1933*. Cambridge: Cambridge University Press.

Schopenhauer, Arthur. (1819) 1883. *The World as Will and Idea*, vol. 1–3. London: Routledge and Kegan Paul.

Sellars, Winfrid. 1963. *Science, Perception and Reality*. London: Routledge and Kegan Paul.

Sperber, Dan. 1996. *Explaining Culture*. Oxford: Blackwell.

_____. 1997. 'Individualisme méthodologique et cognitivisme'. In *Cognition et sciences sociales*, edited by R. Boudon et al., 123–35. Paris: PUF.

Strydom, Piet. 1999a. 'The Challenge of Responsibility for Sociology'. *Current Sociology* 74 (3): 65–82.

_____. 1999b. 'Triple Contingency'. *Philosophy and Social Criticism* 25 (2): 1–25.

_____. 2000. *Discourse and Knowledge*. Liverpool: Liverpool University Press.

_____. 2002. *Risk, Environment and Society*. Buckingham and Philadelphia: Open University Press.

_____. 2006. 'Contemporary European Cognitive Social Theory'. In *Handbook of Contemporary European Social Theory*, edited by G. Delanty, 218–29. London: Routledge.

_____. 2007. 'A Cartography of Contemporary Cognitive Social Theory'. *European Journal of Social Theory* 10 (3): 339–56.

_____. 2008. 'Risk Communication'. *Journal of Risk Research* 11 (1/2): 5–22.

_____. 2009. *New Horizons of Critical Theory*. New Delhi: Shipra.

Trenz, Hans-Jörg and Klaus, Eder. 2004. 'The Democratizing Dynamics of a European Public Sphere'. *European Journal of Social Theory* 7 (1): 5–25.

Turner, Stephen. 2002. *Brains/Practices/Relativism*. Chicago: University of Chicago Press.

Watson, James. 1981 (1968). *The Double Helix*. New York: Norton.

Zerubavel, Eviatar. 1997. *Social Mindscapes*. Cambridge, MA: Harvard University Press.

Chapter 7

PHILOSOPHY AS ANTHROPOCENTRISM: LANGUAGE, LIFE AND *APORIA*

Prasenjit Biswas

Temporality makes liberation dynamic.

—Vaddera Chandidas

The Anthropocentric Subject

The Cartesian-Kantian anthropomorphic subject represents a state of continual immanence in terms of its indefinite and infinite possibilities. The linguistic turn takes an anthropocentric form that has been embedded in the Cartesian-Kantian metaphysics of presence. Wittgenstein, especially, takes language as an enactable rule-governed activity, thereby making it immanent to the 'lived experiences' of the users of language. Heidegger introduces a comprehensive embeddedness of being in language and vice-versa, thereby assigning it a hermeneutical closure. In such anthropomorphic and anthropocentric moves, what is lost is the very ground of reality on which language must act. A project of recovery of the lost grounds between life and language cannot be completed without taking into account the 'constitutive' outside of language, which is the sovereignty of the subject that occupies an indeterminate space between lived reality/time and the time that remains. The time that remains marks what we are in the present. We are always in the midst of profound boredom, which is also projected beyond the present. Postsalvation, we are still in the time that remains between the experience of boredom and the experience of salvation. This Agambenian twist to the nature of subjectivity by an ontological return to a sense of time beyond the temporal allows slippages from subjecthood, as well as from desubjectivation, by shifting the centre of self-consciousness and identity to a state of being free from the metaphysical and ontological burden of bearing any biopolitical substance.

Once subjectivity and language are disentangled from each other, the question that we need to answer is: what comes after the subject as well as language? The answer can be merely 'exploratory' rather than 'explanatory'.[1] Exploratory answers are celebrated in a postphilosophical vein by many philosophers who experience the limit of language. Such limits are no longer explored in terms of 'forms of life'. Instead the mutual embeddedness between life and language acts as a source of 'power-relations' that a regime of truth and subjectivity brings about haphazardly. The play between subject and language beyond the fixed, stable and determinate notion of self/subject takes over the domain of subjectivity in order make it free from its 'core' and throw it up to the open and to the constitutive outside. Such a subject is liberated from the desire to liberate itself; instead it is like a flickering flame of consciousness that flutters and swings with every gentle wind. This subject can be thought of in terms of a 'process of liberation from the minimally disruptive standpoint of its hypothetical scene of origin'. To put it in the language of Vaddera Chandidas, 'It is a possibilisation of an infinite time in an infinite fraction of a moment. The desire that liberates and the liberation that desires are the spiral spinal swinging current […].'[2]

Such a current of temporality, which takes one to the extra time that comes after the consciousness of the temporal comes to an end, can be celebrated in language. This celebration can take two steps. It can be a commentary about the inoperativeness of language as language, as Foucault, for example, expresses in his 'The Thought of the Outside':

> Language is then freed from all the old myths by which our awareness of words, discourse, and literature has been shaped. For a long time it was thought that language has mastery over time, that it acted both as the future bond of the promise and as memory and narrative; it was thought to be prophecy and history; it was also thought that in its sovereignty it could bring to light the eternal and visible body of truth; it was thought that its essence resided in the form of words or in the breath that made them vibrate. In fact, it is only a formless rumbling, a streaming; its power resides in dissimulation. That is why it is one with erosion of time; it is depthless forgetting and the transparent emptiness of waiting.
>
> Language, its every word, is indeed directed at contents that pre-exists it; but in its own being, provided that it holds as close to its being as possible, it only unfolds in the pureness of the wait. Waiting is directed at nothing: any object that could gratify it would only efface it. Still, it is not confined to one place […]. It is in forgetting drawn outside of that the wait remains a waiting: an acute attention to what is radically new, with no bond of resemblance or continuity

with anything else (the newness of the wait drawn outside of itself and freed from any past); attention to what is most profoundly old (for deep down the wait has never stopped waiting).[3]

This idea of language as waiting disengages subjectivity from language and returns it to the pure event of 'waiting'. This waiting promotes a certain kind of sign making. In Eric Gans's words,

> Very briefly, the sign as 'aborted gesture of appropriation' is detached from its worldly temporality as a practical act by the sacred inaccessibility of the common central desire-object. At this point, it becomes an object of attention in itself, not a mere pointing-to but a sign of the object that is, at the same time, a 'sign' to the other participants of the sign-maker's renunciation of appropriative designs on this object.[4]

This is how an anthropomorphic view of language could be overcome by a directedness to the 'sign' that abandons an appropriation of subjectivity, as well as the world, making the anthropological machine dissimulate itself in the open. This is a staging of the sign in order to expose the dynamic interior of a project of liberation. The 'saved night' of this project tells us,

> This subject, 'ever-fractured' by the tension between the resentful periphery and the impossible center, may be described more simply, as linguists do, as the one who says 'I'. In order to become the 'subject' who says 'I', we must understand ourselves simultaneously as center and as periphery, both as the sacred source of language and as one of those 'subjected' to it. Yet 'understand' is not quite the right word, since it implies a cognitive model within which the paradox has already been resolved. Cognition, in the form of originary anthropology, offers us a metaresolution, a minimal model of what the human must be in order to give life to this paradox through a praxis of desire.[5]

This shifting and moving centre of a symptomatic 'I' represents one of the possibilities of a minimal presence of the self, which is far overcome by 'actual' experience of making and using signs that do not necessarily fix a reference with an always-present centre of the self. The centre of the self is subverted when such a centre is fixed, and such a fixed employment of 'self' in a discourse also shows that the self cannot be present there. The closures attained in world views and cultures are thereby open to an interruption by the very 'present' that refuses to freeze itself in the flow of time, a flow that leaves us only as a 'remnant'. The future lies in establishing the self as a remnant of itself, in the rediscovery of the humane as a necessary thought, without which life mourns its essential connection with the infinite possibility of becoming. In the words of Vaddera Chandidas, 'Realities breathe through reality; and, reality is sustained in and through realities. Reality is not personality; whereas realities enjoy the medium of "personality".'[6]

The shifting centre of self establishes a 'personality' in reality, but the shift recreates a new sign outside the 'form of life' and its everydayness that attends to the other. Acting on such a human condition, a perpetual making of reality goes on that renders an anthropomorphic description of 'reality' a static activity. Opposed to such a fixed construction of reality, there lies a temporal flux that gives necessity to the idea of reality. Anthropology as philosophy can delve into this flux of reality in the appearance and disappearance of selves. An anthropocentric notion of self does not posses the ability to inscribe itself in difference, it merely constitutes itself in its already interpellated domain of self-identity. Contrastingly, a nonanthropocentric notion of self in terms of 'temporal' and 'beyond temporal' alterities shall constitute dual powers of repetition in difference and erasure that would never make a full presence. Rather, it would be fragments of various temporalities and its associated remnants. Accordingly, a cultural-anthropological notion of self would move in a repetitive trajectory of emergence and disappearance of the figure of the human. As Foucault suggests,

> It is probably impossible to give empirical contents transcendental value, or to displace them in the direction of a constituent subjectivity, without giving rise, at least silently, to an anthropology-that is, a mode of thought in which the rightful limitations of acquired knowledge (and consequently of all empirical knowledge) are at the same time *the concrete forms of existence*, precisely as they are given in that same empirical knowledge.[7]

This same empirical knowledge now needs to constitute a discourse of anthropocentrism, which by way of its limitations cannot make the self and hence remains suspended in a self–other dialectic that never reaches the full presence as the 'subject' of that discourse. The anthropological machine pits language as prior to a discourse of the 'constitution' of self and reality, but once such a machination is dispelled what arises is only a divestment of language and being in order to substitute the self and the other, by increasing the degrees of responsibility. Anthropology merely increases the degrees of freedom for a nonanthropocentric moment of understanding the human by facilitating a transition from an absolute being to the imperfections and limitations of an empirical human being, who comes after transcendence and for whom there is an extra time that remains after philosophy.

Language

Given this inoperative 'anthropological machine', language only throws up a series of homonyms in order to develop the 'idea' of language. This idea of language lies in setting a limit on the very idea of language as 'immediate', which is a presentation of the very idea of language. The task of this presentation is formulated by Agamben as follows:

> *The task of philosophical presentation is to come with speech to help speech, so that, in speech, speech itself does not remain presupposed but instead comes to speech.* At this point the presuppositional power of language touches its limit and its end; language says presuppositions as presuppositions and, in this way, reaches the unpresupposable and unpresupposed principle that, as such, constitutes authentic human community and communication.[8]

This is a move within and beyond language that presents 'a vision of language itself' at the limit or end at which it touches itself. At the limit of the possibility of signification, language touches itself and by this act of auto-affection, it goes beyond its limit to show itself as the 'immediate'. This immediacy is understood in this manner: '*The taking place of language between the removal of the voice and the event of meaning is the other voice* [...]. [It] *enjoys the status of a no-longer (voice) and of a not-yet (meaning)*, it necessarily constitutes a negative dimension. It is *ground*, but in the sense that it goes *to the ground* and disappears in order for being and language to take place.'[9]

This taking place of language is signifying the signification, it is an overcoming of the dualism between an inside and an outside, that is, the temporal and the manifest speech acts that mean something. In other words, language is the ground of meaning by way of being, as it appears between the 'removal of the voice and the event of meaning' as the 'other', which is always surpassed and which always remains as a yet-to-come. Language, as the ground of meaning, touches its 'limit'. The limit of language is presupposed in every use of language: 'The instant language qua "presuppositional power" touches itself at its limit and end, touches itself where it sees and shows itself as 'a vision of language itself', it absolves and absolutizes itself as "absolute presupposition".'[10]

A vision of language as auto-relation of language to itself is also the ground of being, but the ground is not 'foundational'. It is touching the limit of language, which is 'potentiality not to', which also is a negation of the 'as if' analogy on which being is ontologically grounded, as in Heidegger. The status of 'no-longer' is a negation of the temporally constructed centre of human subjectivity as present in the voice, while 'not-yet' is a suspension of the voice in the availability of meaning, which makes the voice no longer operative. The availability of meaning is the moment of fulfilment of language, which again is the moment of experience of the end or limit of language, which is touching itself. This is as if the subject has taken a perspective on itself and delivered a meaning unto itself, while language has fulfilled itself by touching its own limit. Such a moment cannot be maintained any longer as the voice has been already suspended, so the subject remains a bystander, losing no time in seeing that the time flies by. Such an abolition of subjectivity, which manifests in thought and representation, suspends all its 'content' in the moment of decentring itself in the flow of time as a mere 'spectator'. The subject as spectator has already brought an end to the temporal connectedness between various instants of the time-consciousness and instead produces a lapse and delay between the 'no-longer' and 'not-yet'. Agamben puts it in this way:

> Whereas our representation of [...] time, as the time *in which* we are, separates us from ourselves and transforms us into [...] spectators of ourselves – spectators who look at the time that flies without any time left, continually missing themselves –messianic time, an operational time in which we take hold of and achieve our representations of time, is the time *that* we ourselves are, and for this very reason, is the only real time, the only time we have.[11]

A very different notion of temporality arises here that even surpasses the anthropomorphic notion of the 'open' by way of the experience of limit as it arises in representation of reality and time in human subjectivity. Human subjectivity becomes the 'time *that* we ourselves are'. Following Paul's letter to the Romans, Agamben uses two different notions of time, resurrection and *Parousia*. Parousia is the second coming of Jesus at the end of time, while resurrection marks the 'end of time'. Similarly, the subject as a spectator of time is a resurrected subject at the end of an experiential event of 'time flying'. This resurrected subjectivity at the time of 'time flying' carries no longer the sense of being a spectator, but brings about the infinite possibility of being free of the temporal structure of consciousness and subjectivity. This is not the time of becoming the subject, as such a time has already lapsed in the spectatorial consciousness that the subject has entered into, and it takes the subject to the state of being uncaptivated beyond the 'open' to the not-yet. The following example from Agamben demonstrates this exactly:

> In *The Tempest*, Prospero says to Ariel: 'Be free'. This is the moment when he relinquishes the spirit's charm and knows that the strength he has now is his own; it is the late and final stage when the old artist lays down his pen-and contemplates.

[…] No doubt life without Ariel loses its mystery, and yet somehow we know that now it can really belong to us; only now do we begin to live a purely human and earthly life, the life that did not keep its promises and, for that reason, can now give us infinitely more.[12]

The progress from mere subjectivity to spectatorial subjectivity and beyond leaves life behind, and yet life is given over to the smallest everyday gesture, as if the meaning of an entire existence condenses into a silly moment of 'missing' oneself.[13] It is an old artist laying down the pen and contemplating: a mode of being captivated, but at the same time losing oneself in that state of being captivated. What Agamben posits is the absolute sovereignty of the subject in language, as the very temporal structure of language and thought lead the subject to a state of 'meaning' that is time itself. This is also a seizing of the outside by the subject, where time flies in relation to a subject as spectator. Agamben characterizes this relationship between subjectivity and language as an abolition of 'as':

When one looks closely, the passage from language to discourse appears as a paradoxical act that simultaneously implies both subjectification and desubjectification. On the one hand, the psychosomatic individual must fully abolish himself and desubjectify himself as a real individual to become the subject of enunciation and to identify himself with the pure shifter 'I', which is absolutely without any substantiality and content other than its mere reference to the event of discourse. But once stripped of all extra-linguistic meaning and constituted as a subject of enunciation, the subject discovers that he has gained access not so much to a possibility of speaking than to an impossibility of speaking-or, rather he has gained access to being always already anticipated by a glossalalic potentiality over which he has neither control nor mastery. […] He is expropriated of all referential reality, letting himself be defined solely through the pure and empty relation to the event of discourse. *The subject of enunciation is composed of discourse and exists in discourse alone. But for this very unreason, once the subject is in discourse, he can say nothing; he cannot speak.*[14]

The subject of enunciation is a pure shifting 'I' that is related to the event of being 'I' in disjunction from a centre of subjectivity, which in effect merely experiences the pure event of touching the limit of language, which happens as a pure event of the subject as sovereign. This sovereign and shifting position of subject, both within discourse and outside it, makes it an aporetic remnant that acts as a caesura, dividing the boundary between the past and the present.[15] The notion of 'pure event' is aporetic as the event needs just not a site, but a temporal continuum.

A Critique of Anthropocentrism

Agamben's notion of subject as sovereign produces the possibility of language as a pure event that can break through the limits of time consciousness and representational features of meaning. This is a subject which is in the open beyond the duality of time and space; it is beyond the dichotomy of subjectivation and desubjectivation. The agency of such a subject lies in a language that is not abstracted from its use and context, but it lies in creating a context for itself beyond the play of closure and openness. The idea of the sovereign subject and the way in which such a subject relates itself to various moments of its actualization, which is 'lost' and 'forgotten', needs to be characterized. This 'lost' and 'forgotten' actualization as such is 'unsaveable',[16] and hence the subject 'sees only a closing, only a not-seeing'.[17] This closing is not an apparent closure, it is a relationship of humanity with the cosmos and nature, but it is not saveable on the basis of relation. Agamben elucidates this relationship in terms of its limits:

> The anthropological machine no longer articulates nature and man in order to produce the human through the suspension and capture of the inhuman. The machine is, so to speak, stopped; it is 'at a standstill', and, in reciprocal suspension of the two terms, something for which we perhaps have no name and which is neither animal nor man settles in between nature and humanity and holds itself in the mastered relation, in the saved night.[18]

The saved night of the anthropological machine no longer succeeds in producing the human in terms of a 'mastered relation'; it only throws up an uncertain relationship between the human and nature that is something in-between the two and thereby allows it to acquire the shape of a 'remnant', as Agamben characterized it. Abandonment of the anthropological machine as a coordinated outcome of the progress of the human subject is an aporetic consequence of any ontological characterization of being.

The aporetic consequence can be characterized in terms of a blurring of discourses such as philosophy and literature, which bear family resemblances that can cover the totality of paradigms and discourses. A diachronic mixing up that remains simultaneously hidden and manifest in layers of discourses produces a communicative continuum between subjects bound by various discourses through their cognitive-narrative abilities. This results in a few case histories, counterfactual scenarios and parables within the discourse of philosophy starting from Plato to, say, Austin's speech-act theory. For Derrida, ordinary language is shot through with metaphors, nonserious usages, chance-collocations, parapraxes and such other 'accidental features'. Such accidental features do not allow fixing referents in the world, but the linguistic elements themselves can 'perform' the role of reference. A diachronic mix-up between the referential function of language and its referents is a kind of performance that language does. Derrida uncovers all these accidental features concealed by normal uses of words in order to show how many different routes would be possible from any given point in the discourse. In Derrida's notion of language, each fragment of a language is a part of a larger language, and each such fragment is open to 'receiving' and 'giving' in the process of reconstituting an always-already represented 'referent' or an 'object'. But this opening 'problematizes' a modular notion of language that consists of 'those abstract principles which, when they interface with components *outside* the mind, produce disjoint effects such as language, music and the like'.[19] Such a problematization results into a multiplicity of 'representations', which are not only of a certain genre, but also of 'modulations' of the verb 'to represent'. In Derrida's words,

> It draws attention to a situation in which a context cannot be saturated so as to permit the determination and identification of a sense. […] If there are two conditions for fixing the meaning or overcoming the polysemy of a word-namely, the existence of an invariant beneath the diversity of semantic transformations, on the one hand, and the possibility of determining a saturable context, on the other-these two conditions seem to me in any case as problematical for a living language as for a dead one.[20]

In other words, contexts are never complete in a specific discourse of meaning and reality without a warrant that satisfies the 'truth-conditions' for a representational predicate; in almost the same way, Derrida countenanced the idea of 'representation' from assuming a 'semantic kernel' such as 'truth' or 'meaning'. Derrida indicated that the very function of language lies in not expressing what is 'truth', but to be true to itself. A language remains 'true' to itself by being self-referential, and hence the apparent isolation of the 'being' of language has to be accessed as 'presence'. But such a presence is never auto-telic, or closed onto a reality, it is rather a 'diversity of corpuses, codes, and contexts'. This is a mimetic substitution of the moving multiplicity of language that passes from being singular to being multiple without an ontological reduction to thought or reality into its structural manifold. The situation is illustrated by Wright:

> The form of pluralism […] is one of, roughly, *variable realization*. What constitutes the existence of a number may be very different to what constitutes the existence of a material object. The identity of persons is generally held to call for a

special account, contrasting with that appropriate to the identity of material constituents generally. And what constitutes truth in ethics may be quite different to what constitutes truth in theoretical physics. [...] Evidently there is space for a corresponding contention about truth. *There need be no single, discourse-invariant thing in which truth consists.*[21]

If that is so, and there are no discourse-invariant conditions of truth, then it results in a dis-relation between 'presentation' and 'representation', which is an abandonment of the relationship between event and context without falling either into the trappings of an ontological binary between 'belonging' and 'inclusion' (read: being and existence) or into the fear of 'death' – the disclosure of the 'limits' of shedding an essentialist pluralism that fails in its intellection. Such an intellection, needless to say, is a reflexive failure that fails to subsume performatively its own happening from its context. This is also a shipwreck of the Kantian 'reflexive manner of thinking', when sensations fail to provide any information about an object, but signal the imaginary locales of the subjective mind, a supplementary information without 'representation'. This is a breach between cognitive faculties as well as between the constitution of subjectivity and the conferment of meanings in language. The way Kant formulated this breach still acts as an example of the return to the subject, which in Lyotard's heuristic analysis of 'sublime' is as follows: 'There is not one subjectivity that experiences pure feelings; rather, it is the pure feeling that "promises a subject".'[22] But this can be reformulated in the complex, architectonic picture of human subjectivity as follows: 1) 'either the subjective calculus is ruled through and through algebraically, or there is a hasty subjectivation and a subjective process of certitude'; and 2) the discursive materiality of the production of the subjective is marked by 'the ontological form of anxiety' about the constitution of the very subject. What further promises a subject is its arising after language, which at the moment of its application is 'someone else's' and never one's own. Can language be given or taken between one and the other without a promise?

Wittgenstein's insight into the workings of our language needs to involve the question of representation, which, in his opinion, should be 'surveyable';[23] that is to say, it must allow a 'grammatical movement' (PI, 401). A grammatical movement is movement of composition, as in language and music (PI, 46), which is a movement through various constituents of language. Such a movement is meant to survey various parts of a composition in words in order to 'show the fly the way out of the fly-bottle' (PI, 309). This showing is also a state that gets treated grammatically (PI, 573). This is how one is not bewitched by the resources of language. There are grammatical fictions, such as 'new ways of representation', that Wittgenstein debunks in favour of a common technique of representation that can be taught to someone else. Wittgenstein believed that the 'inner process stands in need of an outward criteria' (PI, 580). This outward criteria is a grammatical criterion. As Wittgenstein argues, 'essence is expressed in grammar' (PI, 371) and 'grammar tells us what kind of object anything is' (PI, 373).

The outward criterion is somewhat a matter of construction. Wittgenstein's example of a dream report during the state of wakefulness throws up 'completely new criterion for the report's "agreeing"' with the content of the dream. In an apparent distinction between the truth of what is dreamt and the truth of the dream report, Wittgenstein's supposed new criterion for agreement would depend on another distinction between 'truth' and 'truthfulness' (PI, 320). The truthfulness of the report establishes the truth of the dream postfacto, as it cannot be established unless one is awake and one reports what one 'sees' in a dream. So the time of the dream and the time of narrating the dream are never coincident; while the notion of truthfulness relates to the 'time of the dream', the notion of 'truth' is related to the telling of the dream.

A similar picture arises in Lacan's notion of 'logical time', which is a construction of time based on construction of truth in close relation to truthfulness. Alain Badiou interprets 'logical time' as 'experiential and lived time', in which one can only describe the breach or disjunction between 'possibility' (which is infinite) and 'actuality' (which is the choice of one or many) in a particular moment separated by the anxiety of being. This anxiety is to find truthfulness in truth, which once again is a terribly anthropocentric anxiety. The anxiety lives up to a different reality beyond the sensation in the subjective by a breached suspension of its fulfilment in the form of a sublime that has an excess over both sides of the breach without a possibility of any reproduction or synthesis. This breach operates as a detemporalized stasis of the subject's signifiers and the temporal becoming of the subjective in the realm of meaning and language. This is a moment of resolving the duality between the subject and its objective constituents by not synthesizing them into one, but by naming them as two, as the 'truth as an effect' of the breach between the ontological 'two' and the ontic 'duality'.[24]

Wittgenstein alludes to this ontic duality as the 'system of reference' and the 'facts of life'[25] that give rise to an 'order', which either precedes or follows it.[26] Such an 'order' is derived by an interpreter in parallel with a pre-existing 'system of reference' that acts as the source of understanding a totally different 'form of life'. Even if such a parallel is not easily available, it is still playing the 'language game' – a play without a game. In Lyotard's coinage, it is 'just gaming', meaning the prereflexive narrative whole of a culture that affects how others 'read' their language and culture.[27] This prereflexive narrative whole is reflected upon through a Wittgensteinian picture that presents the 'rules' of life. These rules of life are constructed by way of reflecting upon what is prereflexively given. This move from the prereflexive to the reflected dimension of life presents the rules with all their 'wrong turnings'. Wittgenstein draws a fascinating picture of such wrong turnings:

> A hero looks death in the face, real death, not just the image of death. Behaving honourably in a crisis doesn't mean being able to act the part of a hero well, as in the theatre, it means rather being able to look death *itself* in the eye.
>
> For an actor may play a lot of different roles, but at the end of it all *he himself*, the human being, is the one who has to die.[28]

Such a picture breaks down the calculus of rules and roles, but in the ultimate analysis, what comes into picture is the life itself with the human being at its centre. In a strong sense, Wittgenstein draws out an ontological situatedness of being human from any rule or role. In the case of facing death, the role of a hero is surpassed by an ontological predicament of dying that supersedes the courage to face death. The fine distinction between looking death in the face and looking death in the eye arises when one moves from the former to the latter, a move from the prereflexive to the reflected that brings out the human predicament of death lying beyond rules and roles, through which one moves toward such a predicament. As a commentary on life, Wittgenstein makes us aware of a different predicament than the calculus of life that exhausts itself in rules and roles and plays itself out, only to be overcome in a typical human predicament such as death. In a sense there is a collapse of the prereflexive and the reflected in a situation such as death, which creates the possibility of acting out a great role in the face of grave danger. But such acts lie on the other side of the ultimate human predicament, an ontological limitation that human beings cannot overcome.

Wittgenstein's anthropological stance is based on a notion of human predicament that arises only as a limit or ultimate possibility in every human transaction. Human transactions assume the form of a game that lies embedded in a distinguishable 'form of life'. The forms of a game, grammatical, logical or mathematical, are necessarily understandable if one understands the language in which they are presented. Understanding language for Wittgenstein is like understanding the rules of a game, a calculus that enables someone to perform certain operations over a well-defined domain of knowledge.[29] It is also like understanding a theme in music.[30] The very phenomenon of understanding is treated by Wittgenstein as 'diffused ability', which enables someone to respond or to do something by way of hearing, receiving or grasping an idea, meaning or intention of the other.[31]

Understanding is diffused in responses; it is never something outside the frame. It is rather locating the place of a word in grammar as well as in real life transactions, and both are intertwined and diffused with each other in being able to give a response. The meaning of a linguistic expression and its grammatically determined use are both embedded in understanding, which itself is a diffused response. Wittgenstein puts it a different way: 'One might say that the concept "game" is a concept with blurred edges. But is a blurred concept a concept at all?'[32]

Such blurred edges of a concept and the diffuse functioning of understanding arise just because 'language is not defined for us as an arrangement fulfilling a definite purpose'.[33] Rather, it is defined as an activity woven into life. This kind of a 'positioning' shifts from a structure-based understanding of language to an action-coordinating mechanism that depends on the 'use' of language. This kind of positioning of language in the midst of activity in a human context makes it simultaneously local and feature-based, and does not immediately conform to any universalistic theoretical or scientific prevarications. Therefore, two of the prevaricating notions of language – namely, representational and fideistic – are both challenged in Wittgenstein's blurring of the edges of language.

Such blurring of the edges becomes a contentious source of linguistic relativity. Jean Francoise Lyotard himself, for example, had read the culture of the Cashinahua tribe (a small South American tribe living on the Peruvian–Brazilian border) in terms of 'rigid designators' that the specific narrative of the tribe draw from the events of the 'now'.[34] The prereflexive character of the 'language game' of another cultural community cannot be reduced under a 'parallel', analogous or single criterion of judgment, 'they' cannot be judged by others from a reflexive knowledge of their language. This impossibility of using a single criterion to judge different 'forms of life' in a reflexive manner is recognized by Wittgenstein, when he comments, 'The relation, connection, between thoughts and reality is given by language through the common possession of expression […]. We have here a sort of relativity theory of language before us. (And the analogy is nothing fortuitous).'[35]

The 'ontic' reality relates to 'facticity' or ascriber-contextualism, while the 'ontological' relates to what Jean Luc Nancy called 'the coming into presence of the immobile heart of things', which in the ultimate analysis is the meaning of being as presence or absence, as part of a system of thought and an inhabitant of language.[36] The question of ontico-ontological difference arises at two levels: at the level of predicates that 'present' being, and at the level of 'conditions of possibility' of that very presence. The presence of being (which is not an object or entity) is different from the mere facticity of an experience of being; it is rather a reflected notion of being that arises from the very intentional constitution of subjectivity that enters into every instances of 'facticity', which is an already-interpreted notion of facts. This already-interpreted notion of things/facts in the intentional reflected notion of being in the subjectivity of the subject overcomes the duality between subject and object, self and other, by way of an ontico-ontological difference that differentiates 'facticity' and 'being'. In this context, Heidegger granted *Dasein*, or being-in-the-world, only the status of 'ontology', while he granted the 'ontic' status to humans as the only creatures that have a being. But this Heideggerian notion of *Dasein* as both 'ontic' and 'ontological' produces the notion of a centred being that *presents* itself in the world qua self-consciousness, which ultimately establishes a connection of necessity between how the ontologically present being understands, interprets and acts in the world. This connection of necessity makes both 'ontic' and 'ontological' mutually co-constitutive, such that the distinction Heidegger draws between *Dasein* and the entities towards which *Dasein* bears a relation of comportment is circumvented by bringing the difference under a co-reductive holism.

Notes

1 Eric Gans, 'Staging as an Anthropological Category', *New Literary History* 31 (1) (2000): 45–56.

2 Vaddera Chandidas, *Desire and Liberation: The Fundamentals of Cosmicontology* (Tirupati: New Directions Press, 1975), 54.

3 Michel Foucault, 'The Thought of the Outside', in *Aesthetics, Method and Epistemology*, ed. James Faubion (London: Penguin Books, 1998 [1994]), 167.

4 Gans, 'Staging as an Anthropological Category', 48.

5 Ibid, 53.

6 Chandidas, *Desire and Liberation*, 25.

7 Michel Foucault, *The Order of Things: An Archaeology of Human Sciences* (London and New York: Routledge, 2002), 270.

8 Giorgio Agamben, *Potentialities: Collected Essays in Philosophy*, ed. and trans. Daniel Heller-Roazen (Stanford: Stanford University Press, 1999), 35.

9 Giorgio Agamben, *Language and Death: The Place of Negativity*, trans. Karen E. Pinkus with Michael Hardt (Minneapolis: University of Minnesota Press, 1991), 35.

10 Agamben, *Potentialities*, 43.

11 Giorgio Agamben, *The Time that Remains: A Commentary on the Letter to the Romans* (Stanford: Stanford University Press, 2005), 68.

12 Giorgio Agamben, *Profanations*, trans. Jeff Fort (New York: Zone Books, 2007), 18.

13 Ibid, 24.

14 Giorgio Agamben, *Remnants of Auschwitz: The Witness and the Archive*, trans. Daniel Heller-Roazen (New York: Zone Books, 2002), 116–17.

15 Agamben, *The Time that Remains*, 74.

16 Giorgio Agamben, *The Open: Man and Animal*, trans. Kevin Attell (Stanford: Stanford University Press, 2004), 82. Agamben invokes here the notion of Benjamin's 'saved night', which is a relationship with something unsaveable.

17 Ibid, 68.

18 Ibid, 83.

19 Nirmalangshu Mukherjee, *The Cartesian Mind* (Shimla: IIAS, 2000), 30.

20 Jacques Derrida, *Psyche: Invention of the Other*, vol. 1 (Stanford: Stanford University Press, 2007), 99.

21 Crispin Wright, 'Response to Commentators', *Philosophy and Phenomenological Research* 56 (4): 924.

22 Jean Francois Lyotard, *Lessons on the Analytic of the Sublime*, trans. Elizabeth Rottenberg (Stanford: Stanford University Press, 2007), 20.

23 Wittgenstein, *Philosophical Investigations* (henceforth PI), trans. G. E. M. Anscombe and P. M. S. Hacker, revised fourth edition by P. M. S. Hacker ad Joachim Schulte (Sussex: Wiley-Blackwell, 2009), sec. 122.

24 Peter Hallward, ed., *Think Again: Alain Badiou and the Future of Philosophy* (London: Continuum, 2004), 87, 183–7, 200.

25 Ludwig Wittgenstein, *Remarks on the Philosophy of Psychology*, vols 1 and 2, ed. G. E. M. Anscombe and G. H. von Wright, trans. G. E. M. Anscombe (Oxford: Blackwell, 1988), sec. 630.

26 PI, 206.

27 Jean Francois Lyotard and Jean-Loup Thébaud, *Just Gaming*, trans. Wlad Godzich (Minneapolis: University of Minnesota Press, 1985), 23–4.

28 Ludwig Wittgenstein, *Culture and Value*, ed. G. H. von Wright, trans. Peter Winch (Oxford: Basil Blackwell, 1986), 50e.

29 Ludwig Wittgenstein, *Philosophical Grammar*, ed. Rush Rhees, trans. Anthony Kenny (Oxford: Basil Blackwell, 1974), 50–51.

30 PI, sec. 527

31 G. Baker and M. S. Hacker, *Wittgenstein: Understanding and Meaning*, vol. 1, 2nd edition (Sussex: Wiley-Blackwell, 2009), 183.

32 PI, sec. 71.

33 Wittgenstein, *Philosophical Grammar*, sec. 137, 31.

34 Jean Francois Lyotard, 'Missive on Universal History', in *The Postmodern Explained to Children* (Sydney: Power Publications, 1992), 33–4.

35 Ludwig Wittgenstein, Manuscrpit 109, vol. 6, Bergen Library, 199.

36 Jean Luc Nancy, 'The Heart of Things', in *The Birth to Presence*, trans. Brain Holmes et al. (Stanford: Stanford University Press, 1993), 187.

Part II

SOURCES OF PHILOSOPHICAL ANTHROPOLOGY

Chapter 8

KANT AND ANTHROPOLOGY

Ananta Kumar Giri

In this chapter, we explore the challenge of rethinking modernist knowledge by looking at Kant's conception of anthropology. Kant taught courses in both anthropology and physical geography, and his book *Anthropology from a Pragmatic Point of View* (1798) was published nearly thirty years after his initial engagement with anthropology. While his lectures embodied his crisis of identity as a professional philosopher, thus facilitating a border crossing between philosophy and anthropology, *Anthropology from a Pragmatic Point of View* was far short of his earlier critique of metaphysics. Kant wanted anthropology to play by universal principles, if not be totally subordinate to metaphysics. The book is especially interesting from the point of view of border crossing: 'In this work Kant comes as close as possible to combining the qualities of English and continental philosophy. The power of the intellect and the attraction of the imagination both merge into a system of common human concern which has more relevance today then it had before' (Zammito 2002). The word 'pragmatic' in the text is important, and nearly two hundred years later new democratic possibilities seem to have arisen from border-crossing dialogue between American pragmatism and Kantian traditions, as in the works of Karl-Otto Apel and Jürgen Habermas. As we shall see in the case of Kant himself, Rousseau was a major influence who inspired him to use the project of philosophical anthropology for the education of mankind. Thus, Kantian engagement with anthropology embodies several border crossings, first between different intellectual and philosophical traditions, and second between academic philosophy and popular philosophy.

Kant begins his *Anthropology* by declaring, 'All cultural progress, which represents the education of man, aims at putting acquired knowledge and skill to use in the world' (1978, 314). He contrasts the physiological and pragmatic approaches to anthropology: 'The first offers a conceptualization of what nature makes of man, while the latter presents what man "does, can and make himself".' Kant pleads for the pragmatic, considering the physiological approach a waste of time. At the same time, the pragmatic study must be systematic and universal: 'Universal knowledge will always precede local knowledge as long as it is to be arranged and guided by philosophy, without which all acquired knowledge can provide nothing but fragmentary groping, and no science at all' (Zammito 2002, 301).

Though Kant seems to subordinate local knowledge to universal knowledge, there are important local details in his pragmatic anthropology about different peoples, nations and characters. Though Kant did not travel much beyond Königsberg, he had an anthropological eye, suggested in the title of his other border-crossing text – one which in fact represented a certain self-critical turn from pure metaphysics to anthropology – *Observations on the Feelings of the Beautiful and Sublime* (1764). His attention to observation is borne out both in his anthropological and philosophical vocations. Notable is his following observant eye, though problematic from the point of view of justice and fairness: 'A young wife is always in danger of becoming a widow, and this leads her to distribute her charms to all men whose fortunes make them marriageable; so that, if this should occur, she would not be lacking in suitors' (1978, 218). 'As for the scholarly women, they use their books somewhat like a watch, that is, they wear the watch so that it can be noticed that they have one, although it is usually broken or does not show correct time' (221). But Kant is not simply male chauvinist, as he himself writes: 'Woman is the monarch and man, the cabinet ministers' (224).

As to the significance of observation in his philosophical vocation, Kant's *Observations* represented a contribution to the analysis of feeling, and the role of observation is quite central here. As one observer writes, 'Kant clearly considered anthropological inquiry *propaedeutic* to fundamental moral philosophical inquiry' (Zammito 2002, 110). Furthermore, 'In *Observations* Kant had abandoned scholarly elitism and accepted Rousseau's call for philosophers to become the "educators of mankind".' But 'there could never be any question of a primitivist reception of Rousseau. The dynamic of social development was programmed into natural man, for Kant' (116). Though Kantian anthropology tries to fulfil man's potential, there is nonetheless an ethnocentric bias, as illustrated in the following comments:

> Patience of a particular kind is shown by the Indians in America who throw away their weapons when they are encircled and, without begging for pardon, let themselves be slain quietly. Does this indicate more courage than the Europeans display, who in such a situation tend to defend themselves to the last man? To me it seems to be just barbaric vanity intended to preserve the honor of the tribe so that the enemy could not force them to lament and beg as vindications of submission. (Kant 1978)

Though Kant's pragmatic anthropology is full of problematic ethnocentric statements and perspectives, at times he gives rather spectacular results of his pragmatic anthropology: 'Drink loosens the tongue. But it also opens the heart wide, and it is a vehicle instrumental to a moral quality, that is, openheartedness' (1978, 61).

Ethnocentrism is not the only challenge in Kantian pragmatic anthropology. Anthropocentrism is another: 'The most important object of culture, to whom such knowledge and skill can be applied, is Man because he is his own ultimate purpose. To recognize him, according to his species, as an earthly creature endowed with reason deserves to be called knowledge of the world, even though he is only one of all the creatures on earth' (Kant 1978, 314).

Kant does not have a disciplinary view of anthropology, as he writes in the very second paragraph of his book: 'Such an anthropology, understood as knowledge of the world, has to be continued after the formal education is over' (1978, 4). Such an anthropology 'is not yet properly pragmatic so long as it contains extended knowledge of the things in the world, such as animals, plants, and minerals in various lands and climates. It is properly pragmatic only when it incorporates knowledge of Man as a citizen of the world' (4). Despite Kant's anthropocentric limitations, such a view calls for a new kind of global or cosmopolitan anthropology beyond the imprisonment in culture, society and nation-state. And if it can cross the borders of anthropocentrism, such a pragmatic anthropology could also transform itself into a planetary and cosmic anthropology involving a fundamental critique and transformation of *anthropos* as well. Such a project would continue the explorations of Kant beyond Kant, as Kant not only gives supremacy to reason, but also extends its limits. For Kant, 'man's rational capacity alone is not sufficient to constitute his dignity, and elevate him above the brutes' (Dowdell and Rudnick 1978, x).

What is important to note is that Kant's pragmatic anthropology contains a critique of egoism and appreciation for pluralism: 'Egoism can only be contrasted with pluralism, which is a frame of mind in which the self, instead of being entrapped in itself as if it were the whole world, understands and behaves itself as a mere citizen of the world. The above is all that belongs to the world.'

Kant and Anthropology: Some Contemporary Considerations

The frequent occurrence of the word 'world' in Kantian pragmatic anthropology should caution us about the multidimensional nature of the world itself – beyond this world being just a 'citizen's world'. As J. N. Mohanty (2000) would suggest, there are worlds and worlds. It is in this context that Keith Hart's elaboration of a Kantian project of anthropology deserves our attention. For Hart, 'Kant saw that the world was moving towards war between a coalition of nation-states; yet he posed the question of how humanity might construct a "perpetual peace" beyond the boundaries of state, based on principles we all share' (2000, 3). 'In order to pursue this goal,' for Hart, 'the world has to be imaginatively reduced in scale and our subjectivity expanded so that a meaningful link can be established between the two' (3). Furthermore, 'We need to feel more at home in the world, to find the means of actively resisting alienation' (3). But feeling more at home in the world today cannot be pursued in a matter of certainty or mastery; it has to acknowledge the fundamentally fragile character of our home and the world, and calls for a border crossing between home and homelessness, worlds and worlds, immanence and transcendence. This calls for a spiritual transformation of Kantian pragmatic anthropology as an anthropology of the world.

As Keith Hart and David Harvey have argued, perpetual peace and cosmopolitanism are important legacies of Kant and important sources of inspiration for a planetary anthropology emerging out of simultaneous engagement with philosophical reflections and fieldwork. But Kantian cosmopolitanism is facilitated by deepening and broadening our engagement and conversations. For Kant, 'Peace will be attained through the inevitable spread of the institutional and legal structure of a "perpetual federation" among independent republican states, each of which respects the basic rights of its citizens and establishes a public sphere in which people can regard themselves and others as free and equal "citizens of the world".' For Kant, establishment of 'strict publicity, further ensured by the presence of an enlightened, critical, and educated world public' would facilitate the realization of peace. For Gandhi, alongside this we need the development of capacity for *ahimsa* (nonviolence), love and Satyagraha. Peace is not just public; it calls for appropriate self-cultivation.

A simultaneous engagement with Kant and Gandhi suggests interesting possibilities for an alternative planetary anthropology. Gandhi's conception of anthropology was not just anthropocentric. Both Kant and Gandhi urge us to understand the significance of moral duty. This would help us transform the current discussions in anthropology about ethics and the ethics of anthropology, as well as anthropological practice. For Kant, realization of moral duty 'would often require self-denial' (1964, 75). But Kant does not explore sufficiently the ontological preparation for self-denial. He does not show us how 'self-denial' constitutes a source of happiness, or what Gandhi calls 'joy' for moral agents: 'A life of sacrifice is the pinnacle of art and is full of true joy' (Iyer 1990, 382). Gandhian suffering can redeem Kantian pure reason, as Gandhi tells us: 'The conviction has been growing upon, that things of fundamental importance to the people are not secured by reason alone, but have to be purchased with their suffering [...]. Suffering is infinitely more powerful [...] for converting the opponent and *opening his ears*, which are otherwise shut, to the voice of reason' (Gandhi as quoted in Narayanan 1968, 202). This suffering is not inflicted on the other, but it is the self-sacrifice of moral agents with the other for the sake of love and justice.

Gandhi reiterates the significance of undertaking suffering for the sake of justice and it is a challenge for Kantian approaches to justice starting from Rawls to Habermas. However, while both Rawls and Habermas look at justice from the point of view of the primacy of the political, both Kant and Gandhi offer a fundamental critique of politics as the project of a desirable anthropology that is most often articulated solely in political terms. Both Kant and Gandhi call for a moral transformation of politics, which should inspire us to transform our predominantly politically engaged anthropology. While, for Kant, the ultimate objective of the moralization of politics is to conquer 'the crafty and far more dangerously deceitful and treason principle of evil in ourselves', for Gandhi it is to bring about 'self-regulation' and a state of enlightened anarchy where 'everyone is one's ruler'. Gandhi calls this Swaraj and it calls for aspiration and struggle for truth, or what Gandhi calls Satyagraha. But while in the Gandhian struggle for autonomy and truth seeking, Swaraj and Satyagraha, there is emphasis on self-transcendence and self-transformation, this seems to be missing in the Kantian ideal of autonomy.[1] The transformation of anthropology calls for a dialogue between Kantian autonomy and Gandhian Swaraj and Satyagraha.

Thus Kantian pragmatic anthropology as an anthropology of the world is now in need of transcivilizational dialogues and planetary conversations, and here a dialogue with Gandhi, to begin with, can help us to broaden, deepen and transform Kantian anthropology from a pragmatic point of view. Such a dialogue has great significance for the whole project of philosophical anthropology as it is, in its dominant version, narrow in its source and inspiration (i.e., mainly Euro-American and Western). Anthropologists who cross over to philosophy in the Euro-American world only look at their own local gods, thus Clifford Geertz (2000) considers Wittgenstein as his *guru*, and Bourdieu (2000) Wittgenstein and Pascal. But the need for planetary conversations here cannot be reiterated strongly enough.

Another important challenge for *Anthropology* that is tied up with the Kantian legacy is the challenge of overcoming dualism. Dualism is entrenched in the heritage of modern anthropology, as in the works of Durkheim and Dumont, for example, and a transformation of modernist anthropology calls for multidimensional strivings for the realization of nonduality, both as an epistemic as well as an ontological engagement. But like Kant's striving for perpetual peace, overcoming dualism is a perpetual journey. Much of anthropological logic is dualistic. While at one point it reflects the finitude, inescapable duality and language limitations of human existence, dualism at the same time is not our destiny. It is possible to cultivate nondual approaches to understanding our simultaneous condition of nonduality and duality. Kant sought to connect the dualism of pure reason and practical reason through aesthetic judgment. Aesthetics has the potential to cross over boundaries, especially those of entrenched dualism, and now it can be accompanied by spiritual cultivation and transformation.

Note

1 As Martha Nussbaum (2006, 410) argues:

> Kant does think that we can hope for peace, in part because it is to the advantage of all; but he does not think that we can hope for benevolence that supports basic life opportunities for all the citizens of the world, or even for all in a given nation. This lack of moral ambition is surprising, given that all these thinkers are surrounded by, and in some cases adherents of, a Christian culture that predominantly advocated spiritual reform and self-change in respect of benevolence and other basic sentiments.

References

Bourdieu, Pierre. 2000. *Pascalian Meditations*. Cambridge: Polity Press.
Dowdell, Victor Lyle and Hans H. Rudnick. 1978. 'Introduction to Immanuel Kant.' *Anthropology from a Pragmatic Point of View*. Carbondale: Southern Illinois University Press.
Geertz, Clifford. 2000. *Available Light: Philosophical Reflections on Anthropological Topics*. Princeton: Princeton University Press.
Hart, Keith. 2000. 'Reflections on a Visit to New York'. *Anthropology Today* 16 (4): 1–3.
Iyer, Raghavan, ed. 1990. *The Essential Writings of Mahatma Gandhi*. Delhi: Oxford University Press.
Kant, Immanuel. 1978. *Anthropology from a Pragmatic Point of View*. Carbondale: Southern Illinois University Press.
———. 1764. *Observations on the Feelings of the Beautiful and Sublime*.
———. 1964. *Groundwork of the Metaphysics of Morals*, translated by H. J. Patton. New York: Harper Torch Books.
———. (1795) 1957. *Perpetual Peace*. New York: The Liberal Arts Press.
Mohanty, J. N. 2000. *Self and Other: Philosophical Essays*. Delhi: Oxford University Press.
Narayan, Shriman, ed. 1968. *The Selected Works of Mahatma Gandhi, vol. 6: The Voice of Truth*. Ahmedabad: Navajivan Publishing House.
Nussbaum, Martha. 2006. *Frontiers of Justice*. Cambridge, MA: Harvard University Press.
Zammito, John H. 2002. *Kant, Herder, and the Birth of Anthropology*. Chicago: University of Chicago Press.

Chapter 9

DILTHEY'S THEORY OF KNOWLEDGE AND ITS POTENTIAL FOR ANTHROPOLOGICAL THEORY

Daniel Šuber

The approach that stands closest to psychic life is anthropology, because it aims to penetrate the concrete nexus of mental life itself.

—W. Dilthey

With some considerable delay, the German philosopher Wilhelm Dilthey (1833–1911) was, in 1986, declared the 'new anthropological ancestor' (Bruner 1986, 4). Although he had been acknowledged as having exerted some influence on major figures of anthropology, like Boas and Benedict well before, the recent turn to Dilthey was meant to go far beyond the historical concern. This move contrasts sharply with the result of an examination of the indexes of relevant textbooks on basic anthropological theory, where Dilthey's name hardly ever appears. What then are the common points of contact between late twentieth-century anthropology and turn-of-the-century German philosophy? In what manner could Diltheyean ideas be useful in overcoming the conceptual shortcomings of contemporary anthropological theories of knowledge, relating back to structuralism or (eventually) Kantian origin? In answering these questions I will, first, resort to some historical-theoretical lines of argumentation, thereby reconstructing the motives of the pioneers of the 'interpretive' and 'reflexive' turn in anthropology (Geertz, Turner). In a second step I will go further in reconstructing the main angles of Dilthey's theory of knowledge and propose it as an adequate model of knowledge acquisition in the social sciences. On that basis, my final reflections shall be devoted to sketching out some family resemblances between Dilthey's concepts and some recently voiced postulations of anthropological theory.

1. Dilthey in Modern Anthropology

Not only among anthropologists, but also among sociologists Dilthey figures, first and foremost, as a co-founder of modern philosophical hermeneutics and, consequently, a paragon of *verstehende* social science (Brown 2005). Thus, he is often mentioned alongside Max Weber and Alfred Schutz (Rabinow and Sullivan 1979, 5; Marcus and Fischer 1999, 30; Geertz 2005, 114). Unsurprisingly, Dilthey became one of the crucial reference points for anthropologists like Clifford Geertz and others who stroke their blows at positivist, functionalist and structuralist approaches of anthropological practice in the 1960s and 70s, the result of which is nowadays known as the 'interpretative' or 'reflexive' turn in anthropology. However, the role of Dilthey in this theoretical movement has yet to be explored, since the recourses to his ideas have been, even in the works of Geertz and Turner, selective, sketchy and unspecified. Also, Dilthey's leitmotifs are frequently fused with philosophical content of American pragmatism (Dewey), as in the case of Turner (1986), or with the late Wittgenstein for the 'linguistic turn' in human science, as in Geertz (2000, xi–xiii). For these reasons, the task of determining the theoretical potential of Dilthey's philosophy for the foundation of modern empirical science remains to be done. It shall provide the opportunity to ward off common misunderstandings of such Diltheyean themes as the notion of emphatic understanding, which is frequently (mis)taken for the keystone of Dilthey's hermeneutics.

Dilthey first became attractive to anthropologists at the moment when the epistemological premises on which ethnographic praxis was grounded were put at issue during the 1960s. Symptomatically, the rhetoric of a disciplinary crisis was sweeping, as was the quest for a new 'radical', 'critical' anthropology.[1] By 1969, what was at the root of the general feeling of nuisance was still hard to determine (Scholte 1999, 430–31). Struggling for an explanation, Bob Scholte hinted at the 'hypothesis' that 'intellectual paradigms, including anthropological traditions, are culturally mediated, that is, they are contextually situated and relative' (1999, 431). From that observation Scholte inferred the necessity to subject the sociocultural contexts of anthropological activity to 'further reflexive understanding, hermeneutic mediation, and philosophical critique' (431). If one recalls the ideological atmosphere that the young Dilthey had already sensed, and which to overcome became the overall aim of his intellectual journey, the parallels are compelling. In a letter to his mother, Dilthey wrote around the early 1870s, 'The great crisis of science and European culture, which we face these days, affects my frame of mind so completely and deeply that it has extinguished any personal ambitions in me' (Misch 1933, vii). The crisis Dilthey alluded to was spurred by the decline of the idealist system and the ideological vacancies this devaluation had left. Philosophy was suddenly in the difficult position of manoeuvring on a completely secular ground, and had to invent new methods and conceptual tools. Thus, a novel theory of knowledge, expressed as the Kant-inspired 'critique of historical reason', was the animal Dilthey was after for the rest of his working life.

The connection between Dilthey's aspiration and the anthropological project becomes apparent from the following quote: 'Only when we succeed in developing anthropological reflection, inner experience, and the human sciences positively can the Spiritual life of Europe receive a new impetus' (Dilthey 1989, 437). The claim at stake in both intellectual domains – nineteenth-century philosophy and postwar anthropology – was to redraw the lines between scientific knowledge and everyday experience, which, naturally, required a fundamental relativization of traditional epistemic foundations. For this purpose, a fundamental 'self-reflection', a term Dilthey had chosen as the watchword of his philosophical endeavour (1931, 192–3), came to be seen as the adequate method by which to answer the question: 'Is a truly universal, objective, and transcultural enterprise ever possible or even desirable?' (Scholte 1999, 432). Although Dilthey, on a programmatic level, eventually solved the question affirmatively, he did so on original conceptual grounds that went philosophically far beyond the conventional concepts of science. These innovations will be treated presently after we have dealt more with the concern of anthropologists for the status of their knowledge.

If we take a closer look at how the inventors of the 'interpretive turn' recount the driving force behind their efforts, we are yet again struck with a peculiar analogy. That is, we can in both instances identify the same adversary that both movements set upon. While Dilthey had, above all, argued against the epistemological positions of positivism (Comte, Mill, Mach, Avenarius), as well as intellectualist versions of idealism (Descartes, Hume, Kant, neo-Kantianism), the late Geertz retrospectively rephrased his theoretical motives in allegorical terms: 'Wearied of slipping about on Kantian, Hegelian, or Cartesian iceflows, I wanted to walk' (2000, xii). Also, with reference to Victor Turner, the architect of the 'anthropology of experience', Durkheim (as an heir of Kantianism) and Radcliffe-Brown (as an associate of positivism) were mentioned as critical foils (Bruner 1986, 4).

Only recently were we reminded that one of the main achievements of Geertz's reassessment of anthropology since the early 1960s is meanwhile often discounted – his 'reconception of its subject matter' (Fuchs 2001, 26). Although the word 'revolution' (Swidler 1996, 301) does seem somewhat hyperbolic, it is much closer to what he had in mind than arguing for the replacement of an ethereal concept of culture with a new, semiotic one (as was indicated in his seminal essay 'Thick Description' [1973, 4–5]). Colson noticed with regret that the 'intellectual history' behind this project remained virtually obscured (1975, 638). As I see it, the revolutionary momentum in Geertz is to be seen in introducing conceptual schemes into anthropology that allowed for seeing various functions and spheres of social life, which so far have been treated independently, as interconnected. To provide some practical evidence of what I mean, I will quote from Geertz's conclusion in 'Person, Time, and Conduct in Bali':

> The close and immediate interdependency between conceptions of person, time, and conduct which has been proposed in this essay is, so I would argue, a general phenomenon, even if the particular Balinese form of it is peculiar to a degree, because such an interdependency is inherent in the way in which human experience is organized, a necessary effect of the conditions under which human life is lead. (1973, 408)

For a more general formulation of that idea, I can hint at another early essay where Geertz argued that his anthropological ancestors were, in their search for cultural universals, deluded by an underlying hinge on a '"stratigraphic" conception of the relations between the various aspects of human existence' (1973, 44). In that model, each sphere of human life was perceived as an independent layer that could, through scientific analysis, be separated from one another. Striving to overcome that archetype, Geertz opted for a 'synthetic' view, 'in which biological, psychological, sociological, and cultural factors can be treated as variables within unitary systems of analysis' (44). Here, we can mark out the most relevant link to Dilthey's attempt at theorizing those practical grounds of human scientific knowledge, thus far ignored by his contemporary epistemologists. Even though Dilthey eventually failed in laying down his ideas in a systematic philosophical form, among a few historians of ideas he has been recognized as the originator of a 'revolution within the general theory of knowledge and theory of action' (Krausser 1968). Dilthey's main epistemological theme was 'to understand various dimensions of the relationships between man and history, individual and society', as has been rightly measured by Jensen (1978, 424). In a similar vein to Geertz, Dilthey thereby worked from certain, namely *holistic*, ideas about the givenness of 'life' in human consciousness. They are perhaps best expressed in his unusual term 'life nexus', which presumes that life is never given to us as a compendium of a multitude of separate aspects, but only as a 'structural coherency', where functions such as 'willing', 'feeling' and 'thinking' are immediately and inextricably present. This notion of 'life' is holistic in that 'it *encompasses* our representations, evaluations, and purposes, and it exists *in the connection* of these constituents. And in each of these constituents, the acquired nexus exists in distinctive connections – in relationships of representations, in assessments of values, in the ordering of purposes' (Dilthey 2002, 102; my emphasis).

Against such interpretations, which emphasize Geertz's alleged distance from any human scientific agenda (Fabian 1984, 273), I would maintain that, regardless of any programmatic affinities, Geertz's key notions eventually hint back to late nineteenth-century theories of human science. As will be indicated in the next section, Dilthey's psychological account as well as his hermeneutics both rested on the holistic notion of life as a structural nexus. It indeed represented the starting point of his critical theory of knowledge altogether: 'Beginning from the universally grasped nexus of psychic life, (it) analyses the single members of this nexus, describes its component parts and connective functions, and examines them as thoroughly as it can' (1977, 57).

What I want to argue for is to recognize Dilthey not only as the inventor of an original, holistic, theory of structure (allowing sociologists like Simmel, Weber, Mannheim and others to ground their discipline upon a nontranscendentalist, non-Kantian bedrock), but also as a promoter (side by side with Dewey and Wittgenstein) of a synthetic approach in anthropology which would not be fixed on cognitive facets alone, but would systematically include emotional, volitive and ideational aspects of human experience. How he came to be relevant for anthropologists can probably best be grasped from Victor Turner's stipulation of a 'dramatical' approach to the anthropology of experience.

Jerome Bruner, who surmised Dilthey's importance to Turner, has, in tune with our proposition, pointed to the motif of refinement of the anthropological notion of 'experience', which accordingly would not only account for 'sense data [...], but also feelings and expectations' (1986, 4). Another statement uttered by the advocates of an anthropology of experience could be viewed as an almost literal translation of Dilthey's eminent declaration that 'the first givens are lived experiences' (2002, 102): 'Lived experience', Bruner writes, 'as thought and desire, as word and image, is the primary reality' (1986, 5). And also in Geertz we occasionally, but certainly not by chance, come upon programmatic references to the same belief that 'the answers to our most general questions [...] are to be found in the fine detail of lived life' (2000, xi). For several reasons related to the conceptual predilections of modern anthropology, in the words of another anthropologist of experience, 'lived experience is robbed of its vital significance' (Rosaldo 1986, 103).[2] Even at the close of his life, Turner could still only 'dream' about a 'liberated anthropology' that overcame the 'systematic dehumanizing of the human subjects' (1988, 72). Maybe even surprisingly to some philosophers, it was Dilthey with whom Turner associated the onset of a distinctive 'epistemological tradition' surpassing the 'Western tradition of philosophy' associated with 'Plato, Aristotle, Descartes, Hegel, Kant and all the anthropological structuralisms' (84). By the end of his search, Turner fathomed the potential of Dilthey's philosophy for his own revolution of anthropology. As can be grasped from the course of his adoption, his interest in Dilthey grew steadily. While he initially drew primarily upon Dilthey's concept of 'experience' (*Erleben*), Turner later acquainted himself with those parts of Dilthey's work which lie beyond standard book learning, such as his *Weltanschauungslehre*, and synthesized his new outlooks together with his earlier approaches into an inclusive 'anthropology of performance'.

What were the teachings Turner took from Dilthey for the benefit of grounding his dramatic approach of an anthropology of performance? Put in one sentence, the answer will probably be seen in the tenacious manner in which Dilthey followed his maxim to view all cultural products as originated in the complex structure of 'life'. Even abstract philosophical doctrines (e.g., metaphysical, religious and ethical dogmas), apparently rid of any 'psychological' and 'experiential' properties, were interpreted as fundamentally related to the 'psychic nexus'. World views, hence, were not to be seen as products of merely human cognitive reflection, but also of volition and affect, as Turner makes clear (1988, 90). Thus, they did not constitute 'theories', but rather 'lived experience'. To an anthropologist who felt 'always struck by cognitive reductionism as a kind of dehydration of social life' (1982, 91), such an outlook must have been appealing.

Turner, as is widely known and therefore shall only be restated summarily here, intended a reformation of anthropology on the footing of those parts of social life that tended to be widely ignored, namely the 'primordial and perennial agonistic mode' of 'social drama' (1982, 11). 'The social drama', Turner defines, 'is an eruption from the level surface of ongoing social life [...]. It is propelled by passions, compelled by volitions, overmastering at times any rational considerations' (1988, 90). In the same vein, he depicted any cultural performance – ritual, ceremony, theatre, etc. – as rooted in social drama (1982, 11) and as 'explanation and explication of life itself' (1982, 13). Through performance the invisible deep structures of a society became articulate, which is why Turner saw it as 'the proper finale of an experience' (1982, 13). Especially from Dilthey's drawings of *Erleben* in his psychological works, Turner was able to deduce a particular structural coherency pertaining to the process of dramatic experience and, in this way, anticipate any attack for founding anthropology on the uncontrollable, irrational and preposterous propensities of humanity. As he demonstrated, social drama was constituted by a sequential structure comprised in four phases: 'breach', 'crisis', 'redressive action' and 'reintegration'. Similar to Dilthey's analysis of world views that systematically correlate their dynamics with the underlying 'psychic structural nexus', Turner presupposed that the total of human experiential apparatus is involved in the process of social drama.

There is, however, another instance where anthropology was informed by Dilthey's rendering of the science/life complex. This time, we have to refer to his hermeneutics, to the category of 'meaning' and to how it was adopted by the founders of the 'interpretive turn'. What Turner deemed compelling in Dilthey's late work was his theory of meaning: 'It is only the category of *meaning* that enables us to conceive an intrinsic affinity between the successive events in life' (1988, 96). In his view, 'anthropological functionalism, whose aim is to state the conditions of social equilibrium among the components of a social system at a given time, cannot deal with meaning'. Apart from the functionalist coinings, Dilthey's version was marked as 'comprehensive' and 'inclusive' (97). From Turner's depiction it becomes evident that, unlike Geertz, he himself had no particular interest in linking anthropological method to hermeneutics. Although it must be left open to doubt whether he did full justice to Dilthey's proper theoretical intentions, Turner certainly was alive to the potential of these ideas for anthropological methodology. This hypothesis can only be determined after we look into the finer points of Dilthey's theory of structure.

2. Dilthey's Holistic Theory of Knowledge

Dan Sperber, some time ago, collected a list of names from contemporary anthropologists when asked for the philosophical forebears of their discipline. The list featured Durkheim, Weber, Marx, James, Wundt, Freud, Hobbes, Montesquieu, Hume and Kant (Sperber 1985, 3). But one could also add, on the basis of more recent statements, Rousseau (Diamond 1999, 410–12), Peirce (Kjaeholm, this volume), Wittgenstein (Geertz 2000, xi) and, as already indicated, Dilthey (Streck 2001, 528). Although such an inspection tells us more about the present than the actual past, it still gives an impression about the current craving for epistemological foundation.[3]

As we have seen from the reconstruction of the main themes of the 'interpretive turn', its initiators shared the movement away from those anthropological quarters which were allegedly entrenched in Kantian philosophy. Although it is rarely spelled out, the heritage of Kant on modern anthropology represents something like an unspoken common belief. In a comprehensive work, Raul Pertierra made an effort to trace Kant's legacy back to such eminent circles as the Durkheimian school, structuralism, British social anthropology (Evans-Pritchard, Leach, Douglas) and also American cultural anthropology 'from Boas to Geertz' (1985, 217). Yet such a broad view upon the matter hardly entails any information at all. For instance, to place hermeneutically inspired anthropological projects on the same epistemological ground as structuralist accounts is more perplexing than constructive. Moreover, such a vision would run counter to the self-positioning of authors like Geertz, Turner, Douglas and others. And finally, as shall be demonstrated now, Dilthey, who on a programmatic level declared himself to be siding with Kant, was first and foremost striving for novel criteria for the constitution and evaluation of human scientific knowledge that went beyond the limitations of Kantian (and neo-Kantian) expositions.

In this section I aim at sketching out the tenets of Dilthey's theory of knowledge, which I will mark as *holistic*. By confronting this with a (neo-) Kantian (i.e., *dualistic*) epistemology, I aim at an unbiased assessment of the theoretical potential of Dilthey's epistemological exertions, which until now were often obscured by preconceptions and misinterpretations.[4] As shall be seen, the methodological differences between Dilthey's epistemology on the one hand, and the Badian neo-Kantian approach proffered by Windelband and Rickert on the other, stem from irreconcilable theories of structure. A theory of structure, or rather *Strukturlehre*, as Dilthey termed it, includes and denotes the basic *ontological* and constituent properties upon which a particular theory of knowledge is erected. It also tells us about the mode of givenness of the constituent parts and their relation to each other. When it is referred to as a *holistic* versus a *dualistic* system of knowledge in the following narrative, we are thus alluding to those *axiomatic* features in contrast to *methodological* strategies.[5]

While Dilthey's theory of knowledge is based upon the ontological position (according to which 'inner' and 'outer experience' cannot be separated, but both pertain to one and the same 'psychic nexus'), Rickert, the head of the Southwest school of neo-Kantianism, sought to establish a novel ontological dualism by introducing the 'sphere of values' (*Wertssphäre*) as an autonomous domain of philosophy. By separating 'values' and 'reality' (*Wirklichkeit*) as two distinct ontological areas, he also introduced an original line of demarcation between philosophy on the one hand and empirical sciences on the other, while Dilthey is famed for founding both human and social sciences upon the 'nexus of lived experience, expression, and understanding' (Dilthey 2002, 109). Rickert himself denounced such premises as a 'metaphysics of immediate experience' (1999, 24), because it would not only reduce the world to a single substance, but, moreover, declare it unintelligible at the same time (23). Rickert instead wrote, 'Science has to be, at least, dualistic' (24).

Our rough demarcation between these two theories of knowledge might be confusing to those readers who have learned from the textbooks that Dilthey was in fact an originator of the methodological dualism between human and natural science. Also, he is regularly ranked as the offspring of an *ontological* divide between the two fields.[6] A closer look would, however, reveal that Dilthey himself rejected such a position and insisted that 'it is clear that the human sciences and natural sciences cannot be logically divided into two classes by means of two spheres of facts formed by them' (2002, 103). Thus, whatever the *methodological* consequences Dilthey drew, his actual *ontological* vantage point, as indicated above, was not dualistic in nature, but rather holistic. To understand the impact of this starting point on Dilthey's further conceptual and methodological ruminations and, hence, its centrality within Dilthey's theoretical architecture, we have to delve deeper into its core.

Here, we encounter the 'principle of phenomenality', which Dilthey deemed the premise of any modern philosophy. It stated, 'Whatever is there for us – because and insofar as it is there for us – is subject to the condition of being given in consciousness' (Dilthey 1989, 246–7). While this postulation can be read as a general concession to Kantianism, Dilthey intended to go beyond rationalist as well as empiricist distortions of this sentence. Where they erred, according to Dilthey, was in their assumption that 'the constitutive elements of reality were mere representations' (1990, 171; my translation). The effect had been a 'reduction of the full, whole human reality' (1982, 379; my translation). Dilthey's alternative solution to the epistemological question was instead built upon the perspective of the 'totality of the spiritual life' (GS xx, 128; my translation). In his famous preface to 'Introduction', Dilthey was more concrete about his goal: 'to explain even knowledge and its concepts in terms of the manifold powers of a being that wills, feels, and thinks' (1989, 50). Thus, the problem of epistemology was not only one of mere cognition, but contained at least two more aspects, namely volition and affect.[7] On that foundation, it was only consequent to conceive a human scientific version of psychology designed for the purpose of objectifying and analysing the complex psychic nexus in which all forms of human knowledge were grounded. As Dilthey pointed out very clearly, the 'descriptive psychology' was actually based upon 'the structure of life' (1982, 345) as its vantage point. Philosophy of life and hermeneutical psychology are in that form interconnected within the frame of Dilthey's theory. In the following extract from his 'Ideen', this trait is profiled further: 'The consideration of life itself requires that the potent reality of the soul *be described* in its wholeness, from its more humble to its highest possibilities' (Dilthey 1977, 40).

The Dilthey of the 1880s hence regarded psychology to provide the perfect means to discern the 'reality and objective accountability of inner experience' (Dilthey 1990, 280; my translation). Not only had the assiduous critique of Dilthey's psychology by Ebbinghaus, a leading German psychologist of the time, left the former with doubts about his approach, but in the 'Ideen' Dilthey finally had to concede that, somewhat contrary to his ambitious claims, the interrelational processes within the psychic structural nexus were not directly attainable, but had to be guessed from systematic observation of, for instance, ingenious personalities (1957, 180). Late in his life, he even noted, 'Psychic life is something unfathomable' (2002, 351). Inspired by the reading of Hegel, Brentano and Husserl, Dilthey afterwards developed a method that would premise on the awareness that inner experience could only be grasped through the mediation of their objectified forms, i.e., 'expressions'. This was, of course, the moment that hermeneutics became most relevant to Dilthey's theory of knowledge. To deflect those interpretations that install a stern dividing line between the psychologist Dilthey on the one hand and the late hermeneutist on the other, I can present a longer passage from the 'Aufbau' that indicates the continuity between both perspectives in Dilthey:

> The first givens are lived experiences. But, as I have attempted to show previously, they belong to a nexus that persists as permanent amidst all sorts of changes throughout the entire course of a life. What I have previously described as the acquired nexus of psychic life emerges from that foundation; it encompasses our representations, evaluations, and purposes, and it exists in the connection of these constituents. And in each of these constituents, the acquired nexus exists in distinctive connections – in relationships of representations, in assessments of values, in the ordering of purposes. We possess this nexus; it operates constantly in us. […] Thus it is always present and always efficacious, but without being conscious. (2002, 102)

What becomes ultimately clear from this text is that the 'structure of life' was not solely grounded in psychology. It also 'embraces the gestures, looks, and words by which human beings communicate, the enduring spiritual creations in which the depths of the creative artist are revealed to the one who apprehends them, and the constant objectifications of spirit in social formations'. More adequately, Dilthey spoke of the 'psychophysical life-unit' (2002, 108).

Now, we can discern what the crucial concepts of 'life' and 'structure' were actually about. From the posthumously published essay 'Leben und Erkennen' we find this somewhat redundant, but at the same time elucidating, depiction: 'Life is a structure. Structure is a vital connectedness' (1982, 355; my translation). Both notions are relational towards each other and cannot really be understood apart from one another. The obscure concept of 'life' did not hint at a metaphysical phenomenon, as in many contemporary populist versions, but instead denoted a concrete and empirical givenness. However, 'life' was not concrete in the sense that it could always be grabbed directly (as could works of art). Rather, it was existent as an all-embracing structured nexus which could only be disclosed 'by the detour of understanding' (2002, 108).[8]

When Dilthey finally based the human sciences upon the 'nexus of lived experience, expression and understanding' (109), this meant not only one single object ('life'), but likewise identified the mode of its givenness as a structural coherency within the human mind. The basic circular formation of human scientific knowledge as it is expressed in formulations such as 'Here life grasps life' (2002, 157) must, as I hope to have justified, be understood from the holistic theory of structure underlying Dilthey's general theory of knowledge. It is also in this light that we can correct a widespread misjudgement as regards his concept of 'understanding'. The textbooks typically place Dilthey among those theorists that bore a premodern, emphatic, mythical notion of 'understanding'. From our perspective one can clearly see that 'understanding' is warranted by the given premise that the subject and object of understanding both descended from the same basic nexus.

A rough outline of the methodological impetus of the outlined starting points shall now close this section. We can only hint at some aspects of the 'revolution within the general theory of knowledge' (Krausser 1968) that Dilthey's modelling of human and social scientific knowledge has brought about. Dilthey himself was quite aware of the challenge he had posed to his nonphilosophical colleagues. But also among contemporary philosophers did he cause some commotion. One of the often underrated implications of Dilthey's epistemological manoeuvres was the devaluation of epistemology as the principal foundational discipline. On the basis of his holistic concept of psychic nexus, Dilthey consequently inferred that cognition as one element of consciousness could not be determined separately, but only in correlation to other 'sides of psychic life'. In fact, Dilthey even went one step further in debasing the autonomy of human cognition by declaring 'knowledge from cognition' as secondary to 'knowledge from experiencing and understanding' (1957, 86; 1990, 327).[9] To put it plainly, 'thought cannot go behind life' (1931, 184; my translation). From here Dilthey went stubbornly on to introduce a novel discipline that would not only account for the reflexive capacities of human consciousness, but also for the other forms of experience: 'This analysis of the total content and nexus of the facts of consciousness, which makes possible a foundation for the system of the sciences, we call "self-reflection", in contrast to "theory of knowledge"' (1989, 268).

It is hardly surprising that the larger plan for a well-founded theory of human scientific knowledge required an elaboration of a multiplicity of very complex philosophical topics: 'epistemology, logic, methodology, theory of value, and ethics' (Dilthey 1931, 183).[10] In negative terms one could object that such an enlargement of the problem of knowledge did necessarily lead to an overstretching of Dilthey's intellectual strength.[11] But, although Dilthey thus bestowed his successors with a compelling, but likewise weighty, baggage, the positive effects outweigh the negative ones. The broad frame of his theory of structure (*Strukturlehre*) that was installed as the ground of human scientific knowledge allowed for the implementation of basic practical human features like emotions, imagination, remembrance, historicity and sociality – topics upon which seminal philosophical figures like Husserl, Scheler, Heidegger and Plessner have dwelled, as did social scientists like Weber, Simmel, Geertz and Turner.

In advancing a 'life-philosophical turn of transcendental philosophy' (Lieber 1974, 30; my translation) Dilthey must be viewed as the executor of a particular theoretical movement that, since the 1850s, strove for a novel '"organic conception of the world" prepared to concede the first and highest place in the sciences to the empirical' (Köhnke 1991, 13). For betraying the 'neo-Kantian consensus' (Rorty 1979, 163), Dilthey became the whipping boy for the various neo-Kantian factions. What is rarely acknowledged until today is his contribution to the establishment of a particularly *modern* notion of science. He not only replaced the traditional (Kantian) notion of the knowing subject with the 'whole person', but furthermore liberated the concept of 'experience' from intellectualist misrepresentations. In his own rendering, every form of knowledge was relative to its socio-historical basis as well as the respective angle from where it was judged. Thereby, Dilthey accounted for the consequence that such categorical strongholds of the classic concept of science like 'universal validity, truth and reality are only determined according to their sense' (1977, 35). He thus became the founder of a relativistic notion of science, despite the fact that he adamantly denounced this labelling. To the science of anthropology, which had been widely and over a long period of time been identified with relativism (Marcus and Fischer 1999, 20), and which refers to relativism as 'the most general and the most generally accepted theory' (Sperber 1985, 8), Dilthey must be attractive. Especially so because, as we have seen above, anthropology is still struggling with overcoming Kantian precepts.

3. The Potential of Dilthey for Current Anthropology

Taking stock of the metatheoretical debates in turn-of-the-century anthropology, one is left with the impression that, after the waning of the strong waves induced by the postmodern turn since the eighties and the concomitant refraining from metatheoretical queries whatsoever, we have by now entered an age of theoretical reconceptualization. Being of an utmost radical nature, the claims range from the 'reconsideration of the philosophical underpinnings of the discipline' (Hastrup 1995, 5) and the 'reconsideration of the whole project of ethnography' (Kuper 1999, 50) to the quest for 'a new anthropological imaginary' (Rabinow 1999, 18). What is remarkable here is the fact that the voices who call for a theoretical renovation of the epistemological foundations of the discipline cannot be reduced to a particular intellectual or generational group of scholars. Rather, it is a transgenerational phenomenon that can even include such exemplary figures as Victor Turner and Mary Douglas, who at the close of their academic careers did not shy away from metatheory, but even explored new epistemological paths. Laying bare some of the ideas and concepts that are currently at issue, I want to hint at such items where the anthropologist in need of advice can benefit from turning to Dilthey.

Above we have pointed to Geertz's labours for a refined notion of human experience which would account for the entirety of the human senses. Authors like Kuper and Hastrup again see the most foundational premises of anthropology compromised in the wake of the linguistic turn, which not only spurred a principal rethinking of the ethnographer's position, but also the category of the 'empirical' altogether (Hastrup 1995, 47). Merging some of the alternative propositions together in one picture, it boils down to denouncing any *dualist* conceptions – such as 'subject/object' (Moore 1996, 4; Fuchs 2001, 46), 'inside/outside' (Fuchs 2001, 46), 'mind/body' (Hastrup 1995, 85), 'culture/action' (85), 'self/other' (51), or 'science/world' (59) – which were at the root of the classic (positivist) notion of science. Fabian recently put it in a catchy instruction: 'We must maintain nonidentity (or negativity) in our conceptions of knowledge' (2001, 24).[12] The royal road to a more pertinent notion of anthropological knowledge is therefore regularly seen in 'a processual theory of knowledge' (24).[13] To quote another informant of a 'repatriated anthropology' (Hastrup 1995, 6): 'We should realise, and creatively exploit, our intricate implication in the world' (51).

What we can observe here appears not only as a restatement of theoretical preoccupations raised by anthropologists in the 1970s, but even a renewal of the debate Dilthey had already been engaged in over a century ago.[14] The disturbing impression that there has been no actual progress in the development of anthropological theory, brought about by its postmodern turn, is fostered by Henrietta Moore's conclusion that 'the debate collapsed into an unenlightened scuffle between the self-declared supporters of empiricism on the one hand and interpretation on the other' (1996, 2). What, thus, still remains to be done, not only in anthropological theory of course, but in all quarters of social theory, is the formulation of a concept of knowledge which is twisted neither by positivist nor by idealist presumptions. Dilthey's notion of 'experience', grounded upon a holistic theory of structure, was intended to avoid both frailties. Likewise, holism in recent debates stands for a formula that is trusted with the potentiality to overcome the fault lines created by dualist conceptions of social science. Perhaps the most optimistic application of epistemological holism[15] to future anthropology is indicated by Kirsten Hastrup: 'it is to acknowledge the fact that people live in real worlds, which may be made up, temporary, blurred, global, narcissist or whatever, but which nevertheless still ground them, connect them to other people, and make sense of the everyday as well as the unprecedented' (1995, 154).

The recent turn to varied philosophical concepts and figures (as indicated in the introduction to this volume) clearly manifests a longing for categories comprehensive of the complexities of human existence and 'nondual modes of thinking' (Giri, this volume). Dilthey himself, in his later works, tried to ground human scientific knowledge upon so-called 'categories of life' (in contrast to the Kantian *a priori* categories for the knowledge of nature). While he singled out such features of life as temporality, historicity, possibility, purpose, meaning, value and coherency, he never laid claim to abundance, since he believed that 'life' could not be captured by any taxonomy in principle. Still, his theoretical move chimes with recent aspirations in anthropological theory to incorporate such aspects of social life into the concept of experience that have not been included in its conceptual horizon so far.

One of the trails blazed in this development has already been brought in above, namely Turner's effort to fume his empirically deduced categories into a 'new synthesis' (Rochberg-Halton 1989, 210), an anthropology of performance which he rated 'an essential part of the anthropology of experience' (Turner 1982, 13). It leaves us with a feeling of discomfort that still today an ethnological programme that would plead for an acknowledgment of the role of passion and ecstatic experience as a condition of anthropological knowledge formation would be viewed as 'scandalizing', as its author himself imparts (Fabian 2001, 31). Fabian, taking up issues raised in present-day debates, reveals a rather detailed set of experiential facets that an epistemological reshaping of anthropology should take into account in the future. Against the keystone of postmodern anthropology to take culture for a text, he promotes a turn towards an 'ethnography of reading' (28) that would account for the communicative nature of ethnographic knowledge.[16] Another point Fabian hints at, mooted by anthropologists before, is the privileging of vision as the most reliable source of knowledge.[17] A 'critique of the visual bias' (30) would not only have to rehabilitate other neglected senses like taste, hearing and smell (and, worse yet, the body in general), but also point to how the focus on vision has served to preserve a particular (Western) type of knowledge since the age of Enlightenment.[18] Finally, Fabian, as already signified, opts for 'giving room in our theories of knowledge to passion and ecstasis' (32) in order to overcome the passivity inscribed in the knowing subject within the traditional model of knowledge.

Since the groundwork for such an enhancement of the anthropological subject matter has long been submitted by Dilthey's critique, any remodelling must therefore not be affiliated with a 'revolution' of the discipline whatsoever. His theory of structure as the common ground of any human scientific enterprise provided, at least, a general theoretical framework which provided for an incorporation of various 'categories of life'.

Lastly, I want to close by relating another current issue in anthropological metatheorizing to a basic motif of Dilthey's, namely the reconsideration of the conception of personhood. Mary Douglas (and her collaborator from political science) departed from a critical disquisition of the roots and usage of this category among varied social sciences to work towards a general 'critique of the social science' (as is indicated by the subtitle of the book; 1998). Douglas, herself a heroine of postwar anthropology, found herself, still at the close of the twentieth century, in a position to respond to the 'paradox that the social sciences' description of the self does not refer to a social being' (89). A similar observation led Geertz (1973, 360–411) and others, following his lead, to reflect upon anthropological (mis)renderings of personhood.[19] Telling the story of the pervasiveness and the career of the *homo oeconomicus* from its onset in Ricardo's analysis of agriculture and its constant reproduction in Western research, Douglas and Ney campaign for its replacement with a notion which accounts for the social and communicative nature of human being, or, as they express with an unintentional borrowing from Dilthey, the 'whole person'. 'No real blood flows in the veins of the knowing subject constructed by Locke, Hume, and Kant' (1989, 50), Dilthey notably charged against empiricist and idealist abbreviations of personhood. Conversely, he placed a programme of 'a developmental history proceeding from the totality of our being' (51). On the ground of the anthropological presumption that the meanings of 'personhood' vary among different types of societies, Douglas and Ney deliver four models of personhood derived from Douglas's well-known four-fold matrix of cultural bias. They are, respectively: 'unpredictable', 'robust', 'in need of structure' and 'under duress' (1998, 109). Leaving aside the discussion of this typology and the apposite question whether they did full justice to the entire fund of social scientific conceptions of personhood, this source again exhibits why it could be profitable to account for Dilthey as an anthropological ancestor.

Notes

1 As a telling document of the critical mood of that period, we can hint at the classic reader edited by Dell Hymes (1999).

2 Instead of confirming this argument by expanding upon the well-known imperfections of the most common anthropological schools, let me again hint at Bruner, who goes

so far as to conclude, 'We systematically remove the personal and the experiential in accordance with our anthropological paradigms' (1986, 9).

3 Knauft (1996, 20) is to a great degree correct in denoting the references to those great European thinkers as an invention of the 1960s theoretical movements in North American anthropology and, thus, a 'myth'.

4 The chief editors of the *Selected Works* concluded in their preface (to all volumes) that Dilthey's philosophy was 'still not adequately recognized' (I, vii).

5 Within the domain of philosophy of social science, the category of holism is generally marked off from atomism (or individualism). Both stand for contrary methodological explanatory strategies with regard to social phenomena. In my usage, the term denotes a particular ontological view of the structure of the world.

6 Already in his lifetime Dilthey was fiercely attacked for this feat. Among these critics, Rickert (1986, 12, 29, 70) and Weber (1968, 12) are the most prominent.

7 Dilthey referred to the 'three sides of psychic life: cognition, affect and volition' (1990, 162; my translation).

8 From its extension, Dilthey's concept of 'life' resembled Hegel's category of 'Spirit', which had also been designed as an almost universal entity that produced nature as well as history. Not coincidentally, both were subject to similar misinterpretations.

9 Most German idealists considered the two approaches, *Verstehen* and explanation, equally valid, though irreconcilable.

10 Rodi (1985) has reconstructed that Dilthey's general agenda had already been worked out as early as 1865 and basically not altered since.

11 Since Dilthey did not succeed in completing the second volume of his 'Introduction to the Human Sciences', which would have contained the actual epistemological foundation, he was and is still widely perceived as a failure.

12 Already in 'The Interpretation of Cultures' Geertz stated in the same vein: 'We need to look for systematic relationships among diverse phenomena, not for substantive identities among similar ones' (1973, 44).

13 See also Rosaldo (1989) and Fabian (1995, 48).

14 For similar reasons, Kuper formulated the view that anthropologists should be prepared to retreat to the 1970s (1999, 55).

15 We can distinguish the 'epistemological' form of holism, in the sense established here, from 'methodological' holism, which had been a topic of discussion before (Thornton 1992; Marcus 1998). In its latter fashion, holism is rather taken for a rhetorical strategy.

16 See Tedlock (1983).

17 See also Stoller (1989, 37–98) and Hastrup (1995, 47).

18 Again, we must cite Stoller's pivotal contribution (1989).

19 See the broad discussion laid out by Marcus and Fischer (1999, 45–76).

References

Brown, Richard Harvey. 2005. 'Dilthey, Wilhelm'. In *Encyclopedia of Social Theory*, vol. 1, edited by George Ritzer, 201–3. Thousand Oaks: Sage.

Bruner, Edward M. 1986. 'Experience and its Expressions'. In *The Anthropology of Experience*, edited by Victor W. Turner and Edward M. Bruner, 3–30. Urbana: University of Illinois Press.

Colson, Elizabeth. 1975. Review of Clifford Geertz: 'Interpretations of Culture'. *Contemporary Sociology* 4 (6): 637–8.

Diamond, Stanley. 1999. 'Anthropology in Question'. In *Reinventing Anthropology*, edited by Dell Hymes, 401–29. New York: Random House.

Dilthey, Wilhelm. 1931. *Gesammelte Schriften VIII: Weltanschauungslehre: Abhandlungen zur Philosophie der Philosophie*. Stuttgart: Teubner.

_____. 1957. *Gesammelte Schriften V: Die Geistige Welt: Einleitung in die Philosophie des Lebens*. Stuttgart: Teubner.

_____. 1968. *Gesammelte Schriften VI: Einleitung in die Philosophie des Lebens: Abhandlungen zur Poetik, Ethik und Pädagogik*. Stuttgart: Teubner.

_____. 1982. *Gesammelte Schriften XIX: Grundlegung der Wissenschaften vom Menschen, der Gesellschaft und der Geschichte: Ausarbeitungen und Entwürfe zum zweiten Band der Einleitung in die Geisteswissenschaften (ca. 1870–1895)*. Göttingen: Vandenhoeck and Ruprecht.

_____. 1989. *Introduction to the Human Sciences*. Princeton: Princeton University Press.

_____. 1990. *Gesammelte Schriften XX: Logik und System der philosophischen Wissenschaften: Vorlesungen zur erkenntnistheoretischen Logik und Methodologie (1864–1903)*. Göttingen: Vandenhoeck and Ruprecht.

_____. 1996. *Hermeneutics and the Study of History*. Princeton: Princeton University Press.

_____. 2002. *The Formation of the Historical World in the Human Sciences*. Princeton: Princeton University Press.

Douglas, Mary and Steven Ney. 1998. *Missing Persons: A Critique of the Social Sciences*. Berkeley: University of California Press.

Fabian, Johannes. 1995. 'Ethnographic Misunderstanding and the Perils of Context'. *American Anthropologist*, New Series 97 (1): 41–50.

_____. 2001. *Anthropology with an Attitude: Critical Essays*. Stanford: Stanford University Press.

Fabian, Johannes et al. 1984. 'The Thick and the Thin: On the Interpretive Theoretical Program of Clifford Geertz' (and Comments and Reply). *Current Anthropology* 25 (3): 261–80.

Fuchs, Martin. 2001. Der Verlust der Totalität: Die Anthropologie der Kultur. In *Kulturwissenschaft: Felder einer prozeßorientierten wissenschaftlichen Praxis*, edited by Heide Appelsmeyer and Elfriede Billmann-Mahecha, 18–53. Velbrück: Weilerswist.

Geertz, Clifford. 1973. *The Interpretation of Cultures: Selected Essays*. New York: Basic Books.

_____. 1974. 'From the Native's Point of View: On the Nature of Anthropological Understanding'. In *Bulletin of the American Academy of Arts and Sciences* 28 (1): 26–45.

_____. 2000. *Available Light: Anthropological Perspectives on Philosophical Topics*. Princeton: Princeton University Press.

_____. 2005. Commentary, in *Clifford Geertz by his Colleagues*, edited by Richard A. Shweder and Byron Good, 108–24. Chicago: University of Chicago Press.

Hastrup, Kirsten. 1995. *A Passage to Anthropology: Between Experience and Theory*. London: Routledge.

Hymes, Dell, ed. 1999. *Reinventing Anthropology*. New York: Random House.

Jensen, Bernard Eric. 1978. 'The Recent Trend in the Interpretation of Dilthey'. *Philosophy of the Social Sciences* 8: 419–38.

Knauft, Bruce M. 1996. *Genealogies for the Present in Cultural Anthropology*. London: Routledge.

Köhnke, Klaus Christian. 1991. *The Rise of Neo-Kantianism: German Academic Philosophy between Idealism and Positivism*. Cambridge: Cambridge University Press.

Krausser, Peter. 1968. *Kritik der endlichen Vernunft: Wilhelm Diltheys Revolution der allgemeinen Wissenschafts- und Handlungstheorie*. Frankfurt: Suhrkamp.

Kuper, Adam. 1999. *Among the Anthropologists: History and Context in Anthropology*. London: Athlone Press.

Lieber, Hans-Joachim. 1974. 'Die deutsche Lebensphilosophie und ihre Folgen'. In *Kulturkritik und Lebensphilosophie: Studien zur deutschen Philosophie der Jahrhundertwende*, edited by Hans-Joachim Lieber, 106–27. Darmstadt: Wissenschaftliche Buchgesellschaft.

Marcus, George E. 1998. 'Imagining the Whole: Ethnography's Contemporary Efforts to Situate Itself'. In *Ethnography through Thick and Thin*, edited by George E. Marcus, 33–56. Princeton: Princeton University Press.

Marcus, George E. and Michael M. J. Fischer, eds. 1999. *Anthropology as Cultural Critique: An Experimental Moment in the Human Sciences*. Chicago: University of Chicago Press.

Misch, Clara, ed. 1933. *Der junge Dilthey: Ein Lebensbild in Briefen und Tagebüchern 1852–1870*. Leipzig: Teubner.

Moore, Henrietta L. 1996. 'The Changing Nature of Anthropological Knowledge'. In *The Future of Anthropological Knowledge*, edited by Henrietta L. Moore, 1–15. London: Routledge.

Pertierra, Raul. 1985. 'Kant and Social Anthropology'. *Dialectical Anthropology* 9: 217–31.

Rabinow, Paul. 1999. 'Iceland: The Case of a National Human Genome Project'. *Anthropology Today* 15 (5): 14–18.

Rabinow, Paul and William M. Sullivan. 1979. 'The Interpretive Turn: Emergence of an Approach'. In *Interpretive Social Science: A Reader*, edited by Paul Rabinow and William M. Sullivan, 1–21. Berkeley: University of California Press.

Rickert, Heinrich. 1999. *Philosophische Aufsätze*. Tübingen: Mohr.

Rochberg-Halton, Eugene. 1989. Afterword, in Victor W. Turner, *Das Ritual: Struktur und Antistruktur*, 198–213. Frankfurt: Campus.

Rodi, Frithjof. 1985. 'Diltheys Kritik der historischen Vernunft: Programm oder System?'. *Dilthey-Jahrbuch für Philosophie und Geschichte der Geisteswissenschaften* 3: 140–65.

Rorty, Richard. 1979. *Philosophy and the Mirror of Nature*. Princeton: Princeton University Press.

Rosaldo, Renato. 1986. 'Ilongut Hunting as Story and Experience'. In *The Anthropology of Experience*, edited by Victor W. Turner and Edward M. Bruner, 97–138. Urbana: University of Illinois Press.

———. 1989. *Culture and Truth: The Remaking of Social Analysis*. Berkeley: University of California Press.

Scholte, Bob. 1999. 'Toward a Reflexive and Critical Anthropology'. In *Reinventing Anthropology*, edited by Dell Hymes, 430–57. New York: Random House.

Sperber, Dan. 1985. *On Anthropological Knowledge: Three Essays*. Cambridge: Cambridge University Press.

Stoller, Paul. 1989. *The Taste of Ethnographic Things: The Senses in Anthropology*. Philadelphia: University of Pennsylvania Press.

Streck, Bernhardt. 2001. 'Wilhelm Maximilian Wundt: Elemente der Völkerpsychologie'. In *Hauptwerke der Ethnologie*, edited by Christian F. Feest and Karl-Heinz Kohl, 524–31. Stuttgart: Kröner.

Swidler, Anne. 1996. Review of Clifford Geertz, 'Interpretations of Culture'. *Contemporary Sociology* 25 (3): 299–302.

Tedlock, Dennis. 1983. *The Spoken Word and the Work of Interpretation*. Philadelphia: University of Pennsylvania Press.

Thornton, Robert J. 1992. 'The Rhetoric of Ethnographic Holism'. In *Reading Cultural Anthropology*, edited by George E. Marcus, 15–33. Durham, NC: Duke University Press.

Turner, Victor W. 1982. *From Ritual to Theater: The Human Seriousness of Play*. New York: PAJ
    Publications.
_____. 1986. 'Dewey, Dilthey and Drama: An Essay in the Anthropology of Experience'.
    In *The Anthropology of Experience*, edited by Victor W. Turner and Edward M. Bruner,
    33–44. Urbana: University of Illinois Press.
_____. 1988. *The Anthropology of Performance*. New York: PAJ Publications.

Chapter 10

MALINOWSKI AND PHILOSOPHY[1]

Peter Skalník

Bronisław Malinowski, the founder of modern social anthropology, was a philosopher by way of his tertiary education at Jagiellonian University in Kraków. He was influenced by Friedrich Nietzsche on the one hand and Ernst Mach on the other. At the height of his brilliant career, he enjoyed a lengthy exchange of views with Bertrand Russell. This chapter will explore the place of philosophy in his innovative contribution, with special emphasis on the relationship between philosophy on the one hand and science, religion, culture, civilization, war and state on the other. The tension between Malinowski's emphasis on empirical research and his quest for theory building is well reflected in all his writings. Philosophy played an essential part in Malinowski's anthropology, but at the same time Malinowski never attempted to philosophize anthropology and should be seen as opposed to his lifelong friend Stanisław Ignacy Witkiewicz ('Witkacy'), whose prolific creativity in art and literature was a strong philosophical parallel.

In Kraków, where Malinowski was born in 1884 and where he attended Sobieski Grammar School and the Jagiellonian University, philosophy occupied an important place in his education. In fact, Rev. Stefan Pawlicki, an outstanding philosopher at the turn of the nineteenth and twentieth centuries, taught Malinowski both at Sobieski and Jagiellonian. Professor Pawlicki's influence on Malinowski was such that, after first studying mathematics and physics, he chose philosophy as his main subject and wrote his doctoral thesis *On the Principle of the Economy of Mind* under Pawlicki's supervision. As Kubica illustrates, Malinowski's conversion happened in the academic year 1904–1905 when, besides the philosophical seminar led by Pawlicki, he attended another philosophical seminar by Maurycy Straszewski, lectures on ethics, introductory philosophy, logics and dialectics and the philosophy of Friedrich Nietzsche.[2] That year he also studied psychology, pedagogy and philology, along with mathematics (among the lectures was theory of analytic functions).

In the next academic year, Malinowski's last at Jagiellonian, he further pursued his philosophical interests (Kubica 1988, 103; Flis 1988, 107). His PhD thesis was completed and his final examination in philosophy and physics took place in 1906. All evaluated with highest honours, but Malinowski was not awarded the degree until 1908, having spent the time in between with his mother in the Canary Islands in order to improve his bad health. The ceremony took place *sub auspiciis Imperatoris* (under the supervision of the emperor – Franz Josef I of Austria-Hungary) in the Collegium Novum of Jagiellonian University on 7 October 1908.[3]

His doctoral thesis was based on a critical reading of Ernst Mach and Richard Avenarius. While Pawlicki was a positivist, Maurycy Straszewski, the other philosophy professor in Kraków, was an empirio-criticist in the vein of Mach and Avenarius. Pawlicki, however, respected scientific findings and also moved towards empiricism. It is indeed impossible to know who of the two professors was more influential on Malinowski's decision to write his thesis on the economy of mind.[4] Characteristically, Malinowski's thesis was never published in his lifetime. It appeared in print only in 1980 in Polish (Malinowski 1980) and 1993 in English (Malinowski 1993). It is therefore necessary to trace its influence on Malinowski's anthropology by searching through all his oeuvre and to question the philosophical ingredients in it. Aside from philosophy proper, the philosophical influence can be traced especially in Malinowski's writing on the methodology of research, sociology, religion, culture and civilization. The two last items are expressed in a particular historiosophy of Malinowski. In the rest of this chapter I will go eclectically through several of these concrete points, as follows:

1) Malinowski's philosophical background: empirio-criticism,
2) Malinowski's functionalism, its influence on sociology and other sciences,
3) Malinowski and philosophy of language (Wittgenstein),
4) Malinowski and religion,
5) Malinowski and ethics,
6) Malinowski and psychoanalysis,
7) Malinowski's philosophy of culture,
8) Malinowski's political philosophy.

It was Ernest Gellner (1988, 164–94), both philosopher and anthropologist, who pointed out that Malinowski was facing the same question as the rest of Europe's modern minds: how to make sense of the gap between modern Europeans and their own preindustrial and premodern past on the one hand and the civilizational gulf between modern Europe and the rest of the world on the other, which in his time became evident with increasing intensity.

The latter appeared to modern Europeans to be as backward as their own past. Gellner operates with two ways of grasping of the modern chasm: Hegel's historical approach and the positivist approach. The former preaches a teleology of history (a historic plan) achieved by mechanisms residing inside the world and not by the external forces of God or similar.

The positivist approach, on the contrary, put forward knowledge as the prime mover, not history. Because of the priority of knowledge, the modern Western cognitive method is superior to both premodern European and non-European cognitive styles. 'Positive' spirit is the highest and most powerful of the methods of gaining knowledge. The question is why. Gellner stresses experience (in Latin *empiria*) as the sovereign tool of knowledge, superior to any transcendental explanations. The impartiality of the empiricist option clears the road for a cosmopolitan view of humankind. Besides, the historical approach was laden with the quest for reconstruction as the key to the explanation of the present.

Gellner argues that Malinowski's predicament was resolved by his adherence to the teachings of Ernst Mach because Mach advocated the explanation of the world as made out of observable facts. Knowledge does not speculate about the world, it is, in Andrzej Flis's words, 'active adaptation, a practical-vital activity', 'a response to biological human needs', 'attained by the least effort' (Flis 1988, 115). This Gellner calls the 'Pragmatist Assumption', which complements positivism. Gellner concludes that Malinowski's thought 'was indeed pervaded, even dominated, by *both* the Positivist and the Pragmatist Assumptions' (Gellner 1988, 175). The response was Malinowski's anthropology, whose synchronist functionalism is its philosophical base, aimed against the fragmentary and atomistic Frazerian study of survivals. Another philosophical base for Malinowski was holism. Malinowski lumped together these philosophical elements so that they enable one to see humankind as a biological and social whole. Malinowski, then, had established anthropology as the integral science of humanity.

But Malinowski did not have a specialized biological education; he was never educated in biology, zoology or physical anthropology. I would maintain that his main concern was not so much the constitution of a multifield anthropology straddling between biological, cultural and social directions, but the creation of a new anthropology based on a different philosophical base, that of a 'functional view of cognition' borrowed from Mach (Gellner 1988, 177).

It is, of course, not incidental that the 'second positivism' of Malinowski's student years coexisted with modernism, in Poland a special brand called 'Young Poland'. And as mentioned above, Malinowski was under its spell so much so that he decided to devote his life to (positivist) science rather than to art. This is an apparent paradox. His friendship with Stanisław Ignacy Witkiewicz, better known as 'Witkacy', was decisive here because the multifaceted artistic talent of Witkacy functioned as an unwitting challenge to Malinowski. In a way, the more the two knew each other, the more Malinowski tried to escape from Witkacy's influence (Skalník 1995). The diaries of Malinowski, as compared to some of Witkacy's writings, are ample evidence for this divergent development, which reached its climax in a row over loyalties to scholarship and the fatherland. The news of the outbreak of World War I reached Malinowski and Witkacy while they were in Australia. While Malinowski, an Austrian subject, chose to proceed with his anthropological research and departed for New Guinea, Witkacy, who came to Australia with Malinowski as his artist-assistant, decided to uphold his duty as a Russian citizen and left to fight on the front (against Germany and Austria). Witkacy opposed Malinowski philosophically and ethically. He was opposed to empirio-criticism and already in his 'Unproductive Dreams' ('Marzenia improduktywa', in Witkiewicz 1977) he 'attacked the monistic vision of reality and Mach in what was a vicious and rather dilettante attack' (Flis 1988, 114). Witkacy, in one of his plays written after the break with Malinowski, attacks Malinowski's scientific/scientistic theory of religion. Through the mouth of the clan chief Aparura, Witkacy charged: 'It does not matter that Malinowski, this damned Anglicized, uncontrollable dreamer, has investigated us. Totems are true, no matter what scientists write about them' (Witkiewicz 1972, 553). Flis explained that, 'irrespective of how prosaic needs may be satisfied by religion [...], it constitutes a sphere of spiritual experiences irreducible to psycho-physical needs. No interpretation or description can shake this autonomy' (1988, 124–5).

The moral, philosophical dilemma continued after World War I. When after the war the renewed Poland, whose citizenship Malinowski accepted, called him to a professorship in Kraków, he declined with reference to his duty towards science. He wanted to finish writing up the results of his research in New Guinea and to keep a modest lectureship at the London School of Economics, as that job gave him enough free time and financial means to concentrate on his writing. Much later, Malinowski departed for a sabbatical year to the US as a British citizen in 1938, but once Poland and Britain entered war with Germany he decided to stay in the US in order to pursue his career and especially to finish his lifetime ambition, a book on the 'scientific theory of culture'.[5] Witkacy returned from the Russian front and from 1917 stayed back in Poland while continuing to write plays and novels, and even published a philosophical treatise. He became a famous, though controversial, modernist painter. Over the years he tried to continue corresponding with Malinowski (Witkiewicz 1981), but the 'Bronio' of their youth was now

Professor Malinowski, who did not share any more the world of his erstwhile bosom friend. Witkacy committed suicide when he learned that Soviet Russia had invaded Poland on 18 September 1939.

In the case of Malinowski, his self-imposed vocation as a scientist – or more precisely his ambition to become the prime agent of the anthropologization of ethnology in Britain and to create a new scientific discipline of social or sociocultural anthropology – had preference above all. Perhaps paradoxically, Malinowski's empiricist and positivist response to his inability to become a famous author or artist did not diminish his quest for artistic success. He still cherished art above science and tried to write his monographs, chapters, forewords and articles in a literary style. In this he is a precursor of Clifford Geertz, who some fifty years later came up with the suggestion that anthropology is a text, a sort of new literary genre.

The explanation of this lasting tension in Malinowski's anthropology is also philosophical because positivism went along with modernism, at least in Poland. As Jan Jerschina (1988, 128–48) shows persuasively, Malinowski's intellectual formation took place in the last two prewar decades, when positivist and modernist ideas amalgamated. Similar to nineteenth-century Polish romanticism, they were a rejection of Hegel's philosophy of history, which indirectly denied the Poles, at that time without their own statehood, both national subjectivity and history. In the Polish Romantic-modernist vision, in contrast to Hegel, the state was to be subordinated to the nation as a cultural community, to be in the service of the people. Malinowski was familiar with both Hegel's philosophy and the Polish poets such as Mickiewicz, Słowacki and Norwid, who were highly valued by the modernist literati and artists. We will see that the philosophy of history and political philosophy were to play an undeniably major role in Malinowski's anthropological writings following Hitler's seizing of power in Germany.

Jerschina argued that it is impossible to determine which of the two – positivism and modernism – was more decisive in the formation of Malinowski's personality. Polish modernism was marked by the critique of Hegel's panlogism and his hierarchical philosophy of history; by historiosophic pessimism (which included decadentism and perception of the decline of modern [European] civilization); interest in the essence of culture as an autonomous entity embracing folk culture, Eastern cultures and aestheticism; fascination with natural beauty, sex and eroticism; a focus on the individual as a monad acting independently in history and society; interest in religion, mysticism, myth and magic; humanism; and democratism, which rejects aristocratic cosmopolitanism, but expounds cosmopolitanism, which appreciates cultural values of others and rejects racism (Jerschina 1988, 130). Is this a list of Malinowski's inclinations and values?

Yes and no. Yes, in the sense that he was well aware of these traits of Polish modernism, and no, in that he did not apply them unreservedly. If yes, then he was selective in putting different emphases on each trait in his work and life. For example, if we analyse his diaries we will identify many traits of Polish modernism in them. There is pessimism, vanity, national nostalgia and even some racist remarks. But we would hardly find any references to democratism, patriotism, cosmopolitanism or an aversion to Hegel's historical conception. They will be found in his academic writing, especially those texts which were written after the National Socialists took power in Germany. At any rate I would not see Malinowski as an agent of Polish modernism. Jerschina concluded that more of Malinowski's theoretical and methodological ideas 'were rooted in modernism than were based on the positivist method, categories, way of thinking and value system' (1988, 145).

Another question, however, is to what extent was Malinowski's sociocultural anthropology a manifestation of modernity and tolerant, if not altogether egalitarian, cosmopolitanism. Here I would argue that Malinowski was very much part of the cosmopolitan modernity. By his pioneering field researches in Oceania and Africa and his theories of various aspects of human behaviour, he globalized the perception of society and culture by proving that 'savages' are part of the modern world.

The evaluators of Malinowski's contribution to anthropology and sociology often dismiss his theoretical input. My position is close to Gellner's in that I firmly believe Malinowski has never been usurped as the archpriest of social anthropology; his position as a founder of the discipline is continuously matched by the inspiration it has exerted on generations of anthropologists since. How many of us today spend our precious time studying philosophical currents such as positivism, empirio-criticism, scientism, pragmatism, holism? They may be part of the history of human thought, yet we (at least those who are interested in authentic knowledge) still insist on spending long periods of time in the field collecting data about what people do and think they do. We may be not aware of how past philosophy influences us, yet we want to know how isolated data make sense, what is the purpose of this or that cultural feature, to gain as complete picture as possible.

Indeed, today we are more aware of the intricacies of producing data as part of the process of cultural construction – we are much more aware of contradictions and conflicts which equally 'well' contribute to the functioning of the social whole, as do the benign cultural features. The wholes are not bounded any more, nevertheless they are 'semiautonomous social fields' to follow Sally Falk Moore. But there would be no such concepts were it not for Malinowski, who first clearly formulated his crude but essential theoretical and methodological functionalism. Science is a continuous process of overcoming previous truths and proposing new ones. In anthropology this is doubly valid.

Malinowski instigated a revolution, saying ethnology was to be substituted by anthropology, which not only suggests new theories of society, but does it by an altogether different method. This method includes synchronicism, which means that the data collected about the present are supreme above those which relate to the past. Synchronicism is closely related to Mach's empirio-criticism, discussed at length in Malinowski's 1906 dissertation. It is part and parcel of the function conceived as the unit of least effort! This is the meaning of 'economy of mind' for anthropology and other social sciences, of which Malinowski at the time of writing the thesis had as yet no certain idea. However, economy of mind concerns all science (i.e., scientific knowledge as such and its universal validity and applicability). Thornton, in his discussion of Malinowski's thesis and his vast review of Frazer's *Totemism and Exogamy*, indirectly points out that both Malinowski via Mach's positivism and Frazer through his comparative study of texts agree that the common denominator of science is practical and intellectual objectification of nature which works, that is, which is true (cf. Thornton and Skalník 1993, 27–8).

It is intriguing that Mach in his popularizing science stressed the vital importance of comparison in science and thought of ethnology as being an eminent comparative discipline (Mach 1898, 238–9; cf. Thornton with Skalník 1993, 28–9). Andrzej Flis, a contemporary Cracovian philosopher, concludes that Malinowski drew mostly on these three philosophical sources: empirio-criticism (mostly Mach), scientism (Pearson) and neo-Kantianism. Mach's philosophy influenced Malinowski in that he searched for functional explanations rather than causal ones and that he strived for an understanding of culture. The concept of function was for Malinowski the main tool of science. From its mathematical meaning Malinowski proceeded to fructify the notion of function by psychological ingredients in his studies on primitive beliefs and forms of social order (Malinowski 1915), finally arriving at the functional theory of culture and society. Flis further argues that Malinowski views scientific knowledge as 'a practical activity of life' which is 'an instrument of the satisfaction of human needs' (Flis 1988, 126). Thus he implements Mach's thesis on the instrumental character of science and creates his own brand of theory of culture. We will come back to the philosophical foundations of Malinowski's 'scientific theory of culture' later in this chapter.

Let us proceed with Flis's arguments about Mach's influence on Malinowski. Flis believes that Malinowski was inspired by Mach, but that it is impossible to find 'empirio-critical or positivist theses' in the functionalism of Malinowski's anthropology. 'Malinowski adopted little, but transformed much', writes Flis (1988, 126), and points out the 'metaphysical' explanations at which Malinowski allegedly arrives in his *Coral Gardens and Their Magic* (1935) and *A Scientific Theory of Culture* (1944). Flis also objects to branding Malinowski as empiricist because not everything in Malinowski's work boils down to experience, and quotes from Malinowski's review of Frazer's *Totemism and Exogamy*: 'The fewer hypothetical assumptions and postulates to be found in a given description of facts, the greater the value of this description, but because every precise description of facts requires precise concepts, and these can be provided only by theory, every description and classification must thus be based of necessity on a theoretical formulation' (Flis 1988, 126; quoted from Ludwik Krzyżanowski's translation in Thornton and Skalník 1993, 127).

Gellner shows quite persuasively that Malinowski was a 'Zeno of Kraków' who showed that the present controls the past, whether in Europe or in the Trobriands. 'The past is another country [...] forever hidden and inaccessible' (Gellner 1988, 178). Malinowski's ahistoricism or synchronicism relies on four pillars, one of which, according to Gellner, is the Zenonic argument that 'any system is responsive only to contemporary constraints, which can and do act on it, but it cannot be responsive to the past or the future. [...] Hence any system can only be explained synchronically' (185). Gellner sees the real achievement of synchronist functionalism in 'its doctrine of stability', which required anthropological fieldworkers 'to account for the present situation in terms of contemporary constraints' and '*obliged them to treat stability as a problem which requires explanation*' (187, Gellner's emphasis). Thus, Malinowski's great discovery is that the present should be explained by the present, in the same vein as Durkheim's tenet that the social should be explained by the social (185). Gellner concluded that the explanatory rigour of anthropology was immensely raised by Malinowski's 'synchronistic approach' (188).

Let us now look more closely at Malinowski's 'scientific theory of culture'. Malinowski placed 'culture' very high on his conceptual hierarchy. The only competitor, as I have tried to show, was 'science'. On 5 January 1910 Malinowski wrote to his tutor Pawlicki: 'I am very keen on going to England for at least a year, for there, it seems to me, culture has reached its highest standard' (Ellen et al. 1988, 204). Jerschina explained this keen interest in culture:

> Some theoretical conclusions, notably his interest in the biological and economic foundations of culture, and some aspects of methodology, are positivist in origin. His concept of culture as a relatively autonomous entity, his anthropocentrism, the wide scope of anthropological interest, his anti-Hegelianism, his whole underlying meta-theory, all of this is modernist in origin. (1988, 146)

There is a hidden controversy behind Malinowski's lifetime ambition to create a truly scientific theory of culture. On the one hand there is hardly any anthropologist who would deny that Malinowski's revolutionary feat consisted in the method of long-term intensive fieldwork. On the other his theoretical contribution about culture, a concept which he consistently put forward throughout his life, has been belittled or even dismissed. I think that Malinowski's culturology, if we may use such a term here, should receive more attention and be put into the context of his overall oeuvre. An additional paradox rears its head here: Malinowski is known as one of the founders of social anthropology. Yet his main thrust was to come to grips with culture as its basic concept. That, of course, put him into contrast with Radcliffe-Brown, the other founder, who was far from any engagement with the theory of culture and who saw anthropology as comparative sociology or the science of social systems.

Re-reading Malinowski today is especially needed if we want to understand better why Malinowski remains our guru. Andrzej Paluch rightly stresses that Malinowski 'viewed anthropology as a science of culture'. In saying so, however, Paluch (and I hasten to join him in this) means that Malinowski first submitted to criticism the existing theories of culture before he posited his own. This he did in a review article on Frazer's *Totemism and Exogamy*, published in Polish during his early London years and in his review of Durkheim's *Les formes élémentaires de la vie religieuse*. In the first pages of the review article, after praising Frazer for various abilities and results, Malinowski stresses that a 'host of scholars' armed with Frazer's 'splendidly collected material […] will perhaps often be able to formulate more precise and more scientific theories than the original author' (1993, 125). He then declares unequivocally that 'the theories set forth by Professor Frazer in the present work cannot stand up to serious criticism. […] They are extremely interesting from a methodological point of view because they possess all the advantages and defects of the English anthropological school.' Further, he claims that Frazer's writing on totemism suffers from 'lack of method' (126–7). Malinowski's overt target is evolutionism on the one hand and implicitly positivism on the other:

> The fewer hypothetical assumptions and postulates to be found in a given description of facts, the greater the value of this description, but because every precise description of facts requires precise concepts, and these can be provided only by theory, every description and classification must thus be based of necessity on a theoretical formulation. (1993, 126–7)

Malinowski then proceeds with a description of totemic beliefs and ceremonies, and concludes with a 'fundamental reproach' of Frazer's method, as he does not give us a clear and objective picture of the state of things, independently of any hypotheses or theories. On the contrary, when describing facts Frazer constantly employs concepts drawn from purely hypothetical and, as it were, personal assumptions and dogmas. He makes no clear demarcation between facts and inferences from facts; there are no clearly noted assumptions. (1993, 135)

Instead, Malinowski reveals his own position, in a way a philosophical view of science, no doubt influenced by Mach's empirio-criticism:

> [...] the aims of exact science do not consist in constructing theories and hypotheses concerning areas beyond the limits of experience, but rather in an exact and accurate description of facts. The interest of an exact scientist should focus on understanding and penetrating the mechanism and essence of social phenomena as they exist at present and are accessible to observation, and not in order that these phenomena should serve as a key to solving the riddle of a prehistoric past about which we cannot know anything empirically. (1993, 140)

And he continues with his credo:

> All of this would be a banal truth for a natural scientist, but in the sociological sciences the interesting but inexact chats about the origins of various social institutions and beliefs should be replaced at last by less attractive but more exact investigations of sociological laws. [...] Methodological philosophizing without a basis in facts is as far off the mark as the uncritical collecting of facts and the construction of often nonessential theories. (1993, 140–41)

What is to be pointed out is Malinowski's identification with 'exact science', which studies social phenomena 'at present' and excludes from the realm of science anything which does not originate from empirical observation. Thus Malinowski's emphasis on the present as the departing point of any social research, what I would call 'presentism' (for which he would become famous at the height of his career), is clearly discernible in 1910 when he began his studies of sociology in London. Anthropology (although he does not operate with the term as yet) is part of the 'sociological sciences', which investigate 'sociological laws' and are opposed to 'methodological philosophizing' and 'uncritical collecting of facts'.

Going into the question of language (as part of culture), Malinowski is contrasted with Wittgenstein. It was again Gellner, in his posthumously published book, poetically entitled *Language and Solitude* (1998), who uses Malinowski's method and philosophy in order to prove once again that Wittgenstein's language philosophy leads us astray into the loneliness of circular arguments. The breakthrough, of course, is fieldwork and the study of concrete languages as specimens for the proof that learning of 'native' language gives insight into the 'native point of view' (Malinowski 1935, 326). Language is part of the broader language of culture and evidence of the philosophical levels that each concrete language and culture displays (Malinowski 1923). But, not being a specialist on language, I choose to refrain from further comment.

A more complex situation obtains with Malinowski and psychoanalysis. As is well known, the heyday of Malinowskian anthropology coincided with heyday of psychoanalysis. Malinowski was befriended by Marie Bonaparte, one of the actors in the interwar psychoanalytic movement. Though an ardent proponent of science, Malinowski experimented with the application of psychoanalysis in anthropology. As a fresh reader in Social Anthropology at the University of London, he published a long article on 'mother-right' family and the Oedipus complex in Freud's journal *Imago*, which specialized in the application of psychoanalysis in the social sciences (*Geisteswissenschaften*) (1924). Later he published a study *The Father in Primitive Society* (1927) as well as the monograph *Sex and Repression in Savage Society* (1927). Malinowski draws on psychoanalytic reasoning, namely the Oedipus complex, when he tries to understand the stability of family in matrilineal societies, such as those of the Trobriands, in contrast to patrilineal societies.

In brief, Malinowski concludes that whereas in patrilineal societies the Oedipus complex means to kill the father and marry the mother, in matrilineal society the wish is to marry the sister and kill the mother's brother (1924, 275). Kinship in his time was seen as a relationship between sexes. Malinowski however was no biological determinist, and Freud's psychoanalysis, a great fashion at the time, seemed to him to be a possible alternative path to better grasping of interconnections between sexuality, kinship and family. The strategic goal of Malinowski's anthropology was to offer the world a new theory of culture that would take into account the vast diversity of cultural forms. By submitting to critical analysis of Freud's theory of emergence of culture through patricide by joint forces of frustrated sons (i.e., Oedipus complex), Malinowski opened the way to his own theory, which would comprise political arrangements, legal norms and even religion.

Malinowski proceeded comparatively. On the one hand he compares Freud's psychologism with the principles of social sciences such as anthropology and sociology, on the other he systematically compares socialization and the development of sexually conditioned behaviour in Western societies with so-called savage societies, using the Trobriand example especially. A specific framework of his analysis is another comparison: mother-right and matrilineal Trobrianders with patriarchal societies of the European (i.e., Western) type.

Freud's theory comes out of the comparison as Eurocentric, moreover anchored in wealthy layers of the advanced capitalist societies. Malinowski admits that Freud discovered new dimensions of human psychology in the relations between members of a nuclear family, but underlines that from observation of 'contemporary savages' it is possible to derive that 'family' differs in various communities and even within different strata of the same community.

Malinowski asks: do the conflicts, passions and inclinations take place in the family according to its structure or do they remain the same for the whole of humanity? He answers that the structure is different in various societies and therefore the nuclear complex of the family cannot be constant in all human races and groups, but must change according to the family structure. Malinowski rightly remarks that data about modern European society do not have the same value as those which he himself collected by way of anthropological fieldwork in Melanesia.

Therefore, he calls for anthropological research in modern Europe and explicitly writes that it is imperative that European data is processed in the same way, as if they were studied with the same methods and judged from the same anthropological viewpoint. Freud in *Totem and Taboo*, however, speculatively supposes a universal origin of culture: totemism and the prohibition of incest, exogamy and sacrifice on the basis of the drama of primeval patricide. Thus Freud tries to explain psychologically a whole range of anthropological categories, for which he has no comparative data originating from authentic fieldwork. His 'terrain' material comes exclusively from psychiatric-psychoanalytical research of the middle and upper strata in Vienna and Central Europe of early twentieth century. Malinowski writes that he found no consistent reference concerning the social milieu in any of the psychoanalytical descriptions. It is evident, thought Malinowski, that children's conflicts in richly furnished bourgeois rooms would not be same as those in the dwelling of a peasant or one-room flat of the poor working man. Therefore Malinowski believes that it is necessary to study lower, less cultivated layers of society, where things are called by their real names, where a child is in constant contact with the parents, lives and eats with them in one room, sleeps on the same bed and where the parent has no 'substitute' who would complicate the image of the family. A substantial part of the monograph gradually analyses comparatively the stages of childhood and adolescence in Melanesia and in modern Western society. It points out that the world of adults in the rich strata of civilized Western society creates in children reflexes of subordination, sentiments of shame and perceptions of indecency, which they would otherwise not feel. On the contrary, childhood, adolescence and adult life in Melanesia take place without cover-up, shame or other types of hypocrisy. In many respects Malinowski agrees with Freud, in other very important points he parts way with psychoanalysis.

Gellner discounts the scientific ambitions of psychoanalysis. For him psychoanalysis is not far from religion. Yet both Malinowski and Gellner admit that religion is an indispensable partner to science. In his published lectures, entitled *The Foundations of Faith and Morals* (1936), Malinowski declares that a sane social life must be based on a credible religious value system. However, that does not mean that all members of a society regulated by religious faith and ethics have to be bigoted sectarians or even mere practicing believers. He himself is unable to accept revealed religion of any sort. But even an agnostic, underlines Malinowski, must live through faith. In the case of those 'prewar' rationalists and liberals like himself, it was the belief in humanity and progress. This allowed him to work for the progress of science and the formation of a community of free men. This faith was shaken by the war and its consequences, as was that of Christians. Science has suffered because it was harnessed for political and party purposes, with catastrophic consequences. As a rationalist and someone who believes in the development of human personality and a liberal community of free men, he finds himself in the same unfortunate position as a believing Christian. It is high time, Malinowski argues, that the old, artificial animosity between science and religion should be put aside, and both become allies in the struggle against the common enemy. Here he clearly hints at National Socialism, fascism and communism – in brief, all kinds of totalitarianism (Malinowski 1986, 145–6).

Malinowski's philosophy culminates in his political and social philosophy, expressed in his articles on war and the book *Freedom and Civilization* (1944). It was passionately written during the last year of his life, culminating in the few months between the attack on Pearl Harbour and April 1942. Before he could make the final touches to the manuscript, he suddenly died in May 1942. The book has five parts. The first is a political prelude, followed by three parts of scientific analysis of freedom, its meaning and as a gift of culture. The fourth part, especially, puts freedom into the framework of culture and civilization. The exposition of Malinowski's political philosophy culminates in the fifth part, entitled 'The Real Battlefields of Freedom'. To Malinowski, freedom is closely connected with democracy and 'proto-democracy'. The latter is typical of primitive tribal cultures which are 'essentially democratic': 'Democracy as a cultural system is the constitution of a community which is composed of collaborating groups [...] a more fundamental definition of the concept of democracy implies the maximum of discipline with the least amount of coercion' (Malinowski 1947, 228). Democracy implies autonomy of institutions, which in turn comprises all other principles of democracy. Malinowski introduces the terms 'tribe-nation' and 'tribe-state'. The first means a culturally united people, the second the political expression of centralization. Power as a concept resides in the tribe-state or nation-state. Totalitarianism is not a return to savagery as savagery is proto-democratic. Totalitarianism is

> the misuse of power in its modern technological developments, through the use of brute force, indoctrination and communication. The elimination of totalitarianism is not a problem of individual psychology or psycho-analysis, such as the elimination of aggressiveness, sadism or pugnacity. The end of totalitarianism can only be achieved through the elimination and prevention of the use of violence and the technique of the *coup d'état*, of the irresponsible armament of partial groups of humanity, and of lawlessness where law must play an active role. (1947, 241–2)

Malinowski shows that war is the expression of the excessive sovereignty of states. He therefore suggests the limitation of sovereignty, surrendered to an international body such as the United Nations:

> In a democratic culture, the state functions as a guarantor of peace, as arbiter in internal disputes and as controller. […] Only when a state, primitive or otherwise, mobilizes part of its resources for conquest and political expansion, which usually also implies economic exploitation, are such phenomena as war, slavery, oppression, and tyranny not only possible bus as a rule inevitable. (1947, 271)

His political credo is perhaps best expressed in the following quotation:

> Political sovereignty must never be associated with nationhood, since this produces the dangerous explosive of nationalism. Indeed, political power, insofar as it is centralized, must be vested in a hierarchy of federal units. Starting from local autonomy, it must proceed through administrative provinces, states and regional federations to a world-wide superstate. (1947, 274)

To conclude, war may have some positive aspects, but it is basically organized crime. It is a large-scale abrogation of freedom: 'one of the most destructive elements in human civilization', which 'has played but a small constructive and creative part in the history of culture'. (1947, 277)

Conclusion

The relationship between Malinowski and philosophy was close, but he kept a sound distance from it by stressing the scientific nature of anthropology. In other words, Malinowski was well aware that philosophy is a nonscientific ingredient helping to make science, in his case sociocultural anthropology, more theoretical, but firmly grounded in the empirical data gained through field research. Malinowski was inspired by philosophy in his writings on religion, ethics, war and politics, and perhaps most importantly culture. But again, he never indulged in philosophizing without empirical data. Philosophy was an auxiliary for him, a methodological tool, but certainly not an aim in itself. Philosophy helped Malinowski to be both a great researcher and theorist. Unlike other authors, I maintain that Malinowski remains an essential inspiration for anthropology and other social sciences because he kept contact with philosophy throughout his career.

Notes

1 This essay was conceived and partly written in 2008 while I was CEEPUS fellow in the Institute of Ethnology and Cultural Anthropology at the Jagiellonian University, Kraków, Poland. It was completed in 2012 while I was guest at the Institute of African Studies, University of Bayreuth, Germany. I am grateful to these institutions and my colleagues for criticism and support.
2 His essay on Nietzsche's *The Birth of Tragedy* originated from this course with Pawlicki (see Thornton and Skalník 1993, 67–88).
3 Andrzej Flis's edition of documents concerning this extraordinary academic and social event was published as appendix 1 in: Ellen et al. 1988, 195–200.
4 In a way, by choosing anthropology as his subject, Malinowski pragmatically applied 'economy of mind' (least effort) to his own career. By sociologizing ethnology he managed in almost no time to revolutionize (make obsolete) ethnology and establish at least in Britain social anthropology as an independent discipline.
5 Those who would interpret this as a lack of national feelings would be wrong, as Malinowski proved more than once that he cherished his ethnic Polishness and was proud of his acquired British status. Not without interest is the fact that his beloved mother, according to contemporaries the main source of his early successes in Kraków, had to die in comparative poverty alone while her son was carrying out his fieldwork on the other side of the globe.

References

Ellen, R., E. Gellner, G. Kubica and J. Mucha, eds. 1988. *Malinowski Between Two Worlds: The Polish Roots of an Anthropological Tradition.* Cambridge: Cambridge University Press.

Flis, A. 1988. 'Cracow Philosophy of the Beginning of the Twentieth Century and the Rise of Malinowski's Scientific Ideas'. In *Malinowski Between Two Worlds: The Polish Roots of an Anthropological Tradition*, edited by R. Ellen, E. Gellner, G. Kubica and J. Mucha, 105–127. Cambridge: Cambridge University Press.

Gellner, E. 1988. 'Zeno of Cracow' or 'Revolution of Nemi' or 'The Polish Revenge: A Drama in Three Acts. In *Malinowski Between Two Worlds: The Polish Roots of an Anthropological Tradition*, edited by R. Ellen, E. Gellner, G. Kubica and J. Mucha, 164–94. Cambridge: Cambridge University Press.

_____. 1998. *Language and Solitude: Wittgenstein, Malinowski, and the Habsburg Dilemma.* Cambridge: Cambridge University Press.

Jerschina, J. 1988. 'Polish Culture of Modernism and Malinowski's Personality'. In *Malinowski Between Two Worlds: The Polish Roots of an Anthropological Tradition*, edited by R. Ellen, E. Gellner, G. Kubica and J. Mucha, 128–48. Cambridge: Cambridge University Press.

Kubica, G. 1988. 'Malinowski's Years in Poland'. In *Malinowski Between Two Worlds: The Polish Roots of an Anthropological Tradition*, edited by R. Ellen, E. Gellner, G. Kubica and J. Mucha, 89–104. Cambridge: Cambridge University Press.

Mach, E. 1898. *Popular Scientific Lectures.* Chicago: Open Court Publications.

Malinowski, B. 1915. *Wierzenia pierwotne i formy ustroju społecznego: Pogląd na geneze religii ze szczególnym uwzglednieniem totemizmu* (Primitive beliefs and forms of social order: A view on the genesis of religion with general consideration of totemism). Kraków: Akademia Umiejętności.

_____. 1923. 'The Problem of Meaning in Primitive Languages'. In *The Meaning of Meaning*, edited by C. K. Ogden and A. I. Richards, 451–510. London.

_____. 1924. 'Mutterrechtliche Familie und Ödipus-Komplex'. *Imago: Zeitschrift für Anwendung der Psychoanalyse auf die Geisteswissenschaften* 10: 228–77. In English published in 1924 under the title 'Psycho-Analysis and Anthropology'. *Psyche: An Annual of General and Linguistic Psychology* 4: 293–332. Reprint in 1995 by Routledge, Thoemmes Press.

_____. 1935. *Coral Gardens and Their Magic: A Study of the Methods of Tilling the Soil and of Agricultural Rites in the Trobriand Islands*, 2 vols. London: Allen and Unwin.

_____. 1936. *The Foundations of Faith and Morals: An Anthropological Analysis of Primitive Beliefs and Conduct with Special Reference to the Fundamental Problems of Religion and Ethics.* Oxford: Oxford University Press.

_____. 1944. *A Scientific Theory of Culture and Other Essays.* Chapel Hill: University of North Carolina Press.

_____. 1947 (1944). *Freedom and Civilization.* London: George Allen and Unwin.

_____. 1980. *Dzieła*, vol. 1. Warsaw: PIW.

_____. 1986. *Bronisław Malinowski: Schriften zur Anthropologie.* Edited by F. Kramer. Frankfurt: Syndikat.

_____. 1993. *The Early Writings of Bronisław Malinowski.* Edited by R. Thornton and Skalník. Cambridge: Cambridge University Press.

Mucha, J. 1988. 'Malinowski and the Problems of Contemporary Civilisation'. In *Malinowski Between Two Worlds: The Polish Roots of an Anthropological Tradition*, edited by R. Ellen, E. Gellner, G. Kubica and J. Mucha, 149–63. Cambridge: Cambridge University Press.

Paluch, A. 1988. 'Malinowski's Theory of Culture'. In *Malinowski Between Two Worlds: The Polish Roots of an Anthropological Tradition*, edited by R. Ellen, E. Gellner, G. Kubica and J. Mucha, 65–87. Cambridge: Cambridge University Press.

Skalník, P. 1982. 'Bronisław Malinowski (1884–1942): Een argonaut uit Kraków'. In *Beroep antropoloog: Vreemde volken, visies en vooroordelen*, edited by G. Banck and B. van Heijningen, 29–41. Amsterdam/Brussels: Intermediair.

_____. 1991. 'Malinowski on War, Nationalism and the State'. In *Ideen zu einer Integralen Anthropologie (Festschrift for K. Mácha)*, edited by S. Bonk, 545–69. Munich: BB Verlag.

_____. 1993. 'Malinowski, la guerre, le nationalisme et l'État'. *Gradhiva: Revue d'histoire et d'archives de l'anthropologie* (Paris) 13: 3–19.

_____. 1995. 'Bronisław Kasper Malinowski and Stanislaw Ignacy Witkiewicz: Science Versus Art in the Conceptualisation of Culture'. In *Fieldwork and Footnotes: Contributions to the History of European Anthropology*, edited by H. Vermeulen and A. Roldán, 128–41. London: Routledge.

_____. 2005. 'Malinowski and Africa: An Opportune Opportunity?' *Azijske in afriške študije / Asian and African Studies* 9 (3): 1–10.

Thornton, R. and P. Skalník. 1993. 'Introduction: Malinowski's Reading, Writing, 1904–1914'. In B. Malinowski, *The Early Writings of Bronisław Malinowski*, edited by R. Thornton and P. Skalník, 1–64. Cambridge: Cambridge University Press.

Witkiewicz, S. I. 1977. 'Marzenia improduktywa'. In B. Michalski, *O idealizmie i realizmie.* Warsaw.

_____. 1978. '622 upadki Bunga czyli Demoniczna kobieta'. In *Dzieła wybrane*, vol. 1. Warsaw: PIW, 45–473.

_____. 1981. *Listy do Bronisława Malinowskiego.* Edited by E. Martinek. Warsaw: PIW.

Chapter 11

GROUND, SELF, SIGN: THE SEMIOTIC THEORIES OF CHARLES SANDERS PEIRCE AND THEIR APPLICATIONS IN SOCIAL ANTHROPOLOGY

Lars Kjaerholm

The Ontological Ground of Peirce's Semiotics: Firstness, Secondness, Thirdness

Far more than a theory of signs, Peirce's semiotics is also an attempt to summarize ontology as seen in his time and in the Kantian tradition in which he is situated. The concepts of *firstness*, *secondness* and *thirdness* sum up the forms and conditions under which anything can exist, within the framework of the ontological tradition that Peirce belonged to. Peirce has various ways of defining Firstness. It is 'what the world was to Adam on the day he opened his eyes, before he had even drawn distinctions, or had become conscious of his own existence' (1.357). This makes Peirce's definition of firstness somewhat difficult to comprehend, since elsewhere he uses the red colour of Lady Welby's servants' uniforms as an example of firstness, in short the quality of being red, which these uniforms embody (Lieb, 1953). However, if we are to take the above quotation literally, which would preclude drawing distinctions in firstness, then even the redness of these uniforms could presumably not be appreciated without presupposing a drawing of distinction between red and other colours? Peirce further says about firstness: 'It avoids being the object of some sensation. It precedes all synthesis and all determination. It has no unity and no parts. It cannot be articulately thought. Assert it and it has already lost its characteristic innocence; for assertion always implies a denial of something else. Stop to think of it and it has flown' (1.357). As Isabel S. Stearns aptly observes, 'Firstness is the most elusive of Peirce's categories, since it signifies the thing itself, or that primary limit to our thought which can never be conceptually grasped in its original state' (Stearns 1952, 199). E. Valentine Daniel, one of the most important anthropologists to successfully use Peirce's semiotics, observes a certain likeness between firstness and Victor Turner's (1967) concepts of *communitas* and *liminality*: 'In this commonness lies much of communitas's and liminality's allure as well as elusiveness, which have moved its admirers to respect and its detractors to scepticism' (Daniel 1984, 240).

However, most readers of Peirce have taken firstness to mean simply a quality, as that modality of existence which cannot exist without being embodied in something else, namely something which exists in secondness, in the world of tangible objects. Suffice it to say about the mysterious concept of firstness, that it is first of all *a limiting concept*, which implies that nothing can exist before, or hidden behind, that which exists in firstness. Thus it is a culturally constructed concept, which makes a firm statement about the modalities of existence. This is most clearly revealed when the Peircean concepts of firstness, secondness and thirdness are brought into contact with another ontological world, the world of double substance thinking, such as Indian Sankhya philosophy, which assumes precisely what Peirce's ontology precludes: that something can exist prior to firstness, and accordingly we stand in need of applying a new concept, *zeroness*, in an understanding of this ontology (Kjaerholm 1993b, 82). I shall return to this discussion below when I review anthropological applications of Peirce's semiotics. In the felicitous wording of Anne Marie Dinesen and Frederik Stjernfelt: 'Peirce's table of categories [...] is constructed in analogy with logic – for Peirce firstness corresponds to the predicate, secondness to the subject, and thirdness to the copula, the connection between the subject and the predicate. Firstness is thus pure predicate without subject – therefore vague, not simple and only possible, not real' (Dinesen and Stjernfelt 1994, 15; my translation).

In contrast, secondness is 'brute fact', that which exists in the material world of objects that embody qualities. Secondness is associated in Peirce's thinking with the concept of *struggle*, since this is where the individual's body comes into contact with the material world of objects. Peirce illustrates it thus: 'Imagine yourself making a strong muscular effort, say that of pressing with all your might against a half-open door. Obviously there is a resistance. There could not be effort without and equal resistance any more than there could be resistance without an equal effort that it resists' (5.45). Also, it is in secondness that awareness of the self comes about. It is 'only in the polarity of secondness that Self and No-Self becomes precipitated out against each other' (1.324; Stearns 1952, 201).

Thirdness is the final modality of existence, which refers to rules, belief and relations between entities, thus it refers to something nonmaterial. Peirce uses the term 'signs of habit' in order to characterize thirdness. Daniel sees a similarity between Peirce's concept of sign of habit and Pierre Bourdieu's concept *habitus*, 'the durably installed generative principles of regulated improvisation, which produces practices which tend to reproduce the regularities immanent in the objective conditions of the production of their generative principle' (Bourdieu 1972, 78). According to Peirce, 'A man is a bundle of habits. But a bundle of habits would not have the unity of self-consciousness. That unity must be given as a centre for the habits' (6.228). Habits are what steer human action and it corresponds thus to Bourdieu's habitus concept, in that both concepts have to be working without being made explicit. Were this to happen, one could begin to doubt the basis of one's choice of action, and doubt is something we wish to avoid: 'Belief is not a momentary mode of consciousness; it is a habit of mind essentially enduring for some time, and mostly and (at least) unconscious; and like other habits, it is (until it meets with some surprise that begins its dissolution) perfectly self-satisfied. Doubt is of an altogether contrary genus. It is not a habit, but the privation of habit' (5.417).

Thus we see how closely Peirce's concept of signs of habit resembles Bourdieu's concept of habitus, in as much as both must be unconscious in order to regulate human behaviour. So maybe these two terms represent the same idea: 'The feeling of believing is a more or less sure indication of there being established in our nature some habit which will determine our actions. Doubt never has such an effect' (5.371).

In many accounts of Peirce's semiotics the concepts of firstness, secondness and thirdness are left out, and his sign concepts are introduced without them, but as we shall see later in this chapter, it is important to establish the ontological ground on which his semiotic theory rests, as these three modalities are the only ones he is prepared to consider. When we take his semiotic ideas and apply them in other cultural worlds such as India, we must first investigate the ontological ground that is to be found to reign there, before we can begin to apply his semiotic method: 'Cultural, linguistic, personal, biological habits not to mention science, belong to the Third' (Dinesen and Stjernfelt, 1994, 16; my translation).

Were we to make a model of Peirce's ontology, a model of secondness, it might look like this:

here there is only one kind of substance, causality and time/space in which the phenomena may manifest themselves. The three categories described above are the basis, the ground for his phenomenology, or *phaneroscopy* (a term used by Peirce to distinguish his phenomenology from other types of phenomenology).

The Sign

Peirce's sign definition is nonlinguistic and is closely linked to his pragmatic philosophy. A sign is simply what you become aware of, and he often uses the term representamen to denote that which a mind becomes aware of, so the sign is not reality as such, but that which is manifested in a mind, such as that individual mind perceives it. The understanding of a phenomenon consists in perceiving the practical consequences which may pertain to the sign or representamen, which is the pragmatic dimension. Understanding of a *phaneron* depends on prior experience and knowledge of the perceiving mind: 'No *proposition* can be understood – unless the interpreter has "collateral acquaintance" with every object of it' (8.184). The example he gives is the word 'soleil', the understanding of which means that you must know more than that it corresponds to the English word 'sun', but what the sun really means in the world of experience.

'My definition of a representamen is as follows: "A *representamen* is a subject of a triadic relation to a second, called its *object*, *for* a third, called its *interpretant*, this triadic relation being such that the *representamen* determines its interpretant to stand in the same triadic relation to the same object for some interpretant"' (1.541). This means that semiosis, the understanding of a sign or representamen, is a potentially perennial process which can lead to new understandings of the same object, as the individual mind perceiving it may change its way of interpreting it over time, and various minds may interpret it differently based on their prior experiences and understandings of phenomena. Thus there is no true understanding of a given representamen, but a never-ending range of understandings, due to the very different conditions for interpreting a sign which may exist in various minds. To take an example, the red dot placed on the forehead by some Hindus, called in Tamil *pottu*, will be interpreted differently by different minds, depending on the prior experience and knowledge of those minds. Furthermore, the individual understandings of the *pottu* may change in individual minds over time, as more knowledge and experience is added. If you are from a remote part of Europe and have no knowledge of India or Hindu customs, the *pottu* may have a vague meaning of something 'exotic' or 'oriental', whereas if you have been inside a Hindu temple and seen how worshippers receive red powder from the temple priest and apply it to their foreheads, the *pottu* means 'Hindu worship has taken place', and if you have furthermore seen a Christian Indian woman buying a self-adhesive red dot in a shop in order to place it on her forehead between her eyebrows, your understanding of the *pottu* is extended, as it can also mean simply 'female adornment without religious implications'. This bears some resemblance to Paul Ricoeur's ideas about the interpretation of 'meaningful action interpreted as text' in the article with the same title, where he states 'discourse is always realized temporarily and in a present, whereas the language system is virtual and outside of time' (1971, 530). For Ricoeur, it is in actual discourse that all messages are communicated, and there is always a subject sending the message and another person, to whom the message is addressed. Discourse always has a 'world' – a social, cultural and historical world in which it has its own life and dynamic function (531). But once discourse, or meaningful social action, is fixed, written down, is noted by somebody, this results in the act escaping its author, and being set free to be interpreted by others in ways that the originator of the act cannot control: 'Only man *has a world* and not just a situation. In the same manner that the text frees its meaning from the tutelage of the mental intention, it frees its reference from the limits of ostensive reference' (535). Thus, acts may be interpreted very differently by those who observe them, because it may have different meanings to them qua their social relation to the author of the act. There is thus never one truth about a social act; it is always open to interpretation. This resembles the dynamics of the sign in Peirce's definition as described in the example above with the red dot, the *pottu* and its use in Indian culture.

Icon, Index and Symbol

Corresponding to the ontological categories of firstness, secondness and thirdness are the sign categories icon, index and symbol. Peirce defines these three types of signs thus: an icon is a 'Sign that represents its Object in resembling it', indices are 'Signs that represent their Objects by being actually connected with them', and symbols are 'Signs that represent their Objects essentially because they will be so interpreted' (4.371). Examples of icons are pictures, diagrams or other images (6.336). The most 'abstract form of an icon is a metaphor. Icons may be found in man-made things, but may also be perceived similarities between natural objects and something else. Thus mimesis, that important part of cultural construction, can be viewed as a special area of anthropological and cultural study (Maran 2003). A photograph is a good example of an icon.

The index is that which exists in the world of matter and which is needed for icons to exist. Peirce gives these examples: 'I see a man with a rolling gait. This is a probably indication that he is a sailor. [...] A sundial or a clock *indicates* the time of day. [...] A rap on the door is an index' (2.285).

The Dialogic Self: Man's Glassy Essence

When many anthropologists (such as Clifford Geertz, Victor Turner and Mary Douglas) began to develop an interest in symbols and began to understand culture as systems of symbols and meanings, and anthropologists began to look for a theoretical underpinning of this, Claude Lévi-Strauss found inspiration for his theory of structure in Saussure's semiological theories, while others looked to Peirce's semiotics in order to find a theory on which to develop a new type of anthropology. Milton Singer proposed that Charles Peirce's semiotic theory would be a more fruitful theoretical approach for anthropology.

The Cartesian notion of the self as a thinking substance is opposed in Peirce's philosophy and replaced by a dialogic self. Peirce deconstructs the self in the sense that the self is constantly in flux, being driven by semeiosis to change and evolve constantly. This is one of Peirce's definitions: 'We have already seen that every state of consciousness [is] an inference; so that life is but a sequence of inferences or trains of thought. At any instant then man is a thought, and as thought is a species of symbol, the general answer to the question what is man? Is that he is a symbol' (7.583). In fact, the self becomes more than the isolated individual, implying that the self is in fact also a bundle of social relations. This is in line with Radcliffe-Brown's conception of the individual as a part of a pattern of social relations, and also with McKim Marriott's (1976) ideas about the Indian *dividual*, as opposed to Western notions of *individual*, as an isolated entity. The use of the term *dividual* is found by Marriott to be a better term for the person in the Indian context, as people in India generally tend to see themselves as parts of social wholes, and as results of interchange and transactions with other people, which constantly 'create' them and shape them. But to Peirce, not only the self is dialogic, but all thinking becomes so, *because* the self is dialogic.

'All thinking is dialogic in form. Your self of one instant appeals to your deeper self for assent' (6.338). Peirce's notion of the self is important, since it shows how his semiotic theories become more relevant for anthropology than Saussure's semiology because, paradoxically, by almost dissolving the self, he opens up the possibility of a dynamic and evolving self, which would be impossible in Saussure's semiology.

Peirce's and Saussure's Sign Concepts

In this paragraph I shall closely follow Gérard Deledalle's (1979) comparison of these two sign concepts, as I find myself in agreement with his assessment of the character and capability of them. Saussure's semiology developed during his linguistic studies and refers mainly to linguistic signs, and nothing was found in his posthumous papers about semiology, so what is known about it is mainly derived from notes taken by his students during his lectures. Saussure distinguished between *langue*, language as a system, and *parôle*, the actual use of the language in discourse and writing. In language, a concept and a sound pattern are united in an arbitrary fashion. Saussure's semiology profoundly influenced Claude Lévi-Strauss's anthropology.

Saussure's concept of the sign has two parts: *signifiant* and *signifié*, the relationship between which is arbitrary and fixed by convention. Peirce argues the social nature of the sign, 'not like Saussure by placing *langue* and *parôle* in opposition to each other, but by simply eliminating the subject in discourse. It is admittedly "I" who is speaking, but this is not and cannot be the "subject"; the "I" is the place of the signs and exclusively the place of the interpretant, a place which is not isolated, on the contrary it is a place in a situation, and any situation is social' (Deledalle, 22–34; my translation). In contrast to Saussure's sign concept, Peirce's sign is triadic, and because his concept of the interpretant is variable, it comprises three different kinds: the immediate interpretant, the dynamic interpretant and the final or normal interpretant. These three types of interpretant are called emotional, energetic and logical and thus correspond to firstness, secondness and thirdness.

In contrast, Saussure's sign theory is dyadic. All his ideas are dichotomies: *significant/signifié, langue/parôle*, synchrony/diachrony. His semiology is a part of 'social psychology and following from this the general psychology' (Saussure 1916, 33). Thus, Saussure's sign concept cannot accommodate experience and praxis, which Peirce's semiotic theory is able to. As Deledalle puts it, 'Peirce's semiotics is at one and the same time the semiotics of representation, communication and signification' (1979, 38). Deledalle poses the question: which semiotic theory should one prefer, that of Saussure or that of Peirce? His answer is that it depends on what you want your semiotic analysis to achieve. The final test of the validity of their theories depends on an analysis of what you are able to do with them. It depends on 'the fruitfulness of the analyses, which the model allows' (39). As Peirce's semiotics is open to experience, history and society it seems better suited to anthropology than Saussure's semiology, although Saussure has had tremendous influence on anthropology, vide its influence on Claude Lévi-Strauss.

Peirce's Typology of Signs

There are nine possible types of subsigns in Peirce's semiotic theory. This comes about because the three types of sign – qualisign, sinsign and legisign – should be seen in three different levels of relations. The sign can be analysed in relation to itself, as a type of representamen (R), in relation to its object (O), or in relation to the interpreting sign (I). This makes it possible to make the following schema of sign types:

1. (R)	Qualisign	Sinsign	Legisign
2. (O)	Icon	Index	Symbol
3. (I)	Rhematic	Dicent	Argument

Out of this typology ten combinations can be made, as stated by Peirce with this diagram (2.264):

(I) *	(V)	(VIII)	(X)
Rhematic	Rhematic	**Rhematic**	**Argument**
Iconic	**Iconic**	**Symbolic**	Symbolic
Qualisign	**Legisign**	Legisign	Legisign

(II)	(VI)	(IX)
Rhematic	**Rhematic**	**Dicent**
Iconic	**Indexical**	**Symbolic**
Sinsign	**Legisign**	Legisign

(III)	(VII)
Rhematic	**Dicent**
Indexical	**Indexical**
Sinsign	**Legisign**

(IV)
Dicent
Indexical
Sinsign

Short definitions of the various terms are needed here. A *rhematic* means the interpretant sign of qualitative possibility. An example of a *rhematic* is a diagram, which can be seen to be a diagram, but which is not completely understood. A *dicent* is an interpretant sign, which for its interpreter points to actual existence, for instance a weather cock, which indicates the direction the wind is blowing, making it a dicent sinsign. *Sinsign* means the individual realization or 'incarnation' of a qualisign. An *argument* is an interpretant sign in thirdness, which for its interpreter refers to a law, and it is a legisign because it is in thirdness: 'Any system, which contains rules which have to be followed, if the system is not to be destroyed [...] is an argument: games, codes, sciences, institutions et cet.' (Deledalle 1979, 19).

Peirce's Semiotics Applied in Anthropology: Some Examples

Attempts to use semiotics of the Peircean kind in anthropology have been few and far between. The first serious attempts at semiotic anthropology, both Milton Singer's *Man's Glassy Essence* and E. Valentine Daniel's *Fluid Signs: Being a Person the Tamil Way*, were published in 1984, but since then there are to my knowledge no major anthropological studies applying Peirce's semiotics.

There is a growing number of articles in which anthropologists apply it in varying degrees, although often there is only a token reference to Peirce and the sign concept, and no real use is made of his semiotic theories. In *Man's Glassy Essence* are found a number of fairly theoretical chapters, the most interesting of which discuss the concepts of self and identity and give a detailed account of Peirce's contributions in this area.

There is in this book not a lot of practical hints to the anthropologist who might wish to learn how to apply Peirce's semiotics in anthropological fieldwork and analysis, as there is little analysis of concrete anthropological material, although there is an attempt in this direction in the last chapter 'On the Semiotics of Indian Identity'. For these reasons Singer's writings have, as it appears, not impacted much on the way anthropological fieldwork and analysis has been carried out in the years following its publication.

In *Fluid Signs*, Daniel shows how he has used Peirce's semiotics as a tool in his fieldwork, applying it in a variety of contexts, thus demonstrating what can be achieved by this. Apart from a long theoretical and historical introduction, the book consists of five examples of fieldwork with a hands-on use of semiotics, which are of great importance for those wishing to follow his example.

In the paper 'Indexicality and the Verification Function of Irreplaceable Possessions: A Semiotic Analysis', Kent Grayson and David Shulman (a cooperation between a marketing expert and an anthropologist) demonstrate that even a limited use of Peircean concepts can yield interesting results in anthropological analysis. They focus on the index in their elucidation of why certain things come to be irreplaceable. They have an interesting discussion about applying the Saussurian model versus the Peircian model, the conclusion of which is that the Saussurian model of the sign seems to be unable to explain why some possessions become irreplaceable. They say: 'Saussure emphasized that both a signal and a signification are psychological impressions and that the meaning process is therefore wholly mental. […] Saussure argued that there is no semiotic basis for preferring one signal to the other so long as either can hold the same place in a particular semiotic system' (2000, 18). This would mean that an heirloom (say, a piece of jewellery) could be replaced by an exactly similar replica, but this is not the case. The heir would definitely not be content if the piece actually worn by their deceased relative were to be replaced with a copy. In Peircian semiotic theory, however, it is possible to view the sign as connected with something in the outside world, and not just within a closed system, as we find in Saussurian semiology. 'Thus, in contrast to Saussure's emphasis on locating a sign semiotically in relation to other signs, Peirce's model emphasizes the importance of locating a sign physically in relation to an objective, real (non-mental) world. This makes it possible for the sign to become embedded not just within a context of mental associations, but also with a less malleable physical context' (18). In their investigation, Grayson and Shulman interviewed 33 individuals and asked them to identify those of their possessions which they found would be irreplaceable, and then linked this to the indexical conditions which were connected with rendering these possessions irreplaceable. Whereas earlier investigations have focused on the capability of objects to evoke memories, Grayson and Shulman reached the conclusion that some objects were regarded as much more able to 'carry' certain memories – or to make these memories more 'real' – because of a connection between the possession and the real world, a connection that is neither unreal nor imaginary' (19).

It is of great anthropological interest to investigate all the possible ways indexicality can be understood as 'linking' persons and objects. Daniel presents material from Tamil Nadu demonstrating the importance of indexicality in the context of houses and those who inhabit them. This is arguably indexicality of another type than the type treated by Grayson and Shulman, as it seems that their informants connected the irreplaceable possessions with particular *events* in their personal history. There is not so much reference to *events* or *social situations* in Daniel's material, but rather a direct relation between persons and houses in the form of *substance exchange*.

Thus, indexicality in the Indian context involves a belief in real and actual substance change of the person involved in indexical contact with the object – in this case, the house lived in. This means that indexicality in the Indian case has consequences for identity and self, and thus is indexicality in a very radical role. Whereas in the case described by Grayson and Shulman, where the respondents are – presumably – Western, indexicality is of another order with a strong element of thirdness, since the elements with which the irreplaceable possessions are indexically connected are more in thirdness than in secondness, since they are situations and evoke personal relations and experiences. So, although there are interesting perspectives in cross-cultural comparison in the area of relations between persons and objects, theoretical work is still required to describe this considerable difference between *kinds* of secondness, which a comparison between Grayson and Shulman's material and the Indian material presented by Daniel reveals. In fact, the differences between Western and Indian secondness may lead us, as Peirce says in 'How to Make Our Ideas Clear', to conclude that if an idea can lead to two very different results, then it is really two different ideas which should have different names. In the ontology in which Peirce's semiotics arose, they cannot be dicent, and Peirce makes his position on this very clear: 'icons and indices assert nothing' (2.291), but this seems to be the case in India. Therefore, we must look for the concomitant difference in ontology which would make icons and indices dicent and meaningful, and thus make secondness a direct

link between different domains of existence. One could demonstrate this
attitude towards iconicity and indexicality with numerous examples. Swami
Narayanananda reads a meaningful message from signs in nature:

> There is a variety of soils in this world and these constitute separate classes
> of their own. A certain kind of mud is found only in certain localities. If we
> try to mix them up, the soil of stronger kind absorbs that of inferior kind and
> the mixture takes on a new form or variety. If we examine a river bed, we can
> observe pebbles, sand and fine earth of different kinds settling down separately
> in different layers. They do not mix up. The fine mud gathers at one place. Sand
> particles will settle down at some other place and pebbles form into a group
> somewhere else. Likewise gold, silver, iron, brass ores, etc. are found in certain
> localities only. This shows that caste exists, though in a crude form, even in earth
> and animals. (Narayanananda 1982, 8)

Thus to his mind, since various substances are distributed apart from each
other in nature, this is evidence that the caste system is based on natural
principles. The conclusion is that there must be a difference in ontology, which
makes it possible for Narayanananda to read signs in a way that is radically
different from Peirce's. To the Indian mind, the geological layers have an iconic
similarity to social stratification; it is a dicent iconic sinsign, which cannot exist
in Peirce's semiotic theory. A clue as to the ontological difference which makes
such signs possible in the Indian context may be found in Sankhya philosophy,
which introduces the idea of a subtle substance, unreachable by the human
senses, but which is the cause of the coarse substance that humans can observe
and experience. Hence, iconic likenesses in coarse substance are signals,
impressions from a world beyond human experience, but a world which is
somehow more important than it: 'Primordial matter is not perceived because
it is too subtle, not because it does not exist; for it is known from its products
(the phenomenal world). And those products are partly like it and partly unlike
it' (Bary 1963, 309).

   Primordial matter is of a higher order because it is not caused by anything;
coarse substance on the other hand is caused by this subtle substance. This
seems to account for the importance of iconic signs and iconicity in Hindu
thought, where omens based on iconic likenesses play an important role in
human life. Thus, if one sees a woman carrying an empty pot, the iconicity of
'empty pot', conveys the message 'no result' to the observer, and a person, when
confronted with such a sight, may put off an important decision till the signs
are better. Similarly, seeing a Brahmin carrying an umbrella is perceived as an
icon saying 'I am protected', and is hence considered auspicious. Ontologies
such as the one found in Sankhya philosophy seem to be widely accepted, and

this may explain why iconic signs and iconicity are considered so important in Hindu culture.

Secondness and Subtle Substance

With the notion of subtle substance as the cause of the observable, coarse substance, secondness seems to be invaded by something which might be termed 'zeroness'. In a certain sense one could describe it as a constant state of 'possession', where coarse substance in possessed by subtle substance, and this would make it logical to pay such attention to iconic signs, since they point to the, somehow more real, world of subtle substance. This is an ontology which also makes the Indian attitude understandable as a communication with a subtle kind of secondness, through the medium of another coarse kind of secondness. Thus, what is termed secondness in Peirce's semiotic theory in the Indian context hides another and more real secondness, so that the coarse secondness is, so to speak, secondness by proxy. The question is whether new semiotic terms should be coined in order to take this into account, or whether it is enough to point out that the interpretant in the Indian context is based on an ontology not accepted in the Peircean system.

I shall describe in some more detail Daniels's findings in the area of person–house relations. In Chapter 2, 'An Ur Known', Daniel describes a substance linking a Tamil person and his place of origin, his *ur*. A businessman from Malaysia, who has never been to the village from which his father migrated, has come back to get to know his *ur*. Daniel suggests that this can be done in a few days, but the businessman plans to spend a couple of months. 'Knowing' his *ur* entails drinking the water drawn from its well, eating the food grown on its soil and so on, so that the qualities, the *kunam*, of this place may enter his body and blend with it, making it possible for him to reach his full potential as a businessman, because the general opinion of his caste is that this particular village has qualities which are particularly compatible with members of his caste. Thus, his father sent him back here so that he could 'know' the village, and we understand that knowing in this case takes place in secondness and is of an indexical nature. He must enter into actual, physical, indexical contact with his village of origin in order to 'know' it.

Joseph Alter presents material from traditional wrestlers in North India which points to a similar substance exchange and hence connectivity through indexicality, as the wrestlers think of their bodies as being in a constant and mutual substance exchange with their wrestling arena, the *akhara*. According to Alter, to live the virtuous and morally superior life of a traditional wrestler is seen by the wrestlers as opposition to a morally corrupt modern Indian state, which does not patronize wrestling in the way the former rulers did.

Living the highly regulated and disciplined life of a wrestler, which involves a very selective diet, makes them morally superior, and through the sharing of substance with the mud of the *akhara*, this particular place comes to share in this moral superiority. When the wrestlers come into contact with the mud, they share in this moral superiority. This process takes place, as it would seem, entirely in secondness. It is not the symbolic value of the wrestlers' discipline alone which makes him superior – although we cannot rule thirdness out entirely – but it seems that secondness plays the most important role in this process of moral-superiority making. As Alter says, 'Muscles do not translate well into metaphors when substance is more at issue than meaning' (1993, 65).

I have – as I realize in retrospect – observed the same during fieldwork in Tamil Nadu, India, where I found that objects that had belonged to deceased relatives were often kept in shrines for the *kula teyvam*, or family deity, in a process where the soul of the deceased would be gradually merged with a *kula teyvam*. Thus, a feeling of connectedness between the family and its family deity, via the deceased family members' belongings, is brought about in secondness, which would explain why precisely a dead aunt's sari or some other belonging would be regarded as irreplaceable. It would not be possible to buy similar objects and replace them with the actual ones (Kjaerholm 1990, 67–87). Although at the time of writing this chapter I did not apply Peirce's concepts of firstness, secondness and thirdness, in retrospect I find that it is useful to reanalyse this material in these Peircian terms, as it shows the importance of secondness in some detail in the cult of the *kula teyvam*. The link in secondness between *kula teyvam* and humans is found also in the soil on which the temple for this deity is built. If a person moves very far away from where his temple is, a new temple for the deity can be constructed provided that a sample of the actual soil from the original temple is placed under the new temple, thus linking in secondness the old and the new temple, which by this procedure become identical in respect to their ability to house and communicate with the deity. There is a similarity here with the soil of the wrestlers' *akhara* as described by Joseph Alter above and the role played by the soil on which the temple stands. The anthropological and other analyses of Indian culture have brought such an enormous amount of examples of this kind that there seems to be endless connectedness along axes in secondness where humans and places and things may be connected. Where does it all end? In fact, in millennia-old works such as the Upanishad, this perspective is unfolded, as illustrated by this quotation from Brihadaranyaka Upanishad (III, vi, I):

'Yajnavalkya', said she, 'If all this is pervaded by water, by what, pray, is water pervaded? By air, O Gargi. By what, pray, is air pervaded? By the sky, O Gargi. By what is the sky pervaded? By the world of the Gandharvas, O Gargi. By what is the world of the Gandharvas pervaded? By the world of the sun, O Gargi. By what is the world of the sun pervaded? By the world of the moon, O Gargi. By what is the world of the moon pervaded? By the world of the stars, O Gargi. By what is the world of the stars pervaded? By the world of the gods, O Gargi. By what is the world of the gods pervaded? By the world of the Indra, O Gargi. By what is the world of Indra pervaded? By the world of Viraj, O Gargi. By what is the world of Viraj pervaded? By the world of Hiranyagarbha, O Gargi. By what is the world of Hiranyagarbha pervaded? Do not, O Gargi,' said he, 'question too much, lest your head should fall off'.

Conclusion

This chapter has argued the fruitfulness in using the semiotics of Peirce in anthropology, but has also pointed to some problems in bringing it to bear in cultures where there are other ontologies which are incompatible with Peirce's classes of possible signs. To point to just one example, the problem becomes acute in Victor Turner's studies of symbols, since (as we see in the Indian material) what to our minds are symbols may in the Indian understanding be indices – direct representations of deities and not symbolic representations of them. If the interpretation, the ground which any given culture refers to in its interpretation of signs, is not brought to bear in an analysis of its signs, then we run the risk of importing our own ontology in the analysis of other cultures. An example is the *yantra*, the geometric design which is thought in a very real sense to represent a particular deity. The *yantra* and its accompanying sound formula, its *mantra*, together are a deity, not a symbol for one. As one text on *yantras* and *mantras* say about Sri Chakra (the *yantra* of the goddess Sri): 'Thus Sri Chakra is verily the body of the mother goddess, her own form' (Rao 1987, 17). A meticulous use of Peirce's semiotics may help us to avoid this, and hence has great potential in anthropological analysis, a potential which is still waiting to be used.

References

Alter, Joseph S. 1993. 'The Body of One Color: Indian Wrestling, the Indian State, and Utopian Somatics'. *Cultural Anthropology* 8 (1): 49–72.
Bary, William Theodore de, ed. 1963. *Sources of Indian Tradition*. Delhi: Motilal Banarsidass.
Beck, Brenda E. F. 1976. 'The Symbolic Merger of Body Space and Cosmos in Hindu Tamil Nadu'. *Contributions to Indian Sociology*, n.s., 10 (2): 213–43.
Bourdieu, Pierre. 1972. *Outline of a Theory of Practice*. Cambridge: Cambridge University Press.
Daniel, E. Valentine. 1984. *Fluid Signs: Being a Person the Tamil Way*. Berkeley: University of California Press.

Deledalle, Gérard. 1979. *Théorie et pratique du signe: Introduction á la sémiotique du Charles S. Peirce.* Paris: Les editions Payot.

Dinesen, Anne Marie and Frederik Stjernfelt. 1994. *Charles Sanders Peirce: Semiotik og pragmatisme.* Copenhagen: Gyldendal.

Graves, Mark. 2007. 'Peircean Approaches to Emergent Systems in Cognitive Science and Religion'. *Zygon* 42 (1): 241–8.

Grayson, Kent and David Shulman. 2000. 'Indexicality and the Verification Function of Irreplaceable Possessions: A Semiotic Analysis'. *Journal of Consumer Research* 27 (1): 17–30.

King, Alexander D. 2005. 'Genuine and Spurious Dance Forms in Kamchatka, Russia'. *Max Planck Institute for Social Anthropology Working Papers* 79: 1–19.

Kjaerholm, Lars. 1990. 'Kula Teyvam Worship in Tamilnadu: A Link Between Past and Present'. In *Rites and Beliefs in Modern India*, edited by Gabriella Eichinger Ferro-Luzzi, 67–87. Delhi: Manohar.

_____. 1993a. 'Body, House, Cosmos: An Application of C. S. Peirce's Semiotics in an Anthropological Analysis of Indian Silpa Sastra'. *Semionordica* 1 (2): 35–63.

_____. 1993b. 'Silpa Sastra: An Indian Expert System in the Light of Peircean Semiotics'. In *The Expert Sign: Semiotics in Culture*, edited by Jan Slikkerveer, Gerard van den Broek, Barend van Heusden, René J. Jorna, 65–82. Leiden: DSWO Press.

Layton, Robert. 2003. 'Art and Agency: A Reassessment'. *Journal of the Royal Anthropological Institute*, n.s., 9: 447–64.

Lieb, I. C., ed. 1953. *Charles S. Peirce's Letters to Lady Welby.* New Haven: Whitlock's/Graduate Philosophy Club of Yale University.

Maran, Timo. 2003. 'Mimesis as a Phenomenon of Semiotic Communication'. *Sign Systems Studies* 31 (1): 1991–2115.

Marriott, McKim. 1976. 'Hindu Transactions: Diversity Without Dualism'. In *Transaction and Meaning: Directions in the Anthropology of Exchange and Symbolic Behavior*, edited by Bruce Kapferer, 109–142. Philadelphia: Institute for the Study of Human Issues.

Moriarty, Sandra E. 1996. 'Abduction: A Theory of Visual Interpretation'. *Communication Theory* 6 (2): 167–87.

Narayanananda, Swami. 1982. *Caste, Its Origins, Growth and Decay.* Gylling: Narayana Press.

Peirce, C. S. 1931–58. *Collected Papers of Charles Sanders Peirce.* Vols. 1–6 (1931–35) edited by Charles Hartshorne and Paul Weiss. Vols. 7–8 (1958) edited by Arthur W. Burks. Cambridge, MA: Harvard University Press.

Pollock, Donald. 1995. 'Masks and the Semiotics of Identity'. *Journal of the Royal Anthropological Institute*, n.s., 1, 581–97.

Rao, S. K. Ramachandra. 1982. *Sri Chakra: Its Yantra, Mantra and Tantra.* Bangalore: Kalpatharu Research Academy.

Rappaport, Roy A. 1992. 'Ritual, Time, and Eternity'. *Zygon*: 27 (1): 5–30.

Reyes, Angela. 2002. 'Are You Losing Your Culture? Poetics, Indexicality and Asian American Identity'. *Discourse Studies* 4, 183–99.

Ricoeur, Paul. 1971. 'The Model of the Text: Meaningful Action Considered as Text'. *Social Research* 38 (2): 529–62.

Rubinstein, David. 2004. 'Language Games and Natural Reactions'. *Journal of the Theory of Social Behaviour* 31 (1): 55–71.

Saussure, Ferdinand de. 1916. *Cours de linguistique générale.* Paris.

Shankar, Nalini. 2006. 'Metaconsumptive Practices and the Circulation of Objectifications'. *Journal of Material Culture* 11: 293–327.

Singer, Milton. 1977. 'On the Symbolic and Historic Structure of an American Identity'. *Ethos* 5 (4): 431–54.

_____. 1980. 'Signs of the Self: An Exploration in Semiotic Anthropology'. *American Anthropologist* 82 (3): 485–507.

_____. 1985. 'Comments on Semiotic Anthropology'. *American Ethnologist* 12 (3): 549–53.

Stearns, Isabel S. 1952. 'Firstness, Secondness, and Thirdness'. In *Studies in the Philosophy of Charles Sanders Peirce*, edited by Philip Wiener and Frederick H. Young. Cambridge, MA: Harvard University Press.

Tsintjilonis, Dimitri. 2004. 'Words of Intimacy: Re-membering the Dead in Buntao'. *Journal of the Royal Anthropological Institute*, n.s. 10: 375–93.

Turino, Thomas. 1999. 'Signs of Imagination, Identity and Experience: A Peircian Semiotic Theory for Music'. *Ethnomusicology* 43 (2): 221–55.

Varenne, Hervé. 1984. 'Collective Representation in American Anthropological Conversations: Individual and Culture'. *Current Anthropology* 25 (3): 281–300.

Chapter 12

RICOEUR'S CHALLENGE FOR A TWENTY-FIRST CENTURY ANTHROPOLOGY

Betsy Taylor

> *Under history, memory and forgetting.*
> *Under memory and forgetting, life.*
> *But writing a life is another story.*
> *Incompletion.*

Ricoeur ends his last major book with the above poem (Ricoeur [2000] 2004, 506). This poem is a dance of paradoxes, vividly conjuring up its author and his long life of philosophical labours – a life remarkable for both generous openness and tenacious continuity. In his distinctive mix of solemnity and playfulness, Ricoeur sets up a game of hide and seek in this poem – between text, author and reader, between life and death, between embodiment and disembodiment.

The overt paradoxes in this poem concatenate with silent allusions to the *aporias* central to earlier works. On the one hand, the poem evokes Heidegger's ideas of humanness as being-towards-death, since Ricoeur would anticipate the readers who would be reading after the irreversible punctuation point of his own bodily death. The English edition of *Memory, History, Forgetting* would be published just one year before his own death in 2005 at 92 years. Ricoeur dedicates the book to his wife, who died a few years before the French publication, suggesting connections between his philosophic labours and the personal work of mourning. On the other hand, this poem evokes his sustained critique of the understanding of subjectivity as being-towards-death in its 'one-sided aspect of Heideggerian resoluteness in the face of dying' (Ricoeur [2000] 2004, 357). Throughout his lengthy oeuvre, Ricoeur turns to ideas of humanness as being towards life, in incompletion and opacity.

He notes Arendt's concept of 'natality' (1958, 357), as developed in *The Human Condition*, as a necessary corrective to Heidegger's ideas of *Dasein* –the vast openness of possible being, which only receives wholeness, authenticity and integrative form through 'the finitude of the horizon of mortality' (355).

But this poem also points towards his running debates with Derrida. On the one hand, it playfully celebrates the trickster powers of texts and textual voices to break from the embodied and given limits of life and death. The final word disputes the ending of his personal or bodily life, his oeuvre and the book itself, even as he anticipates the finality of his own death – setting up paradoxes of authorial authority, like the philosopher who quotes the Cretan who says that all Cretans are liars. Like Derrida, and against Gadamer, Ricoeur celebrates the 'distanciation' of text from life and world.[1] But, on the other hand, Ricoeur is a gentle but strong critic of those who would see the gap between text and life as so impassable as to break the referential powers of language to world and life – like Derrida and the so-called 'poststructuralist' theory.[2]

The poem sets up a paradoxical play between 'life' and 'a life'. It is in this space of paradox that this chapter takes off. Its central *aporia* is the dynamic play between the particularity of 'a life' and 'life' – that is, life processes in general, in a continuum across human and nonhuman. My goal is to see whether Ricoeur's work on time is useful in understanding 1) the temporality of the ecological commons, and 2) what that means for the anthropological project. First, I look at the notion of humanness as ecological, as developed by Herbert Reid and myself (2010), to consider how Ricoeur's notions of text, world, body and action might help us understand the complex and heterogeneous temporalities of humans as ecological beings. Second, I argue that ecological understanding shifts our understanding of knowledge, to emphasize the centrality of public scholarship as stewardship of the life commons through care for knowledge commons (democratically linking multiple knowledges – including local, lay and expert in embodied, emplaced co-participation in the life commons). Third, I put these ideas into debate with the recent call for 'an anthropology of the contemporary' by Paul Rabinow and George Marcus (2008).

Body~Place~Commons

In our book, *Recovering the Commons: Democracy, Place, and Global Justice*, Herbert Reid and I speak of 'subjectivity as intersubjectivity arising in embodied practices in concrete places within heterogeneous temporalities of the ecological commons'. We argue,

> To be a creature – human or non-human – is to be hinged between one's own embodiment
> and the particularity of places which accrue the grounds for life from unruly and ruly cycles

of interdependence, mortality and natality of the ecological commons. Our being is not 'in' us, like something poured in a bag of skin, nor is it 'outside' our skin in signs, economies, machines or powers. The stuff of our being arises as dynamic infrastructures of forms of life which we share with non-human creatures – generative matrices of co-constitution among particular bodies within the chaotic piling up of particular conditions of ecological relations within particular places. (2010, Introduction)

We give the name 'body~place~commons' to these chronotopic infrastructures. We use the tilde (~), following Kelso and Engstrøm, who use it to signify reconciled complementary pairs: human/nature, mind/body (2006). Phenomenology has been a long attempt to overcome pernicious dualisms of Western modernity. In our book, we particularly emphasize Merleau-Ponty's notion of 'flesh' as the preobjective, presubjective dynamic 'hinging' between beings and nature – a matrix of exchange between inorganic and organic processes and the perceptual, agentic and conceptual infrastructures of beings (2010, see especially Chapter 5).

In this article, I want to use Ricoeur's thought to look more specifically at the cultural dimensions of body~place~commons. He is helpful because of the complexity of his understanding of the temporalities that are constitutive of humans and the centrality of culture to the always incomplete resolution of the *aporias* of human time. Ricoeur is famous as a bridge builder, someone who struggles to mediate oppositions and aporias – often through keeping them in dynamic, unstable tension in almost kinaesthetic notions of concrete, practical action. But it should be emphasized that he consistently refuses to let this slip into the kind of postdualism that suppresses the scandalous disjunctions of paradox. He is, therefore, a particularly helpful thinker for understanding body~place~commons because it is constituted in embodied, lived practices that are structured by multiple but *heterogeneous* temporalities. It is crucial not to move too quickly (to use a Ricoeurian phrase) through this heterogeneity – not to minimize the disjunctions between the very different kinds of times which are somehow bundled together into the embodied, emplaced practices of beings in co-constitution with their ecological matrices. This is a complex interpenetration of many different sorts of linear and cyclic temporalities of bodily, ecological and social rhythms.

The Sedimentary in the Temporal Constitution of Subjectivity

This article looks at three kinds of temporality which recur in Ricoeur's understanding of subjectivity – modalities of temporal constitution of being which I label as sedimentary, architectonic or kiltering. Sedimentary time refers to Ricoeur's interest in the ways in which phenomena are laid down as traces, and residues of, occurrences. Despite all his interest in structures and infrastructures (narratival, symbolic, dramatistic, etc.), he is also interested in the ways in which things and meanings *pile up* and take on emergent qualities through a process of composting and accumulation. Some of the greatest passages in his first major work, *Freedom and Nature: The Voluntary and the Involuntary* are on 'habit'. He refuses the simple equation of habit to autonomization that is understood as more primitive than intentionally willed thought or its simple by-product ([1950] 1966, 284). Rather, he emphasizes that, while habit can fall into automatism (296–307), the sedimentation of habits from conscious, 'free' acts can also create a 'second nature' which increases bodily spontaneity and aptness, thus increasing freedom and capacity (288–96). His 1950s work on the phenomenology of the will, then, includes an epigenetic understanding of subjectivity – a kind of concretion of particular characteristics laid down within the particularities of the unfolding temporal career of particular persons. In later work, he continues to attend to the cumulative piling up of personhood as a sort of exfoliation of meaningful occurrences that compost into 'a life' – part of what he calls the constancy of 'character' in the 1960s ([1965] 1986).

This epigenetic temporality of subjectivity is suggested by his notions of the 'hermeneutic circle' as virtuous circle, the 'gift' that symbols in action give to thought, and a 'kinship of thought with what life aims at' ([1960] 1967, 352). But this circle must still be opened up to life as a

> wager that I shall have a better understanding of man and of the bond between the being of man and the being of all beings if I follow the *indication* of symbolic thought. That wager then becomes the task of *verifying* my wager and saturating it, so to speak, with intelligibility. In return, the task transforms my wager: in betting *on* the significance of the symbolic world, I bet at the same time *that* my wager will be restored to me in power of reflection, in the element of coherent discourse. ([1960] 1967, 355)

In his work on narrative in the 1980s, we see this same circling that is really a spiralling – a return but to a beginning that has been transformed by the journey of narrative prefiguration, configuration and refiguration ([1983] 1984, [1984] 1985, [1985] 1988) – a mutual incitement between text and the world through which subjectivity passes with a certain capacity for becoming more itself, precisely through its dislocation, expansion and refiguration by texts.

What I am calling sedimentary temporality appears as the capacity of subjectivity *to accrue being over time* through co-participation in meaning and action in the world. However, this accrual does not, in any simple way, *enstructure an architecture for the self.* It is not a developmental sense of self, like the Freudian, in which strata are laid down in the psyche – like geological strata predictably or catastrophically building from geological processes of deposition. To shift the hermeneutic circling of text and action, of text and world from vicious circle to virtuous circle, Ricoeur speaks of the 'wagers' that are anything but certain, and are frail because they are always subject to 'fault' ([1965] 1986). In a way that is very unfashionable now, this way of thinking about subjectivity combines continuity and tenacity of selfhood, with radical indeterminacy and epigenesis. There is a paradoxical, constitutive and radical openness here – like the post-Derridean views of self as an effect of flux, play and gaps in language.

But Ricoeur sees the constitutive, perilous and radical gaps of subjectivity as precisely the site at which selves make the wagers and receive the gifts to become, not just patients of language, but agents of lives in worlds-in-common, illuminated and made habitable by language. This resembles John Dewey's notion of 'individuality'. Dewey says that the significance of Heisenberg's uncertainty principle 'is generalization of the idea that the individual is a temporal career whose future cannot be *logically* deduced from its past' ([1938] 1962, 151–2) and that 'if we accept the intrinsic connection of time with individuality, [individuals] are not mere redistributions of what existed before' (153). He says, 'The mystery of time is thus the mystery of the existence of real individuals' (156). Reid and I argue that this is a power of 'individuals', to accrue being that is

> an *emergent* quality of co-creation between individual and world which appears at a hinge of interaction which is an open, synaptic site characterized by uncertainty, indeterminacy and contingency, yet, can be known after the interactions have occurred. What makes this a deeply ecological view is that this quality of individuality characterizes human *and non human beings*, and the co-creative unfoldings of evolution. (2010, 170)

To avoid the Western cultural biases towards individualism we recast 'individuality' as 'particularity':

> To encounter the world in its particularity is to encounter beings as mortal. To be mortal is to be actual and material within the flow of time. That is to say, the reality of mortal beings is in their stubborn presence in the present – yet this present exists as emergent from multiple past events and chains of consequences, as inherent in a matrix of simultaneous and contemporary events, while mysteriously pregnant with multiple but incompatible futures. (2010, 171)

The Architectonic in the Temporal Constitution of Subjectivity

This continuity of subjectivity, described above, is both strong and fragile. What I have called sedimentary time is not at all an automatic deposition, not at all a steady piling up of one thing on top of another that leaves stable foundations or boundaries of selfhood. It is for this reason important to make a distinction between 'sedimentary' and 'architectonic' modalities in the temporal constitution of subjectivity. Ricoeur has an extremely complex understanding of the architectonic qualities of subjectivity – an understanding to which *aporias* of time are central. The very capacity of selves to accrue being through the virtuous circles described above is only possible through movements, leaps and wagers that are at best mysterious, and at worst impassable paradoxes that open 'fault' lines within selfhood and collectivities of profound, unspeakable and irreversible tragedy ([1965] 1986).[3] Ricoeur's critique – in *Memory, History, Forgetting* – of the early Heidegger is too complicated to unpack here ([2000] 2004, see especially 352–61). But an overall goal seems to be to dislodge that temporal architecture of Heidegger's *Dasein* that accents the future as 'thrownness' into infinite possibilities, that gains 'authenticity' and 'integrity' from its resolute awareness of the finitude which death will impose – thereby creating a sort of overarching temporal linearity to the architecture of the self. Ricoeur dislikes the way in which this creates a hierarchy of temporalities – in which the thrownness to the future and toward death seems more primordial and authentic. Instead, Ricoeur would emphasize what he calls the 'resources of conditionality' (355) – the matrixical conditionings of the past (in memory and forgetting) and the wagers that radically open to the present. Like Husserl and Heidegger, Ricoeur draws on the Augustinian notion of subjectivity as threefold temporal extension – the *distentio animi* of the soul stretched in three contradictory ways in the 'present of the past or memory, the present of the future or expectation, and the present of the present or attention' (101). Ricoeur is concerned that the linearity of *Dasein*'s thrownness into the future, in *Being and Time*, overwhelms the heterogeneity and dislocations of time, and does not adequately attend to the 'tears' and gaps opened up by the 'dissimilarity of the self to itself' (101) within the often impossible torsions of memory, attentiveness and anticipation.

Kiltering as a Temporal Mode in the Constitution of Self

In Ricoeur's understanding, subjectivity is a constantly changing poiesis of heterogeneous torsions, movements, leaps and agglomerations. But subjectivity is also the capacity to kilter this heterogeneity into an 'I' who promises or who can impute itself into its acts. The movement of 'oneself' into 'another' is the modulation of that component of subjectivity that is always already intersubjectivity, the stretchedness of betweenness that can shift between a 'you', 'thou' or 'we' (Ricoeur 1992). The capacity to unify and integrate into one pronomial position is always an impermanent act that must be continually re-enacted as a moving centre of equilibrium between paradoxes that never can be fully resolved but can be kiltered in practical action in the world – just as a skilled dancer sediments learning into habitualized skills to enable an upright posture within the dualism of up and down, front and back.

The term kiltering is mine, not Ricoeur's. But I think it an apt label for his recurrent explanations for how different forms of subjectivity and intersubjectivity manage to create durable continuity of being – despite the radically decentring and disjunctive tendencies of human being-in-the-world. Herbert Reid and I describe kiltering as the ability to hook together the disjunct temporalities of our being as emplaced, embodied animals, as we 'accrue the grounds for life from unruly and ruly cycles of interdependence, mortality and natality of the ecological commons' (2010, 5).

> The key characteristic of body~place~commons is the power to *kilter heterogeneous temporalities of cyclic, linear and arrhythmic temporalities with spatialities that are recursive, planar, topological, etc. and which integrate sedimentary forms of retention with capacities of protention towards the unexpected, new or the maddeningly or wonderfully same-old.* […] But, kiltering always thrums with unkiltering. Kiltering is the ability to juggle stuff that you did not see coming, or, which just slipped out of your grasp. (2010, 90)

A Detour through the Linguistic Turn and Back

Ricoeur is famous for his detours, and we now need to take a quick detour back through what we have just said before we can consolidate it into an inquiry about human being as constituted in, and through, the temporalities of the ecological commons. It is crucial to remind oneself that Ricoeur never left the phenomenological project which understands subjectivity as intentionality – in its specialized meaning in phenomenology, as the stretching between consciousness and its objects. Subjectivity is always a betweenness, not a thing and not a meaning. When Ricoeur made his linguistic turn in the 1960s and 1970s, he never followed people like Derrida in letting go of this notion of intentionality as primordially constitutive. But this is not some psychologized notion of 'experience' as primordial, but prelinguistic. Somehow, then, it is textualized, or saturated with language. In fact, he criticizes Geertz for the notion of 'extrinsic' symbols and their systems that create a sort of semiotic pattern which is parallel to life patterns, which culture then matches (Ricoeur 1986).

For Ricoeur, human being is a creative stretching of being, which can best be described as creative and embodied *acts*. Language is actional through and through; these acts are constitutively intentional – torsions that cross and recross the only apparent boundaries of body and world. That is because language is first metaphor – understood as a creative act of extension and intention of meaning, in which linguistic structures excite each other through almost fractal-like combinations and decombinations. The labile, unstable dynamism is clear when he says, 'My inclination is to see the universe of discourse as a universe kept in motion by the interplay of attractions and repulsion that ceaselessly promote the interaction and intersection of domains whose organizing nuclei are off-centered in relation to one another; and still this interplay never comes to rest in an absolute knowledge that would subsume the tensions' ([1975] 1977, 302).

The intentionality of language acts entrains human subjectivity and 'reality' in a way that is in no way a simple philosophical realism, a one-to-one equation of word and thing. For Ricoeur, so-called 'literal' meaning is a third-order metaphoric move, which arises first from metaphoric creation of categorical orders, and then an assignation of words to things ([1975] 1977, 22–3). When literal meaning happens, language in some sense dies or freezes because a thoughtful intentionality in the world is always the act of 'thinking *more*', an active, 'productive' imagination that keeps the play of metaphoric motion in a process that is essentially poetic. However, the Derridean move of leaping entirely into language as the site for the lively play of meaning is also a way to kill language. For Ricoeur, a complete dive into nominalism is the flip side of realism. The pivot that keeps language alive is the *intentionality* of humans *in* the world, which is a moving and actional hinge of co-participation *between* humans and reality. When the referential function is lost, the liveliness of language is lost, dying into reification. There is a human tendency in language to reification (whether in a realist or a nominalist direction), but it is the evaporation of thought as one stops thinking *more*. Ricoeur says, 'Metaphor not only shatters the previous structures of our language, but also the previous structures of what we call reality. [...] The strategy of discourse is [...] to shatter and to increase our sense of reality by shattering and increasing our language. [...] With metaphor we experience the metamorphosis of both language and reality' ([1973] 1978, 132–3).

Ricoeur never lets go of referentiality, of the necessary chiasmus of language and reality into each other. But Simms is quite right to point out that in moving across this chiasmus of language~reality, Ricoeur takes 'the long route' compared to Heidegger's 'the short route' (2003, 34–8). Heidegger, especially in his later years, can speak more directly of the ways in which language creates a 'clearing' for being-in-the-world. But, for Ricoeur, the co-constitution of language and world is more like a high wire act, where the artificiality of linguistic fashioning is the balancing bar for the intensely embodied and real-time passages of being-in-the-world. In Ricoeur's theory of narrative ([1983] 1984, [1984] 1985, [1985] 1988), emplotment is already 'prefigured' in praxis as temporal infrastructures of embodied agency in the world (in what he calls the emplotment of $mimesis_1$). But, narrative as text (what he calls $mimesis_2$) also arcs back towards the world as the capacity to project a world, leading to $mimesis_3$, which is a 'refiguration' of imagined worlds into lived ones. There is continuity between the infrastructural forms of praxis as embodied and the emplotment of narrative – both are processes of worlding and both arc towards each other. This theory matters here because it is 1) an argument for cosmogenic structure, or a kind of architectonic proportionality – a world-making capacity – within language, and 2) an argument for infrastructural temporality within praxis that reaches towards a similar architectonic proportionality of forms of life in being-in-the-world. Praxeomorphic emplotment and narratival emplotment incite and require each other.

Ricoeur has a strong sense of the referentiality between language and world, but he also has a strong sense of the powers of narrative to insert an 'as if' that flips open alternative worlds. The phase of narrative that he calls $mimesis_2$ is entered by crossing the threshold of 'as if' into a fictional world that is projected by the complex and specific semiotic mechanisms of narrative that he has studied in such detail. Like the play of young mammals that prepares them for engaging the world in all its real-time and mortal risk, the fictionality of $mimesis_2$ is an important form of expansion and sedimentation of the referential and actional powers of humans. Ricoeur, like many others, took a 'linguistic turn' in the 1960s and 1970s, but he went in a different direction from much social theory. The deconstructionist linguistic turn focused on the gap between signifier and signified – as a dislocation of referentiality. Ricoeur, however, sees this as a distanciation that *increases* our freedom for getting closer to reality. $Mimesis_2$ provides the skills in worlding that allow us to more skilfully and thickly be-in-the-world and for-each-other. The dislocations between signifier and signified *can* be the site for the fault that spins humans into reification, or sterile hermeneutic circles, but it is not the most daunting fault line. More risky (and interesting), for Ricoeur, are the many other torsions, intentions and extensions from which our being arises – the aporias of time, will, self/other and embodiment which he explores as the intrinsic frailty of our being that can rip into 'fault'.

From Subjectivity to Intersubjectivity: World

The implication of the above is that the hinge of referentiality is not the gap between signifier and signified. Rather, it is the power of symbolically mediated action to project and introject 'world'. Despite his prodigious diversity of writings, Ricoeur did not systematically explore the notion of world, even though his arguments repeatedly end with world as the site for the practical action. I think that world, for Ricoeur, is what Heidegger describes as an 'unthought', a driving but unthematized question behind his philosophic corpus. Hannah Arendt (1958) has developed some of the most important and systematic philosophies of world (drawing on Heidegger's more elusive but important thought). Herbert Reid and I start from Arendt's notion of world and expand it to include our ecological articulation with the nonhuman:

> *World is that dynamic mesh of relationships among creatures and their ambient surround that provide durable and livable architectonics for creaturely action and environmental sustenance.* [...] Arendt emphasizes that world is a strange mixture of history as residue from past action and history-in-the-making as sheer openness of new possibilities for action. Human world arises in, and out of, history, with all its particularity and onrush, as people find their lives to be at stake in what happens around them. And so, historical events pile up in traces of meaning and matter – forms of intelligible speech, conscious remembrance, unconscious habit and ecological engagement. And, world is where this piling up happens, and, where it becomes available for us to make and remake individual and collective life in its particularity. *Human world is that durable architectonics of engagement that creates the background which actors need to illumine future and present as coherent settings for action, and, into which acts can transmute into remembrance (or habit) that avails past for future action.* (2010, 8)

Ricoeur's distinctive combination of hermeneutics, phenomenology and narratival theory suggest a way to resituate the hinging of 'a life' – in all its accrued particularity and (in Dewey's sense) individuality – into 'life' as it accrues particularity and pluralities of times of habitable worlds. To achieve landscapes within which history and utopian possibilities can take hold, a certain magma of narrativability must be sedimented into landscapes that connect human and nonhuman life (Castoriadis 1987, 340–44). Heidegger speaks of truth as *alethia* – as we reach to know an object, one part turns towards us, but another part turns away from us. Subjectivity engaging with objectivity is always selective, so the 'truth' of the object requires a plurality of subjective engagements because the foregrounding of something into visibility is a backgrounding of its other side. If the *alethia* of objectivity is this play of forgetting and unforgetting, visibility and invisibility, then the *alethia* of subjectivity would be the fluent play of what Drew Leder (1990) calls the ecstatic and the recessive body. Our embodied intentionality into emplaced life is an ecstasis that has a definite narratival structure, as Ricoeur helps us to understand. The recessive body with its sedimented and habituated capacities for ecstasis needs to be at hand, in a magma of imaginative possibility. This requires an aesthetic ecology that can continually act and re-enact a poetics of embodied landscape that accrues and bestows particularity in subjectivity~objectivity. In the last two chapters of his book *Memory, History, Forgetting*, Ricoeur has an extended exploration of what he calls 'happy memory' and the 'reserve of forgetting' ([2000] 2004). What he is getting at is the way in which the storytelling of memory distils and condenses itself into 'traces' which fall into a kind of collective unconscious – where they are not effaced, but are in latency, available for reactivation.

Public folklorist Mary Hufford gives an exemplary exploration of this in her ethnography of the 'ecstatic ecology of place names' in Appalachian coalfield communities (Hufford, forthcoming). She uses Merleau-Ponty's concept of 'flesh' for the folkloristic study of place, saying it 'espouses an opacity, a grounding, and a vitality that is missing from terms such as "habitus" (Bourdieu), "imaginary" (Castoriadis, Taylor), discourse (Foucault) or "ethnopoetic plenum" (Cantwell)' (2–3). She says of this 'flesh' of place that it is

> sedimented into Lifeworld, which is the prereflective, preobjective common worlds and its landscape, 'former acts of expression' (i.e., known genres of communication) are available for the work of taking up a position within the world of meanings. (7)
>
> [...] The immanent past is part of what lies within the opaque, anonymous, primordial being [...] in which we participate prereflectively and preobjectively, and within which every perception has been deposited, and remains available for reactivation and retrieval. (10)
>
> [...] In land-based communities a cyclical, relational form of time is inseparable from its spaces. Axioms for planting and gathering such as 'plant corn when oak leaves are the size of squirrels ears', and names for wildflowers such as 'farewell summer, assume the continual cycling of time as a process of development – literally 'unveiling' – that moves from emptiness to fullness and dehiscence and back. Cycles of annual, biographical, and generational time can be tethered to the land through chronotopes that are seasonal and intermittent – that is, the spaces defined by cycles of time prompt connections to the matrix through disappearances and reappearances collated with forgetting and remembrance. (26)

Ontology of the Commons

It can be argued that crises of the commons will be the defining challenge of the twenty-first century. The triple crises of climate change, resource scarcity (especially water) and peaking of fossil fuels (International Forum on Globalization 2007) will require unprecedented global cooperation and solidarity – but the solutions and effects also play out in diverse forms of localization. In meeting the intellectual challenges of these multiscalar challenges, Ricoeur's understanding of subjectivity and intersubjectivity provide ways to think through the spatiotemporal problems and possibilities posed by these interlinked crises of the commons.

In his introduction to a useful overview of these issues, Nonini says 'By "the commons" I mean those assemblages and ensembles of resources that human beings hold in common or in trust to use on behalf of themselves, other living human beings, and past and future generations of human beings, and which are essential to their biological, cultural and social reproduction' (2007, 1). The notion of 'assemblage' should be noted. This idea is useful because it suggests what I have described as a 'sedimentary' nature of chronotopes in commons. Commons are enmeshed interdependencies between communities of beings which accrue habitational niches within inorganic nature. These interdependencies and forms of liveability grow *over time* and *in place*. It is for this reason that we see so much emphasis on 'local knowledge' in traditional and emerging systems for common property management (Fischer 2000). Commons are highly placed. They are settled into, and arise from, distinct and sedimented configurations of geological, biological, climatological and ecological adaptation, and cultural forces that have grown together in idiopathic ways.

Ecological patterns assemble and pile up in the manner of bricolage – assembling, reassembling and taking advantage of what is already there. The formative patterns of coevolved ecological communities tend to be strongly 'path dependent' – that is, once an adaptation, symbiosis or use-pattern has been laid down, future patterns tend to follow and deepen the causal pathways already started. This is not a static homeostasis. Rather, it is a constant process of assemblage and reassemblage, with complex cocreation of continuity and perturbation. Perturbation can change things dramatically, but living beings respond by activating sedimented patterns of survival which have proved successful in the past, as well as with innovation. In fact, it is precisely in times of perturbation that sedimented survival patterns can be most strongly activated and most closely articulated with innovation. Ecological resilience depends on the flexibility and diversity of repertoires of crisis response laid down by past successful responses to crisis.

But, the notion of 'assemblage' is problematic insofar as it is borrowed from Deleuze's use of the word to suggest constant decentring, becoming and flux, which does not include a sense of stability of being or habitational matrices which support that stability. Taken to an extreme, Deleuzian notions of assemblage produce radically deconstructive and disembedding ontologies which are blind to the architectonics of what Merleau-Ponty called 'the conservation of being in becoming' (see chap. 3 of Reid and Taylor 2010).

(Inter)subjectivity of Commoners

Ricoeur's thought can be helpful in understanding our constitution as ecological, embodied beings within life commons. He combines temporalities of sedimentation, architectonics and kiltering in his chronotopic grasp of (inter)subjectivity – all of which are necessary for an ecological understanding of who we need to be to be responsible commoners. Herbert Reid and I argue that we need to reshape our political identities to understand ourselves as co-constituted in, and constituting of, the ecological assemblages that are our commons (2010, chap. 7–8). The goods of the commons are, by definition, public goods – too common or too fundamental to individual or collective wellbeing to be parcelled into individual ownership. This means that we feel connected to commons not just as an 'I' having an 'it'. Rather, we experience them in ways that transgress first and third person, singular and plural. Our sense of ownness with them requires an (inter)subjectivity that has pronominal hybridity and fluency across 'I', 'we', 'thou', 'you', 'it' and 'them'. This entails a paradoxical mix of the particular and the matrixical in self-constitution – as described in the discussion of Dewey's notion of the 'individual' above. Individual subjectivity is understood within its matrices – as an 'I' arising from, and returning to, an 'itness' that is as much a part of the 'self' as that which language denotes with the first person singular. Our being as commoners arises from what Merleau-Ponty calls 'flesh' – that hinging of sentient and sensible, of human and nonhuman where these apparent opposites reverse into each other. In addition, this enfleshed hinging is the site for very literal and essential material exchanges – of energy, nutrients, toxins, wastes between creature and creature, between creature and environment. This is why Bollier keeps emphasizing that the exchanges that constitute the commons have the form of a gift economy (2003, 31). To green our economy, we have to stop forgetting that, as Herman Daly says, it connects to nature at both its ends (2004).

Herbert Reid and I argue that it is precisely these chronotopes of the commons that have been effaced by the constitutive ideologies of capitalist nation-states – in their liberal philosophies, but especially in recent neoliberal formations (2006). Povinelli argues that Western modernity was founded on a disembedding of the individual from matrices (Plumwood 1993; Povinelli 2006). The disembedded liberal self (Stivers 2009), with its negative liberties, is necessary for what I have called the 'logics of fungibility' that dominate market, liberal state ideologies (Reid and Taylor 2006). Neoliberal globalization rides on logics of fungibility that can grasp any particular thing and translate it into systems of equivalence (like global economic space) that can relocate it elsewhere, with easy and nonplace or path-dependent forms of valuation and identity. This is a process of disinhabiting, of disembedding items and persons from the idiopathic pathways of their being within the commons. Under these regimes of fungibility, the only way to safeguard habitations at all is through a process of enclaving, in which the bare necessities of daily at-homeness are heavily guarded from a landscape which is more open to fungibilization than dwelling.

Toward an Epistemology of Commoning

In resistance to the fungible landscapes of neoliberal globalization, there are efforts to reclaim ways to resituate anthropological and other knowledges within civic commons grounded in life commons. The worldwide movement for participatory research and planning and public scholarship is, in part, an outgrowth of the fight against logics of mere fungibility (Fischer 2000; Giri 2002, 2004, forthcoming; Kezar 2005; Kezar, Chambers and Burkhardt 2005; Taylor 2008). It tries to build knowledge systems that link local, expert and official knowledges together in order to tend public goods. Anthropology has gone against the grain of disembedding and decontextualizing forms of knowledge because it emphasizes embodied immersion in peoples' everyday routines and the places that are matrixical for them. However, in conversation about future directions for anthropology, Marcus and Rabinow (2008) point out problems with this history. They call for diverse projects which are more collective, longer term, and more like the 'design studios' of architects and planners – embedded in large, ongoing work accountable to places. They suggest the term 'collaboratory' for such studios. However, they only consider collaboration between disciplines. Also crucial is the collaboration among experts, lay thinkers, citizens, government officials and communities. Increasingly effective methods and organizational models for such interdisciplinary, intersectoral, multi-issue collaboration are emerging from the new movements for public scholarship, action and service learning, participatory research and planning.

Notes

1 Influenced by Gadamer's notion, in *Truth and Method*, of the 'distanciation' effected by written texts, Ricoeur moved from a focus on language and symbol to a concern throughout the 1970s and 1980s with textuality and its constitutive narrative structures (Ricoeur [1975] 1977, [1983] 1984, [1984] 1985, [1985] 1988), but always found a productive circling between text and world – which put him into a running debate with Gadamer.

2 See for instance, Ricoeur's critique in *The Rule of Metaphor* ([1975] 1977) of Derrida's essay 'White Mythology' ([1971] 1982), followed by Derrida's response in 'The *Retrait* of Metaphor' ([1978] 1998).

3 By 'fault', he refers to the infrastructural fragilities which are like fault lines, along which personhood can fracture. These lines of potential fracture are the gaps between the paradoxes which constitute us and give us freedom and creativity, but which allow a 'disproportion of self to self' (Ricoeur [1965] 1986, 4). The necessary paradoxes of our being include paradoxes of self/other, gaps between the opacity of our bodily motivations, and our will, etc. These fault lines are where 'evil' can enter.

References

Arendt, H. 1958. *The Human Condition*. Chicago: University of Chicago Press.

Bollier, D. 2003. *Silent Theft: The Private Plunder of Our Commonwealth*. New York: Routledge.

Castoriadis, C. 1987. *The Imaginary Institution of Society*. Cambridge, MA: MIT Press.

Daly, H. E. 2004. 'Sustainable Economic Development: Definitions, Principles, Policies'. In *The Essential Agrarian Reader: The Future of Culture, Community, and the Land*, edited by N. Wirzba, 62–79. Washington, DC: Shoemaker Hoard.

Derrida, J. (1971) 1982. 'White Mythology'. In *Margins of Philosophy*. Brighton: Harvester.

_____. (1978) 1998. 'The *Retrait* of Metaphor'. In *The Derrida Reader: Writing Performances*, edited by J. Wolfreys. Edinburgh: Edinburgh University Press.

Dewey, J. (1938) 1962. 'Time and Individuality'. In *Time and its Mysteries*, edited by H. Shapley, 141–59. New York: Collier Books.

Fischer, F. 2000. *Citizens, Experts, and the Environment: The Politics of Local Knowledge*. Durham, NC: Duke University Press.

Giri, A. 2002. *Conversations and Transformations: Toward a New Ethics of Self and Society*. Lanham: Lexington Books.

_____. 2004. *Reflections and Mobilizations: Dialogues with Movements and Voluntary Organizations*. New Delhi: Sage.

_____, ed. (forthcoming). *Pathways of Creative Research: Rethinking Theories and Methods and the Calling of an Ontological Epistemology of Participation*. New Delhi: Primus.

Hufford, M. n.d. 'The Ecstatic Ecology of Place Names'. Unpublished manuscript.

International Forum on Globalization. 2007. *Manifesto on Global Economic Transitions: Powering-Down for the Future*, edited by Jerry Mander. Washington DC.

Kelso, J. A. S. and D. A. Engstrøm. 2006. *The Complementary Nature*. Cambridge, MA: MIT Press.

Kezar, A. J. 2005. 'Creating a Meta Movement: A Vision toward Regaining the Public Social Charter'. In *Higher Education for the Public Good: Emerging Voices from a National Movement*, edited by A. J. Kezar, T. C. Chambers and J. C. Burkhardt, 43–54. San Francisco: Jossey-Bass Press.

Kezar, A. J., T. C. Chambers and J. C. Burkhardt, eds. 2005. *Higher Education for the Public Good: Emerging Voices from a National Movement*. San Francisco: Jossey Bass.

Leder, D. 1990. *The Absent Body*. Chicago: University of Chicago Press.

Nonini, D. M., ed. 2007. *The Global Idea of 'the Commons'*. New York: Berghahn Books.

Plumwood, V. 1993. *Feminism and the Mastery of Nature*. London: Routledge.

Povinelli, E. A. 2006. *The Empire of Love: Toward a Theory of Intimacy, Genealogy, and Carnality*. Durham, NC: Duke University Press.

Rabinow , P. and G. E. Marcus. 2008. *Designs for an Anthropology of the Contemporary*. Durham, NC: Duke University Press.

Reid, H. G. and B. Taylor. 2006. 'Globalization, Democracy, and the Aesthetic Ecology of Emergent Publics for a Sustainable World: Working From John Dewey'. *Asian Journal of Social Science* 34 (1): 22–46.

_____. 2010. *Recovering the Commons: Democracy, Place, and Global Justice*. Urbana: University of Illinois Press.

Ricoeur, P. 1992. *Oneself as Another*. Chicago: University of Chicago Press.

_____. (1950) 1966. *Freedom and Nature: The Voluntary and the Involuntary*. Translated by V. Kohak. Chicago: Northwestern University Press.

_____. (1960) 1967. *The Symbolism of Evil*. Translated by E. Buchanon. Boston: Beacon Press.

_____. (1965) 1986. *Fallible Man*. New York: Fordham University Press.

_____. (1973) 1978. 'Creativity in Language'. In *The Philosophy of Paul Ricoeur*, edited by C. E. Reagan and D. Stewart, 20–33. Boston: Beacon Press.

_____. (1975) 1977. *The Rule of Metaphor: Multi-disciplinary Studies of the Creation of Meaning in Language*. Toronto and Buffalo: University of Toronto Press.

_____. (1983) 1984. *Time and Narrative (Volume 1)*. Translated by K. McLaughlin and D. Pellauer. Chicago: University of Chicago Press.

_____. (1984) 1985. *Time and Narrative (Volume 2)*. Translated by K. McLaughlin and D. Pellauer. Chicago: University of Chicago Press.

_____. (1985) 1988. *Time and Narrative (Volume 3)*. Translated by K. McLaughlin and D. Pellauer. Chicago: University of Chicago Press.

_____. 1986. *Lectures on Ideology and Utopia*. New York: Columbia University Press.

_____. (2000) 2004. *Memory, History, Forgetting*. Translated by K. Blamey and D. Pellauer. Chicago: University of Chicago Press.

Simms, K. 2003. *Paul Ricoeur*. London: Routledge.

Stivers, C. 2009. 'The Ontology of Public Space: Grounding Governance in Social Reality'. *American Behavioral Scientist* 52 (7): 1095–1108.

Taylor, B. 2009. '"Place" as Pre-Political Grounds of Democracy: An Appalachian Case Study in Class Conflict, Forest Politics and Civic Networks'. *American Behavioral Scientist* 52 (6): 826–45.

Chapter 13

CLIFFORD GEERTZ: THE PHILOSOPHICAL TRANSFORMATION OF ANTHROPOLOGY

Gernot Saalmann

Clifford Geertz (1926–2006) was one of the main figures to build a new kind of anthropology, beginning in the 1960s. In doing so, he borrowed many ideas from philosophy. Although some of his works have been read by philosophers too, the influence of his anthropology on philosophy is negligible. The reception of his thoughts does not conform to the generally accepted significance of his writings, appropriate to their philosophical content. Most often, Geertz is read only superficially and the reading is confined to his two most famous texts – 'Thick Description' (1973) and 'Deep Play: Notes on Balinese Cockfight' (1972).

With this chapter, an attempt is made to treat two questions more deeply: 1) which are the main philosophical concepts that are used by Geertz? and 2) how and why did he succeed in transforming anthropology? The first step in trying to answer these questions has to be a short biographical sketch.

1. A Life of Learning

Looking back on his long and outstanding academic career, Geertz claimed, 'I am an ethnographer, and a writer about ethnography from beginning to end; and I don't do systems' (2000b, x). Because Geertz refrained from expounding a systematic theory, we have to reconstruct his theoretical and philosophical thinking from his many publications.

After World War II, at the age of 20, Geertz began his studies of English literature and philosophy at Antioch College in Yellow Springs, Ohio because he wanted to become a writer and/or journalist. His teacher in philosophy, George Geiger, was a student of John Dewey and he introduced Geertz to the pragmatist way of looking at philosophical problems. Nevertheless, Geertz and his wife Hildred went to Harvard to become anthropologists. His major influence there was anthropologist Clyde Kluckhohn (author of a readable introduction to anthropology 1949 and editor of Malinowski 1948), but Geertz also sensed the enthusiasm of Talcott Parsons and his colleagues for building an interdisciplinary Department of Social Relations. Geertz only took one course, held by Parsons, who at that time had just published his translation of the first part of Weber's *Economy and Society* (1949) and was preparing with Edward Shils the volume *Towards a General Theory of Action* (1951). Many decades later Geertz characterized these and other works as a kind of 'effort to construct a unified, generalizing science of society from which could emerge a practical technology for the management of human affairs' (1995c, 46). Geertz spent most of his time at Harvard working for the 'Five Cultures Project' led by Kluckhohn, producing an evaluation, more than one hundred pages long, of the role that alcohol played in these cultures. After only two years of study at Harvard the Geertz family left for fieldwork in Indonesia. Affected by the spirit of the time for 'modernization', Geertz pursued the Weberian task of explaining the relations between religion and economy in Java (resulting in his doctoral dissertation of 1956, published in 1960). After a few years back in Cambridge at the MIT, in Bali for further fieldwork and in Berkeley as assistant professor, the Geertz family moved to Chicago. On the initiative of Edward Shils, Geertz was to work in the Committee for the Study of New Nations (1995, 111) and at the same time, together with his colleagues at the Department for Anthropology, had to outline a new course structure (114). It was here that Geertz, reading and discussing a lot as well as reflecting on his fieldwork experience (then also in Morocco), developed his own theory of culture.

From 1970 until 2000 Geertz was head of the School of Social Science at the distinguished Institute for Advanced Study in Princeton. With this position his influence in the social sciences and the humanities grew considerably. If we look at the stations of his career it becomes clear that Geertz nearly never worked in a classical anthropological institute. Therefore, his thinking is deeply interdisciplinary. In his typically ironic style Geertz characterizes the differing atmospheres in the various academic settings: 'an eclectic collection of let's-go-on-with-it enthusiasts at après-guerre Harvard […] an equanimous company of long-distance reasoners amid the political tumult of sixties Chicago […] a carefully defended island of specialistic research in manicured Princeton' (1995, 134). By comparing the academic tone in Harvard and Chicago ('The Sociology is About to Begin'; 'Meaning Matters') and the two projects – 'an attempt to rationalize social research along industrial lines; a more patched-together handicraft affair' – Geertz implies that his interpretive anthropology has the same theoretical status as structural-functionalism (1995, 119). This bold claim seems to be justified, if one takes a closer look at the theory of culture that it is based on.

2. A Pragmatist Theory of Culture

Geertz had a good idea of the different ways to conceptualize culture; as a postgraduate he had been proofreading the famous review of culture concepts that Alfred Kroeber and Clyde Kluckhohn published in 1952. And Geertz certainly took some inspiration out of their résumé that symbols play a crucial role in culture (1952, 181). In looking for an answer as to how exactly they do and why, Geertz consulted the latest writings in physical anthropology and philosophy. He wrote several texts on the philosophical implications of the physical nature of man (1962a, 75, 78, 83; 1964d; 1966d, 47ff.) and arguments can also be found in his texts on ideology (1964b, 214ff.), religion (1966a, 99), the person in Bali (1966c, 405) and the book *Islam Observed* (1968). Unlike animals, which are confined to an ecological niche, man is open to the world and can live nearly everywhere. With the exception of basic reflexes and unspecified drives, man has no instincts or other *intrinsic* sources of information how to behave and how to live. Therefore he needs *extrinsic* sources of information, which lie outside of the organism (1966a, 92). This information is laid down in systems of symbols, or 'cultural patterns' as they had been famously called by Ruth Benedict (1934). Symbols are defined as 'any object, act, event, quality or relation which serves as a vehicle for conception' (1966a, 91; cf. 1966c, 362) – conception being the symbol's meaning. Here it is clear to see the influence of Susanne K. Langer, who also spoke of symbols as 'vehicles' (1942, 60, 67, 97; cf. Kroeber and Kluckhohn 1952, 184). The systems of symbols are 'like a blueprint' or 'programs for the institution of social and psychological behavior' (1966a, 92, cf. 62; 1964b, 216ff.). But unlike genes, which only *shape* molecules *to them*, symbolic systems are *shaping themselves to* reality to give it meaning (93).

Other philosophers who had an influence on Geertz are Gilbert Ryle (in his critique of Cartesian philosophy, stating that thinking is 'public' and not something taking place in the head [1949, 25, 51, 58; Geertz 1962a, 55ff.; 1966c, 362; 1973a, 10ff.; 1980, 135; 1986, 76]) and Ludwig Wittgenstein (with his idea that the meaning of something is to be found in its use [1953, 7ff.; Geertz 1995, 46; 1973a, 17]). So, in his famous introductory text 'Thick Description', Geertz defines culture as 'webs of significance' (1973a, 5; referring to Weber, although actually paraphrasing Cassirer 1944, 25), but then goes on to explain that 'it is through the flow of behavior – or, more precisely, social action – that cultural forms find articulation' (1973a, 17; cf.

Ryle 1949, 58: 'people's activities are the way their minds work'). That is, by inspecting events we gain access to symbolic systems: 'Culture consists of socially established structures of meaning in terms of which people do things' (1973a, 12). Culture is an 'acted document' and therefore 'doing ethnography is like trying to read [...] a manuscript [...] written [...] in transient examples of shaped behavior' (1973a, 10). With the metaphor of culture as text, Geertz not so much claimed that culture *is* a text, but that it can be *read* like one, because the symbols used in behaviour form a web (Latin: *textum*). Geertz liked this metaphor because it has the capacity to connect Paul Ricoeur's idea that a text is the result of past action (Ricoeur 1971; Geertz 1972b, 448) and Susanne Langer's statement that the various relationships in the symbolic processes are used 'in weaving the intricate web of meaning which is the real fabric of human life' (Langer 1942, 78; cf. Geertz 1957a, 145: 'culture is the fabric of meaning').

With reference to Ryle, Geertz makes the difference between natural science and cultural anthropology clear. Because identical actions can have different meanings, a superficial description is not enough, but a 'thick description' is needed, which consists in 'setting down the meaning particular social actions have for the actors whose actions they are' (Geertz 1973a, 27; it has to be pointed out explicitly here, that 'thick description' does *not* denote *a method*, but merely an *epistemological argument*). But it is not so much the (symbolic) actions that are relevant to describe, than what 'is getting said' in their occurrence (1973a, 10), or as Paul Ricoeur once stated, 'the meaning of the speech event, not the event as event' (1973a, 19). The difference is like that between the statement 'a seemingly female human being walks along the street with a basket in her hand' and 'Mrs Mukerji goes shopping'. The solution offered by ordinary language philosophy to the problem of social and scientific understanding, taken up by Geertz, consists in the direction of attention first to the *practical* dimension. Human behaviour most of the time is symbolic action, action that signifies (1973a, 10, 23). Single acts and symbols refer to others, building systems of symbols and a whole pattern of life (1973a, 14, 17). Therefore, it is this context (1973a, 14) which gives meaning to the single event. The scientific method consists in building hypotheses of interpretation and seeing how useful they are in reaching deeper understanding. 'Cultural analysis is guessing at meanings, assessing the guesses, and drawing explanatory conclusions from the better guesses [...]' (1973a, 20). This is nothing but the 'hermeneutical circle': 'Better informed and better conceptualized [new studies] plunge more deeply into the same things' (1973a, 25; cf. 1974, 69; and 1983b, 11 for other formulations of the circle). The aim is not to find the 'truth', but 'to make available to us answers that others [...] have given, and thus to include them in the consultable record of what man has said' (1973a, 30).

The theory of Geertz is of particular importance because he does not focus on knowledge or meaning, or on action either. He focuses on that which is 'in between': symbols as vehicles of meaning and the symbolic dimension most actions have. So, it is not some abstract 'universe of symbols' that he is after, but the 'universe of symbolic action' (1973a, 24). The special characteristic of symbols is that they alone have the capacity to combine *is* and *ought* (1957b, 126) to answer the questions of 'what?' and 'how?'. They have the 'double aspect' of being 'model *of*' reality and 'model *for*' reality, being a 'picture' of the world of action and a model for action at the same time (1966a, 89, 93). Symbols express and shape something (95), the Balinese cockfight 'provides a metasocial commentary' because it works at once as 'a description and a judgement' (1972b, 448). Being a text and an event, 'in the cockfight, the Balinese forms and discovers his temperament and his society's temper at the same time' (451). In symbolic formulations the 'model *of*' is transposed into the 'model *for*' and thereby made testable *pragmatically* in circular feedback (1957b, 127). Thus, the meaning of symbols or symbolic acts depends on their 'use in an ongoing pattern of life' (1973a, 17). It is clear, then, that the 'interpretive anthropology' of Geertz is based on a pragmatist theory of culture and that Geertz, often scolded for being an idealist, is a purely Wittgensteinian pragmatist.

3. Anthropology and the Quest for Interpretation

It may be useful to restate the main points of Geertz's outline of cultural anthropology:

1) contrary to many criticisms based on a superficial and highly selective reading of his works, Geertz sketches out a *pragmatist theory of culture*; 2) therefore, he is interested in symbols, not in themselves, but in *symbolic acts*; 3) all these acts are knotted together, they form a web or fabric of meaning – or, stated otherwise, a *text*; 4) this text can be read by the scientist entering into the *hermeneutical circle* between interpretations of the whole and the part which enlighten each other.

Never anywhere does Geertz claim that a culture is homogeneous – on the contrary, he showed that it is fragmented into different cultural systems that have their own dynamic and structure. When analysing symbolic systems he broke with mentalism and looked to symbolic action instead, creating what he once termed 'an outdoor psychology' (1982a, 153). The 'text' formed by cultural actions has got a double aspect of existence – as an objective structure and as a particular reading or interpretation.

The empirical objects of 'interpretive anthropology' are symbolic acts. It is not the *persons* that are saying or doing something that Geertz is interested in, nor the *event* of the saying (and its social context), but the *said*, the *meaning*, contextualized in the particular culture as a whole. His anthropology looks more to the *structural dimension* of meaning than to the *situation* or the acting *subject*, which in part give meaning to symbolic actions too.

Geertz was quite successful in bringing about an 'interpretive turn' (1983c, 233) with respect to the analysis of social life. Fred Inglis even claimed that 'Geertz has given anthropology a new idiom' (2000, 180). To explain this, many reasons have to be taken into account:

1) Most of the texts by Geertz are written in a brilliant and intellectually pleasing style. He is indeed an extraordinarily gifted writer (Bonnell and Hunt 1999, 2). His texts, from the beginning of the 1960s at least, are witty and ironic and are a pleasure to read.

2) Geertz had a knowledge of philosophy that was as broad as it was deep. For instance, he refers to Burke, Pierce, Wittgenstein, Cassirer, Langer and Ryle on a single page of one text (1964b, 208), or to most of these authors throughout 'Thick Description' (1973, 3–19). Trying to build something new out of their thoughts could be appealing to many people.

3) With ordinary language philosophy and speech act theory the audience was prepared for a more pragmatist theory of social life (1975a, 77).

4) The reference to Wittgenstein already had become obligatory and therefore met with the expectations of the reader.

5) Geertz made use of the metaphors that crept in from the literary world into the social sciences – like 'drama', 'theatre' and 'role', which are part of the works of Burke, Goffman and Parsons.

6) While closely connected with the leading social theories on the one hand, Geertz distanced himself from them on the other. Deeply influenced, for example, by the basic ideas of Parsons (the four systems), he never fell for the whole theoretical approach (1957a, 145ff.; 1966a, 91ff.; 1966d, 41ff.). Indeed, he proposed an alternative to functionalism as well as to structuralism, although he still explains the functions of religion (1966a) or looks to the structural and contextual dimension of symbolic action.

7) When speaking of 'interpretation' or 'hermeneutics' Geertz evades the *methodological dualism* of explanation and understanding. He clearly states that there is a *dualism of scientific aims* only – the search for laws or meaning (1973a, 5). Experimental science explains on the basis of descriptions, interpretive science formulates a diagnosis based on thick description (1973a, 27).

8) His ethnographical writings could be read as proof that Geertz had been successful in trying to reconstruct anthropology.

9) After working on the 'Five Cultures Project' as a postgraduate his interpretive anthropology becomes strictly comparative – whether comparing different kinds of Muslims in Java (1960), the differing economic outlook of certain groups of the population (1956b; 1963a; 1965), subsistence or plantation economy (1963), Bali and Java, Indonesia and Morocco (1968; 1972e) or the ritualization of power in Bali and Elizabethan England (1977c).

10) Geertz developed certain rhetorical moves to make his interpretations of ethnographical details acceptable to the reader. The first step is to pose a question of common interest, the second to offer some thick descriptions and the third to show their relevance in answering the question. Inglis describes the three 'crucial manoeuvres of interpretive method' as: 'the circumscription of the field; the translation of the strange into the familiar; the algebraic summary' (Inglis 2000, 127; cf. 111). Nevertheless, this kind of presentation still enables the readers to develop their own interpretation of the ethnographic 'facts' as well.

Contrary to all this, a big hindrance for a broader reception of Geertz's ideas in philosophy might be seen in his combination of analytic philosophy and the hermeneutic tradition. He speaks of 'forms of life' as well as of 'lifeworld', 'way of life' and 'ways of being in the world', likewise. In the discipline itself, such an easy overcoming of the deep opposition between two of the main strands of contemporary philosophy seems impossible.

4. A Sociological Transformation of Geertz's Ideas

Although there are good reasons to revive the theoretical insights of Clifford Geertz, one has to admit some shortcomings. First of all, the theory of culture is incomplete because Geertz stopped to work on it. He was more interested in the 'progress of empirical research' (1995, 115). Secondly, he did not develop a systematic theory of symbols. Geertz did not pay enough attention to the difference between 'symbolic actions' (dealing with symbols) and the 'symbolic dimension of action'. Third: even if all human actions have meaning, not everything is meaningful to the same extent. How could the 'depth' of meaning be evaluated? Fourth: the question of how meaning is constituted is left open by Geertz. He is quite right not to confine himself to the subject or the intersubjective sphere, but to look at action and interaction instead. Nevertheless, it remains unclear where social action gets its meaning from. Even if meaning should be confined to the process of interpretation, there remain open questions. To which extent do we have to look to the situation for an interpretation and to which extent to the structural dimension? If we consider the difference between interpretations of one's own culture and interpretations by an outsider, epistemological arguments are needed to explain differences and similarities between them. Fifth: although pointing to symbolic practice and thick description, both of them nearly never appear in the ethnographic writings of Geertz; we are confronted with his interpretations only. Geertz does not make clear the step from thick descriptions to interpretations. What happens during the process of interpretation? What kind of methods are useful therein – if we are not to leave this to the genius of the interpreter? Sixth: contrary to his pragmatist theory of symbol use and action, Geertz did not outline a theory of practice. Nevertheless, it could be shown that the double aspect of symbols, which Geertz worked at, is highly suitable to supplement Anthony Giddens's thoughts on structure and agency, as well as Pierre Bourdieu's theory of the genesis of practice. All three of these authors laid stress on the double aspect of structures, which are structured by past events and work to structure something in the future.

As can be seen, there is much potential in the basic ideas of Clifford Geertz for sociological (and cultural) theory to be developed in the future.

Works of Clifford Geertz

1956a. 'Religious Belief and Economic Behavior in a Central Javanese Town. Some Preliminary Remarks'. *Economic Development and Cultural Change* 4 (2): 134–58.

1956b. 'Capital Intensive Agriculture in a Peasant Society: A Case Study'. *Social Research* 23, 433–49.

1957a. 'Ritual and Social Change: A Javanese Example'. *American Anthropologist* 59: 32–54. Reprinted in Geertz 1973, 142–69.

1957b. 'Ethos, Worldview and the Analysis of Sacred Symbols'. *Antioch Review* 17: 421–37. Reprinted in Geertz 1973, 126–41.

1959. 'Form and Variation in Balinese Village Structure'. *American Anthropologist* 61: 991–1012.

1960. *The Religion of Java*. Glencoe, IL: The Free Press.

1960a. 'The Javanese Kijaji: The Changing Role of a Cultural Broker'. *Comparative Studies in Society and History* 2: 228–49.

1962a. 'The Growth of Culture and the Evolution of Mind'. In *Theories of Mind*, edited by J. M. Sher, 713–40. New York: The Free Press. Reprinted in Geertz 1973, 55–83.

1962b. 'Social Change and Economic Modernization in Two Indonesian Towns: A Case in Point'. In *On the Theory of Change*, edited by E. E. Hagen, 385–407. Homewood, IL: Dorsey.

1962c. 'The Rotating Credit Association: A "Middle Rung" in Development'. *Economic Development and Cultural Change* 10 (3), 241–63.

1963. *Agricultural Involution: The Process of Ecological Change in Indonesia*. Berkeley: University of California Press.

1963a. *Peddlers and Princes*. Chicago: University of Chicago Press.

1963b. 'The Integrative Revolution: Primordial Sentiments and Civil Politics in the New States'. In Geertz, *Old Societies and New States: The Quest for Modernity in Asia and Africa*, 105–57. New York: The Free Press. Reprinted in Geertz 1973, 255–310.

1964a. '"Internal Conversion" in Contemporary Bali'. In *Malayan and Indonesian Studies*, edited by J. S. Bastinand and R. Roolvink, 282–302. Oxford: Clarendon Press. Reprinted in Geertz 1973, 170–89.

1964b. 'Ideology as a Cultural System'. In *Ideology and Discontent*, edited by D. E. Apter, 47–76. New York: The Free Press. Reprinted in Geertz 1973, 193–233.

1964c. 'Teknonymy in Bali: Parenthood, Age-grading and Genealogical Amnesia' (with Hildred Geertz). *Journal of the Royal Anthropological Society* 94: 94–108.

1964d. 'The Transition to Humanity'. In *Horizons of Anthropology*, edited by S. Tax, 37–48. Chicago: Aldine.

1964e. 'Tihingan: A Balinese Village'. *Bijdragen tot de Taal-, Land- en Volkenkunde* 120: 1–33. Reprinted as: 'Organization of the Balinese Subak', in *Irrigation and Agricultural Development in Asia: Perspectives from the Social Sciences*, edited by E. W. Coward, 70–90. Ithaca, NY: Cornell University Press. 1980.

1965. *The Social History of an Indonesian Town*. Cambridge, MA: MIT Press.

1966a. 'Religion as a Cultural System'. In *Anthropological Studies of Religion*, edited by M. Banton, 1–46. London: Tavistock. Reprinted in Geertz 1973, 87–125.

1966b. 'Modernization in a Muslim Society'. In *Religion and Progress in Modern Asia*, edited R. Bellah, 92–108. New York: The Free Press/Pall Mall. Reprinted in R. O. Tilman, ed. *Man, State and Society in Contemporary Southeast Asia*. New York, 1969, 201–11.

1966c. *Person, Time and Conduct in Bali: an Essay in Cultural Analysis*. New Haven: Yale University Press. Reprinted in Geertz 1973, 360–411.

1966d. 'The Impact of the Concept of Culture on the Concept of Man'. *Bulletin of the Atomic Scientists* 22: 2–8. Reprinted in Geertz 1973, 33–54.

1966e. 'Are the Javanese Mad?' *Encounter* 27: 86–88.

1966f. Book review on C. Hooykaas and Agama Tirtha, *Five Studies in Hindu-Balinese Religion*. *American Anthropologist* 68: 242–43.

1967a. 'Politics Past, Politics Present: Some Notes on the Uses of Anthropology in Understanding the New States'. *European Journal of Sociology* 8: 1–14. Reprinted in Geertz 1973, 327–41.

1967b. 'The Cerebral Savage: On the Work of Claude Lévi-Strauss'. *Encounter* 28: 25–32. Reprinted in Geertz 1973, 345–59.

1968. *Islam Observed: Religious Development in Morocco and Indonesia*. New Haven: Yale University Press.

1968a. 'Thinking as a Moral Act: Ethical Dimensions of Anthropological Fieldwork in the New States'. *Antioch Review* 28 (2): 139–58. Reprinted in Geertz 2000a, 21–41.

1968b. 'Religion: Anthropological Study'. In *International Encyclopedia of the Social Sciences*, vol. 13, edited by D. L. Sills, 398–406. New York: MacMillan.

1968c. 'Village'. *Sills* 16: 318–22.

1969a. 'Myrdal's Mythology: "Modernism" and the Third World'. *Encounter* 33: 26–34.

1969b. 'On the Languages of the Humanistic Sciences'. *Daedalus* 98: 981–92.

1971. 'After the Revolution: The Fate of Nationalism in the New States'. In *Stability and Social Change: A Volume in Honor of Talcott Parsons*, edited B. Barberand and A. Inkeles, 357–76. Cambridge, MA: Little, Brown. Reprinted in Geertz 1973, 234–54.

1972a. Letter of invitation by C. Geertz and P. de Man. Cited in the preface by the editor to Issue 1: 'Myth, Symbol, and Culture' of *Daedalus* 101: v–viii. Slightly changed in C. Geertz, *Myth, Symbol and Culture*. New York: Norton, 1974, ix–xi.

1972b. 'Deep Play: Notes on the Balinese Cockfight'. *Daedalus* 101: 1–38. Reprinted in Geertz 1973, 412–53.

1972c. 'Afterword: The Politics of Meaning'. In *Culture and Politics in Indonesia. Ithaca*, edited by C. Holt, 319–36. Ithaca, NY: Cornell University Press. Reprinted as: 'The Politics of Meaning' in Geertz 1973, 311–26.

1972d. Comment. In *Rural Politics and Social Change in the Middle East*, edited by R. Antoun and I. Harik, 460–67. Bloomington: Indiana University Press.

1972e. 'The Wet and the Dry: Traditional Irrigation in Bali and Morocco'. *Human Ecology* 1: 23–39.

1973. *The Interpretation of Cultures*. New York: Basic Books.

1973a. 'Thick Description: Toward an Interpretive Theory of Culture'. In Geertz 1973, 3–30.

1974a. '"From the Native's Point of View": On the Nature of Anthropological Understanding'. *Bulletin of the American Academy of Arts and Sciences* 28 (1): 26–45. Reprinted in Geertz 1983a, 55–70.

1975. *Kinship in Bali* (with Hildred Geertz). Chicago: University of Chicago Press.

1975a. 'Common Sense as a Cultural System'. *Antioch Review* 33 (1): 5–26. Reprinted in Geertz 1983a, 73–93.

1976. 'Art as a Cultural System'. *Modern Language Notes* 91: 1473–99. Reprinted in Geertz 1983a, 94–120.

1977a. 'The Judging of Nations: Some Comments on the Assessment of Regimes in the New States'. *European Journal of Sociology* 18: 245–61.

1977b. 'Found in Translation: On the Social History of the Moral Imagination'. In *The Georgia Review* 31: 788–810. Reprinted in Geertz 1983a, 36–54.

1977c. 'Centers, Kings and Charisma: Reflections on the Symbolics of Power'. In *Culture and Its Creators: Essays in Honor of Edward Shils*, edited by J. Ben-David and T. N. Clark, 150–71. Chicago: University of Chicago Press. Reprinted in Geertz 1983a, 121–46.

1978a. 'The Bazaar Economy: Information and Search in Peasant Marketing'. *American Economic Review* 68 (2): 28–32.

1978b. 'Stir Crazy (Book Review on M. Foucault, Discipline and Punish)'. *New York Review of Books* 26 January 1978. Reprinted in P. Burke, ed. *Critical Essays on Michel Foucault*. Aldershot: Scolar Press, 1992, 139–46.

1978c. 'Group Report: Sociobiology, Morality and Culture' (with R. C. Solomon, E. A. Gellner, J. Goody, F. A. Jenner, T. Nagel, G. S. Stent, W. Tu and G. W. Wolters). In *Morality as a Biological Phenomenon* (Life Sciences Research Report 9), edited by G. S. Stent, 283–307. Berlin: Abakon Verlags-Gesellschaft.

1979. 'Suq: The Bazaar Economy in Sefrou'. In *Meaning and Order in Moroccan Society: Three Essays in Cultural Analysis*, edited by C. Geertz, H. Geertz and L. Rosen, 123–313. Cambridge: Cambridge University Press.

1980. *Negara: The Theatre State in Nineteenth-century Bali*. Princeton: Princeton University Press.

1980a. 'Blurred Genres: The Refiguration of Social Thought'. *The American Scholar* 49, 165–79. Reprinted in Geertz 1983a, 19–35.

1980b. 'Ports of Trade in Nineteenth Century Bali'. *Research in Economic Anthropology* 3: 109–22.

1982a. 'The Way We Think Now: Toward an Ethnography of Modern Thought'. *Bulletin of the American Academy of Arts and Sciences* 35 (5): 14–34. Reprinted in Geertz 1983a, 147–63.

1982b. Book review on M. Sahlins, *Historical Metaphors and Mythical Realities: Structure in the Early History of the Sandwich Islands Kingdom. American Ethnologist* 9: 583–84.

1982c. Foreword to K. J. Pelzer, *Planters Against Peasants: The Agrarian Struggle in East Sumatra*. Leiden: Nijhoff, vii–xii.

1983. *Dichte Beschreibung: Beiträge zum Verstehen kultureller Systeme*. Frankfurt: Suhrkamp Verlag.

1983a. *Local Knowledge: Further Essays in Interpretive Anthropology*. New York: Basic Books.

1983b. Introduction to Geertz 1983a, 3–16.

1983c. 'Local Knowledge: Fact and Law in Comparative Perspective'. In Geertz 1983a, 167–234.

1983d. Foreword to J. S. Lansing, *The Three Worlds of Bali*. New York: Praeger, vii–x.

1984a. 'Distinguished Lecture: Anti Anti-Relativism'. *American Anthropologist* 86: 263–78. Reprinted in Geertz 2000a, 42–67.

1984b. 'Culture and Social Change: The Indonesian Case'. *Man* 19: 511–32.

1985. 'Waddling In'. *Times Literary Supplement* 7 (4288): 623–24. Reprinted in Geertz 2000a, 89–97.

1986a. 'The Uses of Diversity'. *Michigan Quarterly Review* 25: 105–23. Reprinted in Geertz 2000a, 68–88.

1986b. 'Making Experience, Authoring Selves'. Epilogue to *The Anthropology of Experience*, edited by V. W. Turner and E. M. Bruner, 373–80. Urbana: University of Illinois Press.

1987. Book review of L. Abu-Lughod, *Veiled Sentiments: Honor and Poetry in a Bedouin Society*. *American Ethnologist* 14: 567–68.

1988. *Works and Lives: The Anthropologist as Author*. Stanford: Stanford University Press.

1988a. 'Recollections of an Itinerant Career'. *Bulletin of Indonesian Economic Studies* 24: 31–51.

1988b. 'Citation Classic: The Interpretation of Cultures'. *Current Contents* 20 (33): 14.

1989. 'Toutes Directions: Reading the Signs in an Urban Sprawl'. *International Journal of Middle East Studies* 21: 291–306.

1990a. 'History and Anthropology'. *New Literary History* 21: 321–35. Reprinted in Geertz 2000a, 118–33.

1990b. '"Popular Art" and the Javanese Tradition'. *Indonesia* 50: 77–94.

1990c. Comment on M. Carrithers, 'Is Anthropology Art or Science?' *Current Anthropology* 31: 274.

1991a. 'An Interview with Clifford Geertz' (by Richard Handler). *Current Anthropology* 32: 603–613.

1991b. 'The Social Scientist as Author: Clifford Geertz on Ethnography and Social Construction' (interview with Gary Olson). In *(Inter)views: Cross-Disciplinary Perspectives on Rhetoric and Literacy*, edited by G. A. Olson and I. Gale, 187–210. Carbondale: Southern Illinois University Press.

1993. '"Local Knowledge" and It's Limits'. *Yale Journal of Criticism* 5: 129–35. Reprinted in Geertz 2000a, 133–42.

1994. 'Angestammte Loyalitäten, bestehende Einheiten: Anthropologische Reflexionen zur Identitätspolitik'. *Merkur* 48: 392–403.

1995. *After the Fact: Two Countries, Four Decades, One Anthropologist*. Cambridge, MA: Harvard University Press.

1995a. 'Culture War' (book review on G. Obeyesekere and M. Sahlins). *New York Review of Books*, 30 November 1995: 4–6. Reprinted in Geertz 2000a, 97–107.

1995b. 'The Strange Estrangement: Charles Taylor and the Natural Sciences'. In *Philosophy in an Age of Pluralism*, edited by J. Tully and D. M. Weinstock, 83–95. Cambridge: Cambridge University Press. Reprinted in Geertz 2000a, 143–59.

1995c. (Quotations of an interview Geertz gave to David Berreby) D. Berreby, 'Unabsolute Truths: Clifford Geertz'. *New York Times Magazine*, 9 April 1995, 44–7.

1996. *Welt in Stücken: Kultur und Politik am Ende des 20. Jahrhunderts*. Vienna: Passagen Verlag. In English (1998): *The World in Pieces*. Reprinted in Geertz 2000a, 218–63.

1996a. Afterword to K. H. Basso and S. Feld, eds. *Senses of Place*. Santa Fe: School of American Research Press, 259–62.

1997. 'The Legacy of Thomas Kuhn: The Right Text at the Right Time'. *Common Knowledge* 6: 1–5. Reprinted in Geertz 2000a, 160–66.

1998. 'Deep Hanging Out'. *New York Review of Books*, 22 October 1998. Reprinted in Geertz 2000a, 107–118.

1999a. 'Passage and Accident: A Life of Learning'. In Geertz 2000a, 3–20.

1999b. '"The Pinch of Destiny": Religion as Experience, Meaning, Identity, Power'. *Raritan* 19 (4): 1–19. Reprinted in Geertz 2000a, 167–86.

2000a. *Available Light: Anthropological Reflections on Philosophical Topics*. Princeton: Princeton University Press.

2000b. Preface to Geertz 2000a, ix–xiv.

2000c. 'Imbalancing Act: Jerome Bruner's Cultural Psychology'. In *Language, Culture, Self: The Philosophical Psychology of Jerome Bruner*, edited by D. Bakhurst and S. Shanker, 19–30. London: Sage. Reprinted in Geertz 2000a, 187–202.

2000d. 'Culture, Mind, Brain/Brain, Mind, Culture'. In Geertz 2000a, 203–17.

2000e. 'Indonesia: Starting Over'. *New York Review of Books*, 11 May. Reprinted in HyperGeertz. Online: http://hypergeertz.jku.at/HyperGeertz-2000-2009.htm (accessed 21 May 2013). Reprinted in Geertz 2010, 112–22.

2001a. 'School Building: a Retrospective Preface'. In *Schools of Thought: Twenty-five Years of Interpretive Social Science*, edited by J. W. Scott and D. Keates, 1–11. Princeton: Princeton University Press.

2001b. *The Near East in the Far East: On Islam in Indonesia*. IAS Occasional Papers 12. Princeton: Princeton University Press. Reprinted in Geertz 2010, 160–84.

2002a. 'Interview with Clifford Geertz' (by N. Panourgia). In *Anthropological Theory* 2: 421–32. Reprinted in HyperGeertz. Online: http://hypergeertz.jku.at/HyperGeertz-2000-2009.htm (accessed 21 May 2013).

2002b. '"I Don't Do Systems": An Interview with Clifford Geertz' (by A. Micheelsen). In *Method and Theory in the Study of Religion: Journal of the North American Association for the Study of Religion* 14: 2–20. Reprinted in HyperGeertz. Online: http://hypergeertz.jku.at/HyperGeertz-2000-2009.htm (accessed 21 May 2013).

2002c. 'An Inconstant Profession: The Anthropological Life in Interesting Times'. *Annual Review of Anthropology* 31: 1–19.

2002d. 'The Last Humanist' (book review on E. Gombrich). *New York Review of Books*, 26 September 2002. Reprinted in HyperGeertz. Online: http://hypergeertz.jku.at/HyperGeertz-2000-2009.htm (accessed 21 May 2013).

2003a. 'Off the Menu' (book review on T. Cowen). *The New Republic* 205: 27–30. Reprinted in HyperGeertz. Online: http://hypergeertz.jku.at/HyperGeertz-2000-2009.htm (accessed 21 May 2013).

2003b. 'Which Way to Mecca?' (book review) part 1 and 2. *New York Review of Books* 12 June and 3 July 2003. Reprinted in HyperGeertz. Online: http://hypergeertz.jku.at/HyperGeertz-2000-2009.htm (accessed 21 May 2013). Reprinted in Geertz 2010, 135–56.

2003c. 'Interview with Clifford Geertz' (by J. Gerring). *Qualitative Methods: Newsletter of the American Political Science Association* 1 (2). Reprinted in HyperGeertz. Online: http://hypergeertz.jku.at/HyperGeertz-2000-2009.htm (accessed 21 May 2013).

2004a. 'What Is a State If It Is Not a Sovereign? Reflections on Politics in Complicated Places'. *Current Anthropology* 45: 577–91.

2004b. Interview by A. Macfarlane in Cambridge, 6 May 2004. Keywords in HyperGeertz: http://hypergeertz.jku.at/HyperGeertz-2000-2009.htm (accessed 21 May 2013).

2005a. Commentary. In *Geertz and His Colleagues: A Colloquium*, edited by R. A. Shweder and B. Good, 108–124. Chicago: University of Chicago Press.

2005b. 'Shifting Aims, Moving Targets: On the Anthropology of Religion'. *Journal of the Royal Anthropological Institute* 11: 1–15.

2005c. 'Die Dritte Welt: Vom Fanal der Revolution zur postkolonialen Realitätsbewältigung'. *Lettre International* 69: 46–52. English version in *Dissent* (Winter) 2005, 35–45.

2010. *Life Among the Anthros and Other Essays*, edited by F. Inglis. Princeton: Princeton University Press.

References

Benedict, Ruth. 1934. *Patterns of Culture*. New York: Routledge.

Bonnell, Victoria E. and Lynn Hunt, eds. 1999. *Beyond the Cultural Turn: New Directions in the Study of Society and Culture*. Berkeley: University of California Press.

Cassirer, Ernst. 1944. *An Essay on Man: An Introduction to a Philosophy of Human Culture*. New Haven: Yale University Press.

Inglis, Fred. 2000. *Clifford Geertz: Culture, Custom and Ethics*. Cambridge: Polity Press.

Kluckhohn, Clyde. 1949. *Mirror for Man: The Relation of Anthropology to Modern Life*. New York: Whittlesey House.

Kroeber, Alfred L. and Clyde Kluckhohn. 1952. *Culture: A Critical Review of the Concepts and Definitions*. Cambridge, MA: Peabody Museum.

Langer, Susanne K. 1942. *Philosophy in a New Key: A Study in the Symbolism of Reason, Rite and Art*. Cambridge, MA: Harvard University Press.

Malinowski, Bronisław. 1948. *Magic, Science and Religion*. Garden City, NY: Doubleday.

Parsons, Talcott and Edward A. Shils, eds. 1951. *Toward a General Theory of Action*. Cambridge, MA: Harvard University Press.

Ricoeur, Paul. 1971. 'The Model of the Text: Meaningful Action Considered as Text'. *Social Research* 38: 529–62.

Ryle, Gilbert L. 1949. *The Concept of Mind*. London: Hutchinson.

Weber, Max. 1949. *The Theory of Social and Economic Organization*. Translated by T. Parsons. New York: The Free Press.

Wittgenstein, Ludwig. 1953. *Philosophische Untersuchungen / Philosophical Investigations*. Translated by G. E. M. Anscombe. Oxford: Blackwell.

Chapter 14

BAKHTIN'S HERITAGE IN ANTHROPOLOGY: ALTERITY AND DIALOGUE

Marcin Brocki

For over thirty years, the development of theory in anthropology has been under heavy influence from literary theory, serving mostly as an inspiration in solving certain problems in the research practice of ethnography. This influence first started with the assimilation of structuralism and semiotics into anthropology, with their concept of culture as a collection of texts interacting with one another. The real interdisciplinary dialogue, however, originated with the discovery, received in the field of ethnography with much suspicion and astonishment, that the practice of anthropology is not only collecting and analysing data, but also 'producing texts', and that the textualization of the reality examined is part of that process, too.

At present it is generally, or almost generally, accepted that field data are not 'things in themselves', but a result of the process of gaining them (Rabinow 1977, ix). Hence, neither the experience nor the interpretative activity of a researcher are a 'matrix tool' for reality. In them, we always encounter translation, which can be defined as a negotiation involving at least two subjects (Clifford 1988, 41; see also: Sperber 1996, 16–18). It was found that dialogue and polyphony (the basis of which was discovered in Bakhtin's writings) characterize the process of translation better than analysis or interpretation, which presume the hierarchical and thus morally uncertain relationship between the researcher and the researched (see Fabian 2001, 25; Wagner 2003, 60), and that hierarchy disturbs the rules of 'negotiation', changing the process of knowing into 'colonizing the other', and consolidating the obviousness (common sense) of the researcher's thinking. The 'dialogue', on the other hand, reminds us that what the ethnographer should find out does not exist as a definitive idea and is not clearly given, but it is rather an effect of a dialectical process of producing knowledge. In this process any hierarchy may only be a final effect, and not a presupposed starting point.

As Irene Portis-Winner noticed (1998, 18), the discovery of Bakhtin's idea of dialogism coincided with a crisis of representation and the so-called 'literary turn' in ethnography. Stephen Tyler emphasizes that these parallel processes were 'motivated by longing for a return to an original presence, a return that is bound to be frustrated by the fact that any representation alters what is represented' (Mannheim and Tedlock 1995, 7). In addition, at the time of this discovery (in the mid-1970s), the boisterous discussion on ethical dilemmas of ethnography, its colonial and neocolonial involvement, had been passing through anthropology. The solution to those dilemmas was expected to be found, among others, in Bakhtin's writings. The 'ethical phenomenology' included in his *Philosophy of Act* would be of great import in this context, but anthropologist attention was riveted to the ideas of alterity and dialogism that run through Bakhtin's later writings. I have to stress that as a remedy for anthropology's colonial involvement Bakhtin's works are useless. As Edward Said (1989, 210–14) points out, Bakhtin's dialogism, and other 'fashionable' theoretical proposals alike, are completely unable to get anthropology out of its colonial heritage. And what is more, the fetishization of otherness and difference that accompany the idea of dialogism, instead of clarifying anthropology's 'imperial connections', actually fog the issue. Said's comments are not directed toward a critique of Bakhtin's concepts, but a critique of how those ideas were used.

Bakhtin's ideas are obviously present in anthropology not only while discussing problems of otherness, dialogism and polyphony, but also within debates on 'carnival culture' – the work on Rabelais turns out to be an extremely efficient source of inspiration (Bakhtin 1999). Critical remarks on nonverbal communication, the concept of the sign and communicative acts contained in the book are sometimes found in anthropological works. However, anthropologists' practical attitude toward social issues and culture direct their attention towards the concept of dialogism because it seemed to be perfectly adjusted for the description of real relations between researcher, researched, the text and its reader. Starting in the 1970s, those relations have been called dialectic or dialogic. Moreover, it was recognized that the ethnographic text itself stays in dialogic relationship with the reality it concerns. It is worth noting here that the reality described and interpreted by anthropologists is already someone's interpretation, a social vision (the very fact that comfortably relieves anthropologists from ontological considerations). Therefore, an axis of the dialogic relations extends beyond the model presented above (researcher–researched–text–reader); only the heuristic of anthropological inquiry demands cutting the axis in a particular place in order to avoid the trap of infinite references that obstruct any scientific effort.

František Vrhel noted accurately that anthropology found itself in the concept of dialogism because in fact it is a transformation of the other's voice. In ethnography the 'other's' voice is a voice inside the voice about the voice. It is an anthropologist's statement about his informant's statements. It is, as Bakhtin wrote, 'thought about other's reflections, their acts of will, manifestations, expressions, signs' (Bakhtin 1988, in Vrhel 1993, 8). But a more important feature of dialogism, emphasized by Bakhtin, is that dialogic cognition is a meeting in which the question and the answer are not logical relations that can be fitted in one consciousness; every answer brings out new questions. If the answer doesn't engender new questions it drops out of dialogue and becomes part of systemic cognition that is impersonal in its nature (Bakhtin 1975, in: Czaplejewicz and Kasperski 1983, 235). The opinion of one of the most influential persons among dialogic anthropologists, Kevin Dwyer, is almost a copy of the above thesis. According to this author, the rules of the meeting are indeed as unpredictable and unstable as the rules of the dialogue (1982, 274).

This dialectical process was perfectly described in Paul Rabinow's *Reflections on Fieldwork in Morocco*, where he wrote:

As I began to question Ali about the curing, my scientific categories were modified – I understood more about curing, its tacit assumptions, modes of action, and limits – but my common-sense world was also changed. I knew no curers in New York. Thus the first time I witnessed activities like this one they required greatly heightened attention on my part; they focussed and dominated my consciousness. But as the field work progressed and I witnessed such performances a number of times, I began to take them largely for granted. They increasingly became part of my stock of knowledge, part of my world. Ali's curing activity no longer jolted my consciousness, and I was free to focus elsewhere.

This highlighting, identification, and analysis also disturbed Ali's usual patterns of experience. He was constantly being forced to reflect on his own activities and objectify them. Because he was a good informant, he seemed to enjoy this process and soon began to develop an art of presenting his world to me. The better he became at it, the more we shared together. But the more we engaged in such activity, the more he experienced aspects of his own life in new ways. Under my systematic questioning, Ali was taking realms of his own world and interpreting them for an outsider. This meant that he, too, was spending more time in this liminal, self-conscious world between cultures. This is a difficult and trying experience – one could almost say it is 'unnatural' – and not everyone will tolerate its ambiguities and strains.

This was the beginning of the dialectic process of fieldwork. I say dialectic because neither the subject nor the object remain static. With Richard or Ibrahim, there had been only minor movement on either side. But with Ali there began to emerge a mutually constructed ground of experience and understanding, a realm of tenuous common sense which was constantly breaking down, being patched-up, and re-examined, first here, then there.

This examination, although grounded in and constantly mediated by everyday experience of this new sort, is governed for the anthropologist by his professional concerns. Ultimately this constitutes his commitment; this is why he is there. For the informant, it is a more practical affair, both in the sense that we can assume that his motivations are primarily pragmatic and in the sense that he is developing a practical art of response and presentation.

As time wears on, anthropologist and informant share a stock of experiences upon which they hope to rely with less self-reflection in the future. The common understanding they construct is fragile and thin, but it is upon this shaky ground that anthropological inquiry proceeds. (Rabinow 1977, 38–9)

The irremovable feature of the dialogue is the transformation that participants pass through. An anthropologist and his informants alike start to function within the 'world between' – a 'middle ground' between their worlds – so they transgress a common knowledge and such an experience of their cultures through confrontation in dialogue. Transgression is the precondition of the proper dialogue. In the last parts of Victor Turner's story about his best informant among the Ndembu, Muchona, he wrote that in their long-lasting cooperation Muchona achieved an amazing level of objectivity in relation to the most sacred values of his own culture. Turner was not sure whether or not the radical transformation his informant passed through was caused by their interaction, but had no doubts that such a transformation occurred (Turner 2006, 172). In another part of the book, when the author reports on his mutually enriching contact with Muchona, he reflects on the consequences of living for a long time in the 'world between' for his informant, and he's not the only one to pose the problem. Kevin Dwyer and Vincent Crapanzano are convinced that the dialogue between a researcher and his informants influence their identity, their relationships, their shared values etc., but to prove that the presence of the anthropologist is the crucial – or only element – of an activation of those social processes is hazardous (Lubas 2003, 173).

The inner transformation of participants in dialogue is possible only in the case of openness on both sides – the researcher and his informants. Thus not every kind of contact will result in dialogue. Openness is, above all, the ability and the will to listen – but 'to listen' is a complex metaphor that stands in opposition to another common anthropological metalanguage metaphor of 'observation'. When openness becomes the condition of anthropological understanding, the responsibility for interpretation is shifted from 'method' to the proximity of the researcher-researched relation, the participants' abilities and the will to dialogue.

Paul Rabinow maintains that fieldwork is a complex dialogue between ethnographer, his professional culture, the reader and the 'native'; a dialogue in which all meaning is a result of negotiation. Rabinow showed clearly that the view of a culture emerging from fieldwork is not merely a sum of actions and concepts of persons involved in the research. Neither can it be simply translated into 'familiar and orderly categories' (Geertz 1988, 1) of anthropological metalanguage, as it is 'polyphonic' (see, for example, Mannheim and Tedlock 1995, 2).[1] Such a characteristic perfectly matches the Bakhtinian view of the normal utterance.

> [Bakhtin] defines the boundaries of the utterance in terms of the relationship among subjects, with special reference to the response elicited by the utterance and to responsive nature of understanding: in other words, the boundaries of the utterance are those of the dialogic interrelationship with another utterance, with another text. Therefore, the utterance is an open, dialogic, intertextual unit whose signifying value is determined through its contact with the other. (Petrilli 1998, 210)

According to Bakhtin, 'polyphony' is multiplicity of equal, independent, incoherent voices and consciousness and their worlds that form a unity of a certain event while keeping their autonomy (Bakhtin 1970, in: Czaplejewicz and Kasperski 1983, 353). Although Bakhtin's remarks concern the author and characters of Dostoyevsky's novels, the analogies to anthropological practice are easy to find. He wrote that the main characters in Dostoyevsky's prose are not subjects to the author's authoritative voice, but to their own self-descriptions, which have direct semantic value within the story. Therefore 'the word' of the character is not limited to descriptive or plot-pragmatic functions, just as the author's word is not narrowed to express his own ideological position. The consciousness of the character is given here with all the otherness of other, and at the same time the literary hero is not objectified nor finalized within the author's words – that is the main difference from traditional novels.

Bakhtin maintains that Dostoyevsky invented the polyphonic novel as a radically new genre. It features a hero whose voice is constructed the same way as author's. The character's view of the world and himself is of the same value as author's within the story – it is not subordinated to an objectified view of the character as a descriptive element and it doesn't function as the mouthpiece of the author. It is an independent element within the structure of the story, parallel to the author's voice (Bakhtin 1970, in: Czaplejewicz and Kasperski 1983, 353–4).

The above considerations sum up the most important elements (from an anthropological point of view) of Bakhtin's idea of polyphony: multiplicity of equal subjects forming a particular event; the 'other' as a subject of its own word, a subject as independent and as significant as the author within the text, and an active co-author of the interpreted event.

One may ask what are the consequences for anthropological practice of applying the discussed idea. When portraying the polyphonic picture of culture the author neither objectifies the characters nor transforms their worlds into artifact.[2] František Vrhel notes in this context that the ethnographer should not grant himself with the privilege of a deeper understanding the other's world, but only with an essential, pragmatic knowledge that any ethnographic description cannot exist without. Following Bakhtin, we have to remember that the truth about the world is inseparable from the personal truth. In other words, the 'truth' before the ethnographic manuscript exists only as a personal truth. Thus the monologue is unacceptable as it transforms the personal into an impersonal mute object with its authoritative surplus of author's consciousness (Vrhel 1993, 12).

But there is an explicit, ethically ambiguous, dimension of dialogue that can be transformed into questions about our moral right to evoke doubts in our interlocutor's mind, doubts concerning the essentials of his own common sense that are engendered without any control of the consequences (see, for example, Fabian 1996, 245–6). The positive answer to such a question is possible until the confrontation concerns two subjects, as there is no such moral ambiguity in normal communication. But when the confrontation is guided only by 'professional interests' of the 'researcher', and when those interests are aimed at constructing the other with 'orderly and known' categories of the professional meta-language, the situation is different.[3]

I believe that the profession of anthropology develops special skills, makes scholars especially sensitive to the other and at the same time suspicious of any kind of fixed truth – this attitude anthropologists bring to the field, where they interact as 'normal human beings', subjects among other subjects. But understanding means translation and translation means an asymmetrical relation. Does it mean, then, that we have to abandon understanding to avoid moral dilemmas imposed by 'asymmetry'? The obvious answer is 'no', because there are levels of the ethics of interaction.

I'd like to indicate the fact that the 'ethical dimension' of ethnographic practice, so apparent in the consequences of 'dialectical' or 'dialogical' fieldwork as I have just summarized, was substituted by, or rather transformed into, the technical problem of representation and method, which in turn marginalized the 'ethical'. It happened because anthropologists forgot to detach the question of ethics from the vision of 'scientific ethnography', and were trying to convince us that the 'moral ambiguity' can be removed from their practice by developing more sophisticated methods.

Those who tried to address the problem of otherness to ethics also failed by using the discourse more exclusively and reinforcing the hierarchical relationship between 'author' and 'informer', more so than earlier ethnographers, making the authorial voice even stronger than before (Abu-Lughod 1991, 152).

As I have mentioned above, the 'ethical dimension' was limited to the problem of representation. Many authors ask about the ways of representing the complex dialectics of ethnographic research in an ethnographic text (see, for example: Crapanzano 1980; Dwyer 1982; Rabinow 1977; Tedlock 1979, 1983) and ask how the dialectic of reflection and improvised interpretation can be transformed into a concise picture, the intended result of ethnographic research. They found the temporary salvation in 'polyphony'.

Although the term 'polyphony' was borrowed by anthropologists from Bakhtin's writings, it has been broadened compared to the way it was originally used by its author.[4] In the research practice of ethnography, it relates both to the reality being examined (then, however, ethnology becomes entangled into consideration of the nature of cultural phenomena), the dialectics of field research and the 'multiple' authorship of ethnographic texts. The texts involve the author-anthropologist as the narrator of the story (who describes, analyses and interprets the facts; he always has the fullest knowledge). There is also a reader, who is not directly present in the text, yet the text presumes his presence and thus, in a way, adjusts to it. Finally, there are the protagonists of the story, and the researcher's sources of knowledge – the informers. Yet contemporary anthropology does not agree as to the range and method of understanding (in case multiple authorship is considered a diagnosis of research practice) the postulate of multiple authorship.

Marcus and Fischer, for instance, define dialogicality as a practical effort to present multiple voices within a text, which should encourage the text to be considered from multiple perspectives (1986, 68; see also Ortner 1978, 1; Koczanowicz and Fisher 1995).[5] Dwyer, on the other hand, puts the emphasis on exactly quoting expressions, as well as publicizing his own doubts of a moral, professional and political nature (Geertz 1998, 86).[6] In that case, as Marcus and Fisher warn us, 'it is possible for this sort of inquiry to slide into simple confessionals of field experience, or into atomistic nihilism where it becomes impossible to generalize from a single ethnographer's experience. The danger in both cases is allowing the anthropologist-informant dialogue to become the exclusive or primary interest. Insofar as texts do this, they are of no particular ethnographic interest' (1986, 68). According to Bakhtin, the real subject doesn't have a total and finalizing view of him/herself and others; while the author, whether he/she is a novelist or anthropologist, might have such a view in the case of monological creative activity, in which a finalized vision of the literary hero and a surplus of the author's consciousness is typical. In case of dialogical 'production', this view is consistent with the real one. But such an image of 'dialogism' might lead, and sometimes does, to dangerous (incorrect) conclusions in anthropological practice.

Sometimes dialogism is presented as a desire to reproduce as best as possible, or at least to better reflect, the truth of examined cultural reality. When we consider that contemporary culture is characterized by multiple meanings and multiple voices, and that we live in the era of enhanced communication activity and cross-cultural interactions, where we have a number of tools available to interpret ourselves and others, we may conclude that dialogue and polyphony are closer to reflecting the nature of anthropological knowledge, as they are closer to the nature of things they refer to. The dialogical approach would thus be forced by the nature of reality the researcher encounters.[7] Paradoxically, this sketched approach (method) is directed at a symmetry of description and reality: dialogical, polyphonic reality, correspondent to dialogical representation (evocation) and polyphony in field research. Such symmetry clearly opposes the dialogical ideal of knowledge, while perfectly supplementing ethnographic realism (rejected by dialogical anthropology),[8] which reifies the anthropological metalanguage and thus marginalizes not only the 'ethics' of our practice but the other itself.[9]

However, if we look closer at Bakhtin's idea of the dialogic novel we might notice that the effect of realism is inscribed in the idea. The real character doesn't have a total and finalizing view on himself and others. An author (or anthropologist) has such an insight only in the case of monological creations. The finalizing of the hero and surplus of the author's consciousness are characteristic of this type of work. There is a lack of those elements in dialogic novels (or such an ethnography) so the author's view is closer there to the real one, therefore the novel (or ethnography) becomes more realistic when the author is omniscient.

There were also some attempts to remove the ethical ambiguity of the former 'monological' approach with the methodological directive of a dialogue (which privileges spoken word), but in some cases it looks like an 'expectation to speak' for the researcher – functioning in spite of his presence.

John Van Mannen wrote in this context on the so-called 'jointly told tales' while discussing different modes of narration in anthropological texts. As he showed, the mode does not form a unique genre of ethnographic work (it usually appears within so called 'ethnographic confessions' or 'impressionistic tales'), but it is used sometimes within the plot as a special stylistic device. In jointly told tales the word of the informant has the same rank as the author's and gains additional space without excessive intervention from the anthropologist.

It is an especially effective and practical narrative strategy when the informer casts a critical eye over his/her own culture and exhibits a kind of 'ethnographical sensitivity', triggered by the presence of the ethnographer. Thus, it's claimed, the informer can represent his/her own culture as well as the anthropologist.

George Marcus (1998, 36–7) calls this strategy, 'saying more by letting others say it'. It is worth noting that such a position includes an assumption that there is a truth (i.e., 'more') outside the dialogue, which links the strategy with the pure form of realism, promptly hidden in the terminology of dialogism.

There are more objections to the 'jointly told tales'. The very fact that the informer is an expert in his own culture is a theoretical prejudice that passes over the fact that 'the informer knows best' only about his own way of classifying his world, about his own view on cultural and social reality. This prejudice omits the fact that such a view is limited, as is its representativeness. Here comes to the fore the problem of 'direct speech' in ethnographic text. Direct speech cannot situate the informer as an equal subject to the fieldwork and the whole research process until he has the same potential for explanation and interpretation of his own words as the anthropologist have (see Marcus and Cushman 1982, 44).

The majority of ethnographic works cite the other's words in a form of reported speech that gives the impression of authentic contact, but loses a lot of that contact as well. Sometimes reported speech performs the function of direct speech, but retains its own characteristics. First of all, it is more open to interpretation, as it contains comments and edits from the author so that as much information as possible is included but in a shorter form. Secondly, it is not clear who is the author of the particular information in the reported speech – anthropologist or his informant. In the case of direct speech, it gives the feeling of getting the original sense, of an almost metonymic relation between the text and the reality it is based on (see Sperber 1985, 15–20). Thus, that mode of narration dominates dialogic anthropology, although direct quotation (literally taken dialogue) is not dialogism yet.

But there is another, totally false, assumption, connected with the narrative strategy of 'jointly told tales', that 'writing' is the main source and a tool of oppression of the anthropological 'other'.

For Tyler (1987), there is a clear distinction between a written word (which he believes to be unauthentic, immoral, using instrumental logic, precision) and a spoken one, which is a live negotiation of meanings between interlocutors, where all the elements of discourse are as fluent as the dialogue taking place. According to Tyler, authenticity (in other words, an 'ethically desirable state') exists only in live discourse – the spoken word. But this somehow brings back, clearly contrary to dialogical anthropology, the modernist desire to overcome the anthropologist's presence, so that the privileged word of an examined subject may speak for itself.

Such an attitude, according to D'Andrade (1995, 400), is characteristic for 'morally oversensitive anthropology'. In this research paradigm (although describing it D'Andrade allows many simplifications), the anthropologist acts morally when he lets the examined subject speak.[10] But this ethically correct situation instantly changes when the dialogue is substituted by written text, which is to some extent context independent. As Deborah Battaglia argues:

> Writing, defined broadly as *formalized traces of a materially concrete productivity*, makes an issue of openness. This is because written texts are detachable and transferable from their originary contexts of use; are consequently inclined to repetition. [...] Thus, in contrast to dialogue, such texts run the risk of closing off the exchange of knowledge; their repetition can make them appear as eternal givens, stable truths across contingencies of time and space. However, they also assert ambiguity or open themselves up to different senses being made of them, to the pleasure of coming to familiarity through an experience of the repeatable, to the craft of study, and so on. No matter how thoroughly canonized or firmly inscribed as doxa, writing, in its quality of what Derrida termed 'iterability' exceeds its own stubborn materiality. (Battaglia 1999, 120–21)

But it's worth noting that spoken word can have the same characteristics in the case of 'recorded speech'.

Note that representation is 'innocent' in itself (and thus it is not the most important problem of ethnography), but the uses of it are not – after all Bakhtin found 'dialogics' in the written texts of Dostoyevsky's prose.[11] Even more – representation is the precondition of dialogical relationships, which are 'reducible neither to logical relationships nor to relationships oriented semantically toward their referential object, *relationships in and of themselves* devoid of any dialogic element. They must clothe themselves in discourse, become utterances, become the positions of various subjects expressed in discourse, in order that dialogic relationships might arise among them' (Bakhtin 1963, 183).

So we encounter 'the ethical' of ethnographic practice in the uses of representation – but that draws our attention to the basics: ethnographies emerge from the interaction between subjects; it is fundamentally a dialogical experience, a confrontation of 'subjectivities', so that personal skills and the subjective come to the fore of our practice. Bakhtin is very clear in that point. He distinguishes human (that is, dialogical) sciences, where we deal with subject–subject relations, and natural (that is, monological) sciences, with their subject–object relation. In the case of humanities, the object of investigation is, if it is not the particular other, the 'text' (that is, every bounded, coded chain of signs), which cannot be understood as an external object (a 'mute thing', as it was commonly treated), but must be taken as the objectivized voice of the other, with which the interpreter (researcher) enters into a special dialogue. According to Bakhtin, a necessity of distinguishing between the explanation and understanding steps out from the former distinction. In explanation occurs only one consciousness, one subject. The understanding requires two consciousnesses, two subjects. It is impossible to stay in dialogical relation to the object, therefore the explanation is devoid of dialogical moments, however the understanding has dialogical character. What, according to Bakhtin, does it mean 'to stay in dialogical relation to the other'? It means very simple skills and so obvious an attitude that it might sound naïve: openness, listening, kindness, susceptibility to consensus, an ability to perceive the positive aspects of every proposition, etc. This attitude can be expressed by a syntactic figure of the kind: 'from one side…, but from the other…' (see Zylko 2001). In explanation we easily take the obvious (from our point of view) for granted (the procedure of explanation, scientific metalanguage, etc.), but that immediately sentences the researcher on reification of the metalanguage and method and, in addition, these two often force us to believe that they are symmetrically reflecting reality. In understanding, the most important thing is our readiness to agree.

This way of 'connecting distance and proximity' presumes the kind of engagement that influences both sides of the understanding process ('researcher' and the 'researched'), as it is in the case of Paul Rabinow. And of course it evokes ethical questions, but so that the author has to stop asking questions and abandon understanding to overcome the ambiguity of his privileged position as the representative of the dominant (or simply different) culture. We have to agree that people always negotiate meanings, which implies that power relations are irremovable parts of the communication process itself and we cannot avoid them, but the way some anthropologists (e.g., Rabinow) do it is much better than the one we can observe in the 'scientific' practice of some kinds of ethnography or public/political discourses overfilled with 'fixed truths'.

Moreover, we do in fact need the 'asymmetry' (of power relations also) because it is something that makes the communication reasonable, that enables processes of signification and communication (see, for example: Petrilli 1998, 212). Jurij Lotman showed (1999, 31–4) that there are three possible models describing communicative processes: the first concerns the situation when the exchange of information takes place within the same code ('structure without memory'), when the sender and receiver share the same codes and have no memory, so they understand each other perfectly but the value of an exchanged information is minimal, and the information itself very limited. Complete identification of sender and receiver makes the communication obsolete – 'they have nothing to say'. In the second case, their codes are totally different, so there are no opportunities to communicate because the medium of communication does not exist. But in normal human communication, in everyday use of the language, there is an immanent supposition of the initial difference of sender and receiver. In that case (our third case), the semiotic space of sender and receiver intersects. On the one hand, the sides of a communicative process are interested in making the understanding easier by making efforts to enlarge the common sphere, but on the other hand they are trying to increase the value of the information by enlarging the difference between them. The common sphere ('common ground') is the natural basis for communication, but the information from that sphere is, as in our first case, completely unimportant for the sides of the dialogue. However, it cannot be excluded from dialogue as it is the only medium of translation of the really important information that resides within the 'others' code. So the information most difficult for translation has the highest value, and the 'difference' and 'asymmetry' makes the communication attractive, useful and reasonable. As Bakhtin notes: 'Creative understanding does not renounce itself, its own place in time, its own culture; and it forgets nothing. In order to understand, it is immensely important for the person who understands to be heated outside the object of his or her creative understanding – in time, in space, in culture' (1986, 7).

There is also another type of engagement that nowadays attracts many anthropologists –activism. But this is dangerous for our discipline because it alters the practice of understanding into a tool of symbolic violence by removing the 'distance' necessary to understand the other, by engaged proximity. It also changes the most fundamental feature of our practice: suspicion of our own cultural and professional truths is replaced with full acceptance of them. Such an activity I would never call anthropology, and surely not the understanding of the other.

The fundamental question we should ask ourselves should be neither 'what are we doing there as anthropologists? nor 'what am I doing here as an anthropologist?', because we will sink in the idle discussion about 'anthropology itself'. We should rather ask the same questions without the noun 'anthropologist', substituting it with 'human being', willing to understand the other.

Notes

1 Once it has been realized that culture (as a derivate of research practice, and not an entity in itself) emerges from such dialogical background, the result of ethnographic research appeared as a created, re-created and reproduced cultural (or cross-cultural) practice; that meant that ethnography itself could become an object of ethnographic consideration, and that has opened new perspectives for research in modern anthropology, and strengthened its bonds with literary theory and literary critique.

2 In this case polyphony is an effect of complex situations of creating data and ethnographic facts.

3 I'd like to add that sometimes such an attitude is forced by the formal requirements of the institutions supporting our research.

4 Although even in his own writings one cannot find the ultimate definition as such definitions are unthinkable within his view on what the process of understanding is. For information on how Bakhtin's ideas reached American anthropology and cultural theory see Portis-Winner 1998.

5 Therefore, what they have in mind is 'recognizing the concept of substituting the representation of facts by the ability to recreate, or "evoke", the experience of reality, both of our own, and other worlds' (Kempny 1994, 182).

6 This is one of the reasons why, according to Gellner (1997, 42–3), the dialogicality and heteroglossy of ethnological texts are nothing more than a symptom of the 'hysteria of subjectivism'.

7 Many authors of sociological, philosophical and also anthropological analysis of contemporary culture maintain that the modern ways of classifying phenomena, including our scientific tools, are more and more unsuited to a changing reality which becomes ambiguous, unstable, indefinable, unpredictable and unclear (Bauman 1995). Suitable language, capable of truly describing such a reality, cannot be a language of order: 'An alternative to modern mind is polysemy, cognitive dissonance, incoherent definitions, random judgments and overlapping of opposite meanings' (Bauman 1995, 21).

8 Cf. Olivier de Sardan on anthropologists who 'dramatize' magical-religious phenomena (1999).

9 Bakhtin wrote that the limit of the precision in the sciences is the 'sameness', which consists of a transformation of 'the otherness of the other' into the self – an effect which should be avoided in 'dialogical sciences' (1983, 234).

10 This was reliably proven in the commentaries supplementing D'Andrade's article.

11 Heidegger, commenting on Hörderlin's vision of poetry, wrote that we were given the most innocent gift of the word (representation), but at the same time we received the most dangerous skill – speaking (uses of representation) (Heidegger 1981).

References

Abu-Lughod, L. 1991. 'Writing Against Culture'. In *Recapturing Anthropology: Working in the Present*, edited by R. G. Fox, 137–62. Santa Fe: School of American Research Press.

Bakhtin, M. 1963. *Problems of Dostoevsky's Poetics*. Minneapolis: University of Minnesota Press.

_____. 1983. *Dialog- język-literatura*. Warsaw: PIW.

_____. 1986. *Speech Genres and Other Late Essays*. Austin: University of Texas Press.

_____. 1999. *Toward a Philosophy of the Act*. Austin: University of Texas Press.

Battaglia, D. 1999. 'Toward an Ethics of the Open Subject: Writing Culture in Good Conscience'. In *Anthropological Theory Today*, edited by H. L. Moore, 114–50. Cambridge: Polity Press.

Clifford, J. 1988. *The Predicament of Culture: Twentieth-Century Ethnography, Literature, and Art*. Cambridge, MA: Harvard University Press.

Crapanzano, V. 1980. *Tuhami: Portrait of a Moroccan*. Chicago: University of Chicago Press.

Czaplejewicz, E. and E. Kasperski, eds. 1983. *Bachtin: Dialog, język, literatura*. Warsaw: PWN.

D'Andrade, R. 1995. 'Moral Models in Anthropology'. *Current Anthropology* 36 (3): 399–408.

Dwyer, K. 1982. *Moroccan Dialogues: Anthropology in Question*. Baltimore: Waveland Press.

Fabian, J. 1995. *Time and Work of Anthropology: Critical Essays 1971–1991*. Amsterdam: Harwood Academic Publishers.

———. 2001. *Anthropology with an Attitude: Critical Essays*. Stanford: Stanford University Press.

Geertz, C. 1988. *Works and Lives: Anthropologist as Author*. Stanford: Stanford University Press.

———. 1998. 'Zaświadczające Ja: Dzieci Malinowskiego'. *Konteksty: Polska Sztuka Ludowa* 1: 81–90.

Gellner, E. 1997. *Postmodernizm, rozum i religia*. Warsaw: PIW.

Heidegger, M. 1980. 'Hörderlin i istota poezji'. In *Teoria badań literackich za granicą*, vol. 2, part 2, edited by S. Skwarczynska, 185–99. Kraków: Wydawnictwo Literackie.

Kempny, M. 1994. *Antropologia bez dogmatów: teoria społeczna bez iluzji*. Warsaw: Wydawnictwo IFiS PAN.

Koczanowicz, L. and M. J. Fischer. 1995. 'Rozmowa z Michaelem M. J. Fischerem'. *Konteksty: Polska Sztuka Ludowa* 1: 8–12.

Mannheim, B. and D. Tedlock. 1995. *Dialogic Emergence of Culture*. Chicago: University of Illinois Press.

Marcus, G. 1998. *Ethnography Through Thick and Thin*. Princeton: Princeton University Press.

Marcus, G. E. and M. J. Fischer. 1986. *Anthropology as Cultural Critique: An Experimental Moment in the Human Sciences*. Chicago: University of Chicago Press.

Olivier de Sardan, J.-P. 1998. 'Okultyzm i etnograficzne "ja": Magia czyli uegzotyczniona nadzwyczajność od Durkheima po antropologię postmodernistyczną'. In *Amerykańska Antropologia Postmodernistyczną*, edited by M. Buchowski, 247–67. Warsaw: Instytut Kultury.

Ortner, S. 1978. *Sherpas Through their Rituals*. Cambridge: Cambridge University Press.

Petrilli, S. 1998. 'Bakhtin Research Between Literary Theory and Semiotics'. *European Journal for Semiotic Studies* 10 (1/2): 203–16.

Portis-Winner, I. 1998. 'Does the Image Sparkle? Bakhtin and Contemporary American Studies of Culture'. *Elementa* 4: 17–44.

Rabinow, P. 1977. *Reflections on Fieldwork in Morocco*. Berkeley: University of California Press.

———. 1986. 'Representations are Social Facts: Modernity and Post-Modernity in Anthropology'. In *Writing Culture: The Poetics and Politics of Ethnography*, edited by J. Clifford and G. E. Marcus, 234–61. Berkeley: University of California Press.

Reed-Danahay, D. E. 1995. Introduction to *Auto/Ethnography: Rewriting the Self and the Social*, edited by D. E. Reed-Danahay, 1–20. Oxford: Berg Publishers.

Said, E. 1989. 'Representing the Colonized: Anthropology's Interlocutors'. *Critical Inquiry* 15 (2): 205–25.

Sperber, D. 1996. *Explaining Culture: A Naturalistic Approach*. Oxford: Blackwell Publishers.

Tedlock, D. 1979. 'The Analogical Tradition and the Emergence of a Dialogical Anthropology'. *Journal of Anthropological Research* 35: 387–400.

———. 1983. *The Spoken Word and the Work of Interpretation*. Philadelphia: University of Pennsylvania Press.

Tyler, S. 1987. *The Unspeakable: Discourse, Dialogue and Rhetoric in the Postmodern World*. Madison: University of Wisconsin Press.

Vrhel, F. 1993. 'Bachtinowskie inspiracje w postmodernistycznej etnografii'. *Zeszyty Naukowe Uniwersytetu Jagiellońskiego: Prace Etnograficzne* 32: 7–22.

Wagner, R. 2003. 'Wynalezienie kultury' [Invention of culture]. In *Badanie kultury: Elementy teorii antropologicznej*, edited by M. Kempy and E. Nowicka, 59–72. Warsaw: PWN.

Zylko, B. 2001. 'Paradoksy Bachtina'. In *Paradoksy humanistyki*, edited by O. Kubinska and D. Malcolm, 359–70. Gdańsk: Wydawnictwo Uniwersytetu Gdańskiego.

Chapter 15

THE PHILOSOPHY OF SLAVOJ ŽIŽEK AND ANTHROPOLOGY: THE CURRENT SITUATION AND POSSIBLE FUTURES

Lars Kjaerholm

The Slovenian philosopher Slavoj Žižek has opened up a discussion of the subject and the self and ideology, which is of great interest to anthropology. In the words of Fabio Vighi and Heiko Feldner, Žižek's concept of ideology distances itself from all former definitions because:

> […] instead of ideology falsifying reality for the sake of pathological interests (power strategies), we start from the assumption that there is no way to access and conceptualize reality which has not already been stained by discourse. The term ideology thus becomes redundant, Žižek argues, for what counts in critical analysis is that every ideological stance we assume is always-already parasitized by an intricate network of discursive devices whose function is to structure our point of view in advance, silently bestowing an appearance of necessity upon it. (Vighi and Feldner, 147–8)[1]

This is bound to affect anthropologists, because they have always thought of themselves as being able to 'understand' all cultures around the world, and explain them, but if we are not able to understand ourselves, then how can we begin to imagine that we can understand others without 'tainting' our descriptions and explanations of other cultures with our own 'ideology' (in the Žižekian definition)? An example of this transposing of our own discourse universe on the entire world could be Emile Durkheim's statement that everywhere in the world people distinguish between the sacred and the profane, which has remained an academic truth ever since. Another example is

Figure 1. A *yantra* representing the goddess Sri

the widespread use of the concept of symbol in anthropology; for instance, in Victor Turner's work. If we take a detour through Peirce's semiotic theory, we may well question that what Victor Turner calls a 'symbol' in another culture may not in fact be something else in the ontological world of the people under study. In a paper on Indian *Silpa Sastra*, I argue that although many of the phenomena, which would invariable be called 'symbols' in the practice of this discipline, still in the minds of the people who practice *Silpa Sastra* and Hindu rituals in general there is nothing symbolic about them. A very good example is the *yantra* representing the goddess Sri, depicted in Figure 1.

This is just another example of a *yantra*, which is a Hindu method of representing deities and cosmic principles with lines and diagrams. All deities can be represented thus, each with a unique *yantra*, and this geometrical form can be duplicated with a sound formula, a *mantra*, which likewise *is* the deity, not a symbolic representation. This 'representation' of the goddess is to a Western mind a symbol, because to us it could not represent the goddess in any other way. But we find this statement in an Indian text: 'Thus *Sri Chakra* (another term used for a *yantra*) is verily the body of the mother goddess, her own form' (Rao 1982, 17). Thus the *yantra* is not regarded as a symbol by those who use it, it is an index, something existing in actuality, in secondness, because of the iconic similarities with the deity as they are perceived by the Indian ritual specialist, a topic I cannot go in more detail with in this chapter.[2] Also, E. Valentine Daniel, in his semiotic anthropology, argues that in India there is a predominant interest in indexical signs, signs of actual existence – 'Secondness [...] the area of daily existence' (1985, 241) – as opposed to in the West, where we are more interested in symbols, signs in thirdness: 'Thirdness […] the realm of law, and laws in their most developed forms not merely describe and determine but also predict' (Daniel, 257). So if a Western anthropologist calls a phenomenon in an African or Indian ritual a symbol, even though the people under study think of it as a thing of secondness, actual existence, is this then not an example of symbolic violence? Is this not an expression of how Western anthropology describes, determines and predicts how other cultures are and how people having them would likely behave in certain situations? Is it not another way of saying, 'I do not believe in the actual existence of this phenomenon, but let me tell you what it really is'?

Although Žižek's theory on ideology does not seem to have been applied, it is still possible to find parallel thoughts. An example is Richard Parmentier's interesting analysis of the American museum Colonial Williamsburg, where he applies a method of not only focusing on what is said about the museum by its staff and what is written in its publications, but in true Žižekian fashion he also looks at what the museum *does*, in the sense that there are some nonverbal messages in the functioning of the museum. Parmentier agrees with Thibault that there are nonverbal messages expressed in the indexical world of actually existing things, for instance in the museum's use of 'authentic' artefacts, which lend an aura of authenticity to the entire museum. 'Indexicality' consists of the semiotic contextualization of the 'prediscursive' world:

> An important dimension of the ethnographic study of history as a cultural system is the analysis of locally deployed semiotic mechanisms which regiment people's understandings and experience of the past. These mechanisms, including, for example, textual forms, visual images, behavioral rules, consumption goods, ritual processions, architectural monuments, and museum exhibitions, are instruments of the historicizing institutions of a society. A particularly powerful example of the regimentation of historical consciousness in the United States is Colonial Williamsburg in Virginia. (1994, 135)

Colonial Williamsburg is a reconstruction of the eighteenth-century capital of Virginia, and is populated by people who walk the streets dressed in the style of that century. Visitors can talk with these 'inhabitants', but these dressed-up old Americans are not allowed to discuss things which were unknown in the eighteenth century. So, by using more-or-less authentic artefacts and 'authentic' inhabitants, secondness and indexicality is used to overwhelm the visitors and make them submit to the way the museum tells 'history' through its academic superstructure, its library, its publications and its selling of copies of contemporary furniture, not to mention its accommodation in one of the reconstructed buildings. But there are other messages, which are more interesting and important, but their importance also makes it impossible to express them in words. As Parmentier says, 'The thesis I want to argue is that Colonial Williamsburg's overt educational and recreational functions mask a powerful covert function of reproducing and legitimizing a system of social distinctions in contemporary American society, and that this is accomplished by the promotion of an ideology of scientific transparency that anchors present distinctions in the colonial past' (1994, 136). There are, according to Parmentier, some hidden messages in the way the various buildings and exhibitions are arranged and access to them granted. While most of the buildings are open and accessible to the visitors all day, there are some where access is restricted in various ways, for example some buildings and exhibitions require an additional ticket. 'Like the fine gradations in eighteenth-century fashion, the ticketing system at Colonial Williamsburg requires careful study and practice'. The hierarchic regimentation of touristic experience can be seen in the regulations stipulating visiting hours and reservation 'requirements' (138). The more important the building the more difficult it is to visit. Interestingly enough, the place most difficult access is Bassett Hall, the former summer residence of the Rockefeller family, who are the main founders of the museum and whose vast fortune funded it. 'Though armed with my Patriot's Pass, I discovered that admission is very limited and that a potential visitor must register ahead of time (in a large volume looking like a guest-book) for an "appointment"'. So the message-which-cannot-be-said is that 'At the top of the hierarchy of regimenting historical interpretation stands the home of the Rockefellers, the very agents responsible for the preservation and reconstruction of the surrounding eighteenth-century city' (140). The entire meticulous academic apparatus of the museum lends authority to the way it interprets the past for the present day, and it functions, 'to celebrate their [the Rockefeller family] newly won pre-eminence and partly to construct a retrospective lineage for themselves by buying their way into the American past' (Wallace 1986, quoted in Parmentier 1994, 140). This analysis of the functioning of Colonial Williamsburg comes pretty close to Žižek's view of ideology, but Žižek would claim that ideology, as he defines it, is everywhere in social practice, daily consumption and cultural habits, not just in enclaves under special 'regimentation' such as this American museum.

Self, Subject, Culture

Anthropologists study people and cultures all over the world, and the discipline wishes to understand and interpret the behaviour and culture of other peoples and cultures. Therefore, anthropology must pay attention to current discussions about the self and about culture, and if Slavoj Žižek can present something which the discipline can use as a tool of analysis or contextualization, then anthropologists should of course consider applying his ideas in their work. Anthropology, as a transcultural discipline, is largely a Western phenomenon. It is by and large Western anthropology which works transculturally, wishing to 'translate' other cultures and interpret them for their Western readers. For this reason, the theoretical tools used in anthropological analysis are almost all derived from theoretical work by Western philosophers and theoreticians. Examples are Karl Marx, Emile Durkheim, Pierre Bourdieu and Claude Lévi-Strauss, to mention just a few. Lately Michel Foucault has been adopted as a theoretician in anthropology and his theories have been applied in societies very different from the Western world which Foucault worked in and theorized on. Is the next name on the list of theoreticians supplying anthropology with theory and new ideas going to be Slavoj Žižek? Although Žižek's philosophy can be seen as systematic, and ought to be understood in its entirety, I must refrain from presenting it *in toto* in this chapter, but the ideas which appear to me to be most interesting to anthropology will be briefly introduced. His ideas on the subject are somewhat in conflict with a recent trend to portray the subject as decentred and fragmented. Žižek does not share Descartes's view of the self as being an entity, a thinking substance, a *res cogitans*, whether material or immaterial like the immortal soul of Christianity. Nor does he share Kant's view that there is something unknowable about the transcendental self, since one cannot observe the observer. To Žižek there is nothing hiding in the subject or the self: 'Our point is that the emergence of the "subject" is strictly correlative to the positing of this central signifier as "empty". I become a subject when the universal signifier to which I refer ("ecology" in our case) is no longer connected by an umbilical cord to some particular content, but is experienced as an empty space to be filled out by the particular content' (2007, 131). Because the subject knows that it is something, but it does not know what, it has to 'seek clues to its identity in its social and political life, asking the question of others' (Sharpe, 13). Apart from his ideas on the subject, a very interesting and promising part of his philosophy is about ideology critique, where he resuscitates a concept which was by many considered totally dead, and brings some totally new angles to it.

Although one can find references to texts by Slavoj Žižek in a large number of anthropological papers from the last two decades, it is still not quite clear exactly what anthropology can learn and apply from Žižek's thoughts. In a number of such papers one can find in the bibliography one or two works by Žižek, but it is not made explicit in most of these texts why he is mentioned.[3] On the one hand, there seems to be a great fascination with Žižek's thoughts in anthropology, but on the other hand it seems that this fascination has not yet resulted in an implementation in anthropological fieldwork of his ideas. This is probably due to the fact that anthropological fieldwork is – still – very much done in limited areas, geographically and socially, and rarely do anthropologists venture to generalize about the macroperspective from the microperspective of their fieldwork, and Žižek's thoughts seem to claim validity in a late capitalistic world, not clearly defined geographically. Another reason for the somewhat hesitant attitude of anthropology could be that Žižek's model of the subject is split between a conscious and an unconscious part, and mainstream anthropology seems to shy away from applying such a model to each and every culture in this world. Political science, on the other hand, seems to be more easily able to accept and apply Žižek's subject theory. This hesitance is perhaps also due to a certain anxiety, that once more taking a concept from a Western cultural world and applying it cross-culturally is yet another example of the dominance, the recolonization of the non-Western world through discourse (and ideology, in Žižek's definition). A rather telling example of the postcolonial mode of thinking is from S. Lily Mendoza's *Between the Homeland and the Diaspora*, from which I quote from a narrative by one of Mendoza's Philippine-American informants: 'With the continuing Western monopoly of the world's symbolic capital, it is an easy temptation for formerly colonized academies (such as the Philippines is) to become eager consumers of the West's massive export of cultural products and theoretical productions, not in the modality of total acquiescence, but in the form of more subtle kinds of subservience' (2006, xx).

The narrator then relates how a paper she wanted to present was declared to be 'not updated', because Derrida was missing in her bibliography. And Derrida just had to be there, end of discussion. But the professor, who rejected the paper, 'made no comment on the substantive aspect of the essay [...]. It is this dismissive stance – the formalistic, decontextualized, and ahistorical use of theories across contexts and cultures – that I find necessary to critique' (2006, xx). It will be interesting to see how Žižek will be received by such postcolonial academics, because foisted on them he will be – like Derrida was foisted on Lily Mendoza. But maybe Žižek can be regarded by them as an ally in their attempt to escape the discursive stranglehold of the Western academic world.

Furthermore anthropologists work in a range of societies which are so dissimilar that anthropology shies away from generalizing their findings beyond the relatively narrow boundaries within which most anthropological fieldwork is still carried out. The perspective of anthropological fieldwork is the world of specific interacting human beings and societies studied first hand through participant observation. Anthropology thus has some work ahead of it to clarify the applicability of Žižek's thoughts. Are they equally applicable in postmodern Western societies and tribal and peasant societies around the world? Can some of, or all of, his ideas be applied globally? These questions have to be addressed first before anthropology can comfortably apply Žižek's ideas and perspectives.

It seems that influence from Žižek may be channelled into anthropology filtered through other disciplines, such as political science and marketing, which are not so much concerned with very different types of society and culture as anthropology is, and in political science we find a more direct influence from Žižek.

Some Important Ideas and Themes in Žižek's Philosophy and its Relevance to Anthropology

In modern anthropological debates on individual / dividual, subject and personhood, there has been a conspicuous absence of references to Žižek, which can be attributed to the fact that Žižek's breakthrough to a wider Western readership is fairly recent (Žižek 1989). Thus one could hardly blame such anthropologists as Martin Sökefeld, Jeanette Mageo, Richard Parmentier and Michael Herzfeld for not referring to him, but one could certainly see some interesting perspectives unfolding, had they been able to include Žižek in their discussions on self and subject, something which I will get back to below. However, first I will introduce Žižek's understanding of the self and the subject. He harks back to Descartes and his idea of the self – the *cogito*, the thinking self – which he took as evidence of the existence of the self, which he arrived at after his famous exercise in universal doubt. Everything might be an illusion, a dream, but *cogito ergo sum*, I think hence I am, was to him evidence of the existence of the self, which later philosophers have attacked. Also, anthropology has done its part in criticizing the Western notion of the indivisible and autonomous self, which is the total master of its thoughts and actions. McKim Marriott was the first (to my knowledge) to use the term 'dividual' (at least in anthropology), which he felt was better suited to describe Indian personhood or selfhood, and C. S. Peirce presents us with a more open version of the self, an alternative to the hermetically closed and autonomous understanding of the self, expressed by Lucien Lévy-Bruhl in his writings on totemism. Lévy-Bruhl imagines that the so-called totemists are unable to distinguish between themselves and their totem, and thus they think in a way radically different from modern people: 'To our minds concepts that have nothing in common, far from blending with each other, are mutually antagonistic and exclusive. The Ashanti mind, however, is not dominated by such laws; its methods of thought are different'. He continues, 'To our way of thinking, however complex an individual may be,

his primordial and essential characteristic is that he shall be *one person*. If he
were not this, he would not be an individual, but a being compounded of
several' (1976, 201).

This understanding of the self, the bounded and autonomous 'island',
was to Lévy-Bruhl essential for personhood, but it is deeply unsatisfactory
for philosophical (and anthropological) reasons because, as Tony Myers
points out, if every person is an island and totally in control of their thoughts
and actions, and totally free to do what they will, '[…] the very features of
the individual which seem to confer upon it such blessings are also those
which blight it. This is because the individual conceived in this way is utterly
subjective; everything remains within its dominion and subject to its control.
There is no objectivity at all' (2003, 33). Furthermore, there is also no way
this autonomous individual can share a culture/habitus/discourse with
other members of a given society, so a way out of this cul-de-sac must be
found if anthropology is to stand on firm ground. Early on in the history of
anthropology Radcliffe-Brown offered one solution, as he simply disposed of
the individual in the traditional sense because he distinguished between the
individual, the physically existing person, and the social person, conceived as
a bundle of social relations, which was the object of his style of anthropology.
Much later, E. Valentine Daniel (1984) suggested another solution to the
problem, when he adopted C. S. Peirce's model of the self as a constantly
emerging dialogical self:

> A person is not absolutely an individual. His thoughts are what he is 'saying to
> himself', that is, saying to that other self that is just coming into life in the flow
> of time. When one reasons, it is that critical self that one is trying to persuade
> and all thought is whatever is a sign, and is mostly in the nature of language. The
> second thing to remember is that the man's circle of society (however widely or
> narrowly this phrase may be understood), is a sort of loosely compacted person,
> in some respects of higher rank than the person of an individual organism.
> (Peirce 1932, 3.421)[4]

Peirce's model allows both for openness and plasticity and explains how the
individual can still maintain a sense of subjectivity, whether this is regarded
as illusory or real, and change and evolve constantly. This presents us with a –
relatively – stable and permanent self, while providing a model of it which
would allow it to communicate with other selves and merge new experiences
with past experiences. It might appear strange that Peirce's – and Daniel's –
important contribution to the philosophy of the self should have received so
little attention by the poststructuralists and anthropologists, as he presents
a model of the self/subject which seems to solve the problem of mediation

between a too centred and subjective model of the self, and its opposite, the totally decentred self. There is a certain parallelism between Peirce's model and Žižek's concept of the subject, although Žižek seems to be unaware of Peirce's ideas on the topic. He never makes references to Peirce (at least that I am able to find), for whatever reason that may be.

Although Peirce rejects psychology in his semiotic theory he nevertheless has a concept of the unconscious, which he calls signs of habit: 'Signs of habit, therefore, are largely, if not entirely, unconscious' (Daniel, 25). There seems, thus, to be a model of the self which can achieve about the same as Žižek's, so what *more* can we learn from Žižek, and what is lacking in Peirce's model? What Žižek adds, and which to my mind is necessary, is a theory of desire, derived from Lacan, which can account for the fact that subjects must ceaselessly try to fill up their empty selves with meaning and content from the word around them.

However, this filling up of content is – in Žižek's text – mainly content of a symbolic nature, in thirdness, as it would be termed in Peircian terminology. This is because in the Western world, which Žižek has in mind when writing, one gets the feeling of becoming a subject filled with something mostly from the world of ideas. But there are other cultures around the world where this process of filling the subject with content and meaning is as much or even more on the indexical level of secondness, i.e., in the world of tangible objects and substance. This is what has been demonstrated most clearly in anthropology informed by Peirce's semiotic, such as that of Daniel, who presents many examples of this from his fieldwork in Tamil Nadu. In *Fluid Signs*, Daniel describes in the chapter 'An Ur Known' how a man, the son of a man who migrated to and settled in Malaysia, comes to his ancestral village in Tamil Nadu with the purpose to 'get to know his *conda ur*, "village of origin")'. Daniel suggests that a few days should suffice for this purpose in this small village, but he is surprised to hear that the man intends to stay several months. Only then will he come to 'know his *ur*', because he will absorb its essential qualities by breathing the air, drinking the water and eating the food grown there, so this process of 'knowing' is a very different kind of understanding as it takes place entirely in secondness, where a Western meaning of knowing is confined to thirdness, the abstract level of ideas and symbols. Daniel has other examples, such as the shared substance of houses and the people who live in them, described in the chapter 'A House Conceived'. When setting out to build a house one should make sure that there is compatibility between the house and those who are going to live in it. A house, like an individual person, is conceived, is born, develops and may in time 'die' if it is totally deserted. It also has its own horoscope, which may be very different from that of the owner, so one should compare the horoscopes to find out if the house and the person are compatible. So the road to becoming a subject filled with 'meaning' is rather different in India, as many other examples will demonstrate, such as the widespread practice of possession cults,[5] or the idea that there is already a core of the human soul, which is a part of the divine, and thus from the outset the Indian subject is not entirely empty. In a study of wrestlers in North India, Joseph Alter (1985) finds the way of adding 'meaning' and content to the subject as happening very much in secondness, as the virtuous group of wrestlers through time share this virtuousness literally and in secondness through the shared substance of the *akhara*, the wrestling arena, which makes not only their minds but also their bodies more virtuous, through the practice of the ascetic and controlled lifestyle of the traditional wrestler. There are also so many studies on exchange in India which demonstrate that something in secondness accompanies the objects and substances exchanged, such as food, so that a high-ranking caste person cannot eat food cooked by a person of lower rank, as the process of cooking means that something from the one who cooks will be fused with the food. This is another example demonstrating that the understanding and social and cultural creation of the subject happens very differently in India from the way we imagine this in Western culture. Although there is this substantial difference between subjectology between these two worlds, Žižek's general understanding of the *cogito*, the subject, as being an empty shell in need of being filled is still a possible general theory and model, but anthropological studies show us that this process of filling the subject can happen in very different ways in different cultures. The recent and sudden popularity of *vastu shastra*, the ancient Indian discipline of building and positioning a house so it will benefit most from cosmic and divine forces, shows that the most meaningful processes of subjectology in India are predominantly linked to secondness, because it is linked to a distinct Hindu ontology of personhood.[6] This means that a lot of the subject-creating processes practiced by the emerging Indian middle class have the – perhaps unintended – effect of creating new and deeper divides between Hindus and non-Hindus in India. In one of the recent books on *vastu shastra*, Derebail Muralidhar Rao writes: 'The creator of this universe Lord Brahma gave the knowledge of construction of buildings (houses), the root of all happiness, to a strange being, known as the Vastu Purusha' (1997, 33). This amazing and massive revival of *vastu shastra* has entered the education of architects in India, because although they were rather sceptical about it at first, there was such a demand from the customers, that they could not ignore it, but had to include it in the curriculum.

Commodity Fetishism and the Subject

In an important paper, 'The Supposed Subjects of Ideology', Žižek presents his theory of commodity fetishism, derived from Marx, which he defends.

According to this theory, the social relations are lifted out of the commodity, the product of labour, and 'in other words [...] in the fetishist universe, people (mis)perceive their social relations in the guise of relations between things' (2003, 40). However, there is another level of fetishism, says Žižek: 'Beneath the apparently humanist-ideological opposition of "human beings" and "things" there lurks another, much more productive notion; that of the mystery of substitution and/or displacement: how is it ontologically possible that the innermost "relations between people" can be displaced onto (or substituted by) "relations between things"?' (40). According to Žižek, people do not really suffer from fetishist delusions. We all know very well that things are produced by people in social relationships: 'The crucial mistake to be avoided here is the properly "humanist" notion that this belief embodied in things, displaced onto things, is nothing but a reified form of the direct human belief: the task of the phenomenological reconstitution of the genesis of "reification" is then to demonstrate how the original human belief was transposed onto things' (40). What is necessary for the fetishist illusion to work, although the subjects do not believe in it, is a belief that the Big Other believes in it. In other words, it is belief by displacement or substitution. 'So the answer to the conservative platitude according to which every honest man has a profound need to believe in something is that every honest man has a profound need to find another subject who would believe in his place' (42).

This is a very interesting idea, which may find its way into anthropology. In my own work in India, I have often come into discussions about belief. When I present religious practices and beliefs in India, I have often entered into discussions at symposia and conferences as to who in India actually believes in this or that aspect of Indian ontology. I am questioned about who I think believes in it, how many, which proportion of the population and so on, and I am asked if I am justified in presenting it as if each and everybody in India shares this particular belief. But with this idea of substitution, I find an interesting new angle on the problem of belief in India. I will present some examples to illustrate this.

In the study of the Aiyappan pilgrimage cult, there are legends and mythology which 'explain' to the pilgrims what the origin and purpose of the pilgrimage is. The first pilgrim was a man who had sinned against Aiyappan, and in order to be cleansed of his sin, which resulted in a serious skin affliction, he entered the *sanctum sanctorum* of Aiyappan's temple and literally merged with the statue representing Aiyappan, thus illustrating what the 'ideological' goal of this pilgrimage is supposed to be: the merging of the subject/individual, or dividual if you will, with the divine universal soul, as in so many other types of Hindu worship. However, in the many interviews I conducted with Aiyappan pilgrims, this goal was never presented by them.

They would mention reasons much closer to their daily lives, such as seeking Aiyappan's help to cure a disease, get a job, get a child (many childless pilgrims regard Aiyappan as particularly effective in granting offspring).[7] When I asked them if their goal was the 'ideological' one, merging with the godhead, they were usually startled, as if that had never occurred to them. In other words, it seems they did not really believe in the 'ideology', but that is no problem, so long as they believed that some people believed in it.

In another fieldwork, I studied the composer Tyagaraja and the way the day of his death in mid-January is celebrated with a large music festival, ancestor rituals and more. That is the most important day in the composer's life, because that was the day when he attained *moksha*, i.e., his soul escaped rebirth and merged with the godhead. This is another example of Hindu 'ideology', which I presented to students at the Government College of Music in Madurai when I asked them if they shared Tyagaraja's goal in life: attaining *moksha*, becoming a 'liberated soul'. They certainly did not, and were surprised that I should even mention the religious/ideological aspect of his life and his compositions. Not that it is difficult to see this ideology in his songs, but those who learn them seem to be quite unaware of it. But this is not a problem, so long as they can believe that there are people who believe it, and there are in fact such people who take part in the celebration of Tyagaraja.

At the music festival I noticed that many in the audience, especially women, actually treated this as a *bhajan*, a religious song gathering, and they joined in the singing, which is a transgression of the supposed audience–musician relationship. Many had even brought the texts of the songs with them. In Tyagaraja's house gathers a small crowd of seemingly true believers, since any private person, who so wishes, may enter it and sit down in front of a statue representing Tyagaraja and sing his songs, most of which are in praise of Rama, and in which Tyagaraja expresses his fervent wish to see Rama. So the pious-looking spectators at the concert hall, and those who gather in his house, may seem to others as those-who-believe. On the other hand, these seemingly pious people may just be practicing a habit, as do many school children – especially girls – of the higher castes in Tamil Nadu, who attend Sunday schools where they learn to sing Tamil *bhakti* songs, with similar content as Tyagaraja's songs in praise of Rama.[8] So they may just present a 'sign of habit', as Peirce would call it, which may be just that, but each of these pious and possibly unbelieving persons might still believe that all the others believe in the ideology.

There are many other areas where this function of belief through those supposed-to-believe can be observed in India. In my work on the worship of the *kula teyvam*, the family deity, in Tamil Nadu, I came across frequent stories about how deceased relatives communicate with the women of the family in dreams, and how old family members became possessed by this deity at the annual ritual for the *kula teyvam*.[9] This might seem hard to believe by Westerners, and many times I have been questioned at conferences about this – 'Do they really believe in this? Are they really possessed?' and so on – and with Žižek's idea about belief-by-proxy, we can now answer that maybe nobody in India 'really' believes it, but the belief is still there, since they believe there are some who believe it.

The Subject Supposed to Know

Another example of the substitution which Žižek describes is thus: 'Is not the primordial version of this substitution by means of which "somebody else does it for me" the very substitution of a *signifier* for the subject? Therein, in such a substitution, resides the basic, constitutive features of the *symbolic order*: a signifier is precisely an object-thing which substitutes for me, which acts in the place of me' (2003, 45).[10] The poststructural position, as represented by such philosophers as Jacques Derrida and Roland Barthes, is that language has a determining influence on our understanding of who we are and how we understand reality. 'Reality' is in their understanding a linguistic text, and as texts can be altered and interpreted indefinitely, likewise reality is always out of our grasp and control. This position is, it seems, very close to that of Paul Ricoeur and hermeneutic anthropology, and the very broad spectrum of various brands of social constructionism, so influential in anthropology, political science and other disciplines today. It is also not a far cry from this position to that of Foucault and his theory of discourse and power. Thus, in the poststructuralist thinking, it is not the individual who is sole author of his own speech and his own thoughts, it is rather intersubjective discourses which speak through the individual or the subject, and the subject is thus no longer centred in Lévy-Bruhl's fashion, but decentred. While Žižek can agree on these views to some extent, he still finds that they present a new problem. If the individual cannot come up with anything subjective in thought or words, but is just a mouthpiece for an interpersonal discourse, or ideology, language or culture, then the 'I' ceases to exist, and we cannot make decisions. But the fact remains that we do make individual decisions. It is 'I' who decides whether to speak or not, and it is 'I' who decides which discourse to give voice to. 'I' have an intention with the choices 'I' make. So just as a totally autonomous self is an impossibility, so is the opposite, the totally decentred individual unable to make any choices or decisions.

In anthropology, Lévy-Bruhl represents the autonomous individual concept, and we could point to Fredrik Barth as having a similar view, while representatives of the opposite position are Radcliffe-Brown and perhaps also

Claude Lévi-Strauss. The theories of Pierre Bourdieu and Anthony Giddens may be seen as attempts to mediate between these two extremes. In the case of Bourdieu, individuals are acting according to rules, a *habitus*, an overall strategy, which means that the acts of the individual are determined by the *habitus* or culture within which that individual is situated. But there is still a possibility to make choices, for instance as to *when* to reciprocate in a social game of exchange, where it is given that you must reciprocate, but you may decide yourself, for strategic reasons, how and when this should be done.

It would be worthwhile here to look at a recent anthropological discussion of self and identity presented in a paper by Martin Sökefeld (1999). Although this paper nowhere mentions Žižek, it discusses the same problem which Žižek deals with, and it harks back to Descartes and his *cogito*. He makes the important point that, 'In the conceptualization of the self, the "Western" self, characterized as autonomous and egocentric, is generally taken as a point of departure. Non-Western (concepts of) selves – the selves of the people anthropology traditionally studies – are defined by a negation of these qualities' (417). So in his view, Western anthropologists impose on their objects of study a negative version of their own ideas of selfhood. As a comment to both Lévy-Bruhl and Sökefeld, one can find theories of the self and the individual, such as we find in India, which conceive of the individual as 'compounded of several', which to Lévy-Bruhl's mind would make logical thought impossible. But we do find fairly commonly ideas in various cultures around the world of individuals as 'compounded of several', but this in no way prevents logical thought, as the work of Indian philosophers and mathematicians show. As already mentioned, there is also plenty of anthropological work on exchange, which points to the widespread belief that a part of the person accompanies the objects exchanged, another version of the 'person as compounded of several'. As examples of 'individuals compounded of several' we could also mention the very widespread beliefs in 'possession' found in so many societies.

Sökefeld argues against recent psychological ideas of multiple identities:

> which according to the word's conventional meaning is a contradiction in terms. The contemporary self is depicted as fragmented, essentially fluid and many-sided, as in Lifton's 'protean self', or populated by multiplicities, as in Gergen's 'saturated self'. In the social and cultural sciences, what was once called 'identity' in the sense of social, shared sameness is today often discussed with reference to *difference*. (1999, 417–18)

The theories of the self have indeed come a long way since the days of Lévy-Bruhl! This stress of difference questions conventional anthropological thoughts of shared culture and identity, 'and demands attention to a personal or individual identity which is here called the *self* (Sökefeld 1999, 418). So just like Žižek grants us in the West a *cogito*, Sökefeld feels compelled to grant to the people studied by anthropologists in non-Western societies a *self*. He argues his case through a detailed analysis of one individual in Gilgit, who indeed has a multiplicity of identities to choose from, and who will have to choose different identity variables in different situations. But although his example from Gilgit, Ali Hassan, has to orient his identity very differently in different situations – where language, kinship affiliation, religious affiliation and so on may direct him in very different directions – there must still be a self, Sökefeld convincingly argues, which operates on a higher level and decides which parameters should be selected to guide his actions. As he says, 'Ali Hassan embraced and enacted a number of different identities. [...] These identities are markers of difference, but these differences are not all-embracing. The differences are not separate and do not compartmentalize the person. [...] They are related because they are embraced by the same person/self, and this relation is crucial for their significance' (422). Although Ali Hassan embraced a number of very different and changeable identities, he was still able to *manage* them (424). So, logic demands that Ali Hassan possessed a *self* capable of doing this managing of identities. Jeanette Marie Mageo presents in the paper 'Toward a Multidimensional Model of the Self' a cross-cultural overview of 'self models' (2002, 340) which shows the contribution that anthropology can make towards an understanding, that there are many ways a self can be socially and culturally constructed. This looks a bit like the return of the culture-and-personality kind of anthropology of Ruth Benedict, but is not quite the same thing. Mageo says, 'Cultures can be mapped via an array of continua that represent dimensions of variation in a multidimensional field of self' (339).

She uses the term 'self' 'as a domain term for all dimensions of being a person' (2002, 339). What is new in Mageo's attempt to make such models of selves is that she tries to identify parameters or continua along which various types of selves can be placed. To give just one example of the nine continua suggested by Mageo: 'a continuum along which emotions are conceived to be, to a degree, either individual or social phenomena', and which illustrates with material from fieldwork in Samoa, where emotions traditionally are seen as a group phenomenon. 'Ifaluk people say "we are worried" not "I am worried"' (Lutz 1988, 89, quoted in Mageo 2002, 341). Although Samoans recognize that individuals have their own emotions, these are regarded as very difficult for others to understand. Mageo states, 'To the degree that people experience themselves primarily as group members, subjectivity tends to be obscure' (342). She describes a very interesting result of the Christianization of Samoa, which began in the early part of the nineteenth century. Missionaries reported that there was a long period 'characterized by violent emotional outpourings by converted Samoans' (Freeman 1983, 213, quoted in Mageo 2002, 347). This was a result of the introduction of the concept of hypocrisy by the missionaries: 'The idea of hypocrisy derives from a conception of emotion as a subjective experience with which one's social behaviour may or may not be congruent.' In other words, 'These nineteenth century Samoans were converted to a discourse of sincerity that located emotion inside the person' (347). The examples of very different types of personhood from anthropology show that subjectology of Žižek's variety may be applied, but with due regard for the staggering range of different ways of constructing the person or the subject in various cultures. However, there are other parts of his philosophy which could prove inspirational to anthropology, such as his idea of ideology, which certainly gives us pause to think. If Žižek is right, then anthropology will seem to stand on shaky ground.

Notes

1 This brings to mind Clifford Geertz's famous definition of culture: 'Believing with Max Weber, that man is an animal suspended in webs of significance he himself has spun, I take culture to be those webs, and the analysis of it to be therefore not an experimental science in search of law but an interpretive one in search of meaning' (Geertz 1973, 5).

2 Kjaerholm 1993.

3 An example is the otherwise excellent paper by Nikolai Ssorin-Chaikov, in which we are told in the introduction that he will 'argue' for the usefulness of Slavoj Žižek's notion of 'surplus of signification' in the understanding of the 'cultural production of gender' (1). I have so far not been able to find the place where Žižek's notion is mentioned later in the paper, but *mille pardons* if I have overlooked it.

4 Here Peirce seems to anticipate McKim Marriott's concept of the 'dividual'.

5 Kjaerholm 1982.

6 Kjaerholm 1991.

7 Kjaerholm 1991.

8 Kjaerholm 2008.

9 Kjaerholm 1990.

10 The concept of the symbolic order is borrowed by Žižek from Lacan, and Tony Myers explains it thus: 'The Symbolic is perhaps the most ambitious of all the Orders because its purview includes everything from language to the law, making in all the social structures in between. As such the Symbolic constitutes a good part of what we call "reality"' (2003, 22). Lacan's concept of the symbolic order also seems to coincide with anthropological definitions of culture, such as Clifford Geertz's.

References

Alter, Joseph S. 1993. ' 'The Body of One Color: Indian Wrestling, the Indian State, and Utopian Somatics'. *Cultural Anthropology* 8 (1): 49–72.

Appadurai, Arjun. 1998. 'Dead Certainty: Ethnic Violence in the Era of Globalization'. *Development and Change* 29: 905–25.

Aretxaga, Begoña. 1995. 'Dirty Protest: Symbolic Overdetermination and Gender in Northern Ireland Ethnic Violence'. *Ethnos* 23 (2): 123–48.

Božić-Vrbančić, Senka. 2005. 'After All, I Am Partly Maori, Partly Dalmatian, but First of All I Am a New Zealander'. *Ethnography* 6 (4): 517–42.

Butler, Rex. 2005. *Slavoj Žižek: Live Theory*. London: Continuum.

Bjerre, Henrik Jøker and Carsten Bagge Austen. 2006. *Slavoj Žižek*. Frederiksberg: Roskilde Universitetsforlaga.

Bowman, Paul and Richard Stamp, eds. 2007. *The Truth of Žižek*. London: Continuum.

Brown, Tony. 2005. 'The Truth of Initial Training Experience in Mathematics for Primary Teachers'. *Proceedings of the British Society for Research into Learning Mathematics* 25 (2): 19–24.

Daniel, E. Valentine. 1984. *Fluid Signs: Being a Person the Tamil Way*. Berkeley: University of California Press.

Eagleton, Terry. 2007. *Ideology: An Introduction*. London: Verso.

Freeman, Derek. 1984. *Margaret Mead and Samoa: The Making and Unmaking of an Anthropological Myth*. Cambridge, MA: Harvard University Press.

Geertz, Clifford. 1973. *The Interpretation of Cultures*. New York: Basic Books.

Hage, Ghassan. 1998. 'On "Having" Ethnography: Mimic Me… If You Can'. *Australian Journal of Anthropology* 9 (3): 285–90.

Hamilton, Annette. 2003. 'Beyond Anthropology, Towards Actuality'. *Australian Journal of Anthropology* 14 (2): 160–70.

Kjaerholm, Lars. 1982. 'Possession and Substance in Indian Civilization: Thoughts Emanating from Fieldwork in South India'. *Folk* 24: 179–96

_____. 1990. 'Kula Teyvam Worship in Tamil Nadu: A Link between Past and Present'. In *Rites and Beliefs in Modern India*, edited by Gabriella Eichinger Ferro-Luzzu, 67–87. Delhi: Manohar.

_____. 1991. 'Aiyanar and Aiyappan in Tamil Nadu: Change and Continuity in South Indian Hinduism'. In *Social Anthropology of Pilgrimage*, edited by Makhan Jha, 48–80. Delhi: Inter-India Publications.

_____. 1993. 'Body, House, Cosmos: An Application of C. S. Peirce's Semiotics in an Anthropological Analysis of Indian Silpa Sastra'. *Semionordica* 2: 35–63.

_____. 2003. 'The Passive Revolution and *Vastu Shastra*: The Timelessness of India'. In *The Avatars of Modernity*, edited by H. W. Wessler, L. Kjaerholm, N. Brimnes, 228–66. Delhi: Munshiram Manoharlal.

_____. 2008. 'Tyagaraja: Saint, Composer and Nation Builder: The Tyagaraja Festival and the Classization of Indian Music'. Unpublished conference paper.

Lévy-Bruhl, Lucien. 1927. *La mentalité primitive*. Paris: F. Alcan.

Laustsen, Carsten Bagge. 2004. *Subjektologi*. Copenhagen: Institut for Statskundskab.

Mageo, Jeanette Marie. 2002. 'Toward a Multidimensional Model of the Self'. *Journal of Anthropological Research* 58 (3): 339–65.

Marriott, McKim. 1976. 'Hindu Transactions: Diversity without Dualism'. In *Transaction and Meaning*, edited by Bruce Kapferer, 109–142. Philadelphia: Institute for the Study of Human Issues.

_____. 1989. 'Constructing and Indian Ethnosociology'. *Contributions to Indian Sociology*, n.s., 23: 1–39.

Marriott, McKim and Ronald B. Inden. 1977. 'Toward an Ethnosociology of South Asian Caste Systems'. In *The New Wind: Changing Identities in South Asia*, edited by Kenneth David, 227–38. The Hague: Mouton.

Mendoza, S. Lily. 2006. *Between the Homeland and the Diaspora*. Manila: UST Publishing House.

Miklitsch, Robert. 1996. 'The Commodity-Body-Sign: Toward a General Economy of "Commodity Fetishism"'. *Cultural Critique* 33: 5–40.

Myers, Tony. 2003. *Slavoj Žižek*. London: Routledge.

Parmentier, Richard J. 1994. *Signs in Society: Studies in Semiotic Anthropology*. Bloomington: Indiana University Press.

Peirce, C. S. 1932. *Collected Papers*, vols 1–6. Cambridge, MA: Harvard University Press.

Pessoa, Carlos. 2003. 'Debate: On Hegemony, Post-Ideology and Subalternity'. *Bulletin of Latin-American Research* 32 (4): 484–90.

Rao, Derebail Muralidhar. 1997. *Treasure Trove and More: Vaastu Shilpa Shaastra*. New Delhi: Galgotia Publications.

Rao, S. K. Ramachandra. 1982. *Sri Chakra: Its Yantra, Mantra and Tantra*. Bangalore: Kalpatharu Research Academy.

Sharpe, Matthew. 'Slavoj Žižek'. Internet Encyclopedia of Philosophy. Online: http://www.iep.utm.edu/zizek (accessed 25 May 2013).

Ssorin-Chaikov, Nikolai. 2003. 'Mothering Tradition: Gender and Governance Among Siberian Evenki'. Working paper no. 45. *Max Planck Institute for Social Anthropology Working Papers*. Halle.

Sökefeld, Martin. 1999. 'Debating Self, Identity and Culture in Anthropology'. *Current Anthropology* 40 (4).

Thoden van Velzen, H. U. E. 1995. 'Revenants That Cannot Be Shaken: Collective Fantasies in a Maroon Society'. *American Anthropologist*, n.s., 97 (4): 722–32.

Vighi, Fabio and Heiko Feldner. 'Ideology Critique or Discourse Analysis? Žižek against Foucault'. *European Journal of Political Theory* 6 (2): 141–59.

Warren, Kay. 2007. 'Writing Gendered Memories of Repression in Northern Ireland'. *Anthropological Theory* 7 (1): 9–35.

Žižek, Slavoj. 2003. 'The Supposed Subjects of Ideology'. *Critical Quarterly* 39 (2): 39–59.

_____. 2004. *Organs Without Bodies: On Deleuze and Consequences*. London: Routledge.

_____. 2006. *The Parallax View*. London: MIT Press.

_____. 2007. *The Indivisible Remainder: On Schelling and Related Matters*. London: Verso.

Chapter 16

BORDER CROSSINGS BETWEEN ANTHROPOLOGY AND BUDDHIST PHILOSOPHY

Susantha Goonatilake

This chapter attempts to locate anthropology historically as to its epistemological roots, its critique that occurred after decolonization and its future, as once again the centre of gravity of the world's economic axis shifts to Asia. The position taken in this chapter is that of standpoint theory, namely that all theoretical as well as empirical statements are bound within a social framework and perspective.

Hitherto, in the discussions on the social construction of knowledge, the canvas had either been the small groups within which knowledge is created (for example, in the case of natural sciences in the laboratory, or in the case of publishing in the peer review group) or, sometimes, the larger perspective of a nation. Here, I extend the social framework to the larger civilizational context, noting that anthropology rose out of the West's search at the period of its ascendancy for knowledge on what it considered inferior societies. I also consider the present global shift as also having a civilizational aspect, namely that Asian civilizations would increasingly impinge on the directions of knowledge, including those in anthropology.

Civilizational border crossings in anthropology from Asia would subsume Asian subject matter, as well as an anthropology of Europe and the West from the standpoint of various Asian epistemological, geographical and cultural locations. The various regions of Asia – although not by any means defining Asia's total culture – have once had as a running thread a Buddhist cultural overlay through their histories (the 'Light of Asia' in Edwin Arnold's evocation). Buddhism is taken here both as a belief system as well as an epistemological-philosophical system which has dealt with many of the problems that Western philosophy has also dealt with.

This chapter is divided into several sections: 1) the standpoint of anthropology that was delivered to the world at the time of decolonization; 2) some of the key misinterpretations in the anthropology of Asian societies and Asian philosophical systems, taking as an example Buddhist societies and Buddhism; 3) the false 'facts' and interpretations on Buddhist societies by Max Weber, a founder of social science; 4) contemporary Sri Lankan anthropology as a paradigmatic example of the persistence of Eurocentrism; 5) the unsuccessful attempt to incorporate Asian conceptual elements in the form of a so-called Confucian ethic; 6) the geopolitical landscape of knowledge within the current shift to Asia; and 7) elements of philosophy in Buddhism that could be used within an anthropological enterprise.

1. Standpoint of Anthropology at the Time of Decolonization

Anthropology was the study of Europe's 'other'. Some of these attempts go back to the fanciful stories of the ancient Greeks of hybrid humans with animal parts living in the East, which were clear adoptions from Sanskrit mythology.[1] Later, in the sixteenth century, the Iberian thrust across the globe carried an Inquisition ideology, sanctioned by the Pope, and so a more aggressive and intolerant attitude appeared in describing the 'heathen' other. The baton of colonial control moved to industrializing Britain in the nineteenth century, as anthropology in its modern form began to emerge. Although not that interested in the crusader ideology of the Iberians, it was still a colonial view from the colonizer. Britain was more interested in a global empire where industrial production occurred in the mother country while raw materials and markets existed in its colonies. An understanding of the Asian was now required in a more sophisticated manner, but at the same time under an ideology of domination and superiority of the West. Together with anthropology now also arose the study of the civilizational heritage of Asia, appearing in later years as Indian or Chinese studies.

With the rise of independence movements and the mortal weakening of the West in World War II, independence was now wrested by the hitherto colonies. Shortly after independence, especially in the 1960s, there began a foundational questioning of the role of anthropology, pointing out the close links between colonialism and anthropology, and that the latter was largely suffused by a colonial ideology. By the 1970s, this extensive criticism began to take effect, and there were calls for a more universal science. The subject was attempting to reform, to become more universal, especially in Africa, but not so in all contexts, as I carefully documented in a book on the social epistemology of anthropology of Sri Lanka.[2]

2. Key Misinterpretations in the Anthropology of Asian Societies and Asian Philosophical Systems

Anthropology in its roots was not only governed by colonial attitudes, but also by the prevailing macrosocial theorists who tried to explain the rise of industrializing Europe in comparison with entities elsewhere. When the entities were small like those of isolated tribal or forest-dwelling communities, the explanations were rather easy to make. But when the entities were larger, civilizational ones with long histories, who had at one time been ahead of Europe, the explanations had to then become more elaborate.

The two founding fathers of the most influential strands of social thought in the West were Karl Marx and Max Weber. For Marx, one reason why Asian civilizations were behind was because they were allegedly governed by an Asiatic mode of production. We know today that this was not true, certain parts of Asia having the requisites of some aspects of industrialism.[3] The second theorist, Weber, used cultural factors to explain the rise of Europe and for the lagging behind of Asia, and it is to him that we should now turn.[4]

Max Weber's major contribution discussed the emergence of capitalism through its association with Protestantism. He also examined other religions including Buddhism in connection to economic activities as an important part of his total system of social theory.

Examining the empirical basis of Weber's views of Buddhism is very instructive. I will to take his *The Religions of India: The Sociology of Hinduism and Buddhism*, where he devotes 24 pages to what he terms 'Ancient Buddhism'.[5] His sources are the Pali language, the canon of Buddhist thought together with its commentarial literature and later works, and Asvaghosa's *Buddhacarita*. Apart from the *Buddhacarita*, all his sources are from the Sinhalese Theravada tradition, which was translated to European languages in the late nineteenth and early twentieth century.

3. Weber's 'Facts' and Interpretations

In these two-dozen pages, Weber makes huge blunders. For example, he falsely mentions that the constant companion of the Buddha, Ananda, was the designated successor to the Buddha.[6] Weber describes the founding of Buddhism as when Prince Siddhartha, the Buddha-to-be, leaves his palace to become an ascetic.[7] The Buddhist Order, however, was established only after the attainment of the enlightenment of the Buddha and the subsequent induction of his first disciples.

Weber denotes nirvana as 'absolute annihilation'[8] whereas the Buddha has categorically stated that it is not.[9] One sees nirvana by clear insight into the reality of things.[10] Weber further asserts that in Buddhism, 'What is sought is not salvation to an eternal life, but to the everlasting tranquility of death', again a complete misunderstanding of Buddhism.[11] In Buddhism, satiety either with life or death is foundationally rejected.[12]

Weber further states that Buddhism knows of no consistent concept of 'conscience and cannot know it because of the "karma" doctrine substructuring the Buddhistic denial of the idea of personality'.[13] In Buddhism, the concept closest to conscience in the Christian sense is more complex and includes both the intention, as well as the consequence, of volitional action.[14] Thus, a person is held responsible only when the deed has been done intentionally; that is, personal responsibility and conscience is taken to a more sophisticated level than that of the Abrahamic religions' commandments.

Weber claims that Buddhism lacks 'almost all beginnings of a methodical lay morality'.[15] Buddhism, however, was not a teaching restricted for monks only; it was equally meant for monks, nuns, laymen and lay women – the Buddha's expositions often started addressing all these four categories. There were also lay *Arahants*, that is, those who reached nirvana. In addition, there are a number of discourses by the Buddha specifically dealing with a well-defined lay morality, such as *Sigalovada Sutta*, *Vyagghapajja Sutta*, *Maha Mangala Sutta*, *Parabhava Sutta*, *Dhammika Sutta*, etc.

Sila, the Buddhist precepts, are referred to by Weber as the ethic of nonaction.[16] But as every Buddhist child knows, every *sila* has a negative as well as a positive aspect, actions to be encouraged and others to be discouraged.[17] Weber's interpretation unfortunately takes only the negative aspect of abstention, for example from killing, and misses out the positive aspect of sympathy and compassion for all sentient beings.

Weber states that the Buddhist monastic community 'lacked all firm organization'.[18] The Buddhist monastic community, however, is one of the world's oldest formal organizations. One of the three parts of the Buddhist canon, the *Vinaya Pitaka* reveals a developed monastic life with detailed rules governing the entire life and activities of individuals and of communities. The Buddhist monastic order has a formal hierarchy and tight rules. Training was a compulsory component. The system of promotions was strict: only after ten years will a novice become a *thera*, and after twenty years a *mahathera*. There were also different areas of specialization among monks, namely: *vinaya*, *sutta* and *abhidhamma*. In fact, the organization of the monks' order had several of the characteristics that Weber later saw in the ideal types that define a bureaucratic organization.

Weber implies that propaganda through teaching was originally regarded as a peculiar 'duty for the monks, but this may remain an open question, though it is rather improbable' – again just the opposite of historical facts.[19] The Buddha's exhortation to the first monks was, 'Go forth monks for the good of the many, out of compassion for the world, for the good. [...] Let not two go by one way. Preach O Monks the *dhamma*, both in the spirit and in the letter'.[20] Propagation through teaching was thus a major duty assigned by the Buddha to his disciples.

The great misunderstanding that Weber brought into the social sciences was that Buddhism was an otherworldly religion, a 'specifically un-political and an anti-political status religion'.[21] The Buddha discouraged the involvement of the monks in 'kingly sciences' since these would have distracted them from their main goal. Yet the Buddha on several important occasions spoke on political and socioeconomic affairs, and in other instances advised kings to lead a path of righteousness and nonviolence.

The Buddha admonished that even a universal monarch who ruled the entire earth should do so under the guidance and the authority of the *dhamma*.[22] The ideal ruler maintains political stability and ensures, among others, the right to life and the right to property. According to another *sutta*, social injustices – erosion of moral values, divisions and wars – arise from misdistribution of goods.[23] This *sutta* further makes a pointed criticism of a particular king's approach: 'The king provides for the righteous protection and security of his subjects but neglected the economy.'[24] The best way to end turmoil and disunity and ensure peace and prosperity, the Buddha said, is not by draining the resources of the country on religious sacrifices, but by developing the economy and providing full employment.[25] Elsewhere, the Buddha gives ideas of how, when the ruler follows certain lay prescriptions, both the ruled and the rulers could be happy: 'The king's revenue will go up; the country will be quiet and at peace, and the populace, pleased with one another and happy, dancing their children in their arms, will dwell with open doors.'[26]

Going further on with his Buddhism as otherworldly, Weber claims that 'Buddhism has no tie with any sort of social movement, nor did it run parallel with such, and it had established no "social-political goal".'[27] The Buddha was a major critic of the slave and caste systems and introduced new social and political arguments: 'It is not the birth that makes a Brahmin or a slave but one's action.'[28] The Buddha did not accept the existing system, with its inequalities and caste discrimination, and spoke forcefully against it, and he had defined positions on social and political life.

Weber again misinterprets when he asserts that there is no ethical position in Buddhism against the use of luxuries.[29] The rejection of a luxurious life is, however, a component of the Buddhist way of life, part of the two extremes to be avoided – excessive self-indulgence or total satisfaction of the senses, while the other was self-mortification or total suppression of the sensual desires. The middle path was the only path to liberation.

There are, we see, twelve significant empirical errors in Weber's knowledge of Buddhism of a very basic kind in just the 24 pages that we have looked at (errors in key biographical data of the Buddha, key tenets of the doctrine and of its relation to society). The translations that Weber used do not make these errors, and are generally sympathetic to Buddhism.

Max Weber was writing on Buddhism and Buddhist societies in a faraway country. But recently, there has been an entire school in anthropology on one predominantly Buddhist society, namely the Sinhalese Buddhist society, that has distorted social reality far more than Weber.

4. Sri Lankan Anthropology Studies

Sri Lankan studies took an 'anthropology turn' nearly a generation ago, and these studies – largely by expatriates or Westerners and predominantly on Sinhalese Buddhists – are the dominant social science discourse published on Sri Lanka. In most Western scholarly quarters, this literature replaced the predominant place hitherto taken in nineteenth- and twentieth-century Western scholarship by the study of Pali and Sinhalese texts on Buddhism and Buddhist societies.

The factual, theoretical and methodological shortcomings of these studies are not difficult to trace, as I have done in a book and a series of articles.[30] Even a cursory examination with some background knowledge of Sri Lanka indicates those writings to be faulty. Let me briefly recount their key errors, taking in a few of the major writers in the genre.

Gananath Obeyesekere, of Sinhalese origin but working in the West to explain current Sinhalese society, invented a so-called Protestant Buddhism – defined by Obeyesekere as both a protest and an imitation of Protestantism.[31] This theme of Protestant Buddhism has led to a chain of citations in the international literature legitimizing its validity. It is easy to show Obeyesekere's Protestant Buddhism as fictional.

Thus, Obeyesekere falsely states that the emphasis on rationality in today's Buddhism has been brought by Westerners, primarily the theosophists like Blavatsky and Olcott. But theosophists like Blavatsky were, however, irrationalists criticized for this by local Buddhists.[32] The more rational theosophist, Olcott, was attacked by Buddhists for irrationality and had to apologize for his misreadings of Buddhism. Obeyesekere also invented non-existing episodes, including total fabrications around the well-known monk Vipulasara.[33]

Easy to show facts indicate that Obeyesekere's alleged Protestant Buddhism was not a Christian overlay, as he implies. The nineteenth and early twentieth century's Buddhist renaissance was basically a reaction from a culture with a long historical sense, which in its long history had gone through several such revivals.

Obeyesekere also shows his ignorance of basic Buddhist facts when he refers to Anathapindika, the greatest philanthropist in Buddha's time and benefactor of the Buddha, as the Buddha's great physician (whose name was Jeevaka), who tended to the Buddha as he approached death. His inventions continue when he implies that the goal of Buddhism is a 'permanent state of bliss', a very different take from the Buddha's descriptions of its goal: nirvana.[34] He again misunderstands when he says that South Asian philosophers are 'obsessed with the idea of an ultimate state of bliss'.[35] Obeyesekere makes further errors of a kind which no Buddhist school boy in Sri Lanka would make: He gives as 220 the number of rules of conduct which a monk should follow, the actual figure being 227.[36] And these rules were not foundational to Buddhism, they were introduced gradually, one by one, over the years. He is also uninformed that a number of laypersons attained *arahantship* (enlightenment) in Buddha's time.

Bruce Kapferer made his career on a series of books[37] that he wrote on the presumed characteristics of Sinhalese Buddhists, based, when one carefully examines his data, on a sample of, at the most, two or three people in the south of Sri Lanka who believed in exorcism.[38] He then went on from these presumed characteristics to essentialize and caricature Sinhalese Buddhists. In spite of the longest tradition of continuous history in the entire South Asian region going back to at least the third century BCE, Kapferer considers the Sinhalese Buddhist heritage as only a recent invention constructed by the so-called 'Protestant Buddhism' *à la* Obeyesekere. He bemoans as un-Buddhist the attitudes of Buddhists when they denounce 'astrology, occultism, ghostology and palmistry'. He adduces here a Protestant hand, being unaware that the Buddha denounced these arts directly as unfit. Kapferer wants his Sinhalese to be driven, not by Buddhist thought or practice, but by exorcism.

Tambiah's tract *Buddhism Betrayed? Religion, Politics, and Violence in Sri Lanka* perhaps is the one book by an anthropologist anywhere that was so widely criticized for its sheer invention of facts as exposed in several Sri Lanka newspapers.[39] Tambiah gave without evidence statements on alleged pathological Sinhalese attitudes, such as 'millenarian politicized Buddhism', 'a dangerously simplified racism' and the right to exclude and exterminate others, especially Dravidians. These were all inventions.

Tambiah describes, contrary to well-known facts, Anagarika Dharmapala, the founder of contemporary international Buddhism, as 'an uncharitable propagandist' (though in a later book he seemed to recant). Tambiah falsely blames Migettuwatte Gunananda, the Buddhist monk who defeated Christians in debate, for a riot between Catholics and Buddhists in 1883. But this was a mischievous invention. The findings of a British colonial government's commission of enquiry was just the opposite, blaming the Catholics for the riots.

Kumari Jayawardena implicitly approved the oppression of Buddhists under colonial rule, as she wrote against the Buddhist revival of the late nineteenth and early twentieth century and the public debates between Christians and Buddhists in 1873 after over three hundred years of colonial persecution of Buddhists. One book sponsored by Jayawardena, with the telling title *Unmaking the* [Sri Lankan] *Nation*, denigrates both the nationalist renaissance in Sri Lanka, and worse, denies the historical importance of Anuradhapura, the ancient Sinhalese capital from the fifth century BCE to the eleventh century CE, an important symbol of Sinhalese civilization.[40]

To give a sample of the feel of the distortions of this school, let me highlight a few more authors. C. R. de Silva invents a crude Buddhist Fundamentalism by quoting some of the above writers.[41] While falsifying Sri Lankan facts, de Silva completely ignores the Christian fundamentalists' hold on the US – de Silva's present home. H. L. Seneviratne, again addressing an American audience, has been writing on the need to rewrite Sri Lankan history and to remove Buddhism from the position which even the British accorded it when it annexed Sri Lanka.[42]

Echoing colonial missionaries, many of these writers have also continuously called for foreign intervention in the country. Unique in the postcolonial world, this literature, therefore, has an implicit recolonization agenda.

Having sketched a contemporary anomaly in anthropology, it is useful to recall the civilizational assumptions of classical anthropology and its lessons.

5. The Present Geopolitics of Anthropology: Subjects and Objects

Anthropology has ingrained within it certain philosophical and value judgements of the West, as it attempted to understand it from its own macroepistemological perspectives. But as the world's axis shifts increasingly towards Asia, different macroperspectives will invariably be factored in – often implicitly. A notable attempt was when the first wave of Asian countries from East Asia began to reach high economic growth rates.

By the 1980s, the rapid rise of parts of Asia such as Japan, Korea, Taiwan, Singapore and Hong Kong invoked a Confucian ethic of group solidarity and hard work reminiscent of Max Weber evoking a Protestant ethic. It was said that Confucian values had been the major contributing factor to the sudden upsurge of East Asian economies.[43] But Confucianism had been there for around 2,500 years and no major industrial breakthrough had occurred comparable to the European Industrial Revolution of Protestant countries. Further, there were noncultural aspects at work fashioning attitudes in these countries. Most of these countries had very repressive and/or authoritarian regimes where labour dissent was not tolerated at the time. In the case of Japan, there was a highly internalized authoritarian ethic arising from its earlier experiences with Tokugawa and partially Meiji. Soon the East Asian countries were joined by other Asian countries such as Thailand, Malaysia, Indonesia, India, Pakistan and Sri Lanka (with a vicious terrorist problem), who with backgrounds in Buddhism, Hinduism and Islam were having growth rates reminiscent of earlier Asian experiences.

The presumed unique characteristics of European culture, including a so-called Protestant ethic – which Eurocentrism placed as a prime necessity for economic growth – was being shown to be grossly inadequate, as Asian countries were waking up and growing furiously.

6. The Geopolitical Landscape of Knowledge within the Current Shift to Asia

The fastest growing economies over the last few decades and into the foreseeable future are thus those of Asia. The first industrial nation, Britain, in its first hundred years, grew at a rate of 2–3 per cent.[44] In comparison, these Asian economies are growing at anywhere between 6 and 12 per cent. As a Goldman Sachs study in 2003 predicted, China could be the largest economy by 2040, India will be the third largest, with the United States coming number two.[45] The personal incomes of average Asians would still be lower than in several Western countries. But there is no doubt that the Asian region as a whole could be a much greater economic force than the West, taken as a whole.

This shift of the economic axis of the world is occurring with a global redivision of work. In the initial phase of the economic development of Asia, there was a relocation of brawn work, such as in garment industries, towards cheaper Asian countries. At the moment, a new relocation of brainpower is occurring. The initial development required some rudimentary knowledge of science and technology. But that phase of partial imitation is rapidly vanishing as, in certain industrial sectors, Asian products now lead. Chinese industrial products today flood the Western markets. Software production has emerged as a major growth point in India paralleling the growth of computer hardware in South East and East Asia in the earlier years. And biotechnology is following fast.

There is, therefore, a new relocation of brainpower, and a shift to the Asian cultural region is occurring in science and technology. In addition, thousands of Asians man research facilities in the West, a symptom being the large number of Asian graduate students in American universities. It has been estimated that in Silicon Valley in the United States – the initial breeding ground of information technology – about one third of the scientific and technology personnel are Asians, primarily from East Asia or South Asia.

Science and technology are, however, cultural products, and the ongoing shift in this field is paralleled in other cultural products. For example, designers from Hong Kong, Japan and now Malaysia set Western clothing fashions. And several Asian countries including the Philippines are those who draw 'Western' cartoon films. In addition, the Japanese genre of anime had by the first decade of the second millennium invaded the consciousness of children in the West. At a higher state of consciousness, some of the best novelists writing in that primary carrier of globalization, namely English, are Asians, mostly from the subcontinent. The earlier hegemonic blanket of Eurocentrism in culture is being lifted.

A central finding of the school of the social construction of science was that the creation of the cultural elements that becomes science is governed by social pressures. These occur in the peer group in that particular branch of science, namely peers in the laboratory; in the reviewers who approve the results for publication; in the social pressures brought in from national priorities such as in funding; and in the import of cultural elements to science. With the shift to Asia, significant aspects of the social environment change allowing for new possibilities outside the European context and imagination to emerge in science, as I have elsewhere argued and illustrated.[46] If natural sciences are so culturally impregnated and governed by context, the social sciences, including anthropology, would be far more so. We have already seen the failed attempt to bring in Asian elements by ascribing a Confucian ethic paralleling the Protestant ethic to describe the rise of East Asia. But this attempt did not take any new conceptual matter from the Asian cultural region. It only took into account aspects of the presumed behaviour of East Asians, due to their partial heritage of Confucianism, as a guide to how they behaved. The greater Asian input would be to take into account epistemological elements from Asian cultures.

Before the coming of European influence in recent centuries, Buddhism was one common cultural overlay across most of Asia. Buddhism has both norms of social behaviour as well as, more importantly, developed approaches in epistemology – guidelines for observation and coming to conclusions. The question we have to pose is: are there elements within Buddhist epistemology which can give insights into anthropology as it locates itself in a confident Asia?

7. Elements of Buddhism for Anthropology

Before coming to Buddhism, it is useful to sketch some of the macroperspectives under which a non-Eurocentric, Asian-oriented anthropology would emerge, paralleling, in the first instance, the particular characteristics of Eurocentric anthropology. For our purposes, let us divide, as Scharfstein did, the civilizations having developed philosophies as South Asia, China and Europe. He summarized their common features. All three cultures were ethnocentric in that they viewed those outside their region as barbarians. Paralleling this ethnocentricity was the relative autonomy and insularity of their conceptual views. All three cultures distinguished between appearance and reality, the relative and absolute, and the temporary and permanent. All three cultural regions developed logic and dialectical systems of argument, in the South Asian cultural region and Europe; these grew into complex and formal schemes. All three had sceptical, materialist and empirical philosophers and had philosophical views roughly corresponding to the (European) concepts of realism, idealism and phenomenology.[47] (Here I would like to emphasize that the latter are Eurocentric categories which do not necessarily exhaust the wide varieties of philosophical positions found elsewhere, especially in the South Asian world.)

The attitude of unconscious ethnocentricity from Europe gave rise, as we have seen, to the distortions in anthropology, in both a macroconceptual sense as well as in a narrower empirical sense. Before a truly universal anthropology could emerge, it is essential, therefore, to go through a necessary passage of an ethnocentric perspective from Asian civilizations. The 'modern age' arose in the sixteenth century with the expansionism of the Iberian powers across parts of the world. Even then, there were counterperspectives from the colonized on the Europeans. I will take the example from Sri Lanka, which was then at its weakest point because of internal political dissensions. Sri Lanka had not only been at the crossroads of East-West traffic from pre-Christian times, but also had nurtured intense discussions in Buddhist philosophy, both from the Theravada tradition as well as from the Mahayana one. Even at the nadir of Sri Lanka, European civilization – at least certain aspects of it – was looked at with contempt by the Sinhalese.

This attitude is best seen from the perspective of the enemy. A Portuguese historian of the period, Queyroz, who wrote about the failure of the 'temporal and spiritual conquest' of Sri Lanka by the Portuguese, observed that the antiquity of the kings of Sri Lanka was 'unequalled in Europe' and that 'the people are noble, cultured'.[48] He went on to say that the Sinhalese were 'pride itself' – the first error of the Sinhalese pride being to think that they alone in the world 'observed and maintained the art of government, cleanliness and propriety and that all the other nations are barbarous, low and wanting in cleanliness and propriety – especially Europeans'. He also observed that they indulged in 'endless ablutions' and that those who do not eat as they do are considered the lowest, and those who do not wash properly 'neither clean nor proper'.[49] Elsewhere he mentions that the Sinhalese are 'generally proud and vain' on account of the presumption of a 'celestial descent', of the 'antiquity of their kingdom and nation' and of the riches in the country.[50] He further noted that when they see Portuguese youths praying in the Christian manner, it is a 'cause of laughter' to the Sinhalese.[51] This latter sentiment was also noted by another Portuguese, de Caminha, who in a letter dated 1547 to the Portuguese viceroy said that the king of Kandy 'laughed heartily at the friars and Christianity'.[52]

So any anthropology from a different civilizational perspective should – at least at the initial stages – engrain a perspective from Europe's civilizational others. Although it may seem crude, as an initial epistemological cleansing exercise, it should also incorporate the undercurrents of cultural contempt at aspects of European civilization that are found in several Asian cultures. At a time when the subaltern is breaking free, it would be an unearthing of a subaltern and hitherto silent perspective. The short tract *Barbaric Others: A Manifesto on Western Racism* by Sardar, Nandy, Alvarez and Davies could be a beginning.[53]

Coming to Buddhism, one should note that it was not the otherworldly religion of Max Weber's construct. As a social force, Buddhism went against social injustices, including speaking against the caste system, inequality, false rites, ceremonies and sacrifices.[54] Yet, although the Buddha made several articulations on society, he was of course not a sociologist; his primary intellectual aim was to understand the nature of reality.

There are many comments on society found in several pronouncements of the Buddha, as for example in the expositions on lay ethics *Sigalovada Sutta*.[55] These have been pointed out by many writers. One, a collection by Nandasena Ratnapala provides a useful summary of these attitudes of the Buddha on society, but is falsely designated as *Buddhist Sociology*, which the book is not.[56]

To arrive at Buddhist philosophical perspectives useful for anthropology, we must go to Buddhist epistemology and not to simple pronouncements to the laity on how one should behave. We should note at the outset that Buddhism, in common with all South Asian belief systems, is unlike the Abrahamic religions of Judaism, Christianity and Islam, which are revealed religions – 'revealed' by a supernatural entity 'God' to his respective messengers Moses, Christ or Mohammed. There is always intertwined in Buddhism an observational element which combines with philosophical elements.

There is also outside these philosophical aspects, much borrowing of cultural furniture from the society that gave rise to Buddhism. This cultural furniture would include elements outside the observational realm such as gods and goddesses and realms of being outside the humanly observable. Yet, outside such cultural furniture, the observational could stand on their own – as in descriptions of meditation. The parallel would be with, say, Greek philosophers believing in their gods, but espousing sophisticated systems of philosophy which could stand outside such beliefs. Another example would be Newton, who while articulating his major contributions in physics was also delving into, and writing extensively on, God.

There are elements within Buddhism on how to observe the world while being within it. A good observational metaphor used in Buddhism is that one should be like the lotus leaf floating on water, being both within water as well as outside it. This observational injunction would be ideal for participant observation; the person, the observer, being both within the water of other human beings as well as being above it. But for a truly Buddhist perspective in anthropology, one must go beyond such individual exhortation, and as an anchoring perspective, go to the core of Buddhist philosophy.

Let us first articulate some basic facts on the Buddhist search for knowledge. The Buddha himself articulated the need for scepticism, including scepticism of his own statements, as is well described in his widely known address to the Kalamas.[57] The attitude of the Buddha to nonfollowers was also straightforward: '*ehi passiko*' – come and see for yourself.[58] Buddhism was also always engulfed in debates within and outside of itself on philosophy and the nature of reality, including aspects of social reality. Buddhism had arisen within a period in India of strong intellectual interest and unrest, the Buddha himself identifying 62 different schools of thought that differed from his. Later, Buddhist universities such as those at Nalanda, Takshila, Vikramashila and the Maha Bodhi were important centres of learning and academic discussion. In fact, they were the first universities in the world. The Maha Bodhi, in today's Bodh Gaya, founded in the fourth century CE by a Sinhalese king, was perhaps the first centre of higher learning funded by foreigners. These centres were all destroyed in attacks by Islamic invaders, Nalanda alone burning for six months. Outside the subcontinental mainland, three similar centres of higher learning with thousands of students arose in Sri Lanka. These centres not only studied Buddhist philosophy and practice, but also studied 'lay subjects' such as mathematics, logic, medicine, architecture, astronomy, astrology and painting.[59]

Philosophical positions come to the social sciences indirectly and implicitly. There have, however, been direct transfers of philosophical positions into the social sciences, as for example in the case of Marxist sociology, positivism and, say, in anthropology, Malinowski's functionalism, with its philosophical roots in Ernst Mach's positivism.[60] Mach's core ideas on the nature of the person, we should here recall, resonated well with the Buddhist ideas of the nature of the person, Mach himself admitting as much.[61]

But, before bringing in extra European ideas of philosophy into the essentially Western-born subject of anthropology, it is useful to make some observations on the differences between the two traditions. Greek philosophy is based on a foundational tripod of ethics, logic and metaphysics. In Buddhism, the central view on reality is that the world both within oneself and outside is a flow, with nothing permanent, both the observer and the observed being built-up of constituent elements. The ultimate goal, and so the ultimate ethical foundation of Buddhism, is to realize this. Buddhist ethics are essentially derived from this central position. Consequently, ethics in Buddhism is situational with, for example, in Buddha's own time, a mass murderer, a prostitute and a thief reaching the highest Buddhist goals. So there are differences even in what constitutes foundational assumptions between the European tradition in philosophy and the Buddhist position.

The validity of *some* Buddhist conclusions on mental behavioural processes have been corroborated by Western psychologists and physicians, who have taken these observations at face value and subjected them to the scrutiny of science. This has been most notably shown in that category of mental and behavioural observation which goes under the term 'meditation'.[62] But the contribution of Buddhism we are interested in is to its epistemological position.

Unique among philosophies, Buddhism denies the existence of a self or soul. Through observation, the existence of a permanent abiding 'me' is radically deconstructed in Buddhism. Buddhist observation breaks down the component, physical and mental factors that constitute the psychophysical personality. In the Buddha's own words, 'there is no materiality whatever ... no feeling ... no perception ... no formations ... no consciousness [these five constituting the five Buddhist aggregates] whatever that is permanent, everlasting, eternal, not inseparable from the idea of change ... that will last ...'.[63] And, at another time, 'When neither self nor anything pertaining to self can truly and really be found, this speculative view [of] a permanent, abiding, ever-lasting, unchanging [self] is wholly and completely foolish'.[64] A disciple of the Buddha elaborated further that what one calls 'I am' is 'neither matter, sensation, perception, mental formations nor consciousness'.[65]

Mental phenomena and the external environment are both in a perpetual state of becoming, changing from moment to moment.[66] In Buddhist observation and analysis of identity, there is no individual, only a stream.[67] 'Life is a stream [*sota*], an unbroken succession of aggregates. There is no temporal or spatial break or pause in this life continuity'.[68] This continuity is not through a soul, but through a stream of becoming.[69] These conclusions are obtained by careful observation of both the world outside as well as the internal world of mental phenomena.

Humans are thus considered in Buddhism a process, a collection of swiftly changing mental and physical processes. The conventional view of the person is constructed from such changing aspects to become a stream of conditioned processes.[70] A conventional empirical self is recognized as only a momentary crystallization of a process which interacts with the world outside.[71] The world, including the environment of other humans in which the individual lives, is itself changing and is in a state of flux.

A foundational approach in sociology using Buddhist philosophy would use the platform of a changing observer to examine and come to conclusions about a continuously changing social field. This social field would consist of continuously changing individuals, continuously changing groups and continuously changing classes. The detailed outcomes of such a changed epistemological position cannot be discussed here. We can, however, mention that in the natural sciences such changed epistemological positions have given rise to far-reaching changes in the subject matter. A most notable example is the case of Einstein's use of Mach's position in epistemology (which incidentally had echoes with Buddhist positions), which changed the direction of physics and gave rise to relativity.[72]

A foundational approach using Buddhist philosophy can be articulated only by examining the whole of the sociological project from a Buddhist epistemological underpinning. Such an underpinning would be different from the convention of dividing the world into a subject which cognizes an object from a fixed subjective platform, which then comes to conclusions on the social world. For Buddhism, cognition is basically experiencing the world, but this experiencing does not imply as absolute a subject–object relationship.[73] Apprehending the world outside is not just a reaction to the external stimulus, but an active process where what is sensed is simultaneously given meaning and form.[74] Buddhism also insists on immediately grasping experience – unfiltered. It takes the view that the world is intertwined and conditioned.[75] Our senses, it assumes, deliver to us only limited information under a blanket of indeterminateness.[76] Persons live in a world that is sensed and thought about, and this social world would exist only as a constructed experience.[77] The social world is cognized only through a framework of pre-established data.[78]

Let us illustrate what such a radical reordering of the epistemological field would imply: Buddhism in its injunction of being like a lotus in the act of observation, being both inside and outside the field of observation, subsumes the essence of the participant-observer in anthropology. But clearly, the epistemological take of looking at the changing world from the changing self is a much larger proposition. Although it could, and would, subsume the conventional injunctions of participant observation, where one is expected to internalize aspects of the observational other for purposes of sympathetic observation (in an exercise of *Verstehen*), a Buddhist approach will be foundationally different – foundationally more encompassing.

Buddhist epistemology has some echoes also with postmodernism, which posits that there is no single valid platform for observation. But Buddhist epistemology goes beyond it. The seeming parallels between postmodernism and Buddhist theories of flux and the ever-changing individual have been noted by comparative philosophers. They have then gone on to point out the epistemological inadequacy of the postmodernist perspective in comparison with the larger Buddhist canvas, as well as the limitations of such parallels. The flavour of these comparisons is seen in several articles in the journal *Philosophy East and West*.[79] The Buddhist epistemological perspective goes beyond the limitations of postmodernism.

The Buddhist relationship between oneself and the social other could also be compared with the *Ich* and *Du* (I and thou) relationship of Martin Buber, which had been used in sociological and allied thought.[80] Buber's central thesis is that social life is a dialogical existence, a relationship between pairs such as 'I and thou'. In a Buddhist formulation, the dialogue of existence is between a flowing and ever-changing 'I' and a flowing and ever-changing 'thou', or more correctly with sets of flowing and ever-changing 'thous'.

Conclusion

Just like modern physics, taking a Machian epistemological position, changed physics and gave rise to a new way of looking at the dynamics of the material world, a similar foundational approach using Buddhist epistemology would change the perspectives on the dynamics of the social world.

Notes

1 Wilhelm Halbfass, *India and Europe: An Essay in Understanding* (Albany: State University of New York Press, 1988), 10.
2 For a summary of these discussions, see Susantha Goonatilake, *Anthropologizing Sri Lanka: A Civilizational Misadventure* (Bloomington: Indiana University Press, 2001), 23–8.
3 John M. Hobson, *The Eastern Origins of Western Civilisation* (Cambridge: Cambridge University Press, 2004); Arun Bala, *The Dialogue of Civilizations in the Birth of Modern Science* (New York: Palgrave Macmillan, 2006).
4 The following details on Max Weber and Buddhism is taken from a joint paper by the present author and Hema Goonatilake, a Buddhist scholar, titled 'Max Weber's Social Construction of Buddhism', later published as a chapter in *Contemporary Social Issues: Essays in Honour of Prof. P. K. B. Nayar*, ed. Jacob John Kattakayam (Kerala: University of Kerala Press, 1990).
5 Max Weber, *The Religion of India: The Sociology of Hinduism and Buddhism*, trans. Don Martindale and Hans H. Gerth (Glencoe: Free Press, 1958).
6 Ibid., 224.

7 Ibid., 204.

8 Ibid., 204.

9 F. J. Hoffman, 'Rationality in Early Buddhist Four Fold Logic', *Journal of Indian Philosophy* 10 (1982); J. F. Staal, *Exploring Mysticism* (London: Penguin, 1976); J. F. Staal, 'Making Sense of the Buddhist Tetra Lemma', in *Philosophy East and West: Essays in Honour of Dr. T. M. P. Mahadevan*, ed. H. D. Lewis (Bombay: Blackie and Son, 1976); T. R. V. Murti, *Central Philosophy of Buddhism* (George Allen and Unwin: London, 1955).

10 L. Feer, *Samyutta Nikaya* V (London: Pali Text Society, 1898), 422.

11 Weber, *Religion of India*, 207.

12 Walpola Rahula, *What the Buddha Taught* (London: Gordon Fraser, 1978).

13 Weber, *Religion of India*, 210.

14 Rahula, *What the Buddha Taught*, 32.

15 Weber, *Religion of India*, 218.

16 Ibid.

17 Dines Andersen and Helmer Smith, eds, *Suttanipata* (London: Pali Text Society, 1913), verses 376–404.

18 Weber, *Religion of India*, 229.

19 Ibid., 228.

20 H. Oldenberg, ed., *Mahavagga, Vinaya Pitaka* (London: Pali Text Society, 1879), 25.

21 Weber, *Religion of India*, 206.

22 T. W. Rhys Davids, trans. *The Dialogues of the Buddha*, Part III, 2nd edition (Delhi: Motilal Banarsidass, 1999), 62.

23 T. W. Rhys Davis, trans., *Digha Nikaya*, vol. I (London: Pali Text Society), III, 65.

24 Ibid.

25 *Digha Nikaya* III, 65.

26 *Dialogues* I, 176.

27 Weber, *Religion of India*, 226.

28 Rhys Davids, ed., *Vasettha Sutta, Majjhima Nikaya* (London: Pali Text Society, 1925), 98.

29 Weber, *Religion of India*, 218.

30 Susantha Goonatilake, *Anthropologizing Sri Lanka: A Civilizational Misadventure* (Bloomington: Indiana University Press, 2001); Susantha Goonatilake, '"Buddhist Protestantism": The Reverse Flow of Ideas from Sri Lanka to the West', *Journal of the Royal Asiatic Society of Sri Lanka*, n.s., 45 (2002): 35–71; Susantha Goonatilake, 'Panadura Vaadaya and Its Consequences: Mischievous Association with Fundamentalism', *Journal of the Royal Asiatic Society of Sri Lanka*, n.s., 44 (2004): 87–118.

31 Richard Gombrich and Gananath Obeyesekere, *Buddhism Transformed: Religious Change in Sri Lanka* (Princeton, NJ: Princeton University Press, 1988).

32 Sylvia Cranston, *H. P. B.: The Extraordinary Life and Influence of Helena Blavatsky, Founder of the Modern Theosophical Movement* (New York: G. P. Putnam, 1993).

33 Goonatilake, *Anthropologizing Sri Lanka*.

34 G. Obeyesekere, *Imagining Karma: Ethical Transformation in Amerindian, Buddhist, and Greek Rebirth* (Berkeley: University of California Press, 2002), 128.

35 Ibid., 127.

36 Ibid., 146.

37 Bruce Kapferer, *The Feast of the Sorcerer: Practices of Consciousness and Power* (Chicago and London: University of Chicago Press, 1997); Bruce Kapferer, *Legends of People Myths of State: Violence, Intolerance, and Political Culture in Sri Lanka and Australia* (Washington, DC: Smithsonian Institution Press, 1988); Bruce Kapferer, *A Celebration of Demons Exorcism*

and the Aesthetics of Healing in Sri Lanka, 2nd edition (Washington, DC: Smithsonian Institution Press, 1991 [1983]).

38 Goonatilake, *Anthropologizing Sri Lanka*, 127.

39 S. J. Tambiah, *Buddhism Betrayed: Religion, Politics, and Violence in Sri Lanka* (Chicago: University of Chicago Press, 1992).

40 Pradeep Jeganathan and Qadri Ismail, eds, *Unmaking the Nation: The Politics of Identity and History in Modern Sri Lanka* (Colombo: Social Scientists' Association, 1995).

41 Tessa J. Bartholomeusz and Chandra R. de Silva, eds, *Buddhist Fundamentalism and Minority Identities in Sri Lanka* (Albany, NY: State University of New York Press, 1998).

42 H. L. Seneviratne, *The Work of Kings: The New Buddhism in Sri Lanka* (Chicago: Chicago University Press, 1999).

43 Peter L. Berger and Michael Hsiao Hsin-huang, eds, *In Search of an East Asian Development Model* (New Bruswick, NJ: Transaction Books, 1988).

44 Phyllis Deane, *The First Industrial Revolution* (Cambridge: Cambridge University Press, 1979), 291.

45 'The BRICs Are Coming – Fast; A Goldman economist talks about rapid growth in Brazil, Russia, India, and China', *Business Week*, 27 October 2003; Nicholas Kristof and Sheryl WuDunn, *Thunder from the East: Portrait of a Rising Asia* (New York: Vintage Books, 2001).

46 Susantha Goonatilake, *Toward a Global Science: Mining Civilizational Knowledge* (Indiana: Indiana University Press, 1999); *Technological Independence: The Asian Experience* (Tokyo: United Nations University, 1993).

47 Ben-Ami Scharfstein et al., 'A Critical Comparison of Indian, Chinese, Islamic and European Philosophy', in *Philosophy East/Philosophy West* (Oxford: Basil Blackwell, 1978), 30.

48 Fernao De Queyroz, *The Temporal and Spiritual Conquest of Ceylon*, vol. 1, trans. S. G. Perera (New Delhi: AES, 1992 [1930]), 298.

49 Ibid., 81.

50 Ibid., 23.

51 Ibid., 121.

52 O. M. Cosme da Silva, *Sri Lanka and the Portuguese (1541–1557)* (Colombo: M. D. Gunasena, 1996), 67.

53 Ziauddin Sardar, Ashis Nandy, Claude Alvarez, Merryl Wyn Davies, *Barbaric Others: A Manifesto on Western Racism* (London: Pluto Press, 1993).

54 Walpola Rahula, *Zen and the Taming of the Bull: Towards the Definition of Buddhist Thought* (London: Gordon Fraser, 1978).

55 Narada Thera, trans., *Everyman's Ethics: Four Discourses by the Buddha* (Kandy: Buddhist Publication Society, 1985).

56 Nandasena Ratnapala, *Buddhist Sociology* (Delhi: Sri Satguru Publications, 1993).

57 Soma Thera, trans., *Kalama Sutta: The Buddha's Charter of Free Inquiry* (Kandy: Buddhist Publication Society, 1981).

58 For a perspective from a Christian theological journal on these Buddhist attitudes to free thought, see John Makransky, 'Buddhist Perspectives on Truth in Other Religions: Past and Present', *Theological Studies* 64 (2003), 334–61.

59 Walpola Rahula, *Bhikshuvage Urumaya*, trans. as *The Heritage of the Bhikkhu: A Short History of the Bhikkhu in Educational, Cultural, Social, and Political Life* (New York: Grove Press, 1974), 30–33.

60 Andrzej K. Paluch, 'The Philosophical Background of the Classical Functionalism in Social Anthropology', *Reports on Philosophy* 4 (1980): 25–38.

61 'Mach and Buddhism' in John T. Blackburn, *Ernst Mach, His Work, Life and Influence* (University of California Press, 1972), 289.

62 Representative of this literature are: Jon Kabat-Zinn; Ann O. Massion; Jean Kristeller; Linda Gay Petersen; Kenneth E. Fletcher; Lori Pbert; William R. Lenderking; Saki F. Santorelli, 'Effectiveness of a Meditation-Based Stress Reduction Program in the Treatment of Anxiety Disorders', *American Journal of Psychiatry* 149 (1992): 936–43; Roger Walsh, 'Two Asian Psychologies and their Implications for Western Psychotherapists', *American Journal of Psychotherapy* 42 (4) (October 1988), 543–60; Michael J. Sweet; Craig G. Johnson, 'Enhancing Empathy: The Interpersonal Implications of a Buddhist Meditation Technique. Special Issue: Psychotherapy and Religion', *Psychotherapy* 27 (1) (1990): 19–29; Padmal De Silva, 'Buddhism and Behavior Modification', *Behavior Research and Therapy* 22 (6) (1984): 661–78; Daniel Goleman, 'Buddhist and Western Psychology: Some Commonalities and Differences', *Journal of Transpersonal Psychology* 13 (2) (1981): 125–36; Margaret Donaldson, *Human Minds An Exploration* (London: Penguin, 1992), 227; Greg Bograt, 'The Use of Meditation in Psychotherapy: A Review of the Literature', *American Journal of Psychotherapy* 45 (3) (July 1991): 383–412.

63 'Anicca', *Encyclopedia of Buddhism*, vol. 1 (Colombo: Government Publisher, 1984), 659.

64 Rahula, *What the Buddha Taught*, 59.

65 Ibid., 65.

66 'Anatta', *Encyclopedia of Buddhism*, 567.

67 'Anicca', *Encyclopedia of Buddhism*, 659.

68 D. J. Kalupahana and Koyu Tamura, 'Antarabhava', in *Encyclopedia of Buddhism*, vol. 1, ed. G. P. Malalasekera, 441.

69 K. N. Jayatilleke, *Survival and Karma in Buddhist Perspective* (Kandy: Buddhist Publication Society, 1980).

70 Peter Harvey, *Selfless Mind: Personality, Consciousness and Nirvana in Early Buddhism* (Richmond: Curzon Press, 1995), 76.

71 Ibid., 79.

72 John T. Blackburn, ed., *Ernst Mach: His Work, Life and Influence* (Berkeley: University of California Press, 1972).

73 Herbert V. Guenther, *Philosophy and Psychology in the Abidharma* (Berkeley: Shambhala, 1976), 24.

74 Ibid., 27.

75 Ibid., 3–5.

76 Ibid., 1.

77 Harvey, *Selfless Mind*, 80.

78 Guenther, *Abidharma*, 89.

79 Lan W. Mabbett, 'Nagarjuna and Deconstruction', *Philosophy East and West* 45 (April 1995): 203–25; David Loy, 'Indra's Postmodern Net', *Philosophy East and West* 43 (3) (July 1993): 481–510; Harold G. Coward, 'Speech Versus Writing in Derrida and Bhartrhari', *Philosophy East and West* Volume 41 (2) (April 1991): 141–62; Robert K. C. Forman, 'Paramartha and Modern Constructivists on Mysticism: Epistemological Monomorphism vs Duomorphism', *Philosophy East and West* 39 (4) (October 1989): 393–406.

80 Maurice Friedman, 'The Interhuman and What is Common to All: Martin Buber and Sociology', *Journal for the Theory of Social Behaviour* 29 (4) (1999): 403–17.

Part III

PHILOSOPHICAL ANTHROPOLOGY
AT WORK

Chapter 17

'ANTHROPOLOGY OF PHILOSOPHY' IN AFRICA: THE ETHNOGRAPHY OF CRITICAL DISCOURSE AND INTELLECTUAL PRACTICE

Kai Kresse

Introduction

An anthropological investigation into philosophy can provide us with insights and information about traditions of knowledge and intellectual practice elsewhere in the world, in social contexts very different from our own. The project needs to engage with – and first of all be able to identify – philosophy as part of social discourse, and as a social practice, within any given region. Here, I am carving out one particular approach about how this could work, in relation to the Swahili context and against the background of discussions in African philosophy. Philosophy, as socialized discourse and practice, overlaps with other (more established) areas of anthropological interest, like literature and religion. These overlaps, of genre and of discipline, can be investigated and made useful, as points of orientation. However, one difficulty of introducing the project of an 'anthropology of philosophy' to an interdisciplinary audience with widely disparate expertise and backgrounds, is dealing with all the subject-specific matters and questions in appropriate depth. Here, I am trying to find a balance, presenting several subdisciplinary 'turns' that lead to an anthropology of philosophy. Thus, the interdisciplinary overlaps provide entry points into the characterization of this project.

Towards an Anthropology of Philosophy

Within the last few decades, anthropology has developed various interdisciplinary subfields of research on ever more complex and subdifferentiated areas, thus creating a broader range of 'anthropologies of …' that are investigated in their own right. To push this research ahead, knowledge from other disciplines needs to be brought in, and has indeed become more crucial for anthropology than ever before (Moore 1999, 4). Now, philosophy is a specific field of human activity, an intellectual yet socially contextualized endeavour. As such, it deserves specific attention of anthropological enquiry, just like all the other fields of human activity and interest. For these purposes, the characterization of philosophy as 'the attempt of thoughtful (or intellectual) orientation within the sphere of the fundamentals of our thinking, knowing and doing' (Schnädelbach 1988, 215; my translation) has struck me as providing a particularly useful guideline. Philosophy can be seen as a human practice that responds to the need for intellectual orientation to be found in many different social and cultural terms and contexts. In the case I present here, texts and debates on the nature of philosophy, on African philosophy, and on the relation between philosophy and its cultural and social contexts are prepared to be used for anthropological research on Swahili philosophical discourse.[1]

If the social practice of philosophy falls within the interest of anthropology – in regard to the regionally particular cultural and social contexts of this practice, but also in general as an area of human experience and expression – this interest is, and should be, reciprocated by philosophy itself. In cultural philosophy, the need to base general statements on the available empirical data, and to constantly reassess new reflections against an empirical background, is obvious. This has been highlighted, for instance, by Ernst Cassirer. His *Philosophy of Symbolic Forms*, comprising extensive works on the nature of human knowledge and culture, is based on what he calls a principal double-aspectivity of the human sphere, and man as *animal symbolicum* (Cassirer [1944] 1992). Hereby, all human experience is shaped and determined through their projection of meaning onto the world, in relation (and partly in response) to concrete material forms. Cassirer's approach thus recognizes a combination of *intellectual activity* and *sensuous receptivity* at the core of the distinct human way of being in the world. Accordingly, human beings shape, or 'make', their worlds, through various alternative and coherent frameworks of meaning, the symbolic forms. Indeed, Nelson Goodman's similarly structured 'Ways of Worldmaking' (1978) is based on Cassirer, who himself used the phrase 'ways of understanding the world' (*Weisen des Weltverstehens*) to characterize the symbolic forms as channels for the constitution of human experience and knowledge (Cassirer [1923] 1994, introduction).

As Cassirer's approach sees an interplay of intellectual *and* sensuous capacity at the core of what makes us human, it also provides a framework that situates 'theory' (the intellectual production of focused and general accounts of whatever is reflected upon) in relation to an empirical context from the outset. From this perspective, philosophy itself is always seen as linked to and contextualized within human experience of the world, no matter how abstract its reflections can become. Cassirer's approach can also provide the basis for a nonhierarchical descriptive approach to the general study of cultures and cultural practices worldwide. It does not prioritize any one before the others *per se*.[2] His philosophy bases itself on a general philosophical anthropology, addressing the question 'what is the human being?', which itself is rooted in concrete and specific empirical information, like the ethnographic accounts of cultures and human interaction happening within them. Cassirer himself called for an 'anthropological philosophy' (Cassirer [1944] 1992, 42; 66ff.), while developing his philosophical statements in relation to the available empirical and historical information. He was an avid reader of the anthropological and ethnographic works of his time, and drew from them to illustrate and underpin his theoretical statements.

The need to root philosophy in experience, or at least to contextualize it, can also be applied to self-referential statements by philosophy on itself. As a discipline concerned with the formulation of social and cultural theory by reflection on empirical data collected during fieldwork, anthropology is able to assist philosophy in extending its awareness of its own character and status – particularly from intercultural perspectives, in regard to a variety of different cultural contexts. This implies, of course, that philosophy is not (and should not be) understood exclusively as a Eurocentric project of Greco-Judaic origin, but as a critical and fundamentally reflective practice that occurs worldwide, in many different forms. In this way, an anthropology of philosophy can assist philosophy to attain a wider and more inclusive self-understanding. This is appropriate, particularly at a time of rising awareness about globally operating power strategies and mutual interdependencies, and within suspicions that 'philosophy', as an icon of Western intellectual culture, may be used as a Eurocentric smokescreen for power interests, by way of excluding others. As has often been raised within the debate on African philosophy, to deny others the potential to philosophize is, to some extent, to deny them their humanity (Appiah 1992; Oruka [1972] 1997; cf. Taylor 1994). In a similar vein, in postcolonial African societies like Kenya, the label of 'philosophy' has been used to advertise and commend autocratic rule as a quasi-democratic national consensus of the people (cf. Moi 1986).

Through ethnography, anthropological research can provide concrete details, accounts and assessments of philosophical practice in various parts of the world, in addition to those that sociologies of philosophy – for instance, the illuminating and expansive intercultural study by Randall Collins (1998), itself partly inspired by and drawing from anthropological approaches – or histories of philosophy can offer. Fundamentally, philosophy always remains linked to knowledge, the quest for knowledge, the critique of knowledge, and to the various perspectives from which different forms of knowledge can be described and conceptualized. This is why an anthropology of philosophy has to be developed and to proceed in relation to an anthropology of knowledge. The latter is a general term for a diverse subfield of investigation in anthropology, and thus a concrete pathway of research has to be specified. Here, I follow a hermeneutically inspired approach, as described by Michael Lambek, where various locally relevant forms of knowledge are identified, observed, described and discussed, in relation to social practice (1993, 8–19). A similar approach is provided in Talal Asad's conception of an anthropology of Islam that focuses on Islam as a 'discursive tradition', and investigates the internal diversities of positions and arguments within the Muslim community (1986). As will be seen later in the ethnography, in the context of observing social practice with a focus on reflexive discourses of knowledge (those that we call 'philosophical') and the processes of their production and mediation, it is not always possible to differentiate very clearly between 'philosophy' and 'nonphilosophy', nor is such a rigid categorization the main intention of this study. In fact, perhaps some of the most interesting questions (in regard to the practice of philosophy) emerge from the blurry areas in between: when poetry shifts from didactic to critical language, when a political speech or a religious sermon is focused on reasoning out the basics of human existence. These are discursive instances that are philosophically laden.

On the whole, the notion of *discourse as verbal practice* is important, since philosophy, as critical reflection or the construction of an argument, is always mediated by language. As Asad has made clear, to work out the particular 'discursive tradition' of Islam in a region, the ways in which Islam has been negotiated, practised and justified within the dynamic and internally diverse social history of a Muslim community is of fundamental importance. Then it can be thematized, how, in a particular setting at the East African coast, 'local discourses of Islam' influence philosophical thought and discussion, and how Muslim thinkers and intellectuals are shaped and shape others 'through discourse' (cf. Lambek 1993; Bowen 1993). Recent studies of Islam in Africa have been able to illustrate, against common prejudice, the intellectual vibrancy of Islamic thought in Africa, within a network of long-standing historical connections to other parts of the Muslim world (cf. Reese 2004).

Turn One: From the African Philosophical Discussion to Anthropology

The debate about philosophy in Africa was sparked off by young academic African philosophers in the 1960s and 1970s, who launched critiques of the book 'Bantu Philosophy', written by the Belgian missionary Placide Tempels (1945). Since its inception, the debate led to the development of two antagonistic camps, which the Nigerian philosopher Peter Bodunrin called 'modernists' and 'traditionalists' (1985). He characterized as 'modernists' those who were mainly focusing on social and technological development that could integrate African societies into the 'modern' world. 'Traditionalists', in contrast, were characterized as those who sought moral orientation and guidance through a look at the past, documenting and describing values and traditions, with a sense that they may still be of use. Bodunrin wisely characterized the difference between the two camps rather as a matter of focus and emphasis, and not as a wholly antagonistic opposition for which there was no reconciliation. As this opposition dominated the field, those who wanted to contribute to research on African philosophy (rather than engage in an ideological stand-off) had to develop 'third ways' to overcome this deadlock and produce alternative approaches that combined a 'modernist' insistence on universal, comparative features of philosophy with a 'traditionalist' stance on the unique and specific particulars of African cultures and societies – in the ways that people think, argue and debate as much as their other aspects of acting in daily life.

For academic research on African philosophy today, the deadlock between 'traditionalists' and 'modernists' that dominated the 1970s and 1980s no longer constitutes such a fundamental obstacle. The heated ideological debate between defenders and critics of ethnophilosophy, the quasi-ethnographic project of presenting collective worldviews of ethnic groups as philosophies, has largely subsided and led to a wide variety of projects, among them the development of more complex research and discussions. It is now obvious that a diametrical opposition between the description of folk wisdom and culturally based worldviews, and the production of critical and scientifically orientated treatises on modernization, is misdirected. Approaches with the character of a 'third alternative' (Oruka 1991, 43) or 'third ways' (Oladipo 2002) between these two poles have been developed, promising fresh perspectives for research on the documentation and reconstruction of philosophical discourse in Africa. For instance, culturally specific conceptions of knowledge and belief, self and world, truth, beauty, and politics have been investigated, within explicit and often clearly defined methodological frameworks, such as analytical philosophy (Hallen 2000; Hallen and Sodipo 1997; Wiredu 1996) or hermeneutics (Okere 1983; Serequeberhan 1994; Janz 1996). Also, the reconstruction of culturally specific 'conceptual schemes' of African philosophical traditions has been initiated (Gyekye 1995), as well as the contextualized documentation of philosophical interviews with individual sages (Oruka 1991; cf. Graness and Kresse 1997).

Within African philosophy, pragmatic references to anthropology and ethnographic material have become more common since the 1990s (Masolo 1994; Wiredu 1996; Karp and Masolo 2000; Wiredu 2004). Though substantial interdisciplinary engagement is still rare, this is a significant step forward for a relationship in which anthropology was long dismissed with contempt, or at least regarded with suspicion, because of its historical links with the colonial system (cf. p'Bitek 1970; Asad 1973; Hountondji [1976] 1996, 2002).[3] It was inherently associated with the misconceived and prejudiced notion of an evolutionary, hierarchical order of human societies, from the 'primitive' to the 'modern' (cf. Kuper 1993). Of course this included an *a priori* assertion of the impossibility of culturally immanent traditions of 'real' philosophy in Africa, an assertion which was followed in anthropological writings on African 'thought systems' (Fortes and Dieterlen 1965). Hand in hand, these early ethnographies portrayed a somewhat paternalistic image, speaking 'for the native' from a higher position (Tempels 1959; but partly also Evans-Pritchard 1937; Douglas 1966), an attitude paradoxically taken up later by some African scholars themselves, mostly missionaries (e.g., Kagame [1976] 1985).

Understandably, then, many academic African philosophers have vehemently insisted that philosophy is a universal form of human knowledge and practice, claiming that common human principles underlie 'philosophy' just as much as any other social action anywhere – and, as already mentioned, that to deny philosophy to people from the outset means to deny them part of their humanity. This does not necessarily go well together with the current discourse of 'postmodernism', which, as Appiah has pointed out, sometimes is just a new version of the old paternalistic speaking 'for the others' already inherent in colonial discourse (Appiah 1992). On what grounds indeed should the claim of 'having philosophy' – which in European history has indicated pride in the complexity of one's culture and its advanced intellectual discourse – be denied to others? In Africa, as anywhere else, reason and tradition are not mutually exclusive. On the contrary, the locally competing traditions of reasoning in Africa, in their concrete shapes and forms, and against the background of the social histories, need to be analysed and evaluated. They present occurrences of what Hountondji has called an 'internal pluralism' in society (1983; [1976] 1996, 168), a pluralist framework of reasoned views and opinions that characterizes African societies as much as others. Beyond that, it presents an initial basis for the identification of philosophical discourse. This notion of 'internal pluralism' can be used as a valuable key term for philosophical fieldwork and the interpretation of local discourses and texts, whether written or spoken, whether published or not. Taken seriously, it can help to ascertain that the locally relevant social discourses are followed up, and it can help to remind us that we should seek to discern and understand the internal variety of opinions and positions within a social context, or even a community, that seek to convince others by means of a good argument. Rarely, if ever, will we encounter simple, collective and monolithic structures of belief in a society, in Africa or elsewhere. It is in this sense that Hountondji's expression 'internal pluralism' provides a useful guideline.

The growing openness and interest of African philosophers in anthropology and its ethnographic data seems linked to an internal differentiation, itself marking development in the field: the more specific and subdifferentiated the issues treated in African philosophy have become (in its subfields of aesthetics, morality, feminism, etc.), the more necessary – and thus acceptable – the inclusion of documents and ethnographic data that may provide the specific information for a philosophical interpretation. Interdisciplinary 'philosophical ethnography' was already called for long ago, by Wyatt MacGaffey, in a seminal interdisciplinary review of research on ideology and belief in Africa, in the disciplines of anthropology, religious studies, history, politics, theology and philosophy (1981; cf. 262ff.). There, he noted the emergence of promising works in this area, and increasing discussions among Africans on it. Now, as the previous concurrence between theology and philosophy that MacGaffey highlighted (257) has been reduced, the 'ethnographic shallowness' that he criticized in philosophical works may decrease. African philosophers now integrate ethnographic information – along with historical, political, etc. – into their studies more commonly (e.g., Wiredu 1996; Gyekye 1995, 1998). Overall, however, the lack of an accepted 'common framework' (MacGaffey 1981, 228) between the disciplines, which would be needed for such a project, is still observable today.

My aim here is to contribute to the construction of such a framework, and to move towards an interdisciplinary cooperation between philosophy and anthropology. In this, I feel supported by two newly edited classics of African philosophy: Barry Hallen has noted a 'general lack of technical philosophical content in anthropological literature' (in Hallen and Sodipo 1997, 134); and Paulin Hountondji has observed a 'change' within anthropology while acknowledging its potential contribution to this area ([1976] 1996, xix, viii). Both statements indicate the systematic interest and sceptical caution, which is necessary for a fertile interaction between the disciplines. To push this point further, in a recent collection of essays, Karp and Masolo, an American anthropologist and a Kenyan philosopher, make a forceful argument for closer interdisciplinary relations between anthropology and philosophy:

> Examining the relationships among discourse, knowledge, and everyday life is an inherently interdisciplinary endeavour, one that requires the skills and knowledge bases of both philosophers and anthropologists alike. This interdisciplinary mix

enables us to study what people know and how they express their knowledge as well
as how knowledge and saying are contested or become authoritative. (2000, 13)

This quote signals support for an envisaged anthropology of philosophy, and
it encapsulates some of the central tasks faced by it.

Turn Two: From Philosophy to Anthropology

From the perspective of philosophy as an academic discipline, approaching
African philosophical discourse should not *per se* pose a problem. If it is
reasonable to say that philosophy begins with wonder or puzzlement, as Plato
claimed, or if it is time put into thought, as Hegel said, we are bound to expect
philosophy in any kind of society. These classic definitions are loose and
flexible while still emphasizing a particular characteristic trait of philosophy
taken to be crucial – awareness of the fundamental uncertainties of life in the
case of Plato, and explicit historical consciousness, in the case of Hegel[4] – and
have often been interpreted and put into various contexts of reflection upon
society. As philosophy is defined formally here, these definitions present no
problem when applied to other cultures – where forms of puzzlement appear
as well as categories of time and thought – and thus both definitions could be
used to describe schools of thought and traditions of reasoning.

It can also be said that the idea of an anthropological investigation into
the forms and positions of philosophical discourse outside of the Western
paradigm does not go against the grain of major schools of thought within the
history of Western philosophy – even though these did have a Eurocentric and
sometimes even racist bias. Thus a systematic anthropological inquiry into
philosophical discourse and practice around the world could be supported,
or at least argued for, even from within mainstream philosophy itself. An
example is one of the central pillars of 'Western' academic philosophy: the
German philosopher Immanuel Kant, who is popularly often taken as an
epitome of German Enlightenment or European rationalism. He developed
a conception of philosophy which can be helpful for our purposes here,
differentiating between two conceptions of philosophy: a 'worldly' and a
'scholarly' one (*Philosophie im Weltbegriff* and *Philosophie im Schulbegriff*), which in
their interrelation form the whole of philosophy. Thus, he distinguished two
axes that constitute philosophy on the one hand as a creative and innovative
intellectual activity, and an institutionalized conservative one on the other,
i.e., an originally reflexive and a doctrinal aspect (1930, 753–5, KrV B866–8;
also 1974, 25–30). The doctrinal *Schulbegriff* marks philosophy as a 'system of
knowledge' of scientific character, aimed at the systematic unity of knowledge
in an established tradition; here, the teachings and rules of a school of thought

are more and more finely interpreted, and thinkers are trained ('learning' the rules). Kant characterizes this aspect of philosophical knowledge as 'historical', which for him marks the systematization and standardization of a certain genuine approach: a philosophical school is formed by students acquiring this knowledge, this 'doctrine of skill' (1974, 28), second hand.

On the other hand, the reflexive *Weltbegriff*, the original 'basis' of the meaning of the term, refers to those fundamental areas of knowledge which are of 'necessary interest to everyone'. It is here that genuinely creative philosophical work takes place, namely 'philosophizing', where a 'doctrine of wisdom' is formulated by the thinking individual. It is specifically *worldly* in that, here, the specialist is not privileged over the common man: philosophical questions are principally of equal concern to all of us, and crucial innovative ideas are not necessarily initiated from within the scholarly realm. It is also *worldly* in a 'cosmopolitan' sense, in that general questions concerning all human beings are treated from a perspective that looks beyond the realm of cultural and social boundaries, seeing all humans commonly as 'citizens of the world' (*Weltbürger*), i.e., cosmopolitans. Unlike the historical *scholarly* knowledge, philosophizing in this sense cannot really be taught since it 'can be learned only through practice and the use of one's own reason'. This is why Kant concludes that philosophy, in the 'true sense', is never a given but always a task (*aufgegeben*). For someone following this task, the available historical doctrines within the *Schulbegriff* can be helpful as thought material and points of orientation: 'Every philosophical thinker builds his work, so to speak, on the ruins of another' (1974, 28). Certainly, the availability of others' attempts to create a philosophy, and thus the possibility of referring to them, helps in the construction of one's own. The existence of scholarly traditions makes it easier for the philosophizing individual to specify and clarify a point. But such traditions are not a necessary precondition for the initial development of truly philosophical thought in the *Weltbegriff*. Rather, the latter is initiated by following up fundamental questions on the nature of human existence – i.e., in a philosophical sense, anthropological questions – that every human being is confronted with, in regard to their own perspective on life: 'what can I know?', 'what ought I to do?', 'what may I hope for?' and 'what is man?' According to this passage by Kant, these questions, while signifying the various realms of the philosophical subdisciplines of metaphysics (epistemology), morality, religion and anthropology, together cover the whole field of philosophy. This, in its full scope, is based on and always leads back to (philosophical) anthropology because 'the first three questions are related to the last' (29), in that they contribute to an overall insight on the nature of human beings.

So in two respects Kant's characterizations of philosophy help provide an orientation for an anthropology of philosophy: first, socially and historically situated (and institutionalized) schools of thought, that can be identified and studied in a diverse range of societies around the world, can be linked to Kant's *Schulbegriff* as one significant aspect of philosophy. This, however, is linked to a second, the generation of critical and innovative ideas for orientation in life, *Philosophie im Weltbegriff*, which is expressed by individual thinkers in relation to the former. (This process can be documented and discussed, very much at the core of an anthropology of philosophy.) The heart of philosophical activity, for Kant, lies in the potential of individuals as self-reliant, critical thinkers to deal creatively with fundamental questions of orientation, and to express and communicate their thoughts to others. As such, philosophy is potentially open and meaningful to all human beings; as pointed out above, it addresses questions which are 'of necessary interest to everyone'. Having read these passages by Kant for our current purposes, we could now use and apply them for our project, as both a rationale and a method for an anthropology of philosophy could be gained from here. If philosophy is a distinctly human activity of intellectual self-orientation, then it is likely to occur in all (or many) different cultures and societies. This insight can be employed for two central tasks of anthropological research on philosophical practice: the ethnographic aspect (i.e., the empirical observation of philosophy as a fundamentally reflexive and critical discursive practice in social life) and the theoretical evaluation of the observed socially and culturally specific forms of this practice in relation to a wider and potentially general understanding of philosophy.

The formal distinction that Kant has pointed at is, in principle, applicable to any social context that human beings live in, in any part of the world. In Africa, too, we should be able to identify various institutionalized traditions of knowledge, schools of thought that teach 'doctrines of skill' (the *Schulbegriff* of philosophy), and individual thinkers who develop their own 'doctrines of wisdom' in regard to basic questions of human existence (the *Weltbegriff*). Approaching African philosophical discourse in this way, the ambivalent Kantian distinction between internal worldly and scholarly aspects can help as a guideline in looking for and identifying philosophical practice. Being formal, it can do this without predetermining any concrete form or shape that philosophical thought should take, for it does not prescribe any content for a culturally specific practice of philosophizing, nor does it determine the concrete forms in which culturally specific philosophical thought can develop. It provides formal criteria with which to identify, contextualize and understand philosophical discourse. Such a descriptive and value-free conception of philosophy enables us to approach existing institutionalized traditions ('systems') of knowledge in Africa, and since the historical knowledge of this realm can be taught and learned, it might also be publicly accessible or otherwise recordable by the philosophical fieldworker or the philosophically minded anthropologist. Furthermore, individual intellectuals can be approached and their practice of theory can be evaluated against its context: is it historically given knowledge or genuinely innovative? Is it critical or purely doctrinal? It is in the observation of the interaction between the two aspects of scholarly and worldly conception of philosophy that we can identify a specific tradition of knowledge, and that we appreciate further attempts by individual thinkers, to increase and improve knowledge and theory within that tradition. From a thorough description of the interaction between these two levels, then, we can work out an appropriate understanding of what one may call 'philosophical discourses' in societies, in Africa and elsewhere.

The intercultural project: Recognition of philosophical traditions

A seminal evaluation of the impact of African studies on philosophy came to the conclusion that the interdisciplinary study of philosophical topics in the African context 'provides a model for interdisciplinary analysis in philosophical work' on the whole (Mudimbe and Appiah 1993, 133). Although a systematic model does not yet exist, a multidisciplinary approach is becoming increasingly indispensable to the description and analysis of specific philosophical traditions of Africa. The postcolonial African 'search for identity' within philosophical discourse involves not only reflection upon the interrelationship of the various disciplines that philosophy has historically followed, in terms of institutional processes of self-cleansing and revaluation of what it means to be 'African' (Masolo 1994, 44ff.). It also requires reflexive contributions from other disciplines in order to make the contours and characteristics of Africa's various philosophical traditions fully visible. This is true particularly for anthropology, which aims to illuminate the internal dynamics of the constitution of meaning and the processes of human interaction in other cultures. The search for philosophical identity in Africa has to be informed by that observation and social contextualization of cultural practices, which is the particular task of anthropology. For the reconstruction of the histories of the various (especially the oral) traditions of philosophical thought in Africa, philosophy, anthropology, literature and history need to cooperate (cf. Wiredu 2004).

The relation between philosophy and the multiplicity of cultures, as referred to above, has become an issue of continually growing importance for philosophy itself, particularly in regard to its history of Eurocentrism. In philosophy as well as in other disciplines, 'the empire writes back' (to use a popular phrase), questioning and contesting the imposed evolutionary frameworks in which 'other cultures' have been likened to 'previous stages' of Western culture. Within Western mainstream philosophy, a process of critical rethinking has been set in motion. Charles Taylor, for instance, when addressing the North American curriculum debate vis-à-vis the increasing phenomenon of 'multiculturalism' in Western societies, cautioned that we need to become aware that, as a fair starting point for intercultural discussion or debate, 'we owe equal respect to all cultures' (1994, 66). This claim, however, is merely a preliminary working assumption to which, being largely ignorant about the histories of other cultures and societies, we are morally obliged to start off with. It provides a fair starting point for the empirical inquiries that need to follow. Thus, overall, the 'politics of recognition' that Taylor advocates are based on the initial acknowledgement of *every* culture's potential to contribute to (and enrich) human civilization. As a second step, he demands that we follow up on and find out about the particular circumstances under discussion.

By means of analogy, Taylor's point can be expanded, applied to the field of intercultural philosophy and used for the project of an anthropology of philosophy. What is called for, on a theoretical level, is thinking the relations between philosophy and culture as inherently pluralistic, without giving up the terminological coherence of the concepts 'philosophy' and 'culture' *per se*. Human beings in comparable, but distinct and unique, cultures produce distinct and unique traditions of reflective practices through which self-assertion and conceptual orientation take place. In this way, various culture-correlating philosophical traditions and philosophies come into being. But so far, mutual *recognition* of different philosophical traditions has not been established. It has to be worked out and argued for. From research in African philosophy, contributions to such cross-cultural philosophical interaction on equal terms can be expected (cf. Mudimbe and Appiah 1993, 133ff.; Moore 1996, 3). While engaged in the establishment of such a practice, philosophers who are working comparatively, and 'able to use other languages in philosophical thought, in particular, languages which are very different from their own' are seen as relevant facilitators (Wiredu and Kresse 1997, 42). An emphasis on the use of local languages as the principal medium for philosophical fieldwork, and the use of methods of anthropological enquiry, can assist in approaching and achieving this intercultural goal for philosophy. In the field of African philosophy, a few studies making use of such fieldwork have contributed significantly to the overall debate while dealing with specific regional discourses and their subthemes: for example, on ordinary language usage concerning 'knowledge' and 'belief' in the Yoruba context (Hallen and Sodipo 1997), on Yoruba moral and aesthetic discourses (Hallen 2000), and on Kenyan 'indigenous thinkers', socially acknowledged sages with philosophical qualities (Oruka 1991). During my own fieldwork, I used Swahili as the language of documentation, interviewing and discussion. However, the use of the local language is merely one – if perhaps the most important – aspect of an endeavour to document and discuss philosophical discourse with the fullest possible social contextualization.

Turn Three: From Anthropology of Knowledge to Anthropology of Philosophy

Recent reflections upon anthropological knowledge and theory have expressed a renewed interest in intellectual and philosophical traditions of other cultures. Henrietta Moore, for instance, sees it as a serious shortcoming of anthropology that, even when occupying itself productively with non-European 'modes of thought' (e.g., Forde 1954; Horton and Finnegan 1973) or local theories, it worked under the assumption 'that the theories of non-western peoples have no scope outside their context' (Moore 1996, 2); they were not taken into account, for cross-cultural evaluation and the furtherance of theory on the whole, as contributions to a global project of understanding 'knowledge'. But if anthropology does not want, ultimately, to remain entangled in a Eurocentric stance, it must begin to treat the members of other cultures also 'as producers of social science theory' and not only, and *per definitionem*, as 'producers of local knowledge' (3). In other words, in dealing with a variety of regional traditions of knowledge, anthropology should always include a comparative dimension that looks at their specific contributions to an overall theory of human knowledge. Integrating these perspectives into the globally oriented social sciences is a task for anthropology. In the long run, it also means to initiate a self-critical attitude within such scientific enquiry on a global level, bringing in the theoretical and reflexive dimensions of all regional traditions of knowledge. In any culture 'an ongoing auto-critique of concepts, notions and forms of argument' (6) might be found; at least this cannot be ruled out from the beginning. Such reflexive discourse is often taken as a constitutive trait of philosophy, and so anthropology has to consciously reckon with, and try to integrate into its own apparatus, the existence of philosophical traditions in other sociocultural contexts. Broadening the outlook of social science in this way, while at the same time learning how to identify and understand these intellectual traditions on an empirical level, would be the aim for an anthropology of philosophy.

The call to such an agenda seems long overdue. It is supported by Ortner's overview of anthropological theory, which observed that until the 1980s, 'little effort has been put toward understanding how society and culture themselves are produced and reproduced through human intention and interaction' (1994, 402). Such neglect to focus on the conscious shaping of culture and society by specific individuals was particularly detrimental to the portrayal of African intellectual culture and history. Though much more effort has been put into this since, earlier European prejudice about the supposed intellectual deficiencies of Africans had long-lasting ill effects. Also, the anthropological study of African societies under the paradigm of structural functionalism, due to its focus on collective functional dynamics, had little to say on individual figures (cf. Falk-Moore 1993), thus indirectly reinforcing the cliché of the African as a passive constituent of a collective social entity. Anthropology in Africa, though producing much acute analysis of social structures and processes, was partly guilty of simplifying societies, when 'levelling' African societies by leaving aside their discursive 'internal dynamics' in terms of possible pluralisms to be investigated (Hountondji 1983, 137). Applying the label 'traditional' to Africa in a generalizing fashion (as opposed to 'modern' and 'the West') is directly linked to this issue: it denies even the possibility of theoretical pluralism. As 'closed' systems, without developed awareness of potential theoretical alternatives, and opposed to the 'open' character of scientifically orientated societies based on rational debate (Horton 1970, 153ff.), the kind of theory that African societies were supposed to be able to offer was visualized as fundamentally inferior to a Western conception of science from the outset. Subsequently, the unequal basis for such intercultural comparison was criticized from within African philosophy (Wiredu 1980). Insisting on the inadmissibility of (culturally specific) double standards in philosophy while highlighting the cultural specifics of local intellectual practice has been a key feature of African philosophers like Wiredu, Hountondji and Oruka.

More than half a century ago, Paul Radin used a different approach for his anthropological investigation into philosophy in oral societies among native North Americans. He basically agreed with the positive methodological rule of acknowledging the possibility of philosophical discourse in any society, as I have sketched out above. He stated very clearly that 'there is nothing […] that prevents philosophical formulations from being attempted. Individuals with a philosophical temperament are present, the languages are adequate, the structure of their societies places no obstacle in the way' (Radin 1957, xxviii). Altogether, his work is mainly an extensive collection of insights into life, as expressed in poems, songs, myths and legends, which he then comments upon. However, Radin takes care to emphasize that individual thinkers, composers and commentators, who are not simply representatives of the common world view of their social group, were the creators of these texts. But we gain little insight into the culturally specific ways of composing or performing such literature, nor into ways of how critical reflection, discourse and debate in society was furthered by these texts or their composers. Nevertheless, this study is probably the earliest anthropological attempt to approach philosophical discourse explicitly as a field of investigation in its own right. As such it was emphatically approved by the famous pragmatist philosopher John Dewey, who wrote the foreword (xvii–xx).

Although up to now few anthropological studies have explicitly investigated philosophical discourse, the last few decades have nevertheless borne evidence of much research that focuses on fundamentally related topics and fields, especially in regard to cross-cultural theories of knowledge, emotions, the self and morality. Yet they have rarely focused on the individual thinkers in society, and have rather emphasized more the 'underlying' or unifying structures of social knowledge and discourse. Some dense and cautiously written ethnographies which use local terminology and systematic explanation of fundamental understandings of society as central guidelines have been produced, and for these reasons they are of crucial interest to an anthropology of philosophy. We also come across examples where anthropologists, even if only in passing, note distinctly philosophical activity in the cultures they study. For instance, Clifford Geertz vividly described the widespread 'intellectual activity' and 'philosophical obsession' of Javanese people ([1983] 1993, 60), while on the other hand noted the limited extent of 'philosophical sophistication' in Balinese religion ([1973] 1993, 175). How far these statements are ethnographically adequate can of course not be judged from here, but they do display a rare explicit sensitivity of an anthropologist for philosophical reflection as human activity in potentially any culture. In both cases 'philosophical' refers to a locally embedded reflection of local knowledge, a local reflective discourse on forms of local knowledge.

Shifting the anthropological focus: From 'religion' to 'philosophy'

Like philosophy, religion is concerned with matters of fundamental orientation in the world, and the two spheres are in part overlapping. Although religious practices and beliefs in various cultures differ, they are still open to a common theoretical framework which can supply a comparative basis for a philosophical quest. An explicit, critical questioning of the bases of practices by the way of conceptual reasoning always constitutes a philosophical practice. Ethnographic work, when engaging in explicit discussion with knowledgeable members of society in order to elucidate the frameworks of meaning for religious practice, already displays a general interest in philosophical discourse. The reflective mechanisms of (a certain aspect of) social life are being examined. In attempting to understand the basis of specific forms of ritual, ethnographers have to discuss with individual specialists the theory of religious practice in the culture concerned. Here, the process of producing a reasonable explanation constitutes a philosophical discourse which illuminates religious practice. Now, although this already points to the philosophical potential of local religious experts, the foremost concern of an anthropology of philosophy does not lie in responses to the questions of the investigator (e.g., as visible in Oruka's sage philosophy project), but in the observation and documentation of practices of philosophical discourse among members of the community itself.

Here, the anthropology of religion has always had a philosophical tinge insofar as it claimed to elucidate the basic concepts structuring social life and ritual practice. In this sense, one might speak of a 'hidden tradition' of an anthropology of philosophy in anthropology itself. For instance, Lévi-Strauss's characterization of Boas's Quesalid, the Kwakiutl healer, as *not* a healer but a 'free thinker' (1993, 178) can be understood in this vein: Lévi-Strauss described him as sceptical of the healing practices that he himself performed and his clients believed in, and somewhat outside of the 'social consensus' (180) on the healing procedures of his society. And although Lévi-Strauss himself engages in a socio-psychological reflection on the constitution of Quesalid's status as an accepted healer, this can also be read as a hint at the neglected category of individual free thinkers in anthropological research – and free thinking has been taken as a characteristic criterion of philosophical enquiry, from Kant to Odera Oruka.

More explicitly, Victor Turner's article 'Muchona the Hornet, Interpreter of Religion' provides us with a personal portrait of a 'true philosopher' (1967, 132), who was an expert on various systems of knowledge in his own society (while socially remaining something of an outsider) and at the same time a major source for Turner's articulation of a theory of Ndembu ritual. In this text Turner conveys a vivid impression of the social status of a local intellectual, a veritable 'philosophy don' who seems destined to be permanently misconceived as a 'witchdoctor' within his own society (150). Furthermore, Turner provides a revealing account of the process of intensive discussion between specialist interpreter and anthropologist, a process which finally led to Turner's classic interpretations of Ndembu ritual, which he presented in other texts in a more theoretical, generalising and objectifying manner.

In this respect, Wyatt MacGaffey's ethnography in *Religion and Society in Central Africa* is stimulating in the way that it relates religion to Bakongo society. Its three constitutive parts are a description of social structure and its fundamentals in cosmology, the 'conscious elaboration' that no society can do without (1986, 3), a description of the religious practices evolved in this context and finally constituting 'religion as a political system' (169ff.), and an account on the historical continuities and changes of religious movements in Bakongo society, which pays explicit, systematic tribute to the recognition of the historically grown categories of religious sages and their communal functions in modern conditions (189ff.). The internal dualism of Bakongo cosmology is carefully depicted. MacGaffey quotes individual Bakongo extensively to establish his points from within the social perspective he observes, and overall his way of relating fundamental structures of religious knowledge and practice to social life provides important guidance for philosophically interested research. The same can be said of Lambek's ethnography of knowledge and healing practices on Mayotte. His study exemplifies how practices of spirit possession do not only *not* oppose rational enquiry, but might sometimes even enhance it, as when the healer consults a spirit for further information about adequate treatment, or when a serious discussion takes place between spirit and spouse of the possessed (1993, part IV).

Finally Feiermann, focusing on the intellectual discourse among Tanzanian peasants, and following Gramsci's definition of intellectual activity, supports the point that potentially 'all people are intellectuals', but only some people have a leading, organizational function as intellectuals (1990, 18). This, while applicable to almost any society including the Swahili urban communities, can also be related back to Kant's conception of philosophy in a worldly sense (*Weltbegriff*). Everyone is regarded a potential philosopher, a producer of original ideas, but in a fully socially accepted sense only those who follow a locally institutionalized (i.e., scholarly) tradition of knowledge (*Schulbegriff*) in society are actually considered philosophers. Individual intellectual ability and participation in a publicly instituted school of knowledge, then, are two common aspects to look out for, for an investigation into the practice of philosophy.

As I have tried to show, all of the studies above are open to readings with a particular interest in philosophical discourse. As such, they can contribute to situating and contextualizing the study of African philosophical discourse in culturally specific African intellectual and religious discourses that have already been portrayed in depth. Similarly, the presentation of my own ethnographic research on Swahili philosophical discourse draws from the multitude of available studies and publications on Swahili language, literature, history, culture and society, as well as my own ethnography.

Notes

1 Indeed, this text is an amended version of the introductory chapter to the resultant monograph, an ethnography of philosophical thinkers and debate in the Old Town of Mombasa, following the approach outlined here (Kresse 2007).
2 This cannot be followed up further here; I have investigated this elsewhere (Kresse 1996).

3 The Ugandan poet Okot p'Bitek nevertheless studied social anthropology in Oxford and produced at least one ethnographic monograph (p'Bitek 1971).
4 Which he, as is widely known, claimed Africans did not have (cf. Hegel 1928, 135–45).

References

Appiah, Kwame A. 1992. 'The Postcolonial and the Postmodern'. In *In My Father's House: Africa in the Philosophy of Culture*, 137–57. Oxford: Oxford University Press.

Asad, Talal, ed. 1973. *Anthropology and the Colonial Encounter*. London: Ithaca Press.

_____. 1986. *The Idea of an Anthropology of Islam*. Occasional paper series, Center for Contemporary Arab Studies. Washington, DC: Georgetown University.

Bodunrin, P. O. 1985. Introduction to *Philosophy in Africa: Trends and Perspectives*. Ile-Ife, Nigeria: University of Ife Press.

Bowen, John R. 1993. *Muslims Through Discourse: Religion and Ritual in Gayo Society*. Princeton: Princeton University Press.

Cassirer, Ernst. (1923) 1994. *Philosophie der symbolischen Formen. Erster Teil: Die Sprache*. Darmstadt: Wissenschaftliche Buchgesllschaft.

_____. (1944) 1992. *An Essay on Man*. New Haven: Yale University Press.

Collins, Randall. 1998. *The Sociology of Philosophies: A global Theory of Intellectual Change*. Cambridge, MA: Harvard University Press.

Douglas, Mary. 1966. *Purity and Danger*. London: Tavistock.

Evans-Pritchard, E. E. 1937. *Witchcraft, Oracles and Magic Among the Azande*. Oxford: Oxford University Press.

Falk-Moore, Sally. 1993. 'Changing Perspectives on a Changing Africa: The Work of Anthropology'. In *Africa and the Disciplines*, edited by R. H. Bates, V. Y. Mudimbe and J. O'Barr, 3–57. Chicago: Chicago University Press.

Feiermann, S. 1990. *Peasant Intellectuals: Anthropology and History in Tanzania*. Madison: University of Wisconsin Press.

Forde, Daryll, ed. 1954. *African Worlds: Studies in the Cosmological Ideas and Social Values of African Peoples*. London: Tavistock.

Fortes, M. and G. Dieterlen, eds. 1965. *African Systems of Thought*. Oxford: Oxford University Press.

Geertz, Clifford. (1973) 1993. '"Internal Conversion" in Contemporary Bali'. In *The Interpretation of Cultures*, 170–89. London: Fontana Press.

_____. (1983) 1993. '"From the Native's Point of View": On the Nature of Anthropological Understanding'. In *Local Knowledge*, 55–70. London: Fontana Press.

Goodman, Nelson. 1978. *Ways of Worldmaking*. Indianapolis: Hackett.

Graness, Anke and K. Kresse, eds. 1997. *Sagacious Reasoning: H. Odera Oruka in Memoriam*. Frankfurt: Peter Lang.

Gyekye, Kwame. 1995. *African Philosophical Thought: The Akan Philosophical Scheme*, revised edition. Philadelphia: Temple University Press.

_____. 1998. *Tradition and Modernity*. Oxford: Oxford University Press.

Hallen, Barry. 2000. *The Good, the Bad, and the Beautiful: Discourse About Values in Yoruba Culture*. Bloomington: Indiana University Press.

Hallen, B. and J. O. Sodipo. 1997 (1986). *Knowledge, Belief, and Witchcraft: Analytic Experiments in African Philosophy*. Palo Alto: Stanford University Press.

Hegel, G. F. W. 1928. *Vorlesungen über die Philosophie der Geschichte. Sämtliche Werke*, vol. 11, edited by H. Glöckner. Stuttgart: Fromann.

Horton, Robin. 1970. 'African Traditional Thought and Western Science'. In *Rationality*, edited by B. R. Wilson, 131–71. Oxford: Blackwell.

Horton, R. and R. Finnegan, eds. 1973. *Modes of Thought: Essays on Thinking in Western and Non-Western Societies*. London: Routledge.

Hountondji, Paulin J. 1983. 'Reason and Tradition'. In *Philosophy and Cultures*, edited by H. O. Oruka and D. A. Masolo, 132–9. Nairobi: Bookwise.

———. (1976) 1996. *African Philosophy: Myth and Reality*. Bloomington: Indiana University Press.

———. 2002. *The Struggle for Meaning: Reflections on Philosophy, Culture, and Democracy in Africa*. Athens: Ohio University Press.

Janz, Bruce. 1996. 'Alterity, Dialogue, and African Philosophy'. In *Postcolonial African Philosophy*, edited by E. Eze, 221–38. Oxford: Blackwell.

Kagame, Alexis. (1976) 1985. *Sprache und Sein: die Ontologie der Bantu Zentralafrikas*. Heidelberg and Brazzaville: Kivouvou-Editions Bantoues.

Kant, Immanuel. 1930. *Kritik der reinen Vernunft*, edited by R. Schmidt. Hamburg: Felix Meiner Verlag.

———. 1974. *Logic*, translated by R. S. Hartman and W. Schwarz. New York: Dover Publications.

Karp, Ivan and D. A. Masolo, eds. 2000. *African Philosophy as Cultural Inquiry*. Bloomington: Indiana University Press.

Kresse, Kai. 2007. *Philosophising in Mombasa: Knowledge, Islam And Intellectual Practice on the Swahili Coast*. Edinburgh: Edinburgh University Press.

Kuper, Adam. 1993. *The Invention of Primitive Society*. London: Routledge.

Lambek, Michael. 1993. *Knowledge and Practice in Mayotte*. Toronto: Toronto University Press.

Lévi-Strauss, Claude. 1993. 'The Sorcerer and His Magic'. In *Structural Anthropology*, vol. 1, 167–85. London: Penguin.

MacGaffey, Wyatt. 1981. 'African Ideology and Belief: A Survey'. In *African Studies Review* 24 (2/3): 227–74.

———. 1986. *Religion and Society in Central Africa*. Chicago: Chicago University Press.

Masolo, D. A. 1994. *African Philosophy in Search of Identity*. Bloomington: Indiana University Press.

Moi, Daniel a. T. 1986. *Kenyan African Nationalism: Nyayo Philosophy and Principles*. Nairobi: MacMillan.

Moore, Henrietta L. 1996. 'The Changing Nature of Anthropological Knowledge'. In *The Future of Anthropological Knowledge*, edited by H. L. Moore, 1–16. London: Routledge.

———. 1999. 'Anthropological Theory at the Turn of the Century'. In *Anthropological Theory Today*, edited by H. L. Moore, 1–23. Cambridge: Polity Press.

Mudimbe, V. Y. and K. A. Appiah. 1993. 'The Impact on African Studies on Philosophy'. In *Africa and the Disciplines*, edited by Bates, Mudimbe and O'Barr. Chicago: Chicago University Press.

Okere, Theophilus. 1983. *African Philosophy: A Historico-Hermeneutical Investigation of the Conditions of its Possibility*. Lanham: University Press of America.

Oladipo, Olisegun. 2002. Introduction to *Issues in African Philosophy: Essays in Honour of Kwasi Wiredu*, edited by O. Oladipo. Ibadan: Hope Publishers.

Ortner, Sherry. 1994 (1984). 'Theory in Anthropology Since the Sixties'. In *Culture, Power, History*, edited by Dirks, Eley and Ortner. Princeton: Princeton University Press. Originally published in *Journal of Comparative Society and History* 26 (2): 126–47.

Oruka, H. Odera. (1972) 1997. 'Mythologies as African Philosophy'. In *Sagacious Reasoning: H. Odera Oruka in memoriam*, edited by Graness and Kresse, 23–34. Frankfurt: Peter Lang.
_____, ed. 1991. *Sage Philosophy: Indigenous Thinkers and Modern Debate on African Philosophy*. Nairobi: ACTS Press.
p'Bitek, Okot. 1970. *African Religion in Western Scholarship*. Nairobi: Kenya Literature Bureau.
_____. 1971. *Religion of the Central Luo*. Nairobi: Kenya Literature Bureau.
Reese, Scott. 2004. 'Introduction: Islam in Africa – Challenging the Perceived Wisdom'. In *The Transmission of Learning in Islamic Africa*, edited by S. Reese, 1–14. Leiden: Brill.
Schnädelbach, Herbert. 1988. 'Philosophie als Wissenschaft und als Aufklärung'. In *Philosophie und Wissenschaft*, edited by W. Oelmueller, 206–220. Munich: Shoeningh.
Serequeberhan, Tsenay. 1994. *The Hermeneutics of African Philosophy: Horizon and Discourse*. New York: Routledge.
Taylor, Charles. 1994. 'The Politics of Recognition'. In *Multiculturalism and the Politics of Recognition*, edited by A. Gutman. Princeton: Princeton University Press.
Turner, Victor. 1967. 'Muchona the Hornet, Interpreter of Religion'. In *The Forest of Symbols*, 131–50. London: Cornell University Press.
Wiredu, K. 1980. 'How Not to Compare African and Western Thought'. In *Philosophy and an African Culture*. Cambridge: Cambridge University Press. Originally published in Richard A. Wright, ed. *African Philosophy: An Introduction*. Lanham: University Press of America, 149–62.
_____. 1996. *Cultural Universals and Particulars*. Bloomington: Indiana University Press.
_____. 2004. 'Introduction: African Philosophy in Our Time'. In *A Reader in African Philosophy*, 1–25. Oxford: Blackwell.
Wiredu, K. and K. Kresse. 1997. '"Still in the Making": An Interview with Kwasi Wiredu'. *Issues in Contemporary Culture and Aesthetics* 6. Reprinted as 'Language Matters!' *Polylog: Forum for Intercultural Philosophy* 1 (2) (2000). Online: http://them.polylog.org/2/dwk-en. htm (accessed 25 May 2013).

Chapter 18

ALBINOS DO NOT DIE: BELIEF, PHILOSOPHY AND ANTHROPOLOGY

João de Pina-Cabral

In Mozambique one is often told things about albinos that can hardly be interpreted at face value.[1] These are not, properly speaking, fictionalized narratives of a connected series of events, but rather they are evidence of propositional attitudes pertaining to refer to statements of fact, that is, they are 'beliefs'. Although they are not told to you as 'lies', the fact is that the people who narrate them are often uncertain as to whether they are true. Upon hearing them, I was immediately challenged by the following question: if these beliefs do not meet up with the test of disbelief, what then is the significance of both conveying and holding them?

For a long time the concept of 'belief' and its relation to that of 'knowledge' has been a source of theoretical concern for anthropologists (see Needham 1972). Malcolm Ruel has argued convincingly that the Christian heritage hidden in our anthropological toolkit has made us susceptible to a number of 'shadow fallacies' concerning belief, of which he identifies four: 1) the notion that belief is a central part of all religions; 2) the notion that a person's beliefs form the ground of his or her behaviour; 3) the notion that belief is essentially a psychological condition; and, finally, 4) that 'the determination of belief is more important than the determination of the status of what it is that is the object of the belief' ([1982] 2002, 111–12).

More recent attempts to differentiate between 'to believe in' and 'to believe that' do go a long way in helping us examine this problem (see Pouillon 1982; Talal Asad 2001). To my mind, however, this polarity is insufficient to clarify what is at stake. As a matter of fact, all intellectualist approaches to the concept of belief (see Robbins 2007) are bound to hide how it is deeply intermeshed with the central tenets of our modernist anthropological heritage, which overstressed both continuity *and* schism. To my mind, Donald Davidson's theory of *radical interpretation* (1984, 2001) provides us with a novel way of looking at the role of 'belief'. In ethnographic accounts, thus overstepping many of the scepticist doubts that have haunted anthropological theory over the past decades. In this chapter, I focus in particular on the problem of the *retention of belief*: that is, the way in which all beliefs are dependent on other beliefs that constitute an environment surrounding them.

My example is belief concerning albinos, an interstitial condition within the great 'black/white' ethnic divide so pervasive in colonial and postcolonial Africa. The tone of disgust that often accompanies reports on albinos is characteristic both of colonial racialism and of pervading Bantu attitudes.[2] This symmetry in response (and the disturbing similarity to 'whites') must not go unnoticed in the light of Michael Tausig's well-known analysis of the search for 'white Indians' by American explorers and anthropologists in the Panama region in the 1920s (1993, 274n2).

Albinos Don't Die

In 2001, towards the end of a long car trip in southern Mozambique, we passed by yet another albino on the side of the road. I commented that there seemed to be a lot of albinos around, having previously become aware that this was a favoured topic of conversation. My Mozambican companions readily confirmed that, in Mozambique, there are more albinos than in other African countries. This seems to be a generalized (though necessarily ungrounded) belief. The conversation proceeded naturally. I was told that it is generally believed that albinos do not die: they merely vanish. I asked my companions whether they had ever gone to an albino's funeral; they responded that, as a matter of fact, they had not.

Much like me, the people that were telling me this seemed to be fascinated with it without caring too much as to whether they believed it to be true. So I asked whether they did. The answer was negative but ambivalent, in the sense that they did not want to deny it either. I asked whether albinos were reborn later or whether they were supposed to go to another level. I was trying out, to see if I could fit this tale with other types of patterns with which I was familiar from other sociocultural regions. But both questions were negatively answered.

Already on a more jocular tone, and because they knew of my interest in the matter of cannibalism, they told me that, when there were food shortages during the socialist period, a rumour (*boato*) suddenly went around that 'the Chinese' were killing albinos and selling their meat as if it were pork, due to the similarity of the skin colouring. Relations with Chinese people have always been slightly tense in this part of the world. Already during the late colonial period (1961–75), the financial success of many Chinese people and their ready association with white Europeans (namely via the process of scholarly success) caused friction with the local black population.

The trip continued and the conversation took off again. Apparently, men do not like their wives to give birth to albinos. The 'more traditional husbands', I was told, are prone to divorce their wives 'for suspecting them'. I was not told what this suspicion consisted of – whether it had to do with having had adulterous relations with whites or even more sinister practices associated to witchcraft. What followed, precisely because it was unelicited, was even more puzzling. I was told that the teller had recently met a Euro-African woman (*mulata*) whose parents were *mulatos*, but whose mother was an albino. Apparently the girl 'did not even have bad hair (*cabelo mau*) like ours', 'she looked just like a white person', as she was both albino and mulata. This again was immediately followed by a discourse on how not all black skins are alike, since people from the region of Chokwé are supposed to have a lighter skin colour. Their skin, however, is clearly that of a black person as it has a yellow tone that cannot be confused with the skin of white Europeans.

What struck me about this series of unelicited comments was how each piece of information provided an interpretative context for the previous piece, in such a way as the teller, without wishing to grant his full support to most of them as empirically verified observations, drew out an interpretative plot that clarified their significance to the hearer. His report sketched out a map of ambivalent ethnic relations, in which 'whites', 'blacks', 'mulatos',[3] 'albinos', 'Chinese' and others distinguished among themselves by means of the diacritical signs of skin colour and hair type.

He was not willing to provide, or even capable of formulating, a theory concerning the way in which the supposed mystic properties of albinos, and the corresponding discrimination which they suffer, were associated with this background of racial classification. But, sensing my lack of means to properly contextualize these beliefs, he provided me with examples that might help me to reconstruct the 'web of belief' within which what he told me came to make sense to him and to the people that he heard it from. It seems important to clarify that at no moment was he attempting to make me 'believe'. In what he told me, in the sense that I should expect it to correspond to empirical reality.

Later on, wishing to understand to what extent what I had been told corresponded to generally held ideas, I queried various other acquaintances about it. I was told, for example, of an albino musician who claims that his father abandoned him on a rubbish heap after his birth, only to be saved by his mother's brother, who raised him. Other persons confirmed to me that albinos are said not to die and that 'one is never invited to go to funerals of albinos'.

One lady claimed that it was supposed to be a magic type of disappearance, but that it did not imply a later rebirth or a reappearance in spirit form. Parents, she corroborated, are profoundly unhappy about giving birth to albinos. An acquaintance of hers had given birth to two albino children in a row, whom she killed at birth, before she gave up and decided to raise her third albino child. Apparently there is a kind of 'medicine' which one can give to these babies, such that they grow up to look like mulatos. This informant also expressed the same strong disgust for the skin of albinos that I had heard being expressed more than once.

Finally, an association is made with vitiligo – a skin disorder characterized by smooth white spots on various parts of the body. I was told that this is a form of acquired albinism that results from theft. If someone has stolen something, the former owner goes to a sorcerer who will 'treat' (*tratar*) the thief in this way. An example was given to me of a person who had stolen a duck. Not only did he get vitiligo, but it also affected his children, who had eaten it without knowing its provenance.

Belief and Interpretation

Belief has puzzled modernist anthropologists. From Needham (1972) to Gellner (1974) to Veyne ([1983] 1988) to Tambiah (1990), the more the issue is discussed, the less we seem to be nearing resolution. Essentially, the topic of the definition of what is belief tends to merge with the more general topic of there being a modernist propensity to treat 'belief' as contrary to 'knowledge'. The important question is of the representationalist approach to 'knowledge' – and, in particular, scientific and technological knowledge. By dissociating 'belief' from 'knowledge', the modernists placed us before a quandary that ultimately can only provide ethnocentric results. Belief came to be associated to what 'nonmoderns'. Indulge in, and knowledge as the realm of modern 'Western' science and culture. There are many variants to this polarity and many different forms of theorizing it, but they all make us ultimately incapable of understanding belief. We know it is there, but we do not know what it is.

I was, thus, profoundly challenged by Donald Davidson's theory of radical interpretation (1984, 2001) and the way in which he treats the question of belief. He can help us to see some light at the end of the tunnel concerning a central issue for anthropology: namely, that a necessary condition for the description, analysis and discussion of divergence in human practice is the presupposition of a solid ground of human commonality. As he puts it, a necessary condition for successful interpretation is that 'the interpreter must so interpret as to make a speaker or agent largely correct about the world'

(2001, 152). This is something that all ethnographers know on the basis of their personal experience, that cultural dislocation did not ultimately prevent communication and interpretation: 'Making sense of the behaviours and utterances of others, even their most aberrant behaviour, requires us to find a great deal of reason and truth in them' (1984, 153). Why, then, do we always focus on difference, leaving similarity as the unstated presupposition?

Davidson defines beliefs as 'sentences held true by someone who understands them' (2001, 138). He insists that they are not 'representations' or 'images'. Rather, following Quine, he claims that 'Beliefs […] are states of people with intentions, desires, sense organs; they are states that are caused by, and cause, events inside and outside the bodies of their entertainers' (138). W. V. Quine's initial definition was that belief, as a propositional attitude, 'is a disposition to respond in certain ways when the appropriate issue arises' (Quine and Ullian 1970, 4). For these philosophers, it is important to reject the commonly held notion that 'believing [is] something that a man does *to* something: to some intangible thing which is *what* he believes' (4). To believe, then, is to 'believe true'. Disbelief and nonbelief are consequently treated as cases of belief and of suspended judgement, respectively. Knowledge is belief when it is very well grounded.

What this means is that, for Quine, 'where no confusion threatens, it will be convenient and natural to go on speaking even in the old way of what a man believes, instead of what he believes true. But whenever we are threatened by the philosophical question of objects of belief, we can gratefully retreat to the more explicit idiom which speaks of believing sentences true, or, ultimately, of believing utterances true' (1970, 5).

According to Davidson, therefore, the possibility of communication among humans (and, consequently, the possibility of thought, since there cannot be thought without language) depends on the sharing of a common ground: 'Communication begins where causes converge: your utterance means what mine does if belief in its truth is systematically caused by the same events and objects' (2001, 151). In this sense, therefore, 'belief is in its nature veridical' (146), as otherwise communication would be impossible. Such a theory may seem strange if, by belief, I continue to hold onto the classical definition of belief in things and, particularly, in things that are not true. But, if I adopt Quine's definition and understand that much of what we think in the course of everyday life are beliefs (such as the sky is blue, the ground is underfoot, etc.), I can easily concur with the notion that most of what a person says and implies is necessarily true.

This, of course, does not mean that error and falsity are impossible – quite the contrary. As Davidson puts it: 'there is no general presumption that someone who utters a declarative sentence wants or intends to speak the truth, nor that, if he does, he does it intentionally' (1984, 268). It does, however, have two major implications. The first is to focus our attention once again on the high level of commonality in all human experience. The second is the overcoming of simplistic scepticism by focusing on the fact that reality is not outside human experience (as it were, hidden by culture), but is a necessary part of it. As he puts it, 'The notion of a belief is the notion of a state that may or may not jibe with reality' (2001, 153).

Truth and Beliefs about Albinos

Let us, then, consider the abovementioned beliefs concerning albinos in the light of this theory. If all beliefs are beliefs that x is true, then these statements about albinos either 1) cannot be granted the status of belief or 2) are statements concerning truth.

The first hypothesis seems difficult to hold in as much as people proffer these statements in much the same way as they proffer other statements and use them in precisely the same way. I could, of course, argue that they are metaphors and thus not meant to be understood literally. But they purport to describe actual events – such as that albinos are not buried or that the Chinese sell albino meat as pork. They do not carry any indication of being a simile (x is like y) and, of course, they do not carry labels that say: 'Watch out, I am a metaphor!'

Therefore, I do not see that these statements can have any other meaning than the literal meaning they have (see Davidson 1984, 245–64). If there is a metaphorical intent in their production, it is not in the actual words pronounced, but in the way they were both produced and received. We are here distinguishing between the meaning of the words and the use to which they are put. Now, 'metaphor belongs exclusively to the domain of use' (247), which means that such statements can only be understood as being of the same nature as normal statements of belief. As it turns out, this is confirmed by the fact that many statements of belief can be received both literally and metaphorically *at the same time* – which, again, underlines the point that the metaphor is not in the statement itself, but in the way it is received by whoever hears it.

If, then, we confirm that these statements are beliefs, we are forced to deal with the notion that they are meant to be statements about truth or falsehood. As we have seen, this is problematic, since the very people that proffer them are *uncertain* about their relative truth. The notion of levels of truthfulness is an *ethnographic fact*; that is, it is what we were told. If pressed (for example, 'But are you really sure that that happened?') informants typically provide devious and uncertain answers (for example, 'Well, people say it is true. And indeed,

I do not know of any instance when it was not true… But whether it is true or not, I cannot really say.'). What typically happens is that informants hesitate and beat around the bush when we press them on this point. In the case of the people who talked to me about albinos, two things must be clear: 1) these things were not told to me as 'stories' (i.e., as fictionalized narratives), but as reports about shared belief, 'things *people* believe' – *as pessoas acreditam que…, as pessoas dizem que…, essa gente pensa que…*; 2) I was specifically told by the informants that these things might well not be true.

This has to do with the issue of 'first-person authority'. People are typically far more certain about things they have experienced personally than about something they have heard or deduced from other sources. Such a potential for gradation in belief is a fact of everyday experience. People are open to greater or lesser certainty even about matters of sensory experience. This, then, is a factor that explains how the truthfulness of statements such as those concerning albinos might be more or less diluted. Following Davidson again, we could argue that the fact that they are presented as possibly false statements is precisely what tells the receiver that these statements are metaphors: 'Generally it is only when a sentence is taken to be false that we accept it as a metaphor and start to hunt out the hidden implications' (1984, 258).

But this does not solve our problem; in the first place, because they were not told to us as being false, but as somehow less true; in the second place, because the relevance of such statements does not seem to be exhausted by their literal interpretation. As it turns out, even if they had actually seen the burial of one albino, I am sure that my informants would still be willing to contemplate the more general truthfulness of the statement that 'albinos do not die' and would still go on discussing the issue: in such cases, 'truth and falsity are not immediately to the point; what counts is *circumstantial cogency*, […] the force of prevalent custom' (Needham 1985, 39; my emphasis).

But there is a third consideration: the relative veridicality of beliefs varies with context. This is a fact that has repeatedly been observed, but that is not easily explained: in situations of social crisis, or in situations of heightened personal emotion, people's willingness to interpret literally beliefs that are not grounded on experience often increases. Thus, everyone that I talked to in Mozambique about these issues stressed that, during the period of hunger at the time of the civil war, people were bound to take very literally, for example, the reports concerning the sale of albino meat by the Chinese. Under the more cool-headed conditions of the present situation (the wealthier post–civil war period) people were less likely to stand by the literal truth of such beliefs. Experience tells me that this sort of reduced veridicality is a common feature of all cultural situations. In short, we return to our original quandary: if these are beliefs, what do they tell us about truth?

The easiest solution, of course, would be to give up on truth (see Pina-Cabral 2009). I would classify my informants as belonging to 'another culture', where people actually believe albinos do not die, and would claim that such a culture is essentially incomprehensible to me, a Westerner. This, however, would make nonsense of a series of things that strike me as important, such as: my own fascination with the notion that albinos do not die (that made me hear these reports, record them, hunt out for more details and finally spend a lot of very fulfilling days trying to make sense of them); my own incapacity to determine where 'their culture' and 'my (supposedly Western) culture' begins; and, not least of all, the whole of the history of anthropologically informed ethnography.

Ostensivity and the Web of Belief

Ironically, I believe the solution is to be found in the contrary direction, in what Donald Davidson calls 'the essentially veridical nature of belief' (2001, 175). According to him, not all that I believe need be true, but if most of my beliefs were not essentially correct as a reflection of a shared world, then I would never be able to communicate with another human being, as I would never be able to acquire language. 'The presumption that I am not generally mistaken about what I mean is essential to my having a language – to my being interpretable at all' (99). What this means is that, for me to be able to understand what is on another person's mind, we both have to share a largely correct view of the world. That being the case, Davidson argues, 'There are limits to how much individual or social systems of thought can differ' (39).

If belief is essentially veridical, then, this means that we have to agree with Quine that observation is the boundary condition of belief (1970, 12–20). In other words, beliefs are dependent on *ostensivity* – the association of heard words with things simultaneously observed. I cannot learn a first language and, thus, I cannot learn to think as human, without being with another person in the presence of a shared world.

This 'process of ostension' is essential for the formation of belief, because, in Quine's words, 'learning by ostension depends on no prior acquisition' (1970, 14). But it is also essential for its fixation and transmission to the extent that I constantly check my beliefs with reality and with other persons by means of the process of ostensivity. I will not attempt here to reduce to a few sentences Davidson's complex argument as presented in his essay on the 'Irreducibility of the Concept of the Self' (2001, 84–91). My point at this moment is simply that belief is indissociably connected with ostensivity in its possibility, in its formation and in its fixation and transmission. In this sense ostensivity is a boundary condition of belief. Nevertheless, as Quine graphically argues, 'Observation is the tug that tows the ship of theory; but in extreme cases the theory pulls so hard that observation yields' (1970, 17). In short, in the matter of *retention of belief*, something else seems to be at work – a tendency to retain what 'makes sense'.

Now, this has to do with one of the central characteristics of belief as identified by these philosophers: namely that 'beliefs typically rest [...] on further beliefs' (Quine and Ullian, 1970, 85). Belief is either a part of a chain of belief or it is nothing, for no belief is independent of the beliefs that surround it. Our minds are a web of belief. No belief would have content and identity without reference to an indeterminable but very large amount of other beliefs (see Davidson, 2001, 98). Furthermore, each of our thoughts is directly dependent on the other thoughts that logically situate it, so it cannot be moved from this setting without becoming another thought. This is what Davidson has in mind when he insists that 'radical incoherence in belief is [...] impossible' (2001, 99).

Consider the belief in the existence of albinos, which allows me to recognize someone as an albino. Starting from the ostensive moment in which we saw someone by the roadside whose physiological appearance was that which we normally recognize as that of an albino, I could only make that identification because I have a world of beliefs concerning what living beings are, which of these are humans, what is the normal skin of a human, etc. But then I have to enter into the whole complex area of human reproduction and of the relation between parents and offspring in skin colour, hair type, social status and all sorts of other features. By the time I have to bring into account what is to be considered as a 'black' person or a 'white' person in postcolonial Africa, I have gotten to the point where a good percentage of all my beliefs has had to be brought to the fore in order to 'make sense' of what I understood when I shared with my companions in that automobile the ostensive moment of identification of an albino by the roadside.

We normally form beliefs on the basis of earlier beliefs, in such a way as to construct structures of beliefs that tend towards some sort of conservatism, rather than towards some definite systematicity: 'We form habits of building beliefs such as we form our other habits; only in habits of building beliefs there is less room for idiosyncrasy' (Quine and Ullian 1970, 59). In fact, the strategies for the transmission of belief that we normally adopt should be sufficient to illustrate this characteristic of belief. Quine makes this claim in yet another of his graphic formulae: 'To maintain our beliefs properly even for home consumption we must attend closely to how they are supported. A healthy garden of beliefs requires well-nourished roots and tireless pruning. When we want to get a belief of ours to flourish in someone else's garden, the question of support is doubled: we have to consider first what support sufficed for it at home and then how much of the same is ready for it in the new setting' (85).

Let us take this injunction and look at the way in which my travelling companion declared his albino beliefs. Faced with my potential doubt (both expressed and assumed), he went on to provide me with a set of apparently dislocated comments concerning skin types that were intermediary to the greater 'black/white' divide. If we look at what he told me without expecting it to be a logically integrated sequence, we can immediately see that all the comments he made played with interstitial types (mulatos, albinos, Chinese, people of Chokwé with lighter skin). I believe he was not consciously providing me with a cognitive map. Nevertheless, that is just what he did. He did not make a claim to the authority of ostensivity (in fact, quite to the contrary, as he was uncertain as to whether what he told me actually occurred), neither did he make a claim to logical systematicity (he never told me why he was threading one comment after the other and he would probably claim, if I asked him today, that he had no particular reason for doing so).

As Quine would have it, my travelling companion was planting a tree in my garden of belief. He wanted me to retain it as it made a lot of 'sense'. In his own garden. For that, he was providing me with a whole set of supports. To stretch the metaphor, he was showing me how well it merged with other plants in my garden and how it helped them grow.

He was in the realm of *retentivity* – the tendency for beliefs to interconnect with each other, tending towards systematicity without ever actually achieving it. As Davidson puts it, 'truth is correspondence with the way things are', thus 'there is a presumption in favour of the truth of a belief that coheres with a significant mass of belief' (2001, 138–9). This I call 'retentivity', placing it, together with ostensivity, as a condition of belief (but not a 'border condition', because it does not have the same significance for the original formation of thought and language).

Ostension and Retention

If, then, we treat retentivity as a characteristic of belief, there are a number of points that need to be raised. We will start by looking into the relation between ostensivity and retentivity.

Conservatism

Firstly, there is some conservatism in belief. This is a perfectly reasonable feature of belief. There are private reasons for it, to do with the architecture of belief. Beliefs being connected with all other beliefs, I cannot safely be willing to jeopardize my whole world for one particular wayward observation. There are also public reasons for this, since all thinking creatures are social creatures and have to remain as much as possible within contexts of intersubjectivity. Our conservatism is such that, even before contradictory evidence, we are likely to be slow to alter the context of meaning of which it is a part.[4]

Another effect of conservatism is that what we take to be an observation also depends on the context of observation. Phenotypic observations are an interesting area for that. For example, the way people read other people's skin colour, body features or hair type varies depending on the relevant ethnic boundaries within the context at hand. This came out very clearly to me from being forced to compare the way the categories 'black' and 'white' are used differently in Mozambique and South Africa.[5]

Furthermore, we systematically 'edit observation'. We see a bent stick in water and we correct our visual observation, since we know that water has that effect on the way sticks look. In this case, we do it not because we learnt a theory of refraction, but because we learnt from experience that the stick is straight. In most cases, however, we edit observation without such strong empirical reasons, as when I take it for granted that someone is a northerner (or whatever) because of the way he pronounces some particular sound.

Localism

Secondly, our world of experience is loosely divided into realms or domains. This is an issue about which much has been written. I refer to it here briefly only to point out that there is a localization effect through which one is less willing to confront observations across domains.[6] This applies both to observations and to systematic implications. We are dealing here with a form of retentivity, for it means that the boundaries between these domains are thus reinforced and retained. My travelling companion is a literate person who, when he is helping his daughter do her housework for school, for example, will know not to include examples about albinos who, instead of dying, simply disappear from the face of the earth.

Systematicity

Thirdly, although we are normally rather unsystematic in the way we attend to our 'garden of belief', structural effects in belief can be observed. In particular, we are prone to treat as true many beliefs that are not supported by observation but by the role they play in shoring up a whole area of belief. The case of the beliefs about albinos is a particularly good exemplification of this process: they turn out to be relevant in terms of the way they structure Mozambican notions of ethnicity. Race, class, origin, status, language, aesthetic standards concerning human bodies, education are all interwoven into a complex and conflictive whole that is one of the central areas for structuring the world in postcolonial Africa. Beliefs such as these reported by my companion about intermediary and interstitial categories are central to construct the conceptual framework that supports the greater 'black/white' divide, making it operational on a daily basis for a very complex set of purposes.

World Views, Classifications and Prototypes

This implies that beliefs are not self-sufficient units of meaning. Rather, they are necessarily integrated into networks that 'make sense' of these beliefs. As Wittgenstein would have it: 'Only in the stream of thought and life do words have meaning' (in Needham 1985, 25). This is a very similar notion to Davidson's claim that 'Radical incoherence in belief is [...] impossible' (2001, 99). This being the case, we cannot be surprised to find that whole areas of belief tend to cohere. As Quine would have it, we are prone to 'habits of building belief' (Quine and Ullian 1970, 59). Davidson expresses a similar sort of concern in what could be taken as the perfect definition of *retentivity*: 'there is a presumption in favour of the truth of a belief that coheres with a significant mass of belief' (2001, 138–9).

Without having to go to the improbable extreme of claiming that, at any one point in time, a person's beliefs are systematically structured, we are nevertheless plainly justified in looking for the existence of loose concatenations of beliefs that function as a shared ground for social living. To 'make sense' is not a characteristic of each belief on its own. Rather, it is a function of the use of beliefs – that is, the way in which each belief coheres with others within intersubjectively shared worlds of meaning. Basically, it is suggested that, for the purposes of the comfortable carrying out of everyday life activities and intersubjective engagement, people find it useful to adhere to 'world views' – broad patterns of beliefs that are widely shared by their daily social interlocutors.[7]

Thus, the fixation and the transmission of a belief depends on the way in which it 'makes sense' by relation to a process of sharing of associational paths rooted in a particular sociocultural context. Each belief is simultaneously integrated in the general web of belief of the person in question and in the localized web of belief associated to the domain where it occurs. Moreover, since belief is an intrinsic part of interpersonal communication, its fixation and transmission cannot be dissociated from the communicational context of its occurrence. Each belief, therefore, is deeply dependent on its environment, both in terms of retentivity and ostensivity, since, as Quine would have it, 'what counts as an observation sentence will be relative to the community chosen' (1970, 99). We must, nevertheless, keep in mind Davidson's advice that 'perfect consistency is not to be expected. What needs emphasis is only the methodological necessity for finding consistency enough' (2000, 150).

World views, therefore, are constellations of belief, they do not exist outside their context of enactment. They are geared to social practice both because they are indispensable for a measure of predictability to occur in social interaction and because they do not exist as formed theories, but as tendencies. They are favoured paths through the web of belief, so to speak. The category, therefore, is fully 'etic'. I do not presume that people hold world views in their heads, so to speak, as actual images or as preformed representations. To the contrary, I am suggesting that the classifications and prototypes that anthropologists describe exist statistically (and not mechanically) as tendencies in the way people concatenate belief. These concatenations only exist because they are useful to people in the way they deal with the world and with other people. Thus, these *paths through the web of belief* are constantly being reinforced by their use. They are like jungle paths: they do not pre-exist the process of passage of people that constitute them and without which they would vanish.

One of the central areas of world view construction is the major fault line of ethnic classification. In postcolonial Africa, the heritage of centuries of European colonialism has come to shape social life in such a way as to give rise to a deeply set frame of interpreting people's social belonging and social rights and duties that tends to assume a binary character: 'blacks' to one side, 'whites' to the other. What is 'black' and what is 'white' differs significantly from context to context and from country to country. Nevertheless, in Maputo today, as in most other African cities, the categorical distinction between 'black' and 'white' is almost as important as gender in the implications it has for daily existence and as a framework for interpreting other people's actions and expectations.

In exchanging these beliefs concerning albinos with me, my travelling companion was laying out a pathway in my garden of belief, to use Quine's metaphor. In this sense, the factor of ostensivity was largely irrelevant. The relevance of the beliefs about albinos that he was imparting to me was at the level of retentivity. By exploring the border areas of the 'black/white' binary classification, where ambiguity might arise, he was opening a window into his world view for me – in the sense of putting the classification to practical use, thus instilling in me the context for its relevance. The 'black/white' ethnic[8] divide functions as an integrating principle within which or across which lie the other modes of differentiation (be they based on subethnic, regional, linguistic, religious or class differences). All the ethnic categories to which my travelling companion referred (mulatos, Chinese, albinos, people from Chokwé) can be grouped either outside or inside the major divide, in a number of ways and, thus, can be seen to problematize it.

In terms of the major line of classification, they are all marginal. In some instances, they are dealt with as external to the major binary classification by being treated as categories apart that have nothing to do with the 'black/white' divide. Alternatively, one can place interstitial groups as frontier categories within either of the two camps. In fact, people in Maputo with whom I tried out the concepts in the course of informal conversation often adopted this strategy. When simplicity requires, people are prone to group mulatos, Chinese and even Indians as part of the 'white' group – contrary to what is the case in South African cities where the Anglo-American 'one drop rule' system is usually adopted (see Pina-Cabral 2001 and Fry 2000). In the case of mulatos, this is facilitated by the fact that they are not that many, since a good number of them actually pass either for 'white' or for 'black'; in the case of Chinese, because they are so few and so clearly associated to whites from a sociocultural point of view.

Of all these interstitial categories, however, albinos are the hardest to classify, for they are decidedly 'black' and yet their skin (the major feature of differentiation) is white. Furthermore, by adopting the style of life that normal lower-class 'black' people adopt, they are often more exposed to the sun than their skin permits. Consequently, they suffer a lot from exposure, which means that their classificatory oddity tends often to appear as physical anomaly: a painful assault on notions of bodily integrity. Our sense of sympathy to the condition of our fellow humans means that the lack of bodily integrity in others challenges our own sense of well being, giving rise to all sorts of sentiments of rejection and/or compulsive compassion. I take it that this explains the sentiments of disgust towards albinos and their skin that I repeatedly encountered.

There is an almost structuralist neatness to the way in which, after having problematized the concept of albino, my travelling companion went on to explore the boundaries of the requirements of retentivity of the concept itself: by discoursing, on the one hand, about albinos who are also mulatos and, on the other, about people who are classificatorily fully 'black', but whose skins, while being that of 'blacks', is lighter and thus more 'white' (the people of Chokwé).

Conclusion

What, then, is the relevance for these people of saying that 'albinos don't die'? It would seem that albinos are said not to die, not because they remain alive or active after death, but because they are not buried. Now, in this, as in most other societies, the link to the earth is a major part of the sense of social belonging. The legitimation of citizenship is mediated by a notion of autochthony. That the earth should not consume these interstitial creatures is a very simple (and, for that reason, powerful) symbol of the fact that in Mozambique, today, belonging is primarily marked by the 'black/white' divide, which albinos breach. Indirectly, however, it is also a denial of rights of belonging to 'whites'.

Careless and disconnected as the comments of my travelling companion appeared to be, they turned out to constitute, after all, useful props for the intersubjective sharing of principles of social and moral differentiation. In imparting these beliefs to me, he was counting on my being 'docile when faced with another's world', as Veyne would have it (1988, 42). As it turns out, he was a mulato himself. This does not mean that he is more or less likely to believe these things. However, if my interpretation is correct, he was reflecting symbolically on the tragic condition of those who fall outside the 'black/white' divide. When talking to me about albinos, my driving companion was attempting to open a window to his world view[9] and, at the same time, he was allowing me to understand the painful condition in which interstitial people such as himself find themselves today in Mozambique.

Notes

1 An earlier and less developed Portuguese version of this article was published in Gil, Livet and Pina-Cabral 2004. I am grateful to J. Giannotti and Omar Ribeiro Thomaz (at CEBRAP, Brazil), as well as to the colleagues in Rio de Janeiro (IFICS and Museu Nacional) for their insightful comments, and to the colleagues at University Eduardo Mondlane for providing me with a welcome environment in Mozambique.

2 Cf. Bryant 1949, 117. I am grateful to Adam Kuper for calling my attention to this passage.

3 In Mozambique the word *misto* (literally 'mixed') is often encountered in daily use with a similar meaning.

4 As Quine puts it: 'Chances are that I will waive the one wayward observation, attributing it to unexplained interference, even to hallucination' (1970, 17).

5 See Peter Fry's interesting essay on the issue (2000) and Pina-Cabral (2001).

6 Cf. Veyne's reference to our 'capacity to simultaneously believe in incompatible truths' (1988, 56). 'The different truths are all true in our eyes, but we do not think about them with the same part of our head' (87). Needless to say, I do not follow Veyne's approach to truth, but I am bound to retain this comment as a valid empirical observation, since a 'pluralist' approach is a condition for the possibility of anthropology (for a similar concern to make realism and pluralism compatible, cf. Lynch 1998).

7 Cf. Pina-Cabral 1986, 4–5. For a similar suggestion, see Michael Lynch's use of 'worldview' (1998). Without entering into his debate with Davidson (1984, 31–54), I think that the latter's insistence that there is a limit to the number of beliefs we may attribute to another person that are contrary to our own beliefs is not incompatible with the notion that people's beliefs differ: 'We cannot intelligibly say that [conceptual] schemes are different, neither can we intelligibly say that they are one' (1984). I fully realize that I am bypassing the thorny issue of differentiating 'concepts' from 'beliefs'.

8 Ethnic relations being here understood as discursive traditions concerning belonging, mediated by narratives of common origin.

9 That is, to the paths of belief that constitute the intersubjective terrain in which his life and that of his family is processed.

References

Asad, Talal, 2001. 'Reading a Modern Classic: W. C. Smith's *The Meaning and End of Religion*'. In *Religion and Media*, edited by H. de Vries and S. Wbere, 131–47. Stanford: Stanford University Press.

Bourdieu, Pierre. (1977) 1989. *O Poder Simbólico*. Lisbon: Difel.

Bryant, A. T. 1949. *The Zulu People: As They Were Before the White Man Came*. Pietermaritzberg: Shutter and Shooter.

Davidson, Donald. 1984. *Inquiries into Truth and Interpretation*. Oxford: Oxford University Press.

———. 2001. *Subjective, Intersubjective, Objective*. Oxford: Oxford University Press.

Foot, Philippa. 2001. *Natural Goodness*. Oxford: Clarendon Press.

Fry, Peter. 2000. 'Cultures of difference. The Aftermath of Portuguese and British Colonial Policies in Southern Africa'. *Social Anthropology* 8 (2), 117–144.

Gellner, Ernest. 1974. *Legitimation of Belief*. Cambridge: Cambridge University Press.

Gil, Fernando, Pierre Livet and João de Pina-Cabral, eds. 2004. *O processo da crença*. Lisbon: Gradiva.

Needham, Rodney. 1972. *Belief, Language and Experience*. Oxford: Blackwell.

———. 1985. *Exemplars*. Berkeley: University of California Press.

Latour, Bruno. 1991. *Nous n'avons jamais été modernes*. Paris: Découverte.

Lynch, Michael P. 1998. *Truth in Context: An Essay on Pluralism and Objectivity*. Cambridge, MA: MIT Press.

Pina-Cabral, João de, 1986. *Sons of Adam, Daughters of Eve: The Peasant Worldview of the Alto Minho*. Oxford: Clarendon Press.

———. 1989. 'L'Héritage de Maine: L'érosion des categories d'analyse dans l'étude des phénomènes familiaux en Europe'. *Ethnologie Française* 19: 329–40.

———. 1992. 'Against Translation'. In *Europeans Observed*, edited by J. de Pina-Cabral and John Campbell, 1–23. London: St Antony's/Macmillan.

———. 2001. 'Galvão Among the Cannibals: The Emotional Constitution of Colonial Power'. In *Identities* 8 (4), 483–515.

———. 2002. *Between China and Europe: Person, Culture and Emotion in Macao*. LSE Monographs in Social Anthropology. London/New York: Continuum Books/Berg.

———. 2006. 'Anthropology Challenged: Notes for a Debate'. *Journal of the Royal Anthropological Institute* 12 (3): 663ff.

———. 2009. 'The All-or-Nothing Syndrome and the Human Condition'. *Social Analysis* 53 (2): 163–76.

Pouillon, Jean. 1982. 'Remarks on the Verb "to Believe"'. In *Between Religion and Transgression: Structuralist Essays in Religion, History and Myth*, edited by M. Izard and P. Smith, 1–8. Chicago: Chicago University Press.

Quine, W. V. and J. S. Ullian. 1970. *The Web of Belief*. New York: Random House.

Robbins, Joel. 2007. 'Continuity Thinking and the Problem of Christian Culture: Belief, Time and the Anthropology of Christianity'. *Current Anthropology* 48 (1): 5–38.

Ruel, Malcolm. (1982) 2002. 'Christians as Believers'. In *A Reader in the Anthropology of Religion*, edited by Michal Lambek, 99–113. Oxford: Blackwell.

Tambiah, Stanley Jeyaraja. 1990. *Magic, Science, and Religion and the Scope of Rationality*. Lewis Henry Morgan Lectures. Cambridge: Cambridge University Press.

Tausig, Michael. 1993. *Mimesis and Alterity: A Particular History of the Senses*. New York: Routledge.

Veyne, Paul. 1988 (1983). *Did the Greeks Believe in their Myths? An Essay on the Constitutive Imagination*. Chicago: University of Chicago Press.

Chapter 19

ANTHROPOLOGY, DEVELOPMENT AND THE MYTH OF CULTURE

Robert Feleppa

Anthropologists have become increasingly involved as participants on development teams, but their great potential to promote sustainable development is hindered by vestiges of one of cultural anthropology's founding myths. It is the notion of cultures construed as self-contained symbol systems, conceptually opaque to all but true insiders, with an implied notion of correct translation, which makes it an 'all or nothing' matter. This notion is also linked to long-standing concerns in the field with moral relativism, value neutrality and colonialism. As a result, within the community of anthropologists working in development, two somewhat opposed positions have arisen: one holds that anthropologists should simply provide cultural knowledge (be 'knowledge brokers' as some put it); the other holds that anthropologists should adopt a more partisan stance which, given value relativism's resistance to imposing values from without, compels anthropologists to be advocates of the interests of those groups receiving assistance. I shall consider several ways in which these concerns figure in development controversies, and give reasons why they, and the ideological stances they validate, are unnecessary impediments to progress. I will then offer a pragmatic view of interpretation in the hope of resolving some of these difficulties.

I shall also consider how these methodological problems are compounded by concerns with the political-social impact of anthropological inquiry – concerns which can lead to an overemphasis on these (albeit important) issues, while eclipsing the epistemological challenges which primarily motivate appeal for anthropological input by development agencies. This in turn leads to some unfortunate conflation of political with epistemological issues, when, for instance, cultural belief-system integrity, as an epistemological thesis, is motivated by concerns to preserve a group's political integrity. Although obviously linked, these are obviously not the same. These problems are made especially difficult by the fact that, as I shall argue, 'success' in translation is not easily sorted into epistemic and ethical components.

Anthropology and Development

Some anthropologists term this kind of fieldwork 'participatory development', a label which reflects the theoretical roots many of them have in the ethnoscience and new ethnography movements of the past. The emphasis these approaches placed on participant observation nurtured research skills which seem ideally suited to development. Much of the impetus for anthropological participation in development originated outside of anthropology, in philosophical shifts by some developmental agencies from 'top-down' interventionist perspectives to 'bottom-up' or 'grassroots' participatory ones – shifts motivated, as Paul Sillitoe remarks, by 'mounting evidence of resources wasted in ill-conceived, frequently centrally imposed schemes that have not only failed to improve matters in less developed countries but which have also on occasion made them worse, arrogantly sending in the eggheads to sort out local problems' (Sillitoe 2002a, 1). Anthropologists on development teams are expected to provide an understanding of local beliefs, values and customs which enables these teams to understand the problems they face; to effectively communicate, learn and teach; and, ultimately, to create a sustainable, positive impact. Sillitoe sees the primary objective of participatory-development anthropology as achieving 'technology transfer [...] now not as a top-down imposition but as a search for jointly negotiated advances' (1998, 224). This provides an objective measure of interpretive success, while also complicating the political aspects of the anthropologist's role.

These developments, some commentators think, have brought cultural anthropology to new and 'interesting times' insofar as they seem to have both beneficial and harmful potential for the discipline. What adds to the interest is the inheritance of a number of long-standing theoretical tensions associated with participant-observation methodologies. One especially troubling notion is that meaningful communication and action rest on systems of symbolic meaning whose elements are holistically interrelated in a way which resists understanding by outsiders. And even if one disavows the idea that the discourse in question is impenetrable, or even systematically organized, even the more modest idea that grasping the holistic interconnections requires thorough analysis presents serious obstacles both to anthropology's potential contribution to development teams, given the latter's typically short project time frames, and to mainstream anthropology's acceptance of the work of developmental anthropologists working under such constraints (Sillitoe 1998, 224ff.).

Anthropologists trained in participant forms of analysis see themselves as especially qualified to meet development objectives, insofar as their training sensitizes them to ethnocentrism's various and subtle forms. Failure to understand cultural context leads both to misunderstanding and undervaluing of local knowledge traditions – a failing to which natural scientists are especially prone, according to Sillitoe: 'The lack of respect for others' knowledge traditions manifested by many Western scientists, underpinned by the assumption that technological superiority implies answers to all difficulties, is a considerable barrier to development' (1998, 227). However, this prudent reflection on the differences and relative merits of scientific and indigenous knowledge forms unfortunately invites engagement in controversies about the universality of 'scientific rationality'. As developmental anthropology's criteria of success involve attainment of sustainable development results, and not the revelation of the potential scope of human conceptualization and valuation, the derived resistance to Western science can be a serious problem.

The root problem here has to do with the way in which the evident need to contextualize information seems, if symbolic holism is understood in a certain way, to create insurmountable access problems. Sillitoe remarks,

> It is not just a question of the time it takes to learn language, cultural repertoire, social scenario, and so on, but also a matter of the investment needed to win the trust and confidence of people who frequently have reason to be extremely suspicious of foreigners and their intentions. The central anthropological dictum of holism underlines the need for a long-range perspective and anticipates the dynamic and negotiated status of indigenous-knowledge research. While the interconnectivity of issues is acknowledged in development contexts, as is evidenced in approaches such as 'integrated rural development' and 'farming systems research', this insight has fallen foul, under the time pressures of development, of holism's all-encompassing contradictions. These starkly demand that socioculturally speaking we know either everything or nothing. It is the functionalist conundrum that has long faced anthropologists of striking a balance between the requirement of achieving a detailed understanding of something, which by definition implies narrowing the field of enquiry, without becoming too narrowly focused and overlooking connections to other issues. In indigenous-knowledge research it amounts to maintaining a broad sociocultural perspective to contextualize the tightly focused view of technical specialists. (1998, 235)

Sillitoe is right to warn against the tendency of natural scientists in development projects to 'behave as if it were possible to pluck information relating to their specialisms out of cultural context and treat it as independent technical facts', while overlooking the fact that 'other cultural activities may influence production activities, from social arrangements to religious observances' (1998, 228). However, what justifies the rather extreme claim that we know 'everything or nothing'? Commenting on Sillitoe's discussion, Roy Ellen agrees with his concerns, but notes a problem that can engender mistrust not only on the part of the target populations, but also colleagues from other disciplines, about the anthropological agenda:

> The difficulty – and danger – here is that an uninformed researcher collecting data during a short time frame and as part of a highly structured organisation is not able to know *a priori* what can be accurately and safely reported as knowledge and recycled in useful ways. The result is that many so-called indigenous-knowledge reports radically disembody particular bits of proclaimed useful knowledge from the rest of culture in a way which does a profound disservice to its potential importance. But to criticise by simply asserting that 'all knowledge is culturally embedded' invites the response that this is no more than a shibboleth which conveniently protects the interests of a particular professional cadre – namely, anthropologists. (1998, 238)

This presents anthropologists with a serious practical problem. The development agency contemplating employment of anthropologists can dismiss the claim as a shibboleth, and perhaps undervalue anthropology's potential contribution to the appreciation of divergent viewpoints as a result. Or it can take seriously the epistemological worries that motivate the 'all-or-nothing' idea and see that as a reason to be discouraged about anthropology's potential value!

The aforementioned problems are further compounded by cross-cutting concerns with knowledge and power issues. Mark Hobart – whose highly influential essay from 1993 is commonly cited, by friend and foe alike, for its emphasis on knowledge/power issues in development – argues that 'the production of knowledge [...] is acutely political, because [quoting Foucault] "what is excluded and who is qualified to know involves acts of power"' (1993, 9). Johann Pottier, another influential author and volume editor in recent developmental anthropology, approvingly cites this remark of Hobart's, adding that 'an empirically grounded understanding of how knowledge(s) is (are) produced through the mediation of unequal power relations and processes of translation is a prerequisite for any serious attempt to instigate dialogue and make *all* stakeholders benefit from development initiatives' (2003, 3).

Pottier approvingly cites Sillitoe's point that scientists cannot simply 'pluck information relating to their specialisms out of cultural context', but places much more emphasis on the knowledge and power implications which can easily be overlooked if this is seen simply as concerning correct interpretation and knowledge transfer. She remarks that the 'emphasis on power in the study of local knowledges inevitably means that questions must be asked about profit and compensation' (2003, 8). Drawing on examples from Fairhead's research (1992) and his own (1997), in which apparent disagreements rooted in technical knowledge are actually about political and economic issues, Pottier argues,

> What is interesting here is less that men think this, or women think that, but (a) that as an agro-ecological process 'suppression' is locally understood and probably underlies many practices; (b) that differences of opinion (in applying this principle) exist, and these differences may reflect different politico-economic experience as well as technical experience, and (c) that it is quite common to find political or gender disputes (e.g. over access to and control over resources) being argued in an ecological idiom. (1997, 4)

These political factors are thrust into greater prominence by the reform agendas of funding organizations, whose misunderstanding of relevant political-social factors in recipient societies is often what leads to failure to achieve sustainable results. This has led inquirers to adopt many roles – as interpreter, advocate, facilitator, etc. Indeed, in developmental anthropology even the traditional reference to ethnographic players as 'inquirers' and 'informants' has given way to talk of 'knowledge brokers' and 'stakeholders'. But overemphasis on such factors threatens to cause a loss of theoretical purchase on questions bearing on the epistemological aspects of ethnography – i.e., accuracy of representation of the symbolic content of the thoughts and actions of the subjects of inquiry.

Concerns about political factors, and appreciation of their inseparability, to some extent, from epistemological ones, can lead to some unfortunate conflation of epistemological and political issues. For instance, Purcell and Onjoro (2000) argue for 'parity' between Western and indigenous perspectives, and like others conflate political and epistemological issues. Concerned that Western development agencies will put indigenous peoples in positions of social/political inferiority – indeed, of subjugation – in the very act of social/ environmental reform, they recommend respecting parity:

> [...] seen as the ability of a group to make autonomous decisions about its future based on a set of principles derived from its own collective ontology – its own 'truth'. Local judgments about the integration of 'outside' knowledge must derive from people's understanding of the world rather than from imposed assumptions. Parity, in this sense, is inherent in self-determination and consistent with cultural relativity. (2000, 163)

But although these are related, the truth of a group's collective ontology and its political integrity are not the same. Moreover, these authors are led to regard the epistemological inappropriateness of science to indigenous knowledge as axiomatic, when this is evidently a question whose answer depends on context.

Sillitoe criticizes others (such as Agrawal 1995; Smith 1999; and Goonatilake 1999) for holding kindred views to the effect that 'that talking about indigenous knowledge may weaken others' rights as non-scientists to be treated as equals and for their views and position to count' – and disparages this 'politically correct criticism' – as does Schönhuth (2002), who sees these attitudes as 'slightly disingenuous' in light of developmental aims (Sillitoe 2002b, 112). Indeed, simplistic respect for 'insider' viewpoints may well preserve traditional unjust power asymmetries existing within the recipient culture. Sinha (2000) and Alatas (2000) are insightful on this point, while also sensitive to concerns to liberate development from assumptions associated with the Anglo-European perspective.

Hobart goes so far as to deny that the divide between knowledge-systems can be bridged by more concerted efforts at communication, since this presupposes 'a model of knowledge as communicable propositions and presumes rationality to be shared' and invokes a 'mirage of perfect communication' (1993, 11). I will argue against his general position by showing that the best way to dispel the illusion of perfect communication of propositions is to reconsider the implicit concept of correct interpretation which underlies it.

Holism, Relativism and the Charity Principle

One problem with typical conceptions of culture is that they make diversity and change difficult to explain. Hobart's view is criticized by Grillo who contends that it implies 'cultural solipsism' (1997, 14), which, he argues, itself 'reflects a surprising ethnocentrism' and 'is also grounded in a "victim culture"' (1997, 21). (cf. on this latter point Olivier de Sardan 2005, 47.) Grillo also notes that despite Hobart's protestations that he does not harbour 'romantic fantasies' about indigenous knowledge, 'there is the real danger of assuming that ignorance is one-sided [and] that indigenous knowledge is seen as complete, accomplished, and hence static and unchanging' (24–5).

The culprit to which I would like to call attention is the view that semantic holism creates the possibility of incommensurability of conceptual schemes and the worry that values defining progress cannot be understood sufficiently, ever, for productive dialogue to take place. This attitude about holism underwrites belief in a standard of interpretive correctness other than the success in social interaction which interpretation is meant to facilitate.

Put briefly, the holism thesis is that the meaning of any one expression is determined by its relationships to other expressions, and it appears essential, if one is to understand a group's language and other symbolic interactions, that one understand the way the mutually defining concepts of its language fit together.

Although the hermeneutic issue here is a very old one, given the influence of ethnoscience on participatory development, it will help to see the issues as they emerge in that tradition. Adapting the phonetic/ phonemic contrast in phonology to semantics, Pike, Lounsbury, Goodenough and other founding figures of the ethnoscience and new ethnography developed an 'etic/emic' contrast, which burdens inquirers with the task of understanding cultures in terms of the concepts of ethnographic subjects ('cultural insiders') and not in the 'etic' terms of 'cultural outsiders'. Understandably, given the strong relativistic elements of the language-and-culture tradition spawned by Boas's work, there emerged a concern that the categorical distinctions in a social group's discourse might differ so deeply and broadly that contrasts seen by the unattuned Westerner as 'natural' – say, between scientific or practical discourse and religious or magical discourse – might not be shared by that group, creating the potential for unpredictable 'side-tracking' problems, as Olivier de Sardan calls them, if, say, the development professional or assisting natural scientists fails to take account of the religious significance of what to them is a practical issue of farming technique.

Returning momentarily to Grillo's worry that Hobart sees indigenous knowledge 'as complete, accomplished, and hence static and unchanging', this remark brings to the fore the wedding of mentalism and relativism which characterizes ethnoscience, and which is a benchmark of the Boasian, language-and-culture tradition in anthropology. However, as Friedman (1994) notes, Boas himself was aware of the problematic ahistoricity which mentalism entails:

> we ought not to forget that Franz Boas, father of cultural relativism in anthropology, was quite clear about the degree to which the elements making up any culture are imports. For the once pure cultures that now interact across borders have never existed as such […] and in Boas's work it is the way in which the elements are integrated that is essential rather than their historical sources.

Indeed,

> If culture is always a practiced product, it cannot be understood as an autonomous object that has somehow become heterogenized. Boas is aware of this, even if

his model of integration is primarily psychological. What changes is the play of interpretations, or of attributions of meaning that must be understood in terms of changing social contexts. (1994, 75)

In this psychological emphasis lies the root of the problem, since it imports philosophical confusions about the nature of meaning – particularly as embodied in what is termed 'mentalism': roughly, the view that meaningfulness is best understood in terms of a relationship between a symbol and an idea in the mind. The reconsideration of interpretation I want to offer here derives from philosophical critiques of this view by Wittgenstein, Quine, Davidson and others. However, it is also important to keep in mind Friedman's and Boas's point here, namely, that culture is a *product*, not a pre-existing system of ideas so tightly interconnected as to assume an ideal, unchanging status.

Quine's work on what he terms the 'indeterminacy of translation' is especially illuminating here because its primary target is precisely the notion that meanings are objects (concepts, propositions) underlying the intelligibility of symbolic behaviour, and that translation is a matter of discovering those antecedent relations. He challenges belief in their antecedent existence by showing that the behavioural evidence on which translation rests could not warrant this belief. Quine framed the indeterminacy thesis at one point in the form of a thought experiment in which a translator is imagined as trying to understand a completely alien language, bearing no relationships to any other – the so-called 'radical translation' argument (Quine 1960, chapter 2). According to this thesis, translation is underdetermined by all *possible* evidence, thus leaving translators free to defend divergent but non-equivalent translations of the language. One line of argument for this thesis depends on semantic holism: roughly, since the translation of individual terms or sentences depends on the translation of an interconnected set of expressions, one can easily defend a particular translation, despite apparent counterevidence, provided one makes appropriate adjustments in related translational hypotheses. Quite silly beliefs could be attributed to people, provided one made the right adjustments in auxiliary hypotheses. Only a charity principle, to the effect that people should not be interpreted as holding obviously false beliefs or making illogical inferences without compelling evidence to the contrary, could be relied upon to eliminate these interpretive options. Behavioural evidence alone could not provide this – no matter how much one gathered. Quine did not invent the principle, which is a component of standard interpretive practice: what he did was to draw attention to its philosophical significance.

The thrust of this complex and controversial thesis is this: Quine attacks the idea that there is any determinacy of meaning by showing that there is no empirical basis for believing there are any objective synonymy relations to ground interpretation. If there were some pre-existing set of holistically interrelated synonymy relations, which constituted the meaning of the network of expressions being translated, then it should be possible to identify a uniquely correct translation manual given a sufficient quantity of behavioural evidence. But if we are left with divergent, incompatible translation manuals, even with all possible behavioural evidence at our disposal, then the notion that translational correctness depends on capturing or expressing these pre-existing synonymy relations is wrong-headed. What follows from this is *not* that objective translation is impossible, but that the underlying assumption that correctness of translation is a matter of describing such pre-existing synonymy relations is incorrect. What needs to be rethought, then, is what it means to call a translation 'correct'.

There is simply, as he puts it in various places, 'no fact of the matter' or 'nothing to be right or wrong about' when it comes to validating interpretation. Now this is not to say that behavioural evidence cannot be relied upon to determine that some translations are wrong. They surely have predictive force. However, what perplexed Quine was that there could be *so many* divergent, but empirically correct answers. The core of the problem for him was that reliance on behavioural evidence was insufficient to settle on a correct translation, and that other, extra-empirical criteria had to be applied – the most significant one being the charity principle. However, he also acknowledged that other, extra-empirical criteria would also be necessary – such as the preference for simpler translations over empirically equivalent but more complex ones.

Translation and Social Coordination

It is important to provide an answer to a question constantly raised by critics of Quine's arguments: why does the indeterminacy thesis show that translational hypotheses are not really hypotheses? Evidence underdetermines any scientific theory, and it is essential to apply other extra-empirical criteria of adequacy in validating theories, such as opting for the simpler or more general theory, or opting for the more familiar construction over the less familiar, if the two are equal on other scores. Why not see charity as being just such an extra-empirical element? Why is interpretation in some distinct category, as Quine seems to claim?

I suggest that these worries are best addressed by developing Quine's insights in a different way (see Feleppa 1986, 1988). Rather than view interpretations as descriptive hypotheses with shortcomings, I should view them as more akin to rules. They are proper parts of anthropological theories, but they are better viewed as contained in their prescriptive, rather than descriptive, components.

Just as speakers get along in discussions in their own languages by adhering to accepted, conventional patterns of usage, often codified in dictionaries, interpreters formulate translation rules which enable speakers of one language to get along with speakers in another language. The process of codifying usage respects behavioural evidence, but follows a pattern of justification distinctly different from that associated with descriptive hypotheses. The result is not to make interpretation unscientific, but to see it as more akin to other prescriptive elements of an empirical theory, such as theoretical definitions and methodological rules. Like these prescriptive elements, its function is *enabling*.

I suggest that translation be regarded as a kind of codification which improves the functioning of an existing set of conventions by increasing the degree to which the expectations of speakers are enhanced and social coordination is improved. Users are justified in following a manual's translational prescriptions only if they are reasonably sure that speakers of the language being translated will conform to certain conventions (whether explicitly acknowledged or not) in such a way as to fulfil mutual expectations. The important difference is that the rules that source-language speakers follow are clearly not the translational rules that manual users follow. Assuming for the sake of argument that the source community has a fairly well-codified language, what speakers follow are the codified and uncodified conventions of linguistic usage of that language. The translation manual allows receptor-language speakers optimally to conform to source-language conventions and reap all the practical benefits thereof without consciously following those conventions. Thus translational codification is a more complex affair, but otherwise the basic dynamics are the same. While it is responsive to earlier established practices, the manual's structure is partly dictated by what facilitates the various tasks of manual users – its correctness does not hinge on its describing pre-existing semantic relations.

This involves a different notion of interpretive objectivity – one that I think fits the political shift in perspective in the development literature, which trades the traditional roles of inquirer and subject in for that of stakeholders, and better fits the mix of epistemological and political considerations which constitute interpretive 'success' – especially given the complexities of agent-agendas which characterize developmental contexts.

By showing how translations could fail to be hypotheses but still respectable and working parts of empirical inquiry, I think we can address concerns which Quine shares with Hobart about viewing interpretation as the capture of propositions. It seems to me that for all the strong mentalism one finds in remarks about the aims of emic analysis – to penetrate the minds or psyches of others – there is a recurring, and more guarded behavioural definition common to many proponents of emic analysis. In voicing a central concern not to allow preconceived Western notions of 'what is going on' to guide their research, Boas, Pike, Kay, Goodenough and others argued for sensitivity to how the people they studied discriminated reality. For instance, in his discussion of the use of 'emic primitives' in studying cultures, Goodenough sometimes speaks as if there were some sort of conceptual identity between his ethnographic concepts and those of the people he studies, while at other times he speaks, more guardedly, of defining emic concepts 'in terms of whatever criteria enabled me to distinguish [...] in a manner consistent with the distinctions [...] people [...] seemed to be making' (1970, 79). Indeed, both attitudes are implicit in the following definition:

> A society's culture consists of whatever it is one has to know or believe in order to operate in a manner acceptable to its members. Culture is not a material phenomenon; it does not consist of things, people, behavior, or emotions. It is rather an organization of these things. It is the form of things that people have in mind, their models for perceiving, relating, and otherwise interpreting them. (1957, 167)

What I am suggesting is that the problematic mentalistic entanglements involved in Goodenough's related notions of emic concepts and culture are best dropped. What we should 'inherit' from ethnoscience is not its broader, and problematic, mentalistic commitments, but its methodological commitment to training interpreters in the skills of 'getting along'. My view is that we follow Quine in being suspicious of the explanatory value of speaking of 'forms people have in mind', but hold on to the insight that culture consists in what one needs to know in order to get along. For this is a definition that outlives what it was meant to define, as it makes perfect sense of the aims of translation in the 'culturally mixed' settings of developmental anthropology. 'Getting along' for the developmental anthropologist involves, as Sillitoe says, 'a search for jointly negotiated advances' (1998, 224). I think this general definition of interpretive success can be developed constructively for anthropology in general, and is especially useful in application to the complex mix of political and interpretive issues that characterize modern developmental anthropology.

My attitude toward interpretation is reflected in Turner's critique (2002) of contextualism. Against Brandom's inferential semantics, which explains the intelligibility of discourse by making explicit its underlying set of interconnected inferential and normative commitment-making rules, Turner argues that there is no 'it' to be made explicit at all. In considering a case of interpreting the meaning of the silence of a Chinese interlocutor, he argues that the interpretation of silence as expressing dislike of what had previously been said 'is a model instrumental rule of translation':

> It tells someone having one kind of expectation to construe some sign, in this case silence, as having a different meaning. Whether this is a scientifically warranted interpretation or whether an anthropologist would have come up with this characterization does not really matter. It is a quite practical rule for dealing with a situation in which one simply needs to know what people are acting as if they mean. This rule is an 'as if' in two senses. When a Chinese is silent it is 'as if' he is telling me he doesn't like what he hears, and it is an 'as if' rule in the sense that it does not depend on the sort of claim that the Chinese actually have 'in their heads' something corresponding to this rule. It is enough to know that they behave 'as if' they were following this rule, and that one can interpret what they are saying by keeping this 'as if' rule in mind, and not get into trouble.

Indeed:

> There is no particular reason that everyone would have to have the exact same interpretive hypothesis in order to understand one another, if *understand* means to get by in interacting with other people. [...] The Chinese learn something that makes them behave in a tolerably predictable way in connection with these silences, and, given this behavior, it is possible to formulate this 'as if' rule in such a way that one can more or less successfully deal with the Chinese. But there is no 'it' to be made explicit. There is a job of translation, which is governed by our imperatives or my imperatives in explaining them to you, and all this machinery such as talk about presuppositions is misleading, at least potentially, if we think of it as out there, as having independent reality and structure, and as being a domain to be described. (2003, 156)

My way of developing Quine's insights about the import of our need to rely on extra-empirical considerations to narrow down an indefinitely large range of translation manuals leaves open the possibility that there may well be a multiplicity of 'correct' interpretations guided by divergent interests of various stakeholders. Also, my emphasis on the social coordination of cultural insiders and outsiders carries no obligation to identifying any purely *emic* rule systems, nor does it compel us to consider the people being interpreted as having systematic belief sets. It may well be that their form of knowledge might turn out to be 'tacit, intuitive, experiential, informal, uncodified' as Ellen and Harris (2000, 28) claim (cf. Fischer 2004, 20).

Furthermore, I think that in carrying no commitment to identifying emic rule systems, this account largely sidesteps the concerns of Hobart and others about the universality of rationality. Although proper treatment of this controversy is outside the scope of this chapter, I would argue that the thorny issues here largely concern whether cultural groups ascribe to principles of rationality akin those familiar to what Whorf termed the 'standard average European'. My enabling account of interpretation depends more on whether people conform to such standards. We can avoid entanglement in many aspects of debates which seem to force upon us the unfortunate choice between the 'ethnocentrism of anachronism' and the 'ethnocentrism of exoticism' (see Lukes 2002 and Borofsky 1997 on the controversy about the demise of Captain Cook).

The Complex Contexts of Development

My arguments are very much in step with those who see Quine's holism considerations as entailing a significant degree of interest relativity implicit in notions of empirical correctness. This has to be the attitude one takes to development contexts. Perhaps the most significant point about these contexts is the multiplicity of intersecting agendas of the various interest groups and individuals involved, compounded by the fact that development teams rarely enter anything remotely resembling pristine cultural territory. Indeed, as Olivier de Sardan remarks, these projects 'take place in a milieu that has already experienced previous interventions which have left their mark', and this history of interaction 'is also interlaced with tales of corruption, patron–client relationships, bureaucratic tyranny and incompetence – four fundamental themes' (2005, 139). As a result, much of what determines the direction and prospects for success and failure of a project is constituted by environmental and social factors outside of the development team's control. Thus it is important that development teams realize that, whatever their perceptions of their role might be, they are likely players in a number of different social scenarios, and *what* they are doing and *how* it is assessed will be understood differently in light of differing agendas. Moreover, the contrasting agendas are not simply those of the team as opposed to the target population. These differing agendas define what Olivier de Sardan terms 'various levels of coherence and compatibility': 1) the internal coherence of the team's technical model; 2) the project's compatibility with the economic policy of the nations involved; 3) its conformity to the norms of the funding agencies; 4) the project's own 'internal dynamic' – i.e., 'its "organizational logics", its specific constraints, its dysfunctions, its "informal economy", which are quite different from the official flowchart'. It is in this last context where phenomena he terms 'selection' (that is, the inevitability that target groups and individuals will select from the 'development package' what they deem useful) and 'side-tracking' (the deviation of target groups from development agency expectations owing to the fact that the reasons target groups adopt development measures often conflict with the reasons development experts have for proposing those measures) are most clearly manifest: how well the project achieves its intended goals is going to depend on how it is adapted by target populations to *their* purposes (2005, 141, 144–5). The culture-concept's limitations as a diachronic tool of analysis, noted by Boas, become increasingly problematic, given the complexity of the social interaction involved in development contexts. Developmental anthropology presents us with a more complex set of coordination problems, insofar as a wider range of stakeholder groups, with their respective, potentially contrasting aims is involved. A complex multiplicity of coordination problems is involved in the developmental anthropologist's interpretive efforts. The complexity, and the very open possibilities of 'side-tracking', stem both from the social milieu of the recipient group and from the multiplicity of theoretical and political agendas imported by the development team.

I argue that translational correlations are more akin to the prescriptive, rather than the descriptive elements of scientific theories. That is, they are more akin, not to hypotheses or observation statements, but to rules of inference and hypothesis acceptance, theoretical definitions, etc., which make up the prescriptive component of theories; and although the adequacy of these elements still hinges in large part on the empirical success of theories, they are not 'confirmed' in the ways that descriptive items are. Their relationship to the observational base is different. To regard translations as rules and not as descriptive hypotheses, and to regard the charity principle as a rule, not a description of mental or neural structure, is only to shift each from the descriptive component to the enabling, prescriptive component of empirical explanation. As such, their 'correctness' is measured in terms of how well they facilitate interaction. In adapting Goodenough's definition of internal understanding as knowing what one needs to know in order to 'get along' in a society, I draw no sharp line between novices and cognoscenti. There is no pre-existing set of structures which one has grasped and the other has not. The sophisticated interpreter gets along in a wider range of contexts than the unsophisticated.

It is especially important to realize that I invoke the notion of correctness as enabling one to 'get along' in a way which does not import the various problematic assumptions associated with the culture myth. I take seriously Olivier de Sardan's concerns with the 'culturalist' assumptions of many anthropologists, assumptions he sees as obstructing the understanding of the multiplicity of competing interests typical of developmental contexts, a feature which makes the understanding of appropriation and the anticipation of side-tracking the primary objectives. It is wrong to assume that the culturalist emphasis on in-group similarities and out-group differences is somehow validated by the way things are. That is the culture myth at work.

Olivier de Sardan finds more useful for understanding development contexts the agency models of Arce and Long (see, for example: Arce and Long 2000, Long and Long 1992), which organize interpretation around the understanding of various agents and their interests, and which derive from conflict models of sociology associated with Gluckman and the Manchester school, which was first, he argues, 'to accord systematic attention to social reality seen from the angle of conflicts' (2005, 188). Depending on the degree to which anthropology is still wedded to the culture myth, it would be wise to consider whether the conflict models inspired by Manchester-school sociology may be more fruitful for development application.

If success in interpretation is measured in terms of how well it facilitates 'our' capacity to 'get along' (a complicated matter, especially in development contexts), then ethical political considerations play an undeniable role as criteria of adequacy. A government agency applying criteria which derive from an overtly oppressive political agenda could rest on a slipshod interpretation of social discourse. Or the resulting interpretation could serve the mutually reinforcing interests of the government agency and certain dominant figures within the social group being studied; or it could serve the coalescing interests of a local agency, a Western political interest group and local figures, etc. Imagine the most oppressive situation you can – imagine success being measured in terms of 'getting along', as effectively promoting its agenda. These measures of 'getting along' might well be at odds with those of other groups – and simply *wrong* as measured by any feasible ethical standards. Translational correctness has to go beyond the mere capacity to 'get along', and be rooted, finally, in ethical/political evaluation. Once we dispel the illusion that there is some pre-existing symbol system which defines cultural identity, we eliminate the basis for axiomatic assertions of inevitable victimization of recipient groups, or for axiomatic demands to attribute epistemic parity. Each case has to be considered on its merits.

References

Agrawal, A. 1995. 'Dismantling the Divide between Indigenous and Scientific Knowledge'. *Development and Change* 26: 413–39.

———. 1999. 'On Power and Indigenous Knowledge'. In *Cultural and Spiritual Values of Biodiversity*, edited by D. A. Posey, 177–80. Nairobi: United Nations Environment Programme and London: Intermediate Technology Publications.

Alatas, S. H. 2000. 'Intellectual Imperialism'. *Southeast Asian Journal of Social Science* 28: 23–45.

Arce, A. and E. Fisher, eds. 2003. 'Knowledge Interfaces and Practices of Negotiation: Cases from a Women's Group in Bolivia and an Oil Refinery in Wales'. In *Negotiating Local Knowledge: Identity, Power and Situated Practice in Development*, edited by J. Pottier, A. Bicker and P. Sillitoe, 74–97. London: Pluto Press.

Arce, A. and N. Long, eds. 2000. *Anthropology, Development and Modernity*. London: Routledge.

Beteille, A. 1998. 'The Idea of Indigenous People'. *Current Anthropology* 39: 187–191.

Bicker, A., P. Sillitoe and J. Pottier, eds. 2004. *Development and Local Knowledge*. London: Routledge.

Borofsky, R. 1997. 'Cook, Lono, Obeyesekere, and Sahlins'. *Current Anthropology* 38: 255–82.

Brandom, R. 1994. *Making It Explicit: Reasoning, Representing, and Discursive Commitment.* Cambridge, MA: Harvard University Press.

Cleveland, D. 1998. Comment on Sillitoe, 'The Development of Indigenous Knowledge'. *Current Anthropology* 39: 237–8.

Ellen, R. 1998. Comment on Sillitoe, 'The Development of Indigenous Knowledge'. *Current Anthropology* 39: 238–9.

_____. 2002. '"Déjà Vu, All Over Again": Reinvention and Progress in Applying Local Knowledge to Development'. In P. Sillitoe, A. Bicker, J. Pottier 2002, 235–58.

Ellen R. and H. Harris, eds. 2000. 'Introduction: Indigenous Environmental Knowledge and its Transformations'. In *Indigenous Environmental Knowledge and its Transformations*, edited by R. Ellen, P. Parkes and A. Bicker, 1–34. Amsterdam: Harwood Press.

Fairhead, J. 1992. 'Indigenous Technical Knowledge and Natural Resources Management in Sub-Saharan Africa: A Critical Review'. Paper commissioned by the Social Science Council, New York.

Feleppa, R. 1986. 'Emics, Etics, and Social Objectivity'. *Current Anthropology* 27: 243–55.

_____. 1988. *Culture, Translation, and Understanding: Philosophical Problems in the Study of Culture.* Albany: State University of New York Press.

Fischer, M. 2004. 'Powerful Knowledge: Applications in a Cultural Context'. In *Development and Local Knowledge*, edited by A. Bicker, P. Sillitoe and J. Pottier, 19–30. London: Routledge.

Friedman, J. 1994. *Cultural Identity and Global Process*. London: Sage Press.

Goodenough, W. 1957. 'Cultural Anthropology and Linguistics'. In *Report of the Seventh Annual Roundtable Meeting on Language and Linguistics*, edited by P. Garvin, 36–9. Georgetown University Monograph Series in Language and Linguistics, no. 9. Washington, DC: Harper and Row.

Goodenough, W. 1970. *Description and Comparison in Cultural Anthropology*. Hawthorne, NY: Aldine.

Goonatilake, S. 1999. *Toward a Global Science: Mining Civilizational Knowledge*. Bangalore: Vistaar.

Grillo, R. D. 1997. 'Discourses of Development: The View from Anthropology'. In *Discourses of Development: Anthropological Perspectives*, edited by R. D. Grillo and R. L. Stirrat, 1–33. Oxford: Berg.

Grillo, R. D. and R. L. Stirrat, eds. 1997. *Discourses of Development: Anthropological Perspectives*. Oxford: Berg.

Hobart, M. 1993. 'Introduction: the Growth of Ignorance?' In *An Anthropological Critique of Development*, edited by Hobart, 1–30. London: Routledge.

Long, N. and A. Long. 1992. *Battlefields of Knowledge: the Interlocking of Theory and Practice in Social Research and Development*. London: Routledge.

Lukes, S. 2002. 'Different Cultures, Different Rationalities?' *History of the Human Sciences* 13: 3–18.

Olivier de Sardan, J. 2005. *Anthropology and Development: Understanding Contemporary Social Change*. London: Zed Books.

Pottier, J. 1997. 'Towards An Ethnography of Participatory Appraisal'. *Discourses of Development: Anthropological Perspectives*, edited by R. D. Grillo and R. L. Stirrat, 203–27. Oxford: Berg.

_____. 2003. 'Negotiating Local Knowledge: An Introduction'. In *Negotiating Local Knowledge: Identity, Power and Situated Practice in Development*, edited by J. Pottier, A. Bicker and P. Sillitoe 2003, 1–29. London: Pluto Press.

Pottier, J., A. Bicker and P. Sillitoe, eds. 2003. *Negotiating Local Knowledge: Identity, Power and Situated Practice in Development*. London: Pluto Press.

Purcell, T. and A. Onjoro. 2000. 'Indigenous Knowledge, Power and Parity: Models of Knowledge Integration'. In *Participating in Development: Approaches to Indigenous Knowledge*, edited by P. Sillitoe, A. Bicker and J. Pottier, 162–88. London: Routledge.

Quine, W. V. 1960. *Word and Object*. Cambridge, MA: MIT Press.

Richards, P. 1993. 'Cultivation: Knowledge or Performance'. In *An Anthropological Critique of Development*, edited by M. Hobart, 61–78. London: Routledge.

Schönhuth, M. 2002. 'Negotiating with Knowledge at Development Interfaces: Anthropology and the Quest for Participation'. In *Participating in Development: Approaches to Indigenous Knowledge*, edited by P. Sillitoe, A. Bicker and J. Pottier, 139–62. London: Routledge.

Turner, S. 2002. *Brains/Practices/Relativism: Social Theory After Cognitive Science*. Chicago: University of Chicago Press.

Sillitoe, P. 1998. 'The Development of Indigenous Knowledge: A New Applied Anthropology'. *Current Anthropology* 39: 223–52.

_____. 2002a. 'Participant Observation to Participatory Development'. In *Participating in Development: Approaches to Indigenous Knowledge*, edited by P. Sillitoe, A. Bicker and J. Pottier, 1–23. London: Routledge.

_____. 2002b. 'Globalizing Indigenous Knowledge'. In *Participating in Development: Approaches to Indigenous Knowledge*, edited by P. Sillitoe, A. Bicker and J. Pottier, 108–38. London: Routledge.

Sillitoe, P. and A. Bicker. 2004. 'Introduction: Hunting for Theory, Gathering Ideology'. In *Development and Local Knowledge*, edited by A. Bicker, P. Sillitoe and J. Pottier, 1–18. London: Routledge.

Sillitoe, P., A. Bicker, J. Pottier, eds. 2002. *Participating in Development: Approaches to Indigenous Knowledge*. London: Routledge.

Sinha, V. 2000. 'Moving Beyond Critique: Practising the Social Sciences in the Context of Globalization, Postmodernity, and Postcoloniality'. *Southeast Asian Journal of Social Science* 28: 67–104.

Smith, L. T. 1999. *Decolonising Methodologies: Research and Indigenous Peoples*. London: Zed Books.

Chapter 20

NOTIONS OF FRIENDSHIP IN PHILOSOPHICAL AND ANTHROPOLOGICAL THOUGHT

Heidrun Friese

Within the Western philosophical tradition, the notion of friendship indicates relations to the *self*, an *other* and the political *community*. It is a practice constituting subjectivity, personal, partial and particularistic bonds, and at the same time it articulates specific moral/ethical expectations of behaviour and universalistic demands.[1] Friendship fosters goodness, reciprocity and generosity, entails mutual trust, solidarity and cooperation. Thus, it creates both social ties and is related to the political order of a community, its ethical prerequisites and the ways in which common matters are negotiated.

Given that friendship cross-cuts what is considered as making up the Western subject and the social and political realm, historical notions and cultural practices of friendship should be at the centre of social and political thought. Theoretical and methodological decisions, however, have impeded a comprehensive engagement with these relationships.

In social and political thought, competition, struggle, conflict and antagonism were seen as basic features of society and the political. From Hobbes's anthropology – the understanding of the state of nature as *bellum omnium contra omnes* in which the desire to winning fame, rivalry and suspicion reign – to modern versions of liberalism and utilitarianism: human beings act according to self-interest and are tied by the beneficial consequences of agonistic behaviour in the public sphere. They are calculating agents who assess gain and loss and opt for profitable preferences, as theories of rational choice assume. Marxist concepts of interests, contest and class struggle regarded – in accordance with classical economic theory – conflict, profit and competition for economic and political supremacy as the driving forces of society, and thus, solidarity develops merely as a function of antagonism as well. Similarly, and related to Antonio Gramsci's concept of 'cultural hegemony', antagonism and conflictual negotiation constitute the political (Laclau 1990, 35). Not least, Carl Schmitt's famous opposition between 'friend and enemy' (1994) reflects theoretical approaches emphasizing conflict and antagonism as main components of the political.

Accordingly, notions of friendship have hardly ever attracted anthropological attention. This astonishing blind spot is part of both methodological procedures and theoretical assumptions. The notion is bound to methodological decisions and modes of othering that develop between oppositions such as subjectivity, particularity and emotion vs distance, objectivity and generality. This is particularly evident if we consider that during anthropological fieldwork intimate relations to a singular other develop (Kulick and Willson 1995), whereas anthropological discourse discloses such experiences of amity and friendship. It is bound to theoretical decisions, such as the relegation of particularistic, personal relationships to a secondary aspect of social and political organization: the other was hardly seen in his irreducible singularity, but as representing social structures, systems of symbols, cosmologies and cultural imperatives (and it was the task of the anthropologist to decipher the principles, cultural grammars and symbolic orders). The aim of ethnographic representation, therefore, was to neglect the particular in order to grasp social structure (its rules, functions, etc.) and the generalized other. Secondly, social integration was seen either as the result of normative consensus (as in the Durkheimian or the Parsionian versions), or as a result of the resolution of structural conflicts, as in theories of conflict, and thus, to latent or manifest (political) antagonism between social groups. Whereas 'the gift', positive or negative reciprocity, has been identified as one of the fundamental mechanisms of social bonds and social life (Osteen 2002), solidarity and generosity have been almost exclusively attributed to kinship relations or to antagonistic practices of expenditure.

In order to engage with these tensions, and given that we always already speak 'within the tradition of a certain concept of friendship' (Derrida 1998, 634), in the following, some aspects of the notion within the Western philosophical legacies will be addressed. As will be shown, anthropological engagement with these relationships (Bell and Coleman 1999) cannot escape this heritage, even if it is by no means homogenous or without rifts and ruptures. Notions of friendship therefore, are inhabited by various tensions: the tension between particularistic and universalistic orders; between closeness and distance, the private and the public; between self, other and the community; between autonomy, self-government and interdependence and relatedness; between solidarity, mutual trust and antagonism and conflict.

The argument developed in the following will proceed in two steps. In the first step, dimensions composing the philosophies of friendship (section 1) will be addressed: the relationship that the individual entails with him- or herself (friendship and selfhood), the relationship with others (friendship and the other) and finally the relationship to the political (friendship and the community). Against this background, the politics of friendship (section 2) will be sketched in order to show that anthropological engagement cannot escape the tensions between obligation and voluntariness, profit and generosity, as well as between universalism and particularity, which have marked the Western philosophical notions of friendship until today.

1. Philosophies of Friendship

Friendship and selfhood

In the Western convention and in a long and entangled historical movement, friendship (*philia*, *philos*) is emancipated from kinship, in which virtue, mutuality, reciprocal support and emotions are interrelated. However, in the philosophical tradition and bound to 'self love', the constitution of the 'self' is associated with a bond to the friend. Friendship requires not only an amicable relationship with oneself, but allows for a mirroring of the self in the other and enables one to recognize oneself as 'alter ego' (*allos autos*).

In the *Nicomachean Ethics*, Aristotle distinguishes three forms of friendship, a distinction that was widely accepted through the seventeenth century and is influential until today. The first one is characterized by 'pre-eminence' and 'excellence', and establishes the noble and virtuous friendship, in which one wishes the friend excellence and the best for his own sake. The second one is 'pleasure', a friendship in which one loves the other due to his wit and enjoyable nature. Finally, the third one is established by 'utility', a friendship from which one profits (Aristotle 1934, 218 [*NE* 1156b9–28]). And as only the first of these categories is not based on accident, lacks superficiality and contingency, and has an enduring character, it is the sole form which can be called true friendship; only with it are the requirements of friendship truly and entirely satisfied. The two other types of friendship can thus be seen as modifications of true friendship and share characteristics including the responsibility of 'help' and 'reciprocity'. With an evident reference to Plato, it is also bound to self-love, as complete friendship with oneself. Friendship with the self is prerequisite for friendship with an other, just as is concern and 'care for the self' (Foucault, 1989). A fundamental element of true and noble friendship – differentiating it qualitatively from benevolence and sympathy, which one might well harbour for others – is 'self-recognition' and the friend is a mirror allowing for self-recognition.

'We are not able to see what we are from ourselves […] as then when we wish to see our own face we do so by looking into the mirror, in the same way when we wish to know ourselves we can obtain that knowledge by looking at our friend', states Aristotle in the *Magna Moralia* (1915 [*MM* 1213a15–24]), an insight which will be re-read in the Western tradition (not least by Friedrich Nietzsche). Self-recognition is hardly understood as psychological introspection, but primarily signifies the recognition of the reciprocally shared. Being with oneself is thus equitable with being with an other and belongs to *eudaimonia*, the practical achieving of the virtuous good life that approaches humans to the divine and its order.

When Aristotle exclaims (with Socrates), 'Oh friends, there is no friend', he addresses this tense relationship which would dominate later philosophical debates as well: as only the few are so virtuous, only few appreciate the friend for its own sake. True friendship is more than a rare entity; friendship, in the sense of completeness, is exclusive and hardly possible 'with many', and it needs time (1915, 223 [1158a9–28]). *Eudaimonia*, the good life, is inconceivable without friendship: 'for no one would choose to live without friends, but possessing all other good things'. Additionally, friendship appears to be the bond of the state; and lawgivers seem to set more store by it than they do by justice, for to promote concord, which seems akin to friendship, is their chief aim (1934, 451–3 [*NE* 1155a4]).

Since Plato and Aristotle, friendship does not belong to the realm of passion and its poignant, affecting intensity, but on the contrary, to that of wisdom, ethics and virtue. From this perspective, ideal friendship is possible only among men and between equals in degree and value. Accordingly, and bound to a long tradition of images of mythic-heroic male friendship – which is basically related to warfare, danger, brotherhood in arms and solidarity against an enemy (Vincent-Buffault 1995, 15), as in the examples of Orestes and Pylades or Patroklos and Achilles – the social *imaginaire* does not supply images of friendship among women. The 'natural' relationship assigned to women is that to man and children, female subjectivity is constituted through the devoted care of husband, house and family. At the same time, friendship is bound to autonomy, which women, due to their pre-ethic nature and dependant position, cannot seize. The concept of friendship thus mirrors the orders of gender, it is inscribed into the extensive and widely branched (symbolic) separation of autonomy and dependence, external and internal, male sociality and female spheres.

This relationship is marked by a doubled exclusion in the ethical-political-philosophical arena. First, it rules out the possibility of 'friendship between women', and second, it excludes the friendship 'between a man and a woman' (Derrida 1988, 642). The philosophical paradigm imputes a – more or less – sublimated form of male homosexuality and constructs a space defining the sexual identity of human beings (Vincent-Buffault 1995, 15).

Friendship has historically been a component of kinship. Subsequently the particular relationship to an other became an independent, sovereign relationship that is to mark human autonomy, self-governance and free will. It allows for the constitution of subjectivity and self-recognition, it involves both (male) camaraderie and a long-lasting reciprocal and ethical bond, and yet it is problematic and precarious. Simultaneously, mutual entrustment is its core feature and includes reciprocity, care, recognition and respect. Selfhood and subjectivity, therefore, are relational: they are constituted in an interpersonal space created by equality, trust, (spiritual) proximity and mutuality, solidarity and recognition.

Friendship and the other

For Aristotle, 'all friendship [...] involves community' (1934, 497 [*NE* 1161b15]) and friendship is primarily bound to the community and the obligations of its different legal relations and terms of agreement. As such, its demands are required of travel companions, comrades in arms, among companions, between man and woman, children and parent, brothers and sisters – even hospitality belongs in this set.[2]

Yet friendship is still differentiated from other social relations. As opposed to the ascriptive relations of kinship, friendship is not assigned by birth, but is – both as a moral/ethical relationship and as a relationship of liability – freely chosen and thus belongs to the realm of human autonomy. Friendship cannot be forced; like a gift, it is given voluntarily and refers to human autonomy as well as – in its actual realization and its practice – enhances virtue and allows for human perfection.

'In every friendship there are additionally the dimensions of relating to an other that appears as concrete, irreplaceable singular person' (Eichler 2000, 220): this relationship proposes an other in his irreplaceable singularity, and just this singularity, the unmistakable character of the relationship to an other, enacts the community of friends. This relationship not only implies autonomy, but equality as well – such as the progeny of natural rights discourse with its emphasis upon universal philanthropy. Ideally it dissolves the hierarchies and differences in social status, and binds equals who recognize each other as equal. The basis of this relationship is proximity, mutual care and both recognition and reciprocity. Between apparent unequals, such as the literate and the uneducated, the poor and rich, there is likely to be, Aristotle notes, 'friendship based on utility [...] for a person desiring something which he happens to lack will give something else in return for it' (1934, 483–5 [*NE* 1159b]).

In Christianity the primacy of friendship is dissolved. St Augustine demands love of the friend in god, *philia* and *amicitia* become *caritas* and the love of god unites humankind (Eichler 2000, 216). However, at the threshold of modernity and with reference to his friendship with Étienne de la Boétie, Michel de Montaigne describes not only antique forms of friendship – that of kinship, sociability, hospitality – but assesses this extraordinary relationship. Whereas, in his view, familial relationships are dictated by nature and defined by law – love to women is volatile and erratic, marriage a business arrangement serving 'other ends' (Montaigne, 1994, 136) – friendship develops through free choice. It is oblivious to 'sexual need or personal greed', is not a relationship which originates in or is maintained for 'public or personal necessity'. Relationships that are less 'beautiful and noble as other reasons, purposes and expectations are blended together' (Montaigne, 1998, 99). In friendship there is no business and no trade, it is concerned exclusively with itself, it is lasting, and reaches – as *eudaimonia* – its fulfilment in endurance and the lack of instrumental functionality.

The practices that make up friendship and its substantial articulations, as well as the implicit or explicit demands and expectations that are to avoid disappointment and conflict, given that obligations cannot be sued, has been subject to historical change (see, among others, Langer 1994). Philosophical inheritance however, maintained – albeit in historically different manners – the differentiation between 'instrumental' and noble, virtuous, 'altruistic' friendship.

Still, Kant's imperative to view the other as a goal in itself, and not as a means to an end, confirms such a view. Kant resumes the familiar tension between instrumental and unconditional friendship, between universalism and particularism, between binding security and emancipating freedom. The categorical imperative and its universalism seem to prohibit both the concept of eudaimonism as well as the particularism of the unique character of amicable relations. However, Kant treats friendship as the highest responsibility of co-humanity (*Mitmenschlichkeit*). Mutual recognition – 'equal mutual love and respect' – as purpose (*Zweck*) 'does not produce the complete happiness of life, the adoption of this ideal in their disposition towards the other', however, includes 'the dignity [*Würde*] of being happy' (Kant 1996, 584–5). Simultaneously, Kant relates the relationship with an other to that with the community, given that he sees 'moral friendship' as the perfect realization of human sociability (Kant 1996, 586; 1997 A152).

Friendship is considered a relationship based on the affirmation of a shared conviction (i.e., an ethically based alliance, a union between men) that was thus founded on a doubled exclusion: 'female nature' is to exclude friendship between and with women. The public-political sphere is governed by autonomy, will, volition and rational choices, in sum: the male subject. Ideal friendship should be separated from sexual attraction and so the question as to whether friendship can exist between man and woman at all was discussed well into the nineteenth century.

Friendship is a relationship which – in historically different ways – develops between profit, leanings, desires and universal principles, the absence of purpose, between private bonds and public politics, a relation which was fashioned in Hellenistic and ancient Roman philosophy (Cicero is certainly the most striking example). In this context, the relationship between the articulations and moral duties of friendship and social responsibilities to the state and community – and connected to that, the question of particularity and universalism – have constantly been reiterated. This voluntarily given, accepted and reciprocated relationship is, on the one hand, always singular and particular, and due to uniqueness cannot be universalized. On the other, it became a model for the political.

Friendship and the community

If 'all friendship [...] involves community', then its demands are required of travel companions, comrades in arms, among companions, between man and woman, children and parent, brothers and sisters; even hospitality belongs in this set. However, the three types of friendship are as well related to the political constitution of the *polis* and the way it allows for having things in common (1934, 229 [*NE* 1159b29–1160a16]). Aristotle distinguishes three basic forms of government: kingdom, aristocracy, timocracy; and corresponding subordinate forms: tyranny, oligarchy and democracy. Forms of friendship exist in all *polis* forms, although in tyranny 'where there is nothing in common between ruler and ruled, there can be no friendship between them either' (1934, 497 [*NE* 1161a]). In democracy, on the contrary, this exists to a much greater extent because 'citizens being equal have many things in common' (1934, 497 [*NE* 1161b]).

Friendship had long been one of the 'determinant categories of social ethics [...] within which traditions of the ancient and Christian ethics did survive as well as did elements of natural law and political thought' (Mauser and Becker-Cantarino 1991, vii). With the old dualism of 'community and society', friendship has been allocated a space where behaviour, state and social order are bound and friendship becomes a model for the political order.

Especially in romanticism, it was settled in a political space (and educated women embodied a community in which equals and elective kin could encounter in friendship and love).

However, Western liberal political theories maintain the primacy of individual free choice and the protection of the individual's legitimate interests. Thus liberal political orders cannot postulate binding norms and values (i.e., that of friendship), but only propose formal procedures which permit democratic negotiation of interests and public welfare. In the contemporary socio-philosophic confrontation of liberalism and communitarianism the controversy over substantial or formal political order is invigorated. In this debate we may discover the first points of reference for regaining the qualitative and substantial significance of particular relations, loyalties, cooperation, trust and mutual engagement of concrete individuals (Eichler 2000, 234) that negates universalistic ethics based on formal procedures.

The mediation of equality and singularity is that which should also characterize democracy, and Derrida outlines a *Politics of Friendship* (1994) that considers singularity as an irreducible part of justice and of a democracy always yet to come, in which hardly ascriptive relationships (family, nation, culture) are decisive as to 'who is heard in the public sphere' (Critchley 1998). What is vital here is not the perspective of equal treatment of everyone, but on the contrary: the particular individual in his difference to all others, and it is precisely this difference that enters into tension with equal treatment. 'An appropriate social form in which the experience of this tension of the general and individual particularity can be made, is friendship' (Eichler 2000, 236). On the one hand, friendship seems to be 'essentially foreign and unamenable' (Derrida 1998, 641) of the *res publica*, whereas on the other, philosophical discourse has related friendship to virtue and justice, ethical and political reason. The inexhaustible thought of thinking friendship thus allows to cross-cut established oppositions, it allows for a political thought beyond these dualisms and its boundaries.

However, social sciences discourse inevitably operates within this context, it cannot elude Western philosophical inheritance and constantly rewrites its inherent tensions.

2. 'Politics of Friendship'

When Friedrich Tenbruck rediscovered 'friendship' as an object for (at least German) sociology, and lamented that sociology and specialized sociologists hardly ever addressed 'friendship and personal relationships', he related this remarkable void to the perception of friendship as a merely 'private, a non-regulated relation of choice' that can be 'explained only by individuality'.[3]

Sociology, on the contrary, is orientated toward 'the society' and does not deal 'with the individual'; it examines social institutions, 'power, social stratification, economy, family and similar realms of being', that are 'prerequisites of living together' (Tenbruck 1964, 435).[4] At the same time, amicable relations have been inscribed into the paradigm of social differentiation and increasing individualization of modernity, which dramatically changed the meaning of friendship. According to this paradigm, friendship lost its all-encompassing meaning in modernity, and serves to maximize personal gain while losing the connection to the common and, thus, to the political.

Yet in this discursive tradition friendship is based on that which people have in common, it is based on that which human beings share, and these relations and bonds are made up by mutual trust, solidarity and recognition. Characteristics and important criteria of the relationship are additionally autonomy and singularity as well as equality, reciprocity and the dimension of temporality.

Obligation and voluntariness

From a 'classical' anthropological (and sociological) perspective, the most important human relations are kinship, corporative groups and institutions that are based on territorial, ethnic and religious belonging and the allocation of political power. Inscribed in different theoretical approaches, anthropological research focussed on – more or less – sanctioned forms of relationships. Anthropological perspectives thus privileged forms of relationships similar to kinship which are (ritually) certified, formalized and sanctioned. Therefore, institutionalized forms of friendship such as bond friendship, blood-brotherhood, the creation of 'fictive kin relationships' and godparent–child relationships attracted anthropological attention (Paine, 1969). The actual function of these relationships was seen as a possibility to express emotions beyond the immediate circle of kinship, allowing for psychological, economic and social advantages. Even if injury of expectations and trust could not formally be sanctioned, the duty to honour this relationship was seen as a functional part of the moral order in a given society. Accordingly, reciprocal duties were to include hospitality and security for the traveller, gifts, services in burial ceremonies, support in (legal) confrontations, the prohibition of approaching the other's woman, the commandment not to mock, the commandment not to deny a daughter in marriage, etc. In short, in this view the blood brother was recommended to support, and this relationship was thus considered a mechanism to broaden relationships (see Evans-Pritchard 1933; Firth 1936).

These institutionalized and ritually concealed relationships have been portrayed as voluntary and particularistic, as they bind specific men with their individual, special and unmistakable characteristics. If from this perspective the character of individual 'chooseness' is evidenced, then it is only to be immediately minimalized, because the observation of the substantial contents is instantly reduced to a social function. These forms of relationships thus were assigned the function of mediating tensions within societies.

Bound to theoretical orientations that stressed structure, function and social integration, anthropological attention was primarily on friendships that strengthen alliance, trade and exchange in societies based on kinship relations. Additionally, the 'savage' non-Westerner was hardly considered as a singular human being or as an individual, but as a 'representative' of unquestioned traditions, blindly repeated customs and timeless institutions. Correspondingly, the idiosyncratic, affective and nonpolitical dimension of these relationships was hardly ever addressed. The above-mentioned tension between generality and particularity defined the concept and interpretation of friendship and this dichotomy 'has always separated the experience, the notion and the interpretation of friendship', and dictated additional oppositions such as 'secret, private, invisible, unreadable, apolitical' as opposed to the public, visibility, decipherable and political (Derrida 1994, 194–5). Given the bias on the political already at work in philosophical perspectives, friendship among women, therefore, could hardly attract anthropological attention. This tension was also internalized and perpetuated if friendships were situated between 'profit and generosity' and – not surprisingly – anthropological perspectives largely privileged to envision one form.

Profit and generosity

The dualism of profit and altruism has been of special interest in anthropological research addressing so-called 'complex societies', particularly peasant societies of Latin America and the Mediterranean. Eric Wolf distinguished between 'expressive-emotional' and 'instrumental' friendships (Wolf 1966; Reina 1959). This perspective sets 'true friendship', being-with, companionship, trust, intimacy and the sharing of secrets, respect and recognition, reciprocity and solidarity which form a moral space against calculation, and the promotion of social and economic advantage. Stressing these aspects, friendship is thus hardly a personal preference, but a result of strategy, calculated personal interests and gain. The humanistic ideal of 'true friendship' –endowed, as we have seen, with a long tradition and certainly not based upon strategic considerations for ones own profit and personal advantage – is inverted. Once established, this dualism became very difficult to transcend. If not explicit, it was implicit in almost all accounts (reflecting ongoing anthropological discussions on the 'pure gift', altruism and benefit as well).

Subsequently, the tension between personal advantage, altruism and generosity had significant influence on perspectives – such as network analysis or 'the theory of practice' proposed by Pierre Bourdieu – stressing the dynamics of the establishment and the maintenance of friendship and mutual exchange. According to these perspectives, instrumental relationships are bound to specific forms of social organization – basically in the Mediterranean – that are to be based upon the primacy of family solidarity, agonistic segments and a strong local identification. The political and economic spheres in these societies – in which the weak central state could establish neither a monopoly of violence, nor universalistic mechanisms of administration and control – are to be based upon the daily politics of 'friends of friends' (Boissevain 1978) and short-term, goal-oriented 'action-sets' (Meyer 1966), coalitions and alliances. Political and economic power is the outcome of networks and the exchange of personal 'favours', the 'social capital' (Bourdieu) of friendship hardly ever disinterested.

With increasing mobility – relations crossing local or national borders, 'globalized friends' and transnational networks – friendships that are to guarantee economic advantage, distinction and social benefits have been emphasized. If women largely seem to be excluded from these networks, then friendship is a relationship which develops between personal bonds and public politics, it is a relationship that is always coded according the (symbolical) orders of gender.[5] However, these dualisms forcefully illustrate a theoretical constellation that relates the singular human being to the political order and juxtaposes particularity and universality.

Universalism and particularity

In most accounts, 'modern' liberal democratic and market-oriented nation-states are to perform according to impersonal and universalistic principles. These are to be legally anchored and to operate independently from concrete individuals and circumstances. Accordingly, liberal economic market structure is defined by the impersonal mechanisms of supply and demand. Political power is delegated and limited by the rules of representative democracy (and the separation of powers). Bureaucracy functions according to rules of rational authority and business in pursuit of instrumental rationalities (Weber 1921/22).

In 'modern' societies in which universalistic rules prevail, as Shmuel Eisenstadt (1956) argued, (ritualized) friendships become obsolete and (alleged) 'traditional' relations are situated in opposition to 'modern' societies. Such a modernization paradigm prevailed for a long time and determined anthropological understandings of friendship. Once inscribed into the scheme of modernization and development, friendships could be considered only as 'residual' or at best 'supplementary' (Pitt-Rivers 1976).

Developing on the work of Georg Simmel, for whom friendship can only be 'differentiated friendship' in fragmented modern life, Friedrich Tenbruck (1964, 453) described this relationship as a 'supplement of an incomplete social structure' and as a paradigm for personal relationships whose overall, comprehensive meaning is dissolved with progressive social differentiation and individualization in modern society. In such a social constellation, partial relationships serving specific and instrumental purposes dominate.

Additionally, anthropological perspectives have – normatively more or less based upon Max Weber's ideal type of rational-bureaucratic rule (*Herrschaft*) and its (alleged) impersonal, impartial and universalistic mechanisms – assigned personal and amicable relationships in specific paradigms and theoretical frameworks. Defined as 'dyadic relationships' (Foster, 1961), as a 'real' system opposing the 'official' system (Galt, 1974), located as a part of 'social networks' and 'egocentric' coalitions and 'non-groups' (Boissevain and Mitchell, 1973; Boissevain, 1978), and as a specific aspect of social practice or a specific historical configuration in the political context, these approaches share commonalties as far as they consider personal and particular relationships and profit-maximizing friendships as being to opposed to universalistic mechanisms of law, rule and administration.

Concepts of 'friendship' have thus been seen as being opposed to (historically specific) notions of a political and economical order and its relationships, which are not based on impersonal and universalistic principles and procedures that are to guarantee impartiality. Friendship is located in a space in which personal relations challenge universalistic mechanisms of rule and control (or, as has been argued, they are to create an authentic personal space opposed to abstract equality and the 'iron cage' of bureaucracy, which might even have a 'subversive' effect). From this point of view, claims of (liberal) universalism become self-deceptive and are opposed to the demand that personal and particular relations of friendship should be taken into account.

Tied to philosophical notions, the concept 'friendship' is methodically bound to the poles of subjectivity and objectivity, emotion and distance, particularity and generality. Within the framework of social and political theory, friendship has been – although in different ways – inscribed into paradigms of social structure, function and integration, the maximizing of profit and instrumental strategy; and thus, their substance and quality has been reduced, flattened and missed. Friendship in societies organized by ties of kinship has been related to obligation and voluntariness; whereas in 'modern' societies the tension between 'profitability and propensity', individual strategies of calculation and advantage, and the validity of universalistic rules as opposed to particularistic relationships has been emphasized. Friendship has thus been subjected to the paradigm of (alleged) 'traditional societies' vs. individualization in so-called 'modern societies'. At the same time, however, it is again liberated for the relation to an irreducible and singular other.

Friendship creates a personal bond and a social link. However, it crisscrosses and troubles the current predominant narratives of social and political thought. The anthropological engagement with these human bonds cannot escape its philosophical legacy. Anthropological thought, however, might endeavour at subverting these established dualisms and the inherent discursive components, the deeply rooted symbolical references and normative narratives that sustain and perpetuate them. What is vital, then, is not trying to find a position 'outside' these powerful narratives, but a critical reworking within that matrix and a critical genealogy of its own practices. A reflexive anthropological engagement with these human bonds, and the constitution of what is considered to be the common, might open a space in which the established dualisms in the Western philosophical legacy to which it has been tied can be destabilized.

Notes

1 My thanks go to Maurice Aymard, who in 2001, generously as ever, allowed me to stay at the Maison des Sciences de l'Homme and to engage with the topic. I would like to thank as well the organizers and participants of the graduate school on friendship at the Albert Ludwigs-Universität Freiburg for lively discussions and a very inspiring stay during the winter term 2006–2007.
2 On friendship, see Friese 1998, 2010; on hospitality, Friese 2003, 2004, 2009.
3 Cf. Nötzoldt-Linden, 1994 and Vowinckel, 1995.
4 During the interwar period however, 'community and occupational studies' developed in the United States already examined the importance of 'primary relationships', i.e., familiar relationships and friendships within the context of 'modern' Western societies (Allan 1979, 1–5; Pahl 2000).
5 This aspect has been only recently recognized. The anthropologist Gilmore still notes: 'In Spain, while studying male camaraderie […] I was unable to document female friendships, although I suspected they were just as important as those of men' (Gilmore 1982, 195; cf. Gilmore 1975).

References

Bell, Sandra and Simon Coleman, eds. 1999. *The Anthropology of Friendship*. Oxford and New York: Berg.

Allan, Graham. 1979. *A Sociology of Friendship and Kinship*. London, Boston and Sydney: Allen and Unwin.

Aristotle. 1915. *Magna Moralia*. Translated by S. T. Stock. Oxford: Clarendon Press. Online: http://openlibrary.org/books/OL7196173M/Magna_moralia (accessed 19 June 2013).

———. 1934. *The Nicomachean Ethics*, Books I–IX. Translated by H. Rackham. London: Heinemann.

Banton, Michael, ed. 1966. *The Social Anthropology of Complex Societies*. London: Routledge.

Berking, Helmuth. 1999. *Sociology of Giving*. London: Sage.

Boissevain, Jeremy. 1978. *Friends of Friends: Networks, Manipulators and Coalitions*. Oxford: Basil Blackwell.

Boissevain, Jeremy and Clyde Mitchell, eds. 1973. *Network Analysis: Studies in Human Interaction*. The Hague and Paris: Mouton.

Bourdieu, Pierre. 1980. *Le sens pratique*. Paris: Minuit.

Critchley, Simon. 1998. 'The Other's Decision in Me (What Are the Politics of Friendship?)'. *European Journal of Social Theory* 1 (2): 259–79.

Derrida, Jacques. 1994. *Politiques de l'amitié*. Paris: Galilée.

———. 1998. 'The Politics of Friendship'. *Journal of Philosophy* 85 (11): 632–44.

Eichler, Klaus-Dieter. 2000. 'Zu einer "Philosophie der Freundschaft"'. In *Philosophie der Freundschaft*, 215–41. Leipzig: Reclam.

Eisenstadt, Shmuel. 1956. 'Ritualized Personal Relations: Blood Brotherhood, Best Friends, Compadre, etc.: Some Comparative Hypothesis and Suggestions'. *Man* 96: 90–95.

Evans-Pritchard, E. E. 1933. 'Zande Blood-Brotherhood'. *Africa* 6 (4): 369–491.

Firth, Raymond. 1936. 'Bond Friendship in Tikopia'. In *Custom is King: Essays Presented to R. R. Morrett*, edited by L. H. Dudley Buxton, 259–69. London.

Foucault, Michel. 1984. *Histoire de la sexualité, Vol. III: Le souci de soi*. Paris: Gallimard.

Foster, Georg. 1953. 'Confradía e compadradzgo in Spain and Spanish America'. *Southwestern Journal of Anthropology* 9: 155–64.

Friese, Heidrun. 1998. 'Friendship and Politics: A Preamble'. *European Journal of Social Theory* 1 (2): 255–8.

———. 2003. 'Der Gast: Zum Verhältnis von Ethnologie und Philosophie'. *Deutsche Zeitschrift für Philosophie* 2 (April): 311–23.

———. 2004. 'Spaces of Hospitality'. *Angelaki: Journal of the Theoretical Humanities* 9 (2): 67–79.

———. 2009. 'The Limits of Hospitality'. *Paragraph* 32 (1): 51–68.

———. 2010. 'Freundschaft: Leerstellen und Spannungen eines Begriffs'. In *Strong Ties, Weak Ties: Freundschaftssemantik und Netzwerktheorie*, 17–38. Heidelberg: Universitätsverlag.

Galt, Anthony. 1974. 'Rethinking Patron–Client Relationship: The Real and the Official System in Southern Italy'. *Anthropological Quarterly* 47 (2): 182–202.

Gilmore, David D. 1975. 'Friendship in Fuenmayor'. *Ethnology* 14: 311–12.

———. 1982. 'Anthropology of the Mediterranean Area'. *Annual Review of Anthropology* 11: 175–205.

Kant, Immanuel. 1974. 'Kritik der praktischen Vernunft. Grundlegung zur Metaphysik der Sitten'. In *Werkausgabe*, vol. VII, edited by Wilhelm Weischedel, 107–302. Frankfurt: Suhrkamp.

———. 1996. *Practical Philosophy*. Translated and edited by Mary J. Gregor, introduction by Allen Wood. Cambridge and New York: Cambridge University Press.

———. 1997. 'Die Metaphysik der Sitten'. In *Werkausgabe*, vol. VIII, edited by Wilhelm Weischedel, 309–634. Frankfurt: Suhrkamp.

Kon, Igor S. 1979. *Freundschaft: Geschichte und Sozialpsychologie der Freundschaft als soziale Institution und individuelle Beziehung*. Translated by Valeri Danilow. Reinbek: Rowohlt.

Kulick, Don and Margaret Willson, eds. 1995. *Taboo: Sex, Identity, and Erotic Subjectivity in Anthropological Fieldwork*. London and New York: Routledge.

Laclau, Ernesto. 1990. *New Reflections On the Revolution of Our Time*. London: Verso.

Langer, Ullrich. 1994. *Perfect Friendship: Studies in Literature and Moral Philosophy from Bocaccio to Corneille*. Genève: Droz.

Mauser, Wolfram and Barbara Becker-Cantarino, eds. 1991. *Frauenfreundschaft – Männerfreundschaft: literarische Diskurse im 18. Jahrhundert*. Tübingen: Niemeyer.

Mauss, Marcel. 1978. 'Die Gabe: Form und Funktion des Austauschs in archaischen Gesellschaften'. In *Soziologie und Anthropologie*, vol. II, edited by W. Lepenies and H. Ritter, 11–144. Frankfurt, Berlin and Vienna: Ullstein.

Mayer, Adrian. 1966. 'The Significance of Quasi-groups in the Study of Complex Societies'. In *The Social Anthropology of Complex Societies*, edited by M. Banton, 97–122. London: Routledge.

Meyer-Krentler, Eckhardt. 1991. 'Freundschaft im 18. Jahrhundert. Zur Einführung in die Forschungsdiskussion'. In *Frauenfreundschaft – Männerfreundschaft: literarische Diskurse im 18. Jahrhundert*, edited by Wolfram Mauser and Barbara Becker-Cantarino, 1–22. Tübingen: Niemeyer.

Montaigne, Michel E. de. 1994. *The Essays* (Great Books of the Western World 23). Translated by Donald M. Frame. Chicago: Encyclopaedia Britannica.

Nötzoldt-Linden, Ursula. 1994. *Freundschaft: Zur Thematisierung einer vernachlässigten soziologischen Kategorie*. Opladen: Westdeutscher Verlag.

Osteen, Mark, ed. 2002. *The Question of the Gift: Essays Across Disciplines*. London: Routledge.

Paine, Robert. 1969. 'In Search of Friendship: An Exploratory Analysis of "Middle-Class Culture"'. *Man* 5: 505–24.

Pahl, Ray. 2000. *On Friendship*. Cambridge: Polity Press.

Pitt-Rivers, Julian A. 1976. 'Ritual Kinship in the Mediterranean: Spain and the Balkans'. In *Mediterranean Family Structures*, edited by John Peristiany, 317–35. Cambridge: Cambridge University Press.

Reina, Ruben E. 1959. 'Two Patterns of Friendship in a Guatemalan Community'. *American Anthropologist* 61 (1): 44–50.

Schmitt, Carl. 1994 (1932). *Der Begriff des Politischen*. Berlin: Duncker and Humblot.

Schrift, Alan D., ed. 1997. *The Logic of the Gift: Toward an Ethic of Generosity*. New York: Routledge.

Tenbruck, Friedrich H. 1964. 'Freundschaft: Ein Beitrag zur Soziologie der persönlichen Beziehungen'. *Kölner Zeitschrift für Soziologie und Sozialpsychologie* 16: 431–546.

Vincent-Buffault, Anne. 1995. *L'exercice de l'amitié*. Paris: Seuil.

Vowinckel, Gerhard. 1995. *Freundschaft und die Gesellschaft der Fremden: Grundlagen menschlichen Zusammenlebens*. Darmstadt: Buchgesellschaft.

Weber, Max. 1921/22. *Wirtschaft und Gesellschaft: Grundriss der verstehenden Soziologie*. Tübingen: Mohr.

Wolf, Eric. 1966. 'Kinship, Friendship and Patron-Client Relations in Complex Societies'. In *The Social Anthropology of Complex Societies*, edited by Michael Banton, 1–22. London: Barnes and Noble.

Afterword

THE RETURN OF PHILOSOPHICAL ANTHROPOLOGY

Fred Dallmayr

As is well known, and as the editors emphasize, the topic of philosophical anthropology has fallen on hard times in recent decades, to the point that it virtually ceased to occupy the attention of both philosophers and professional anthropologists. This neglect stands in stark contrast to the situation prevailing in Europe in the early and middle part of the last century, which can be described as the heyday of philosophical anthropology.[1] The basic aim of the present volume is to rescue the topic from oblivion, and more specifically to recover the older European legacy while transforming it in the light of more recent experiences and intellectual developments.

It so happens that my own youth and early intellectual development stood strongly under the influence of the cited European legacy. A major intellectual figure shaping my early years was that of Max Scheler – certainly a leading mentor of philosophical anthropology at the time. It was Scheler's central ambition to overcome the dualisms marking modern Western thought, including the bifurcation of a shallow empiricism and an abstract (Cartesian/ Kantian) rationalism – an aim which brought him into the proximity of the early Heidegger. Through his study *Die Stellung des Menschen im Kosmos* (The place of man in the cosmos, of 1927), Scheler had established himself as the leading protagonist of a perspective in which the more elusive universalist accents of Enlightenment philosophy were fruitfully combined with the more concrete concerns of anthropology and human biology. Above all, his notion of the human 'person' or 'personhood' – a notion opposed both to the Cartesian *cogito* and all forms of empirical reductionism – allowed Scheler to emerge as spokesman of a spiritual, yet concretely situated 'humanism', a humanism able to serve as an ethical benchmark during the darker years of European history. In correlating philosophy and human life, his thought did not subscribe to an indiscriminate amalgam, but rather envisaged a complex texture of dimensions corresponding to different levels of human experience. One aspect of this texture was the triadic structure of human knowledge, where Scheler differentiated between empirical-instrumental knowledge (*Leistungswissen*), humanistic understanding (*Bildungswissen*), and reflective-speculative insight (*Erlösungwissen*), a structure departing in important ways from the traditional dichotomy of natural and human sciences.[2]

To be sure, Scheler was not alone in inaugurating and solidifying philosophical anthropology. His efforts were ably supported, and also modified, by a number of European intellectuals. Foremost among the latter were Arnold Gehlen and Helmuth Plessner.[3] The differences between the two were striking, testifying to the broad range of possible conceptions of philosophical anthropology. Basically, Gehlen's conception was more restrictive and closed, while Plessner's view was flexible and dynamic, pointing towards open-ended horizons and possibilities. Both thinkers accepted the thesis of the 'premature birth' of humans and their resulting instinctual deficiency and vulnerability; however, their conclusions were radically divergent. For Gehlen, instinctual deficiency was something to be overcome or domesticated, and the latter could be achieved only through the resolute institutionalization of social and cultural patterns and the routinization or standardization of role expectations; from this vantage point, human frailty urgently needs to be compensated through social and political stability. By contrast to this 'conservative' outlook, Plessner favoured a more 'liberal' or emancipatory perspective perceiving human beings as precariously located between nature and culture, a position requiring constant creative adjustments in light of deeper aspirations for 'meaning'. One of Plessner's central notions was that of the 'eccentricity' or 'eccentric positionality' of human existence, a notion not far removed from Heidegger's thesis of the 'ek-static' quality of human being-in-the-world.[4]

Among the various protagonists, my own distinct preference at the time was for Plessner – even to the point of trumping my admiration for Scheler's work. As I pointed out in an essay of 1974 – meant as a contribution to his eightieth birthday – Plessner's writings signalled for me a resolute stride beyond the Cartesian mind/matter or spirit/nature dualisms, a paradigm which still lingered in recessed form in Scheler's 'spiritualism'. What attracted me particularly to Plessner's approach was his ability to correlate (without total fusion) the natural-biological situatedness of human beings, with their capacity for creative interpretation and transformation. This aspect was clearly illustrated in *The Unity of the Senses* (1923) – a study which, as I came to see later, anticipated in many ways Maurice Merleau-Ponty's *Phenomenology of Perception* (1945). How was it possible, the book argued, for phenomena to have an impact on human sensory organs unless the latter are seen as interpretive and sense-finding organs (and not simply as passive instruments)? Rather than being viewed as mute receptacles, sensory organs had to be seen as sensible media in the distillation of meaning out of the multitude of opaque stimuli. In some of his later writings – especially *The Stages of the Organic World and Man* (1928) and *Conditio Humana* (1961) – Plessner articulated the concept of human 'eccentricity', a quality partially attributable to the 'erect position' of humans. As I wrote at the time: the human condition for Plessner 'is doubly mediated and "reflexive" by virtue of man's "ex-centric" status in regard both to himself and his environment. [...] Rather than being safely enmeshed in a life cycle or the stimulus–response nexus, man has to "lead" his life by designing a web of cultural and symbolic meanings – patterns which provide him at best with a fragile habitat.'[5]

As mentioned previously, philosophical anthropology fell on hard times in the latter part of the last century. Several factors account for this development. Not aiming to be exhaustive, I want to single out two main factors: the first of a chiefly philosophical nature, the second of a more political or geopolitical character. The first is related to the rise of (what is loosely called) 'postmodernism' after 1968, with its pronounced antihumanist bias. During its early phase, the postmodern agenda resounded with such catchwords as 'the death of the subject' and 'the end of man' – slogans coined as countermottos to the earlier reign of existential 'humanism' and which clearly implied also the end of philosophical anthropology. No one was more eloquent and zestful in proclaiming this agenda than Jacques Derrida. In an essay of 1968 provocatively titled 'The Ends of Man', Derrida took aim at two possible meanings of the phrase: one accentuating 'end' in the sense of goal or *telos*, the other accentuating 'man' as a compact creature. Under the first rubric, the essay 'deconstructed' the idea of a philosophical or historical teleology of the human species; under the second rubric, the accent was shifted from *telos* to finitude, ending or termination. Despite a complex interlacing of meanings, it was the second aspect which finally overshadowed and dominated the essay's argument. Taking his lead from Nietzsche's *Zarathustra*, especially the distinction between the 'higher man' and the 'overman', Derrida affirmed that the latter 'overcomes' the human itself and thus is no longer 'humanist' in any sense. Rather than cultivating past memories, the overman 'burns his text and erases the traces of his steps; his laughter then will burst out, directed toward a return which no longer will have the form of a metaphysical repetition of humanism'.[6]

Referring to the events of 1968 and their aftermath, Derrida noted a radical rupture of philosophical dispositions. Prior to these events, he wrote, it was 'the tide of humanism and anthropologism that covered French philosophy'. During that earlier period, it was humanism and anthropologism that served as 'the common ground of Christian or atheist existentialisms, of the philosophy of values (spiritualist or not), of the "personalisms" of the right and left, and [even] of Marxism in the classical style'. Using a broad brush, he asserted that humanist anthropologism was 'the unperceived and uncontested common ground of Marxism and of Social Democratic or Christian-Democratic discourse'. Since 1968, however, things have changed. What followed was an 'antihumanist and antianthropologist ebb' and an intense 'questioning of humanism'. In fact, the critique of humanism and anthropologism has become 'one of the dominant and guiding motifs of current French thought' (at the time of Derrida's writing). Inspired by the 'new' Nietzscheanism, what Derrida complained about was not this critique itself, but rather its half-hearted character and the lingering persistence of humanist traces in current discourse. What particularly chagrined him was the continued humanist reading of such thinkers as Hegel, Husserl and even Heidegger, a reading tending to 'amalgamate' these thinkers with 'the old metaphysical humanism'. As he pointedly observed, 'Among those who do practice this amalgamation, the schemas of the anthropologistic misinterpretation from Sartre's time are still at work, and occasionally it is these very schemas which govern the banishment of Hegel, Husserl, and Heidegger into the shadows of humanist metaphysics.'[7]

The second main factor accounting for the 'ebb' of humanism and philosophical anthropology was the accelerating pace of globalization. Although incipiently heralded by two world wars, globalization in the second part of the last century took the form of an increasingly relentless pursuit of global economic, cultural and political-military agendas. Under the impact of steadily expanding markets and communications networks, national and cultural traditions or frames of reference were inevitably placed under siege; the same developments also put pressure on older conceptions of humanism and of philosophical anthropology. Given the growing awareness of cultural and religious differences (fomenting a possible 'clash of civilizations'), how was it possible to discern something like a shared humanity or humaneness – beyond the level of a technological *homo faber* and the global uniformity of consumerism? Were all assertions of a universal 'human nature' not inevitably tainted by an ethnocentric, perhaps Eurocentric, bias? Under these circumstances, how is it possible to renew a conception of philosophical anthropology which does not elope into an abstract transcendentalism (or spiritualism) while at the same time resisting the lure of biological or ethnological reductionism? As it appears, humanism as well as philosophical anthropology are bound to be stranded on the proverbial 'horns' of the dilemma between universalism and reductive particularism – unless an alternative path is found, a path which cannot invoke any 'top-down' formula, but must rely on the experiential process of 'globalization from below'.[8]

In the meantime, the 'ebb' of antihumanism and antianthropologism (diagnosed by Derrida) is itself beginning to ebb. What we are experiencing today is not, to be sure, a high tide of old-style humanism, but the tentative resurgence of a subdued, self-critical and non-Eurocentric (that is, nonhegemonic) view of the 'human' on the far side of absolute affirmation and absolute negation. Several factors again account for this resurgence. One is the danger of antihumanism to slide into inhumanity and the denial of human rights – a slide which is utterly unacceptable given the upsurge of a new form of imperialism, of state-sponsored and privately sponsored forms of 'terrorism', and of the widespread violation of elementary standards of human rights in many parts of the world. Another factor is the immense pressure placed by advances in the biological sciences on acceptable conceptions of the 'human' or 'humaneness' – a pressure evident in the programs of genetic engineering, cloning and stem cell research. What also needs to be taken into account is the rediscovery and revitalization of such resources of philosophical anthropology as social phenomenology, hermeneutics and various modes of social psychology.

All these factors combined have inspired a number of writers to pay renewed attention to this domain of inquiry, neglected for some time. A prominent example is Jürgen Habermas, a participant in the earlier vogue of philosophical anthropology. In a series of essays on 'the future of human nature', Habermas has directly confronted the challenge posed by certain ambitions of genetic engineering. As he observes, in the face of these ambitions, it was 'an urgent matter' to initiate 'a public discourse on the right understanding of cultural forms of life. And philosophers no longer have any good reasons for leaving such a dispute to biologists or engineers intoxicated by science fiction.' Without explicitly invoking the label, Habermas's intervention clearly gives a boost to the resurgence of philosophical anthropology at this new stage of development. In his view, what philosophy can contribute in this context is its capacity for reflective judgment, its ability to illuminate the 'ethical self-understanding of the species' – certainly no small matter. In the assessment of Nikolas Kompridis, Habermas's intervention has in a way corrected his own leanings toward a rationalist universalism: 'By speaking in the name of the human future, Habermas has helpfully (if unintentionally) exposed the cost of adhering to a proceduralist conception of philosophy.' In doing so, it has exposed the 'limitations of a sharp distinction between morality and ethics, between justice and the good life', by showing that the morality of reason is itself sustained 'by a prior *ethical self-understanding of the species* shared by all moral persons'.[9]

In the field of political theory, William Connolly has recently launched an initiative whose parameters mesh with philosophical anthropology, broadly conceived. In his study entitled *Neuropolitics: Thinking, Culture, Speed* (2002), Connolly endeavoured to reconnect and mutually interpolate 'nature' – traditionally the domain of exact science – with 'culture', the central domain of the humanities and philosophy. As he writes, 'Every theory of culture bears an implicit relation to biology and biological theory' – a relation which has tended to be sidelined both by hard scientists and cultural 'idealists', giving rise to various kinds of one-sided reductionism. 'In their laudable attempt to ward off one [biologistic] type of reductionism', he adds, 'too many cultural theorists fall into another: they lapse into a reductionism that ignores how biology is mixed into thinking and culture and how other aspects of nature are folded into both.' Among philosophers, Connolly invokes chiefly the legacies of Henri Bergson, William James, Merleau-Ponty and Gilles Deleuze, while in the field of neuroscience his chief mentors are such practitioners as Antonio Damasio, Joseph LeDoux and V. S. Ramachandran. The reconnection that his text envisages is not so much a harmonious symbiosis as, rather, a fragile and tension-ridden bond where insights garnered from different fields rub against each other and thereby release new energies and horizons. In its emphasis on openness, contingency and shifting horizons, the text in a way harkens back to earlier philosophical anthropology, especially to Plessner's notion of the 'eccentric positionality' of human existence.[10]

Of late, my own thinking has also returned to the issues raised by Scheler, Plessner, and other protagonists half a century ago. In my case, the return was mainly prompted by the debilitating effects of a radical antihumanism celebrating the 'death of the subject', effects evident especially in the areas of public life and political agency. Another motivating factor was a resurgent interest in the legacy of Merleau-Ponty, a legacy sidelined for several decades by the 'postmodern' vogue.[11] These and related motives lead me back to perhaps the central concern of philosophical anthropology: that of 'human nature' and the meaning of humanism. Chastened by the experiences of intervening decades, my endeavour was to renew some older teachings without, however, validating their frequent derailment into a compact, self-possessed and hegemonic (perhaps Eurocentric) humanism. In an essay titled 'Who Are We Now? For an "Other" Humanism' (2009), I sought to clear a path beyond anthropocentrism and antihumanism, a path which also avoids derailment into (biological or idealistic) modes of reductionism.[12] As I point out in that essay, the interlude of antihumanism may actually have served the salutary purpose of cleansing humanism of some of its traditional arrogance. Seen from this angle, the presumed 'end of man' is in effect 'nothing else but the continuous and ever renewed beginning of a journey' – a journey in search of the 'human'. What the deflation of anthropocentrism makes possible above all is 'a released openness to others, to nature, and the recessed ground of being(s)'. I invoke at this point Heidegger's famous *Letter on Humanism*

(1946) where we read: 'If we do keep the label, the term "humanism" signifies that human nature is indeed crucial for the truth of "being" – but crucial precisely in a way where everything does not depend on "man" alone or as such'.[13] In lieu of this dependence, what comes into view here is a complex mode of interdependence between humans, nature and the world.

Notes

1 Regarding the original meaning of philosophical anthropology, I still find Jürgen Habermas on target when he writes that it 'integrates and digests the findings of all those sciences which – like psychology, sociology, archeology or linguistics – deal with "man" and his works', while it is 'not in turn a specialized discipline'. Perched 'between empiricism and theory', its task is 'to interpret scientific findings in a philosophical manner'. See his article 'Anthropologie' in Alwin Diemer and Ivo Frenzel, eds, *Fischer-Lexikon: Philosophie* (Frankfurt: Fischer Verlag, 1958), 18, 20.

2 See Max Scheler, *Die Stellung des Menschen im Kosmos* (Bern: Francke Verlag, 1927); and his *Die Wissensformen und die Gesellschaft* (Bern: Francke Verlag, 1926). Compare also Manfred S. Frings, *Max Scheler* (Pittsburgh: Duquesne University Press, 1965), and Wilfrid Hartmann, 'Max Scheler's Theory of Person', *Philosophy Today* 12 (1969), 246–61.

3 Other important figures were Jakob von Uexküll and Adolf Portmann. Uexküll's contribution resided especially in the demonstration of the closed ecological milieu of animals and the fixed linkage between their instincts and external stimuli, while Portmann's research documented the 'premature birth' of human beings and their initial developmental retardation. Both writers left their imprint on the enterprise of philosophical anthropology. Compare, for example, Adolf Portmann, *Animals as Social Beings* (New York: Viking Press, 1961); *A Zoologist Looks at Mankind*, trans. Judith Schaefer (New York: Columbia University Press, 1990); Jakob von Uexküll, *Theoretical Biology* (New York: Harcourt, Brace, 1926); *Die Lebenslehre* (Potsdam: Müller and Kiepenheuer, 1930).

4 For some of Gehlen's major writings, see *Der Mensch: Seine Natur und seine Stellung in der Welt* (1940), 8th edition (Bonn: Athenäum Verlag, 1966); *Die Seele im technischen Zeitalter* (1949), revised edition (Hamburg: Rowohlt, 1957); *Urmensch und Spätkultur* (Bonn: Athenäum Verlag, 1956); *Moral und Hypermoral* (Frankfurt: Metzner, 1969). For some of Plessner's major writings, see *Vom Anfang als Prinzip transzendentaler Wahrheit* (Heidelberg: Winter, 1917); *Die Einheit der Sinne: Grundlinien einer Ästhesiologie des Geistes* (Bonn: Bouvier, 1923); *Die Stufen des Organischen und der Mensch* (1928), 2nd edition (Berlin: Walter de Gruyter, 1965); *Lachen und Weinen* (Bern: Francke, 1941); *Conditio Humana* (1961), republished (Pfullingen: Neske, 1964) and *Philosophische Anthropologie* (Frankfurt: Fischer, 1970). For a critique of Gehlen, mainly from Plessner's perspective, see Habermas, 'Arnold Gehlen: Nachgeahmte Substantialität', in *Philosophisch-politische Profile* (Frankfurt: Suhrkamp, 1971), 200–221. Regarding Heidegger, compare Helmut Fahrenbach, 'Heidegger und das Problem einer "philosophischen Anthropologie"', in *Durchblicke: Martin Heidegger zum 80. Geburtstag* (Frankfurt: Klostermann, 1970), 97–131.

5 Fred Dallmayr, 'Social Role and "Human Nature": Plessner's Philosophical Anthropology', in *Beyond Dogma and Despair: Toward a Critical Phenomenology of Politics* (Notre Dame: University of Notre Dame Press, 1981), 73 (69–93). My statement would need to be corrected for gender bias.

6 Jacques Derrida, 'The Ends of Man', in *Margins of Philosophy*, trans. Alan Bass (Chicago: University of Chicago Press, 1982), 136.

7 Derrida, 'The Ends of Man', 116–19. As one should add, Derrida did not entirely absolve the work of the mentioned thinkers from harbouring humanist leanings and thus encouraging the 'anthropologistic misinterpretation'.

8 On 'globalization from below', see especially Richard Falk, 'Resisting "Globalization-from-Above" through "Globalization-from-Below"', in his *Predatory Globalization* (Cambridge: Polity Press, 1999), 127–36.

9 Jürgen Habermas, *The Future of Human Nature*, trans. William Rehg, Max Pensky and Hella Beister (Cambridge, MA: MIT Press, 2002), 15, 39–40, italics in the original. See also Nikolas Kompridis, *Critique and Disclosure: Critical Theory Between Past and Future* (Cambridge, MA: MIT Press, 2006), 166.

10 William E. Connolly, *Neuropolitics: Thinking, Culture, Speed* (Minneapolis, MN: University of Minnesota Press, 2002). Compare in the context Antonio R. Damasio, *Looking for Spinoza: Joy, Feeling, and the Feeling Brain* (Orlando, FL: Harcourt, 2003); Damasio et al., eds, *Unity of Knowledge: The Convergence of Natural and Human Science* (New York: New York Academy of Sciences, 2001); Joseph LeDoux, *The Emotional Brain* (New York: Simon and Schuster, 1996); LeDoux et al., eds, *The Self: From Soul to Brain* (New York: New York Academy of Sciences, 2003); V. S. Ramachandran and Sandra Blakeslee, *Phantoms of the Brain: Probing the Mysteries of the Human Mind* (New York: William Morrow, 1996).

11 See in this respect Diana Coole, *Merleau-Ponty and Modern Politics After Anti-Humanism* (Lanham, MD: Rowman and Littlefield, 2007); also my 'Return of the Repressed: Merleau-Ponty *Redivivus*', *Political Theory* 37 (2009), 713–19.

12 Dallmayr, 'Who Are We Now? For an "Other" Humanism', in *The Promise of Democracy: Political Agency and Transformation* (Albany, NY: State University of New York Press, 2009), 211–36. Compare also Heidegger, 'Letter on Humanism', in *Martin Heidegger: Basic Writings*, ed. David F. Krell (New York: Harper and Row, 1977), 193–242.

13 In *Martin Heidegger: Basic Writings*, ed. Krell.

www.ingramcontent.com/pod-product-compliance
Lightning Source LLC
Chambersburg PA
CBHW020333270326
41926CB00007B/158